The New Worlds of Thomas Robert Malthus

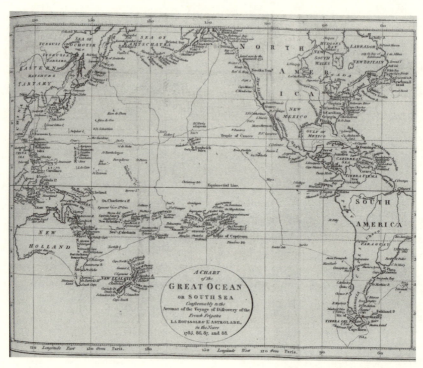

Frontispiece. The new worlds of Thomas Robert Malthus in a map of 1798 produced by his publisher in the year his *Essay on the Principle of Population* made its debut. *A Chart of the Great Ocean or South Sea . . .* (London: J. Johnson, 1798). Courtesy of the John Carter Brown Library at Brown University.

The New Worlds of Thomas Robert Malthus

REREADING THE *PRINCIPLE OF POPULATION*

Alison Bashford and Joyce E. Chaplin

PRINCETON UNIVERSITY PRESS

PRINCETON AND OXFORD

press.princeton.edu

Jacket image: *A Chart of the Great Ocean or South Sea Conformably to the Account of
the Voyage of Discovery of the French Frigates La Boussole & L'Astrolabe, in the
Years 1785, 86, 87, and 88,* (London: J. Johnson, 1798).
Courtesy of the John Carter Brown Library at Brown University.

ISBN 978-0-691-16419-9

Library of Congress Control Number: 2016931919

British Library Cataloging-in-Publication Data is available

This book has been composed in Sabon Next Lt Pro

Printed on acid-free paper ∞

Printed in the United States of America

1 3 5 7 9 10 8 6 4 2

CONTENTS

ILLUSTRATIONS

TABLES

Introduction

For more than two hundred years, people have loved to hate Thomas Robert Malthus, but have they done so with reason and (even if so) for the right reasons? The British moral philosopher and professor of political economy (1766–1834) is too often diminished and dismissed as a mere "parson." Although described as warm and engaging in person—all the more impressive, given his harelip, cleft palate, and speech defect—he has nevertheless been thoroughly vilified. Why? Just as there are characters in books, so there are characters created by books, and Malthus was one of the latter. In his case, he was a character of his own creation. He is famous for one idea, a bleak correlation between population growth and starvation, first set out in his *Essay on the Principle of Population*. In 1798 this was a thesis that seemed to entrench and naturalize rather than ameliorate poverty, just when a new generation of utopians was imagining a brighter and better future. Subsequently, his identification with the hypothetical mismatch between potential population growth and available resources became so strong that, even within his lifetime, his name came to signify it: "Malthusian" (by 1805) and "Malthusianism" (by 1833).[1]

That stark claim about population has been persistently interpreted within a European context, even as Malthusianism is today thought of overwhelmingly in relation to the developing, extra-European world. This distortion is compounded by the problem that Malthusianism has been analyzed far more than the historical Malthus. When historians have sought to contextualize Malthus's ideas, they have defined his "life and times," as a rule, in the political spaces either within England or between Britain and France. This is both unsurprising and correct, not least because Malthus explained the first iteration of his *Essay*, published in 1798, as a response both to William Godwin and to the marquis de Condorcet, and he explained it in his preface to have been prompted by "conversation with a friend" about the future improvement of humankind. We know that this debate was with Malthus's radical father, devotee of John Wilkes and friend of Jean-Jacques Rousseau. The father and son envisioned very different futures at a critical historical moment. In the year of their conversation, Great Britain was at war with France—Nelson defeated the French fleet at the Battle of the Nile that year—and English "Jacobins" and "anti-Jacobins" were also at war. They fought, in large part, over the poor. What had been done, and what could possibly be done, about poverty, about future social "happiness," and about the perfectibility of social organization? In Great Britain, this argument revolved around core economic and political business—the Poor Laws and later the Corn Laws—and Malthus had much to say about both, against the former and for the latter. Quite rightly, radical politics of the 1790s, the Napoleonic Wars, and the ethics and economics of British policy on the poor have long been the historiographical frames in which Malthus and his *Essay* have been assessed. He was, after all, a key figure in the transition from a political economy informed by moral philosophy and to an economics shorn of such philosophical concerns.[2]

Looked at another way, however, Malthus was, all along, a theorist who looked beyond England and especially at new worlds over which Europeans (and settlers) had been fighting long before Bonaparte drew breath. The distinguished population historian and geographer E. A. Wrigley once conceptualized Malthus as "standing between two worlds." Wrigley meant that Malthus stood between two temporally distinct economic systems: the premodern organic and agricultural economy, from which and about which Malthus wrote, and the modern industrial and manufacturing economy, just beginning to accelerate. But what if we were to cast these "two worlds" not just chronologically but also into the geography of Malthus's own life and times, the old world and the new? In fact, he defined his population principle in relation to the new world primordially within his 1798 claim that British North America provided a case study of rapid population growth, and even more significantly in the expanded second edition of his *Essay*, published in 1803. Starting with that revision, and in each that came thereafter, Malthus began with the Atlantic and the Pacific "new worlds," not with Europe. But why? And how does recognition of the new worlds of Thomas Robert Malthus significantly change our understanding of the most famous book on population ever written, or ever likely to be?[3]

The unusual nature of new world societies has been deeply ingrained in examinations of those places, even as their respective scholars may have missed their significance to Malthus. Despite the initial mistaken comprehension of the first new world, the Americas, as part of the East Indies, subsequent Western understanding of them was as places distinctly unendowed with Asia's long-settled, economically complex, and large populations. To the European eye, many parts of the Americas seemed underpopulated, with land and other resources consequently underutilized, and this would remain a central prejudice about them. English descriptions of North America as *wilderness* transformed that term's original connotation of "wild," as populated by wild things (plants, animals, people) to mean also deserted, desert, waste. Thus an invidious description of new worlds was born, one that not only assumed a low person-to-acre ratio—"thin," as it was often put—but hinted at the desirability of separating indigenous persons from their acres, and hypothesized their eventual demise in any case. All imperial zones and schemes are unjust, but the way in which instrumental ideas about abounding land and receding native population informed the empires of the Americas was the distinctive element of their injustice and would generate a model for succeeding new world colonies in Australia and other parts of the Pacific. In the most extreme form of these claims, the concepts of *res nullius* and *terra nullius* asserted that new world zones were literally "nobody's land," free for the taking.[4]

So rich has this distinctive population-land element been within scholarship on new worlds that it has borne many names since "wilderness," "wasteland," or "terra nullius." Within the historiography on the Americas, Frederick Jackson Turner's idea of the *frontier*, as a cultural interaction zone in which shrinking native populations and expanding settler populations clashed over land, has prevailed since the late nineteenth century and been exported to explain frontiers elsewhere, including the Pacific. By the middle of the twentieth century, Latin Americanist Herbert Eugene Bolton modified the notion of a frontier with the concept of a *borderland*, originally to describe the boundary zones between New Spain and British America, later to identify a broader array of cultural participants within those zones, including Indians. Whatever the post-Turnerian criticisms that these concepts tend to reduce native peoples to a historically inaccurate invisibility, *frontier* and *borderland* have continued to be terms of art. Analysis of creoles, the descendants of Europeans who settled in the Americas, has likewise promoted a sense that, within these zones, and especially once the zones' creole inhabitants fashioned nations independent from Europe (beginning with the United States in 1776 and unfolding as wars of independence in "Latin America" that concluded circa 1825), native populations played secondary roles. More recently, definitions of *settler colonialism*, in which the rights and privileges of settlers are instantiated in ways that subsume those of original inhabitants, has formed a more forthright criticism of settler ideologies. This concept has been used, beginning in the latter part of the twentieth century, to interpret ongoing instances of territorial occupation as well as historic cases, with attention to the nineteenth century settler usurpation of land in new worlds stretching from the Atlantic to the Pacific.[5]

Our study reinterprets Malthus's "principle of population" within these connected histories and historiographies, which have interrogated the dynamics of power in new world places that were perceived by settlers as land abundant and population poor. North America constituted Malthus's primary example of just how rapidly population growth could occur, whenever land fit for agriculture was first exploited by Europeans. New world places and their native peoples were then analytically essential within editions of the *Essay* from 1803 onward. From selected studies of indigenous people, Malthus argued that population numbers were always kept within the limits of resources (the "principle of population") by epidemics, starvation, and human violence, and by deliberate measures to control births. And yet Malthus used his principle of population to conclude—against prevailing opinion—that for settler populations to extirpate or subsume indigenous ones was unjust. In this regard, the Reverend T. R. Malthus, long decried as scourge of the English poor, has an unexpected, if intermittent, persona: defender of native peoples.

New worlds were therefore cautionary tales for Malthus. He recognized the allure of lands that seemed to have been previously unused, with new worlds seeming to offer fresh beginnings for humanity, or at least parts of humanity. Yet he warned against the assumption that material plenty would always beckon—the enduring fantasy of new world places—and he was well aware that white settlers would be quick to claim territories that were actually being used by their aboriginal inhabitants. When read in relation to the histories of the new worlds, Malthus's "principle of population" carries a double moral: fresh starts for humanity often rely on misleading promises about natural resources, and the human beings in question are themselves quite often ethically compromised. The *Essay* is therefore an examination, in equal measures, of nature and of human nature, nowhere better exposed in their starkest forms than in new world places.

* * *

While Malthus himself never traveled across the Atlantic or into the Pacific, people from those worlds entered his book. Two of them best capture its new world dimensions, embodying in very different ways the significance of colonized worlds within British intellectual history of the late eighteenth and early nineteenth centuries. It is well known that Malthus inherited a kernel of an idea about rapid population growth from Benjamin Franklin, the British colonist (later independent American), who in 1751 developed a theory of rapid population growth and natural carrying capacity within British North America. Nonetheless, in Malthus studies, Franklin and America are quickly ushered off the stage after a brief mention, obscuring how America (and Franklin) remained central to Malthus's arguments in all subsequent editions of his *Essay*, as well as to debate among Malthus's critics. Far less well known is the presence of another new world man in the *Essay*: Bennelong, a senior member of the Wangal people, whose land had recently been colonized by the British and renamed Sydney. Both Franklin and Bennelong visited London, and while neither met Malthus (so far as we know), their textual meetings in the *Essay* distill what our book is about. Their manifest difference is the point. They represent the two faces of new world history, both of which shaped the *Essay*, both of which engaged Malthus, and both of which have been the objects of major historical inquiries that need to be brought to our understanding of Malthus, the *Essay*, and the world in which it was composed and received.[6]

Benjamin Franklin represents the significant case of British colonization of North America, the ensuing settler population growth, and the white population's celebration of the consequent displacement of the indigenous population. Bennelong represents the Pacific new world, but more profoundly he was an indigenous presence in the *Essay*. The fact that Bennelong spent two years in London in the mid-1790s, but was then reduced by Malthus to an exemplar of savage economy, signals a deeper ambivalence about indigenous new world societies in the *Essay* itself. Placing Franklin, Bennelong, and the disparate views on new world empires those two men exemplified at the conceptual center of our approach to Malthus's *Essay* makes the picture of that text suddenly shift from a British or European axis, to require a new world and imperial axis of analysis.

To what extent has this been done to date? Appraisal of the non-European context of Malthus's *Essay* has tended to be ex post facto—pursued from the perspective of the modern social sciences—or else fleeting, with only a glancing realization of the fuller worlds he inhabited and assessed. Some scholars have intermittently considered him as an early ethnographer, for example. His ideas about Australian Aboriginal people have been noted, sometimes within the tradition of historicizing "prehistory," on occasion within analysis of Enlightenment exploration and encounter, and particularly in terms of indigenous people's decline. The twentieth-century demographer J. C. Caldwell intriguingly wondered why Malthus had focused so much on the "new worlds" at the expense of Asia. At the beginning of his career Donald Winch connected political economy to empire with some discussion of Malthus and colonization, and more recently Eric Richards has discussed Malthus on emigration. John Toye has noted that the new scope of the second edition situated Malthus at the very beginning of what became development economics. These are the small steps that have been taken in thinking of the *Essay on the Principle of Population* beyond both British economic history and a late Enlightenment French-British controversy.[7]

In this book, we take the bigger leap. There is a pressing need to do so, not least because Malthus himself addressed new world societies so directly. We take account of, and account for, the primary materials on these new worlds that informed Malthus and that he actively incorporated into his long edition. These sixteenth- through-eighteenth century works themselves signaled the wider context that must also be considered. The French Revolution and its British opponents and proponents, the Poor Laws, the Corn Laws, were all important contexts, to be sure. But Malthus's life span, 1766–1834, also encompassed world-changing developments in other hemispheres.

* * *

Malthus wrote about how the old world and the new world related to one another at the turn of a new century—unsurprising, given how formative those centenary developments were to domestic British economic and political matters. That North America had contributed significantly to British wealth—the colonies that in part created its economic "great divergence"—was as apparent to contemporaries as it has become to historians. Grain-producing acres that had once been part of the British Empire were, by Malthus's late childhood, instead within the United States of America. Growing reliance on American grain unsettled British economists and was certainly to worry Malthus. The extension of the Napoleonic Wars to the Americas, waged in Malthus's adulthood, altered geopolitical relations yet again. The Louisiana Purchase was negotiated just as the second edition of the *Essay* came off the press in 1803: France relinquished its status as Britain's new world adversary even as the United States doubled its territory. Shortly thereafter the Spanish monarchy lost most of its American territories as those places broke into the independent nations of what is now called "Latin" America.

The so-called swing to the East after the American Revolution had in the meanwhile focused attention on the new economic and strategic possibilities of the Pacific Ocean. The exploration and charting of the South Sea by Bougainville, Cook, Vancouver, and La Pérouse all took place in the first half of Malthus's life. Indeed these explorers each appear in his *Essay*, often in long passages of verbatim quotation. In 1788 the colony of New South Wales was established, to which convict populations already considered "surplus" were deported. New South Wales thus made its way into the second edition of the *Essay* in 1803, and that year British rule over indigenous people in the antipodes escalated with new penal settlements in Van Diemen's Land (Tasmania). In Tahiti and New Zealand too the British initiated commercial and missionary endeavors, building, from 1769 onward, atop James Cook's charting of these places. Even the "free" province of South Australia, enacted by Parliament the year Malthus died (1834), fell within his purview. The new idea of "systematic colonization" was of interest to him, not least because it installed the value of labor, relative to the value of land, at its core.

The antipodean colonies began as maritime ventures, closely hugging coastlines and initially lacking any clear plan to cultivate continental interiors. They were not, at first, an attempt to replace the great grain-producing acreage of the lost North American colonies. Over Malthus's lifetime, however, especially after the Napoleonic Wars, the antipodean colonies did turn into vast agricultural ventures and commercial pastoral holdings, returning considerable wealth to Great Britain and receiving emigrants in return, often from Scotland and Ireland, where linked agrarian reform was underway. Accordingly, Malthus's *Essay* and the whole population question itself were tied up with the settler colonial enterprise of the late eighteenth and early nineteenth centuries. The emigration of English, Scottish, Welsh, and Irish settlers, and the transportation of convicts to the new antipodean colonies, replacing the earlier trade to British America before 1776, was often figured as a mitigation of pauperism. It was part of the massive movement of Britons, domestically and internationally, that characterized the era. Some economists and statesmen thought siphoning off at least some out-of-work laborers and unemployed urban poor to the colonies was useful in keeping the price of labor high. Malthus himself was ambivalent about the economics of emigration and colonization. The morality of such endeavors also occasionally troubled him.[8]

In relation to new worlds, the *Essay on the Principle of Population* was also a book about the human cultivation of land, and of the limits (in an age of "improvement") to which yields could be enhanced. New world colonial sites constituted for British consumers millions of what are now called "ghost acres." In *The Hungry Planet: The Modern World at the Edge of Famine* (1965), Georg Borgstrom defined ghost acreage as the actual extent of food-providing territory that a nation had at its disposal, including whatever lay beyond its direct area of sovereignty. To determine the amount of food that a country could command, it was necessary, Borgstrom argued, to take into account its trade, its fishing, and its agriculture, even though the final unit was usually the only component that was calculated—and typically only within the nation itself, not including its imperial dependencies. Ghost acreage was in contrast the "computed, non-visible acreage which a country would require as a supplement to its present visible agricultural acreage in the form of tilled land in order to be able to feed itself." Borgstrom differentiated between fish acreage and trade acreage as indeed qualitatively distinct, depending on whether a nation had fishing rights in any available body of water (freshwater sometimes, but more typically ocean) or instead had to trade with other nations for its fish. Borgstrom further distinguished among kinds of food imports, substitutionary versus complementary. The first category encompassed items that a nation could produce but might not have done, either to reserve domestic resources for other activities, or else because a crop had failed and a substitute had to be sought. The latter category included items that could not be grown in the country in question, often because (in relation to countries in temperate climates) they were tropical or otherwise climate dependent.[9]

Although the concept of ghost acreage is recent, the economic historian Kenneth Pomeranz has pointed out that, when European nations possessed imperial zones, their leaders quite obviously thought in congruent terms. The whole aim of most early modern empires had been to gain territories and shipping zones in order to procure complementary products (spices especially; sugar eventually) and sometimes substitutionary ones, as Great Britain had done with American grain and Irish beef. Indeed, population theories since the Renaissance (at least) had incipiently analyzed the value of ghost acres. For modern empires, ghost acreage was of staggering importance. Pomeranz has estimated that by around the year 1830 Britain's ghost acres were in the neighborhood of 25 to 30 million. Even before that time, in the late eighteenth and early nineteenth century, West Indian sugar cultivation alone constituted over 1 million acres for England and Scotland, reaching closer to 2 million for the entire United Kingdom. Nor was ghost acreage restricted to food. Although forests in most parts of western Europe would not be seriously depleted until the eighteenth century, people had, by the late Middle Ages, begun to state their perception that wood was running out. There were two solutions. The Republic of Venice sought its wood elsewhere, in the ghost acres of its regional empire. An alternative strategy, original to the German-speaking lands, was to cultivate and conserve forests at home. England would implement both solutions, though notably the Venetian one. North American forests provided an abundance of wood for building British merchantmen and warships, for example. Britain's imperial ghost acres for timber (principally in Upper and

Lower Canada) have been estimated as comprising just over a million acres by the early nineteenth century.[10]

In relation to the question of ghost acres, Malthus's *Essay* was an ethical treatise about who gets to cultivate whose land in other hemispheres and on other continents. The great agricultural ventures in North America and later in the Australian colonies were key parts of the global environmental shift over the eighteenth and nineteenth centuries, first from forest to farm, and then from grassland to grainland. This involved "clearances" not just of new world land, but also of new world people. Sometimes the latter was organized, sometimes haphazard; sometimes actively violent, at other times passively so. But the displacement of indigenous people was most often a deliberate and formal policy. Two of the most notorious outcomes of such deliberations took place in 1830, within Malthus's lifetime—the Indian Removal Act in the United States and the so-called Black Line in Van Diemen's Land. Malthus had anticipated, and deplored, such events in 1803: "The right of exterminating, or driving into a corner where they must starve, even the inhabitants of these thinly peopled regions, will be questioned in a moral view." To be sure, Malthus was interested in the effect of "new land" on the emigrant population, those neo-Britons who were busy replenishing the Earth. But it turns out that he also recognized the cost of all this replenishment in the new worlds. Indeed, as a contemporary of these global trends, he recognized their significance perhaps more keenly than many twentieth-century historians.[11]

Malthus was, therefore, at times, and unexpectedly, a critic of both the imperial project and the politics of extermination, protection, or assimilation of indigenous peoples who came under foreign rule. For him the problem was unfolding on a global canvas, one that highlighted the distinctive tragedy of new worlds. "To exterminate the inhabitants of the greatest part of Asia and Africa, is a thought that could not be admitted for a moment," he argued, even as the reverse of this statement revealed that the thought of extermination could be (and was) openly discussed in relation to the inhabitants of new worlds.[12]

Malthus also worried about the Atlantic slave trade, the other ethical problem peculiar to new world societies. His *Essay* was written and rewritten at the most politicized moment of Atlantic abolitionism and emancipation, from US abolition of the slave trade, as written into the Constitution of 1789, to passage of the British 1807 Slave Trade Act and the Slavery Abolition Act of 1833. Indeed, Malthus revised appendixes to the *Essay* just as William

Wilberforce was arguing through abolitionist bills in Westminster. Although the *Essay* was occasionally used to defend the slave trade, Malthus himself favored abolition. Yet he addressed slavery reluctantly and belatedly in his *Essay*. Most surprisingly, given the status of the West Indian colonies, his corpus as a whole failed to assess the sugar islands as economically meaningful parts of the empire; in effect, it failed to assess new world slavery at all. In this regard, it is significant that Malthus spent most of his adult life at the core of Britain's institutional imperialism: the East India Company. Not just his income but the very roof over the Malthus family head was provided through his long-standing position as professor of general history, politics, commerce, and finance at the East India Company College, Haileybury. There, from 1805 until his death in 1834, Malthus trained generations of young men to be company clerks and sent them to India. In this way, Malthus participated in the British sanitization of imperial activity, away from the slave-trading and land-grabbing model of new worlds and toward an exploitation that, in contrast, parasitically attached itself to existing populations. The new style of imperialism would make what has become known as the Second British Empire distinctive, reflecting considerable effort in reforming and justifying empire, as well as greater confidence in the results, whatever their injustices to extra-European peoples. Perhaps for this reason, Malthus's objections to the moral hazard of taking aboriginal lands in new worlds had been only timidly stated and were gradually superseded by other concerns.

* * *

Why has the centrality of new worlds to Malthus's population principle not been perceived before or, more correctly, not been perceived as important? The block in the past has been partly intellectual and partly about publishing logistics. Many people, including many scholars, have simply read the first, short edition of the *Essay*. And although all Malthus scholars know that the long 1803 edition is altogether different in both scale and content, the early chapters—the fascinating, if not horrifying, studies of indigenous people in the Atlantic and Pacific new worlds—have nevertheless been omitted in widely used abridged reprints. For this reason alone, the frequently omitted sections warrant special focus. It was Patricia James, Malthus's most diligent biographer, who could see at least the antiquarian delights of inquiring into the seventeenth- and eighteenth-century voyagers' accounts on which Malthus relied so heavily: "I wonder nobody has ever produced an annotated edition of the second version of the *Essay* simply as an excuse for the pleasure of thoroughly studying the sources." But these sources were far more than traveler's tales, and their contents are often unpleasant. From those accounts, Malthus received and reproduced a historically specific image of the savage, the foundational actor in his era's universal history, denizen of the first economic stage within the development of commercial civilization, and typically sited within the new worlds, first America, later the Pacific.[13]

Malthus's focus on new worlds was thus a way to consider the question of how resources might be divided among human populations that were (or seemed) different at the time of their historical contact. His major ambition was to establish a universal, mathematically expressed, and therefore scientific principle about all of humanity, and to do so he knew he needed to canvass the inhabited world and find a way to theorize his worldwide exempla. To organize and give meaning to his global survey, he relied to a large extent on stadial theory, the conjectural four stages of human development from hunting and gathering to pastoralism, agriculture, and finally commerce. Malthus did not simply use stadial theory but reconfigured it to place population dynamics at its core, drawing from the late Enlightenment theorists of universal history—Hume, Montesquieu, Kames, Smith, Gibbon, and above all Robertson—in order to do so. The *Essay* is thus important as a contribution to a historically significant (and still-running) debate over the nature of humanity: are human beings more similar to each other than they are dissimilar? Malthus attempted to define a universal principle for all humans, yet he did so during a period of intense racism and by using sources that reflected (if not participated in) the imperial activities that seemed to naturalize cultures as superior and inferior. The result was a profound meditation on the problem of human inequality, though not a solution to it.

The *Essay* for that reason contains both a universalizing history of civilization and a dead-end history of savagery, a paradox contained within Malthus's new world examples and one that he never reconciled. He cited instances from the world over, and from representative societies of all stages of development (past and present). The multiple case studies distilled his thesis and reduced it to its barest and, for him, clearest, principles: by what means are the inhabitants of any society reduced to such a number as can subsist? Just this question, he insisted, should be asked of "the best peopled countries in Europe and Asia." But the universalization of this question did not mean that Malthus believed that the peoples of Europe, Asia, Africa, and the new worlds were equal to each other. The Americas and the Pacific new worlds were formative of Malthus's universal principle because they were distinctive in displaying a contrast between indigenous savagery, a hunter-gathering

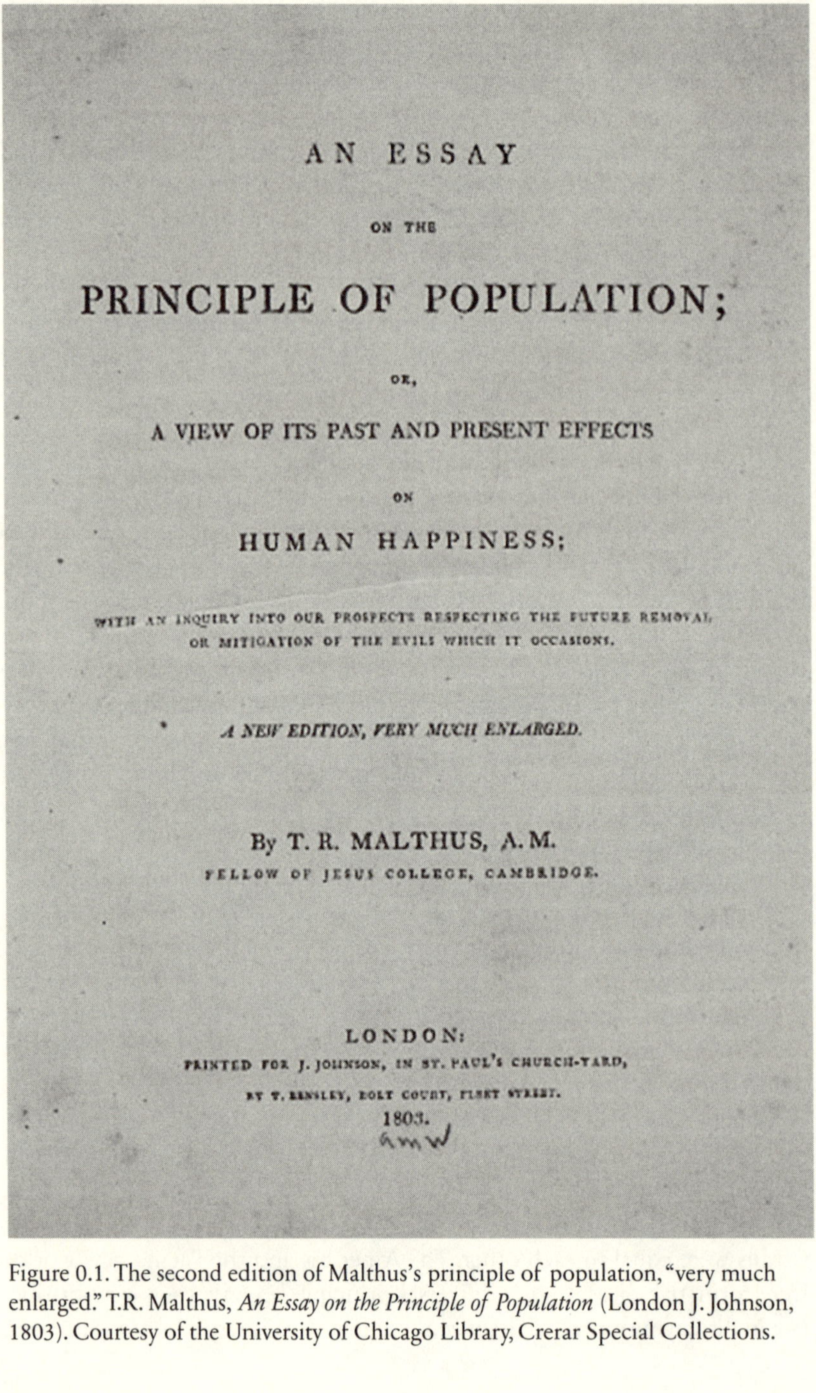

AN ESSAY

ON THE

PRINCIPLE OF POPULATION;

OR,

A VIEW OF ITS PAST AND PRESENT EFFECTS

ON

HUMAN HAPPINESS;

WITH AN INQUIRY INTO OUR PROSPECTS RESPECTING THE FUTURE REMOVAL,
OR MITIGATION OF THE EVILS WHICH IT OCCASIONS.

A NEW EDITION, VERY MUCH ENLARGED.

By T. R. MALTHUS, A. M.
FELLOW OF JESUS COLLEGE, CAMBRIDGE.

LONDON:
PRINTED FOR J. JOHNSON, IN ST. PAUL'S CHURCH-YARD,
BY T. BENSLEY, BOLT COURT, FLEET STREET.
1803.

Figure 0.1. The second edition of Malthus's principle of population, "very much enlarged." T.R. Malthus, *An Essay on the Principle of Population* (London J. Johnson, 1803). Courtesy of the University of Chicago Library, Crerar Special Collections.

economy that elsewhere had become a pastoral economy, and the agrarian, commercial, and civilized economies that settlers had introduced. The essentially new-world contrast in socioeconomic forms, meaning the clash between them, was at the heart of the principle of population, in which one group of humans, settlers, grew rapidly, while the other, the indigenes, underwent collapse, processes observable nowhere else in the world. The second edition of Malthus's principle of population, "very much enlarged."[14]

The six editions of the *Essay*, the books that Malthus read and cited, his private correspondence, his other publications and public testimony, and the writings of a variety of people who knew him or about him are the central evidence of our study. The slimness of the personal Malthus archive (some letters, almost no manuscript versions of his writing intended for publication), particularly compared to his contemporaries, is somewhat mysterious. But many sets of documents that were never gathered into his personal collection, which remain dispersed across multiple archives, are nevertheless highly revealing. So too are many of his underexamined public statements, including his evidence at the 1826–1827 Select Committee on Emigration. His intellectual development within his family is likewise significant; his early tutor, the sometime poet Richard Graves, evoked members of a Malthus family intent "on books; with maps and globes surrounded." That early and global education seems to have mattered, along with the intellectual genealogies that went into it. Finally, and perhaps most important, a close reading of the new world sections of Malthus's *Essay* offers important revelations into its author's logical force.[15]

The New Worlds of Thomas Robert Malthus begins with an analysis of the population studies that antedated the *Essay* and inspired the genesis of Malthus' central ideas. Chapter 1 traces the long and rich tradition of analyzing population dynamics in relation to empires and to the Americas, through the eighteenth century. Next, chapter 2 closely examines the contexts in which the first edition (1798) and the expanded second edition (1803) were written. Three subsequent chapters (3, 4, 5) explore the new world sites with which Malthus opened the 1803 edition; his study of indigenous people in New Holland, in the Americas, and in the Pacific Islands respectively. We consider how theorists,' voyagers,' and colonists' accounts shaped the *Essay*, carrying forward, well into the nineteenth century, the problem of reconciling universality and particularity within theories of human development.[16]

The next three chapters consider Malthus and his editions of the *Essay* in relation to three important historical contexts. Chapter 6 explores the *Essay* in terms of one of the era's most acute discussions of freedom, tyranny, and economy: slavery and the slave trade, with particular focus on the British debates in which Malthus was directly implicated. The penultimate chapter (7) turns to Malthus's larger thoughts on colonization as succeeding British governments considered the political economy of actively distributing "surplus" British populations to new colonial destinations. Upper Canada was one option; the antipodes another. Toward the end of his life Malthus engaged with various colonization schemes and schemers and with colonial policy architects who were particularly concerned with Scotland and Ireland. He eventually agreed with their expectation that emigration and colonization solved domestic problems of poverty and pauperism. Finally, chapter 8 explores the reception of Malthus in new worlds, especially the Americas, where his text enjoyed robust circulation and commentary, but also in the Australian colonies, where his name and thesis likewise had impact. It is notable that new world settlers in these places did not always read or use his population principle as he had intended. Uptake of his criticism of the usurpation of indigenous lands in particular was revealingly uneven. (In terms of the book's division of labor, the two authors worked together on the introduction; Joyce Chaplin was primarily responsible for chapters 1, 2, 4, 8, and the coda; Alison Bashford for chapters 3, 5, 6, 7.)[17]

This book has implications for the history of Malthus and political economy, for the history of universal theories of human societies, and for the history of colonialism and population. Above all, Malthus was a crucial figure in the identification of the cost of European population growth on new world indigenous peoples, a point that is worth making in relation to ongoing debates about global population growth and the limits of natural resources, however much the latter may seem to offer materially new frontiers. Historians know that, after 1492, total world population grew while new world indigenous populations declined. Malthus recognized both trends and analyzed them as they were unfolding within his lifetime. He did so within the most-discussed population text of all time, if not always in terms we would now accept and often with a diffidence that undercut their critical force. The convergence of imperialism and economics within his *Essay* demonstrates that colonial history is always part of economic history and that political economy is never just a domestic matter. The concept, if not the fantasy, of new worlds is central to these realizations about the impact of the "old world" on the rest of the planet. The new world, for Thomas Robert Malthus, had revealed, as no other part of the world could do so well, that human population expanded, struggled, and collapsed within limits set out by nature, and the new world had indeed suggested the possibility of that notorious principle of population in the first place.

PART I

Population and the New World

Chapter 1

Population, Empire, and America

THERE WAS NO ONE ELEMENT WITHIN Thomas Robert Malthus's principle of population that was wholly new, and yet he managed to make everything about it seem new. He did not invent so much as select from received observations about population and innovate within existing modes of demographic analysis. In intellectual terms, he was a magpie, a thief and reweaver of whatever he stole. That should not diminish his achievement—far from it. His use of familiar features of population analysis, if anything, gave his conclusions added power. But the extent to which he drew upon established modes of inquiry about population, adopting some elements while rejecting others, must be understood in order to appreciate his own and singular contribution: placing new worlds at the heart of population analysis.

Most historians of population studies look too late in the history of the field to make sense of Malthus. In identifying demography as a modern science, they trace its origins to the early modern period, often as late as the eighteenth century, with perhaps a little background on earlier periods. But population had concerned political and religious commentators since ancient times, most notably in Judeo-Christian Scripture. Those traditions of analysis did not cease in the early modern period. Rather, they were overlaid by subsequent and eventually more secular forms of analysis. Because Malthus would draw upon the scriptural and secular, the ancient and the modern, beginning at the beginning of the history of demography (long before it bore that name) is essential to understand his ideas about population and to understand how his contemporaries read them.

Four intellectual strands would be crucial to European comprehension of empires, new worlds, and population, and to Malthus's own eventual work on these long-connected topics. First, there was a natural theology of human generation, an interpretation of material things and processes that explained them as parts of divine mandate; this natural theology of population stressed that humanity had a genealogy precisely because of Adam and Eve's fall from grace and expulsion from Eden, a paradise that the new world was sometimes believed to resemble. Second, reason-of-state arguments from the

Renaissance presented population as a tool of statecraft, one that was particularly relevant for rulers who had or wanted imperial territories. Third, political arithmetic, the early modern ancestor of demography, used statistical analyses to define knowledge of what populations existed, their sizes, and whether they were rising or declining (and why). Fourth, political economy analyzed modern commercial society in terms of whatever had economic value, including land, commodities, and labor; as such, it depended on a stadial theory of society in which a commercial stage was thought to be the last in a series of ever more sophisticated social forms.

From the discovery of the Americas through the US War for Independence, each of these intellectual idioms would define the new world as particularly important for an emerging, modern science of population. A variety of experts would contribute to each tradition. But even more important, some commentators would synthesize what was familiar in order to generate a new kind of understanding. That was what Malthus would do in relation to the Americas (later the other new worlds of the Pacific), and in this regard he would draw upon the most important synthesizer and theorist before him, the American-born Benjamin Franklin.

* * *

Assessments of the peoples within worlds that Europeans categorized as "new" had taken initial form in relation to the Americas, with a mounting sense that the modern empires located there were qualitatively different from ancient empires, notably Rome's, and that these new worlds therefore constituted sites of natural experiments in the differential capacity for various populations to utilize natural resources and to increase their numbers, or else fail to do so. Because of this perception of a new quality for the population dynamics of these new worlds, there had also been a serious question of their relation to the story of humanity's origins as given in Christian Scripture, an emphasis that made especially clear that analysis of population was always an interrogation of the linked qualities of nature and human nature—specifically, of whether there ever could be redemption in the material world.

Natural theology interpreted the material world, including human beings, according to God's will and divine plan. That plan introduced an important and long-lived trope, the breeding pair. European Christians were aware that the Book of Genesis had commanded a primordial dyad, Eve and Adam, to "increase and multiply," eventually to "fill the Earth" as part of their divine mandate to exert dominion over nature. Humanity's scriptural parents heard that admonition while still in Eden, though they would not actually fulfil their duties until they had sinned, were expelled from paradise, and apportioned painful and gender-specific obligations. "In sorrow," God warned the apple-eating Eve (and her daughters), "thou shalt bring forth children." Meanwhile, "cursed is the ground for thy sake," God told Adam: "in the sweat of thy face shalt thou eat bread," torn from the ground through daily toil. God would repeat the command to "increase and multiply" to Noah and his family after they survived the Deluge. The sons of Noah were presumed to have repopulated the world after God had drowned Adam and Eve's other descendants. Exactly which of Noah's sons had settled in what parts of the world fueled debate, especially the critical question of where Ham (or Cham) had gone after being cursed for looking upon his father's nakedness. Ham and his descendents were doomed to be the hewers of wood and drawers of water for anyone who could extract such labor from them.[1]

Scripture had thus provided Christians with a global genealogy, though one that designated human nature as fallen, postlapsarian. The population imaginary that survives even into the twenty-first century, of the fateful impact one breeding pair might have for the entire globe, does not always bear a religious cast, but it definitely did for the Reverend Malthus and his contemporary readers. The original sin of a divinely created pair of humans had ordained that producing children and feeding them would be painful human obligations, equally unlikely (it seemed) to create a surplus either of people or of food. A subsequent set of sins and a punitive deluge had restarted the process of human generation and divided the globe among different lineages described as unequal, some destined to labor for others. The latter point became notorious as justification for the enslavement of sub-Saharan Africans, on the assumption that Ham's seed, Canaan, had settled in Africa.[2]

The European discovery of the Americas nevertheless challenged the scriptural explanation of how the Earth had been peopled. As evidence accumulated that the lands Columbus described and explored after 1492 were not, as he claimed, parts of Asia but new worlds entirely, it became difficult to explain how these places had acquired human inhabitants. Which of Noah's lineages had ventured that far, and why had God not explained them to the Christian faithful, as He had done for all parts of the "old" world? The idea of a separate creation of human beings, *polygenism*, was technically heretical. Another part of Scripture made that clear: God "hath made of one blood all nations of men for to dwell on all the face of the earth, and hath determined the times before appointed, and the bounds of their habitation."

Native Americans had to come from the same stock as Europeans—but how? In some ways, that the primordial breeding pair had dispersed progeny so far away compounded the wonder of human procreation, but the Americas also confounded Christian faith in the idea of a unified human lineage and destiny.[3]

For that reason, the Americas could be represented either as another Eden, a newly revealed reminder of God's creative beneficence and possible repository of human innocence, or else as a demonic counterfactual, the long-hidden realm of the devil and ultimate proof of the fallen state of humanity. There would be a rich tradition of associating American Indians with the scriptural past, even with paradise: Columbus was not unique in believing that Eden was located in the lands he had first explored. His descriptions of native Caribs as "guileless," moreover, set off a long convention of regarding Indians as primordially innocent, living sweetly naked in free-giving natural worlds, as if released from Eve and Adam's original sin. But equally commonly, the natives of this new world were depicted as Satan's prey and pawns. Suspicion that the peoples of the new world were cannibals was one of the most powerful of prejudices about them. Their presumed anthropophagy indicated both an inversion of European social norms and a desperate appetite unappeased by American foodstuffs, whether due to natural want or social depravity or both.[4]

Theodor De Bry's massive and influential *Grands Voyages: Americae* (1590–1634), for example, reinforced both interpretations. The frontispiece to the seventh part of this compendium on European reconnaissance of the new world displays the title flanked by an Indian man and woman, each gnawing a severed human body part; an infant tied to the woman's back reaches hungrily toward his mother's awful meal. This male-female dyad only reproduces human beings by consuming them, with no net gain. Their postlapsarian state is echoed in another illustration, this within the first part of De Bry's work, in a portrayal of the Fall and expulsion from paradise. Adam and Eve are in the foreground, just about to taste fruit from the tree of knowledge, and their fallen selves are in the background, performing their divinely mandated tasks. Eve nurses an infant Cain in a primitive hut while Adam scores the ground with a primitive hoe. Through the visual twinning of the two illustrations, the peopling of the world is connected to the peoples of the new world, with Edenic and satanic implications depicted in ironic juxtaposition, a new problem for the Christian faithful.[5]

All the same, from 1492 and through the seventeenth century at the least, a central principle of natural theology remained in place: God had created

Figure 1.1. The new world's cannibal parents. Theodor de Bry, *Grands Voyages*, part VII (Frankfurt, 1599). Courtesy of the Library of Congress.

Figure 1.2. Global parents, Adam and Eve, in new world context. Theodor de Bry, *Grands Voyages,* part I (Frankfurt, 1590). Courtesy of the Library of Congress.

a world uniquely suited to its human inhabitants, howsoever many of them there might be. Interpretation of the Americas was important, therefore, in the globalization of that argument from design, a test of Christians' faith in the idea of *plenitude*, which Scripture had promised. Although several new world landmasses were still missing from European globes and world maps, the still-expanding extent of South and North America already showed just how much land existed. That raised the question of how fully it might be populated. Were the inhabitants of the new world fulfilling the mandate to increase and multiply, to subdue the Earth? If not, how many more people could fit into their territories, once these were supplied with dutifully procreating European migrants equipped with intensive and commercially oriented forms of agriculture?

* * *

Before 1500, Europeans typically regarded population growth as a welcome development, if not a moral obligation. Despite recurring premodern fears about food shortages and concomitant sociopolitical instability, these were regarded as local problems. Ghost acres were important to nations or empires precisely as solutions to these localized difficulties. But incipient concepts of the labor value of property stressed that land was useless without people. Dramatic population decline, as with episodes of famine or plague, for that reason threatened the social order. And the larger argument from design and belief in plenitude for the moment held firm: God would not have created a globe inadequate to the terms of his command that humans should endeavor to fill it up.[6]

Greater fears were expressed about the failure to thrive than about any possibility of overrunning natural resources. Leaders of Protestant nations, including England (later Britain), contrasted their pious fulfillment of the duty to increase and multiply against the Catholics who (the antipapist stereotype went) locked their fertile sons and daughters in monasteries. All the same, Scripture had seemed to warn human rulers that only God should take numerical stock of their peoples: God had punished King David for following Satan's temptation "to number Israel." Together, these dictates indicated that sexual reproduction was a divine mandate, so sacred that secular rulers should not involve themselves overmuch in the result. It is notable that Malthus, a clergyman, was to profoundly ignore both these tenets, instead criticizing population increase as documented by censuses that, like King David's, dared to number the nations. For those innovations, he would be beholden to Renaissance theories about population and the power of states.[7]

During the sixteenth century, reason-of-state arguments for the benefits of a large population began to augment the religious duty to multiply. According to these political texts, any nation, as a territorial unit, was worthless without population. That almost commonsensical warning was then elaborated as a strategy of statecraft. Traditional reason-of-state arguments stressed static measures of political health, as with steady harvests, production of commercial goods, and maintenance of population, three signs of vigor in the body politic. Through their own personal bodily industry, individual humans generated wealth and revenue for the state. Men filled out armies and navies; women nurtured children who would continue those patriotic tasks in future; all worked to create subsistence and foster commerce. Still, overpopulation was recognized as a problem. Niccolò Machiavelli, not least, warned that overcrowding would eventually weaken a nation, only to be corrected by the natural occurrence of "[in]undations, pestilences, and famines":

> . . . for nature, as in simple bodies, when there is gatherd together enough superfluous matter, moves many times of it self, and makes a purgation, which is the preservation of that bodie; so it falls out in this mixt body of mankinde, that when all countries are stuffed with inhabitants, that they can neither live there, nor go other where, because all places are already possessed and replenish'd, and when the subtilty and wickedness of man is grown to that fulness it can attain to, it holds with reason, that of force the world be purged by one of these three waies.

It was a dire warning, an indication that competent rulers ought to monitor how extensive their populations were and how fast they might be growing.[8]

To that end, in his *Les Six livres de la République* (Six Books of the Commonwealth, 1576), French political philosopher Jean Bodin denied that to take a census was to commit a sin. David had been punished not for numbering his people but for counting his warriors only, omitting the priestly tribes. He had lacked faith in God's favor to Israel, which required the priesthood. The moral, Bodin argued, was that earthly rulers ought to know their *whole* populations, with censuses taken as often as they might benefit a commonwealth. Bodin identified another troubling question about populations, ancient or modern: did slaves count? He said yes, slaves were in fact citizens, however inferior ones, an answer that would continue to perplex rulers of composite populations, especially those acquired by means of imperial expansion, as in the Americas.[9]

Starting with the Jesuit-trained writer Giovanni Botero, reason-of-state arguments stressed not only stability but growth. In his *Delle cause della grandezza delle città* (On the Causes of the Greatness of Cities) of 1588, Botero launched an important defense of large, dense human populations. Human fecundity was the ultimate source of power: one young couple in Mesopotamia (the presumed site of Eden) had produced all the people in the world, even "to the countries we call the New World." Against the prevailing assumption that a great nation needed a large territory, Botero countered that "the multitude and number of the inhabitants and their power" mattered far more. The bigger the population, the greater the nation and its concomitant military and economic powers—more people allowed intensive and extensive growth, the former necessary for the latter, an important piece of advice for princes. This was an Italian perspective, by which people from a small but densely populated territory criticized the easy assumption that Spain and France were becoming powerful as national (and global) presences because they had greater territory. The assumption that geographic extent did not mean everything would, likewise, prove attractive to the English, denizens of a small but ambitious nation and later pioneers in population analysis.[10]

Botero was careful to specify how climate and human customs affected population, two criteria that would continue to be debated well into the modern period. He accepted prevailing environmental descriptions of human populations, distinguishing between hotter and colder climates as preconditions for human health and power. In the end, however, he stressed the significance of natural resources, which attracted people who would turn those resources into wealth, which then continued to attract (and sustain) population. Likewise, he believed that marital customs, and the treatment of women and children, were critical to a state's fostering of population. He believed that monogamy was the most effective form of marriage— most Christian theorists did—because polygamy denigrated women and their reproductive capacity. These opinions clearly expressed anti-Muslim antagonism. The kernel of the argument, in favor of a married dyad devoted to their common offspring, in which the wife/mother was acknowledged to have rights and deserve respect, would remain a strong element of European population theories, often prejudicial to all non-Christian peoples.[11]

Whatever their advice about fostering a large population, political commentators nevertheless warned that people could outstrip available natural resources, especially land: Malthusianism existed before Malthus. These proto-Malthusian hypotheses represented some of the earliest attempts to define what would later be called *carrying capacity*, the ability to sustain life, interpreted in this case in terms of the whole Earth. No one assumed that the world had infinite carrying capacity; plenitude depended on an optimal level of people, the fulfilment of God's design. Botero thought that the world's population had peaked three thousand years before he wrote and could never grow beyond that size because "the fruits of the earth and the plenty of victual doth not suffice to feed a greater number." Thomas Hariot, the mathematician and astronomer who lived in England's colony at Roanoke (probably present-day North Carolina), calculated the number of people who, descended from a primordial pair, could "inhabit the whole world" or (in a very different measure) could "stand on ye face of ye whole earth." For the latter case, Hariot thought that, if 6 million people could stand within a square mile, then just over 42 trillion could fit onto the Earth's available land. He estimated only the rate of human reproduction and the physical size of the globe, without analysis of what that globe could produce. But the nightmare image of 42 trillion people crowded elbow-to-elbow begged the question of how a growing global population might feed itself. It was from reason-of-state texts, therefore, that the idea of population varying with the means of subsistence became a commonplace both in small nations (including the Italian lands) and large (including mighty Spain).[12]

This was one reason why empires, as early as the sixteenth century, were described as outlets for any excess population. Bodin recommended that national censuses identify not only the quantity of people but their value as workers or warriors, "thereby to expell all drones [a beehive's nonworker bees] out of a commonweale." Persons without function at home could be exported via imperialism, their capacity to increase wealth and power (according to reason-of-state arguments) thus broadcast over greater territory. To visualize this export, Botero introduced an important metaphor, which might be called the *vegetable imaginary*, in which humans were equivalent to plants. Just as plants multiplied when "transplanted into open ground," so the ancient Romans had benefited from colonies, where the proliferating poor were sent for their further multiplication and production of goods. That scenario imagined land that was somehow clear of other inhabitants, an imperial fantasy (in contrast to the reality of conquest in ancient empires) that would have a long and troubling life in relation to new worlds. The three possibilities that Bodin and Botero had outlined—that empires both required and fostered population growth, that colonial territory must lack significant indigenous population, and that enslaved people had to be taken into account somehow—would continue to influence British-American understandings of colonial populations into the eighteenth century.[13]

Above all, there was new fear that populations could outbreed the resources in their natal lands, hence the need, possibly urgent, for colonies. Again, it seems to have been the unexpected existence of the Americas, and the ongoing discovery of the sizable extent of those new worlds, that teased out this question about the finitude rather than the plenitude of the globe. The idea of scarcity, and its potential transoceanic remedy, had never been defined on the same scale before the age of early modern empires. And because it was the European empires in the Americas that depended on settlement of European colonists (unlike the imperial zones in Asia and the Near East that for the moment had only small trading enclaves), it was the new world that presented the best modern potential for population-dependent colonies. Bodin's and Botero's arguments for the linked benefits of colonies and population increase would therefore influence an array of authors, as well as imperial schemers.[14]

It was not always certain, however, that Europeans could multiply overseas, whatever their fecundity at home. Because early modern medical theories stressed that human bodies were physically adapted to their natal places, global environments and human populations were not thought to be interchangeable. Rather, contemporary geographies, drawing upon ancient Greek texts, stressed the immense variation among potential sites for human life, from pole to pole via the Equator. Extremes of temperature were disparaged; western Europeans lauded the temperate zones, where they lived, as best for humans. As Europeans correctly observed, the largest populations (which they also deemed to be the most civilized ones) were found at the temperate optimum, as in Europe and China. But if members of those populations were unlikely to thrive elsewhere, they would be unable to expand their power outward. That fear rendered questionable migrants' contribution to the imperial might of modern nations, which, since the discovery of the Americas, had greater scope for expansion. Since the Deluge, the original peopling of the world had required slow movement outward from Mesopotamia ("little by little," as Botero put it), which had permitted gradual climatic adjustment. But modern migrations occurred rapidly. Colonists risked the rough transition known, to the English, as seasoning. Foreign places might kill them faster than they could reproduce.[15]

Anxiety on that score may have encouraged close assessment of new world settler and native populations, especially comparisons between them. It did not reassure Europeans that American Indian populations, whatever their size before contact, failed to thrive afterward. Spanish policy to take Indians' lands was accompanied by strategies to extract labor from them, in order to grow crops and mine precious minerals. But almost immediately, beginning in the greater Caribbean, native populations dramatically declined. Scandal over mistreatment of the Indians, particularly enslaved ones, would culminate in debates at Valladolid, Spain (1550–1551), to determine the justice of imperial treatment of new world natives, establishing a link between Indian mortality and Spanish imperialism. The Black Legend of Spanish cruelty would thus have a Spanish pedigree. But even as it exposed abuse of Indians, the legend also generated a powerful idea of the delicate Indian body, an emphasis that had a moral function: how much worse to brutalize such a fragile people? The idea of the delicate Indian would have profound implications for subsequent European (and settler) interpretations of the new world, as populated by a people doomed to melt away at the slightest physical provocation. Compared to them, Europeans, however displaced from their homelands, seemed destined to thrive.[16]

The English counted on that possibility—quite literally. Beginning with thorough head counts in the English settlement at Jamestown in Virginia, the first in 1623, population censuses were taken earlier and more often in Anglo-America than in England itself. After several earlier parliamentary attempts to count the English population, England would at last organize its first national census in 1801, whereas in British America before 1776 there would be 124 colonial censuses, including twenty-one of the twenty-six colonies that existed before the American Revolution. Add to that the local histories, governors' letters, militia musters, town bills of mortality, and hundreds of other sources that assessed colonial populations, sometimes with actual enumeration of all persons, and occasionally including Indian populations. The concern to count heads was the result, at least in part, of early fears about the first tiny English settlements, with their notorious "starving times."[17]

Anxiety quickly gave way to confidence. As early as the first part of the seventeenth century, English colonists claimed "a facultie that God hath given the Brittish Ilanders to beget and bring forth more children than any other nation in the world." The chauvinism was foundational to a racialized theory of population dynamics. Ever since Alfred W. Crosby's analysis of "virgin soil epidemics" in the post-Columbian Americas, scholars have known that such epidemics, disastrous causes of Indian population decline, resulted from lack of native immunity to the contagions that Europeans introduced after 1492—plus settler abuse of Indians. But colonists themselves had a different idea. Starting in the seventeenth century, English settlers hypothesized that the epidemics did not result from their arrival (and introduction of diseases such as smallpox) but instead represented outbreaks of endemic maladies. Colonists' superior survival amid these new world hazards thus showed their better and heritable bodily hardiness, a racialized trait that proved their providential ability to live in American environments, compared to Indians. Even in the Caribbean, where Europeans died at appalling rates, colonists pointed out that they outsurvived the indigenous populations, some of which approached extinction. The idea of native American fragility in response to disease would have a long afterlife, not least in Malthus's own principle of population.[18]

Early analyses of Indian subsistence and reproduction added more racialized elements to the comparative dimensions of emerging population analysis. Probably because the earliest accounts of North America were written by men who did not observe Indian women in childbirth, they generated a stereotype that laboring women did not experience pain, or even require assistance, as if they were exempt from God's curse on Eve. Likewise, Indian women were credited with performing most of the agricultural labor—even when pregnant or newly delivered—as if Indian men were released from the curse to delve in the earth for food that had been placed on Adam and were free to hunt (which in Europe was a pastime of the male elite). Altogether, the natives of North America seemed to defy Christian expectations about the constraints on human material existence, the painful businesses of childbearing and digging in the dirt for subsistence. English accounts were in consequence highly disapproving. Could Indian women really be free from Eve's curse yet damningly ignorant of Scripture? That only made sense to Christians if the special status indicated a diabolical rather than Edenic condition.[19]

Finally, it became near-gospel, and a very damaging prejudice, that North America had been underinhabited at the time of contact with Europeans, with a thin native population that declined still further after contact, guaranteeing the cleared ground that Botero had defined as exceedingly advantageous to nations with imperial designs. Although the Spanish discovery of large Indian populations in Central and South America would be famous, alongside the fact that some of these natives lived in densely populated and wealthy cities, Europeans tended to consider the Americas beyond these zones as lightly settled, engendering a debate, which still continues, over the size of the pre-Columbian population. Hariot had pondered these issues in relation to the native Roanok in early Virginia, concluding that the high land-to-inhabitant ratio guaranteed that the English, with methods of more intense agriculture, could easily insert themselves into the landscape. The earliest settlers of New England shared that view. Of the area around Plimouth Plantation, now in Massachusetts, Edward Winslow marveled at the lack of people and considered it an invitation for further English arrivals. "The country wanteth only industrious men to employ," he reported to correspondents back in England, "for it would grieve your hearts if, as I, you had seen so many miles together by goodly rivers uninhabited, and withal, to consider those parts of the world wherein you live to be even greatly burdened with abundance of people."[20]

As a second strand within pre-Malthusian population theory, reason-of-state analysis continued the scriptural, agrarian definitions of human activity and duty to thrive, while elaborating the significance of these activities to the state. The tradition reached an apex with John Locke's famous statement that "in the beginning all the World was *America*." His assertion cleverly echoed the scriptural tradition of creation (the paradise-dwelling human dyad, later expelled from a garden where they had labored not, and cast out into a world of nothing but labor) while establishing America as a prime example in the history of property. In Locke's labor theory of value, human beings used their bodies to convert natural resources into property. This was the point that political arithmeticians and political economists would subsequently elaborate in relation to human population and what it was good for, with a focused attention on what America represented, past and future.[21]

* * *

The modern science of population would draw upon natural theology and reason of state, even as it began to develop a statistical apparatus. Censuses had in several parts of Europe been used to assess national, regional, and urban populations. The English have been acknowledged as the pioneers in using the numbers that were collected to define modes of analysis that represented populations not only as they existed statically but as they might change over place and time. The new political arithmeticians, as they would be called, continued to stress population's significance to government, and they sometimes had connections to the English court and state that made apparent how their calculations were of public consequence.[22]

John Graunt was the pioneering analyst of demographic developments as they evolved through time. His dataset was London's bills of mortality, the lists of the dead that city officials in fact produced in several parts of Europe. The bills had gained notoriety with recent outbreaks of plague in London; other Europeans evidently regarded them as distinctively English. Graunt recognized that the dead could hold a mirror up to the living. At times of average mortality, the numbers of the dead could be used to estimate the total population; during epidemics, the lists revealed which populations (as defined by area of residence, by gender, or by age) suffered most, results that could challenge or reinforce prevailing ideas about disease. Also, rates of death, especially if correlated with their cause and with the age of the deceased, could predict the future size of the population; die-off among the young was more foreboding in this regard than that among the elderly.

Graunt gathered this research into his *Natural and Political Observations Made upon the Bills of Mortality* (1662), which became a model of statistical analysis of population for any place with the requisite lists of the dead.[23]

One of Graunt's main contributions was to generate tables of aggregate death statistics that correlated age and mortality. Although London's bills of mortality would not until 1728 list the ages of the deceased, Graunt deduced age from the stated cause of death, distinguishing among maladies associated with either young or old. The age-specific rates allowed him to focus on the political significance of the populations capable of performing service to the state, including the able-bodied men who could become soldiers and the fertile women who could become mothers. Population grew, he noted, even during epidemics. Such was the unstoppable force of human generation that it could, Graunt estimated, "double" a population every 64 years—thus inventing an arresting statistical hypothesis of geometric progression, expressed as doubling, that would be central to Malthus's analysis, and well beyond. Married Christians underpinned the fastest doubling. Adam and Eve had managed, "by the ordinary proportion of Procreation," to populate the whole planet within 5,610 years. So it continued, with Christians producing a more equal ratio of female to male children (he claimed) than Muslims. However London-bound his data pool, Graunt's thoughts were clearly global.[24]

Was London a universally representative sample? Graunt confined his statistical comparisons to urban London and rural Hampshire, which did not admit much variation into his conclusion. He was typical in this regard. As Lorraine Daston has noted, many early modern statisticians who analyzed populations, frequently through probabilistic calculation, tended to assume a universal mortality rate. The "life table" for actuarial work, which Edmond Halley would develop, based on Graunt's own tables, would continue to present life-spans as unvarying averages. Certainly, this standardization of death made it easy to attach insurance and annuities to individuals at predetermined rates. While the tendency to regard human death as a regular hazard may have seemed convincing within Europe, the Americas presented different possibilities, analysis of which would require the admission of variation in birth and death rates across the different populations that lived in colonized zones.[25]

The relevant pioneer here, William Petty, not only analyzed geographic and cultural variation but did so within an imperial context that included North America. Petty was an Englishman who had acquired Irish lands during Oliver Cromwell's invasion of Ireland, which he managed to keep even after the restoration of the monarchy. A founding member of the scientifically oriented Royal Society of London (1662), Petty merged his imperial and economic interests into a learned inquiry into the statistical analysis of population. He coined the term *political arithmetic* to describe his method of population analysis, with the political half of the term acknowledging that his new science descended from the tradition of reason of state, at this point expressed explicitly to account for empires that stretched beyond oceans. His imperial focus was deeply influenced by religion. Petty said that "God's first and greatest command to Man and Beast was *to encrease and multiply to replenish the Earth*. Why therefore should this duty bee put off?" His faith in plenitude was firm. Human subsistence was assured until world population averaged one person per three acres, which he estimated would not occur for another one thousand years.[26]

Petty's early comparisons of English and Irish populations, and of English-colonized Ireland and Pennsylvania, identified the imperial dimensions of political arithmetic. He gave numerical precision to the accepted contrast between English colonial increase and American Indian decline, using a hypothetical unit of one thousand Pennsylvania Indians, which dwindled as settlers increased. He contrasted that differential to Ireland. Although the native Irish had been reduced in number during the English reconquest of the 1640s, they were recovering, whereas Indian populations had shrunk due to natural causes (he thought), principally disease and low birthrates, with no signs of recovery. In that situation, the native Irish remained a source of labor, particularly for agriculture, while native Americans did not. (Petty ignored the fact of English enslavement of Indians precisely for work on plantations.) He also hazarded that intermarriage between English and Irish, part of an older pattern of assimilation, might create a strong composite population within England's growing Atlantic empire. His confidence in the basic Irish physical similarity to the English was perhaps the most obvious contrast between Petty's visions of Ireland and of North America; he offered no scenario of intermarriage for the latter.[27]

In his *Political Arithmetick* (1690), Petty continued to assess colonial populations and their value to empire. He estimated that Britons doubled in number only every two hundred years. That statistic made him wary about extending the nation's people over more extensive territory. He noted that the decline of Ireland's population was offset by colonial gains across the Atlantic. "The accession of *Negroes* to the *American* Plantations (being all Men of great Labour and little Expence) is not inconsiderable," he observed, a statement about the merits of slaves to imperial population and economy that would be fervently debated. Among the free colonial peoples, he believed that population increased particularly rapidly in New England. There, "few or no Women are Barren, and most have many Children, and . . . People live long, and healthfully," which had "produced an increase of as many People, as were destroyed in the late Tumults in *Ireland.*" Small but growing, the American colonies contributed, by Petty's estimate, half a million people to the king's total stock of ten million subjects. But Petty questioned the lasting value of colonial populations. "May not the superfluous Territories be sold," he asked, "and the People with their moveables brought away?" He meant New England's population in particular, which would benefit England if transplanted back to the homeland.[28]

That idea betrayed Petty's top-down vision of empire, acquired from his military experience in Ireland and typifying the preference for "garrison government" that emerged under the later Stuarts and would prove contentious in the American colonies. Petty's vision of New England's Congregationalist settlers, as transients to be ordered back to a land where they would suffer religious discrimination (under the Church of England their ancestors had fled), matched that trend. Petty had a similar garrison-government view of the Caribbean, which he thought the most valuable part of the empire. The sugar islands, intensively cultivated by an alien and subordinated population, black slaves, could generate imperial wealth more efficiently than any scattering abroad of free English people. For all this to work, different colonial populations had to be brought under command, something that neither New Englanders (who had the right to self rule through a colonial house of assembly) nor black slaves (whose acts of rebellion were making the Caribbean a byword for imperial instability) were likely to welcome. Petty's technical achievements in political arithmetic must be understood, therefore, as parts of a metropolitan vision of empire that few residents of England's new world colonies would have welcomed.[29]

A maturing plan for the surveillance of overseas populations was nevertheless evident in the gathering of information. English travelers were instructed to observe and estimate foreign populations, especially in places that offered some commercial or imperial opportunity to their nation. In his 1665 "General Heads for a Natural History of a Country, Great or Small," the natural philosopher Robert Boyle urged travelers to assess the human population of any place they visited, including the "Fruitfulness or Barrenness" of its native women. Even at this rather early moment in the history of what would become the British Empire, Boyle distinguished between the "*Natives*" of a place as well as "*Strangers,* that have been long settled there."

He thus acknowledged that travelers could themselves become inhabitants of extra-European parts of the world, not least as colonists, and that their descendants, if settled abroad long enough, could become natives of a kind. That possibility had already been registered with the Iberian coinage of the word *criollo*, in English "creole," to designate a person of old world ancestry born in the new world. Creole ascendency would be a reality by the time Malthus was born, in 1766, when well over a million individuals who traced descent from Britain lived in the Caribbean and North America. But their potential benefit to Great Britain's empire would depend on victory within the largest conflict that gripped the world to date.[30]

* * *

Malthus would write his *Essay on the Principle of Population* toward the end of a period that historians have called the Second Hundred Years' War, and his concerns would be framed accordingly. As in the medieval Hundred Years' War, the modern conflict embroiled France and England, the latter becoming, after 1707, Great Britain. Beginning with the War of the League of Augsburg and concluding with the Napoleonic Wars, the 125 years from 1689 to 1815 constituted a period of intense imperial rivalry, overwhelmingly over land. The territories in question included parts of Europe, but imperial zones also and new world places particularly were at the heart of the long controversy. The conflict would set preconditions and political ideologies for both the American and French Revolutions and their aftermaths. It also intensified questions about empires and colonies: what, if anything, were they good for?

Within this context, debates over population were crucial. It would be wrong to conclude that all writings on the topic were mere reactions to the Second Hundred Years' War; it would be equally wrong to suppose that they were disinterested. Even so, at a distance of three centuries, the differences between the French and British now seem less significant than their shared concerns, as Emma Rothschild has established in her work on Adam Smith and the marquis de Condorcet. In terms of population, two analytical dimensions interested everyone: the populations of ancient versus modern nations or empires and the comparative values of the different populations that lived within modern empires, slave and free, non-European and European. What was at first a basic debate over the varying virtues of ancient versus modern societies would develop into two analytic fields, one historical, about the stages of progress (or decline) in human society, and the other economic, about the value generated within commercial society, thought in this proto-industrial age to be the terminal stage for human social organization. These lines of inquiry, stadial theory and political economy, were interconnected. Political economy had a historical definition. It was underpinned by stadial theories of humanity as progressing through different modes of subsistence until it reached the commercial state, though it was debatable whether this represented rise, decline, or some kind of trade-off. That this was a question at all revealed the continuing connection between moral philosophy and political economy. Only once the modern economic condition was generally assumed to be good (perhaps toward the end of Malthus's lifetime, if then) would economists push the history of humankind, as the history of morals, out of immediate sight and focus merely on the presumed good of the present.[31]

Early modern political theorists had already postulated a theoretical originary state of nature and had sometimes examined contemporary "savages" as living representatives of a historic past. The Americas were critical to these intellectual developments. Savagery and barbarism had been ancient categories of assessment (and disparagement). American Indians became modern prototypes for both, but especially the former, and this was particularly true for the peoples of North America and the Caribbean, who were invariably described as hunter-gatherers who lived in small bands. These were the populations that the earliest European accounts had categorized as Edenic or satanic, sometimes both. By the end of the sixteenth century, as Anthony Pagden has pointed out, discussion of Indians as savages had devolved into the rudiments of comparative ethnology. Within this intellectual framework, societies that Europeans deemed primitive were compared to each other but also to the European civilization thought to be superior. They served as reminders, however, of what Europeans might have been in the past: as ancient Britons had been to the Romans who conquered Britain for their empire, so Indians were to the modern Britons who were conquering America for theirs.[32]

The grand synthesis of this ethnohistoric analysis appeared in Joseph François Lafitau's analysis of North America, *Moeurs des sauvages amériquains comparées aux moeurs des premiers temps* (Manners of the American Savages Compared to Those of Past Times) of 1724. In making a case for contemporary savagery as a historical state, comparable to that of a remote past, Lafitau emphasized the roles of language, belief, and symbolic systems to the manners (*moeurs*) of different peoples, what later ethnographers would call culture. Lafitau argued that similarities between native Americans and ancient Greeks proved humanity's monogenetic origins, therefore Indians' descent from Adam and Eve. Hugely influential, *Moeurs des sauvages* would be widely cited (not least by Malthus) for its myriad examples of native American practices, even as Lafitau's emphasis on nonrational aspects of human belief fell out of step with the criteria with which many Enlightenment theorists preferred to analyze humanity. Nonetheless, the key point that American Indians, as scattered and migratory savages, belonged to a historically prior condition, a hypothesis that Malthus would accept, was the product of several earlier centuries of description and debate about the Americas.[33]

A parallel debate considered Europe's own history and possible destiny as overlords of new world empires that might outdo their ancient prototypes in extent and grandeur. The initiator of this discussion, Charles-Louis de Secondat, baron de La Brède et de Montesquieu, endorsed the widespread opinion that the ancient Mediterranean must have been better peopled than its modern counterpart. He raised this point in his *Lettres Persane* (1721), developing it further in his 1748 *L'Esprit des loix* (The Spirit of Laws). He did not assent to another common opinion, however, that nature was losing its ability to sustain human life. Rather, he described contemporary laws and customs as brakes to reproduction that the ancient world had lacked. Within Europe, he blamed Christianity (especially clerical celibacy and the lack of divorce) for embargoing sexual desire. Modern empires, moreover, oppressed their denizens. The "Negroes" who labored in the Americas had never "filled" them; conquest had diminished American Indians without a compensating growth of colonial populations. That was because humans were adapted to their native climates, so that "the ordinary effect of colonies is the weakening of the countries from whence they are drawn, without peopling that to which they are removed." Montesquieu questioned whether state power could ever boost population. Centralized domination, including imperial conquest, discouraged marriage and family.[34]

David Hume was skeptical that the moderns were less populous than the ancients, which indicated potentially greater power for modern empires. In his essay "On the Populousness of Ancient Nations" (1752), he questioned a longstanding organic analogy between the Earth and the human body, which held that the former must decline in vigor as surely as the latter was known to. There was no empirical reason to accept that analogy, Hume pointed out; just as many ancient sources indicated small and feeble populations as suggested the opposite. Contemporary admiration of classical culture notwithstanding, he concluded that Rome's population must have been small, its empire overstretched, and—crucially—the ancient world's dependence on slaves deplorable. Hume believed that modern society, with its superior technical and financial skills, combined with "the discovery of new worlds," had expanded humanity's capacity to produce and trade the materials for a good life. In comparison, a merely agricultural society, as the ancient world had been (he thought), was a poor material foundation. In modern times, if every man who thought he could support a family went ahead and did so, "the human species" would "more than double every generation." And yet despite his clear preference for Europe's commercial societies, Hume raised the question of whether the fastest population increase might not occur "in every new colony or settlement," a possibility that again stated the distinctiveness of new world places.[35]

Hume's immediate critic, Robert Wallace, instead extolled the ancient world, particularly its empires, with a troubling endorsement of its slave-inhabited new world counterparts. (Wallace, who served in the Church of Scotland, would be the last ordained minister before Malthus to publish an influential population analysis.) Natural theology inspired his preference for the hypothesis of a long-lost ancient vigor. His *Dissertation on the Numbers of Mankind, in Ancient and Modern Times* (1753) opens with the peopling of the world from a primordial couple. From this original pair, the world's population might have doubled in number within thirty-three and a half years, roughly half the scriptural measure of "three score and ten" (seventy years) as a human lifetime. Wallace gave tables to illustrate the possibility, while conceding that this rate was unlikely to have lasted the full twelve hundred years he used as his temporal unit. "The distressed circumstances of mankind" had (and would) consistently undercut natural increase. At any moment disease, famine, natural disaster, war, corrupt rule, and vice could kill the living and retard their replacement.[36]

Wallace proposed an oscillating pattern of rise and fall. The world's first "rude and barbarous" peoples had not cultivated land for food. It was the ancient civilizations of the Near East and greater Mediterranean—agricultural societies with limited trade—that first achieved large food supplies and population to match. But the Roman Empire, through conquest, domination, and political corruption, destroyed these foundations by making agriculture unrespectable. Population had therefore peaked "about the time of *Alexander the Great* and before the *Roman* empire had enslaved the world." Wallace realized his admiration of the remote ancients might repel readers, as when, in response to Hume, he argued that ancient slaves had been well treated and therefore reproduced. "God forbid! that I should ever be an advocate of slavery," he protested, and yet "the ancient slaves were more serviceable in raising up people, than the inferior ranks of men in modern times." Somewhat incredibly, Wallace thought that slavery in the British plantations proved his point. Caribbean planters were determined, he said, to maximize the number of creole slaves, and equally eager to end the slave trade. Both impulses showed their care for slaves' physical well-being. However questionable Wallace's ideas, even for the time, they reveal how slavery was becoming a flash point of debate about Atlantic empires and their populations.[37]

But Wallace was otherwise unconvinced that the new world contributed to population growth. Rather, the discovery of the Americas had helped to "drain" people from Europe. Nor did he think commerce added to national strength; hands devoted to trade would be better used to grow food. Piety and virtue, not economic development, were the sources of greatness. "'Twas simplicity of taste, frugality, patience of labour, and contentment with a little, which made the world so populous in ancient times." Luxury "must of course prevent marriage, give check to the increase of mankind, and hinder millions from ever seeing the light." Economic development above the agrarian level was, in short, a sin, a circuitous violation of the divine command to increase and multiply.[38] Wallace was religiously orthodox as well, in believing in nature's plenitude, a topic he developed in his *Various Prospects of Mankind, Nature, and Providence* (1761). Were material conditions optimal—lands fully populated, people justly governed, religions devoted to marriage and family—nature would be generous. Even so, he warned that the Earth was not nor had ever been perfect—its capacity to sustain population had a limit, if as yet unreached.[39]

The general debate over historic population trends and their implications for economic activities were to gain precision after a series of mostly Scottish theorists defined stages through which human civilizations developed. These stadial theories proposed a universal history of succeeding methods of subsistence that expanded the material base for population. Humans, the theory went, had advanced from small populations that hunted and gathered, to somewhat larger groups that practiced nomadic pastoralism, to settled and denser communities that undertook agriculture (presumed to have made subsistence easier and population swell), and then to the commercial society of modern times, in which trade in edible goods as well as other commodities allowed populations to increase in size as well as sophistication.

The resulting schema tended to be analytic rather than constituting a historical narrative. It had seventeenth-century antecedents, not least Locke's contention that "in the beginning all the World was *America*," meaning that all societies began without definitions of property, and only began to develop them, barely, in the hunter-gatherer social economies that American

Indians still inhabited. Several other writers had posited historical stages, including Montesquieu, who had traced the increase of population from pastoral through commercial economies, concluding that countries below these modes of subsistence and "inhabited by savages[,] are usually thinly peopled, from the aversion they almost always have to labour and the cultivation of lands." Male "savages" wanted to hunt, not farm; females preferred abortion to childbirth. But the concept underwent its most intense development in the 1750s, with Adam Smith and Henry Home, Lord Kames cited as pioneers. By the 1760s, many British historians used stadial analysis within conventional narratives; William Robertson and Edward Gibbon are the most famous exemplars. Much of stadial theory drew on primary sources, particularly travelers' accounts of the Americas.[40]

"Stadial theory" as a label somewhat overstates its coherence, however. There was never one theory, and no unified school resulted. Rather, the idea of human history as progressing through modes of subsistence represented an analytic lens, a general way of understanding historical change without consensus over the particulars. The shared element of the strategy may have been simply to criticize older modes of historical narration that had used faith and authority to impose coherence, and to substitute material criteria as the means for historical transformation instead.[41]

Although the four-stage theory was supposed to apply universally to all humans, societal differences across time and space were sometimes difficult to assimilate to it. There was lively debate over who occupied the lowest stage of humanity and whether they could ever move to a higher stage, with the "Hottentot" (Khoisan) people of South Africa and the inhabitants of Tierra del Fuego most frequently designated as such and described as if incapable of change. Conversely, some theorists adapted classical Roman admiration for savages, including the ancient Britons and Germans, into an ideal of living noble savages, with native Americans as frequent exemplars. But the largest question that stadial theorists did not answer—indeed, disagreed over—was that of race, the belief that human difference was rooted within the body and its characteristics transmitted over the generations. Most Europeans held these assumptions, even as they differed over the degree to which they ought to, or should, act according to them; stadial theory emerged alongside and in dialogue with arguments against chattel slavery and concomitant attacks on heritable debasement. Some stadial theorists were forthright in their belief that race explained societal differentiation. Kames, for example, was a polygenist who declared that nature dictated which people were doomed to savagery and which destined for commercial civility. In this extreme case, stadial theory did not conjecture progress but instead stasis. Kames had his admirers, for his elision of race and culture; he had vehement critics, for the same reason.[42]

Precommercial human populations, past and present, functioned as didactic reminders of misery transcended or virtue abandoned, always in such a way as to bring the focus back to Europeans' true interest: themselves. Jean-Jacques Rousseau was for this reason an important theorist of humanity's natural state. Rousseau did not dispute that primitive society might be miserable; his hypothetical state of nature has an unappealing loneliness and brutality, and the stage he thought occurred after that, among people who had learned to hunt collectively, was not much better. And yet humans in these states, though little differentiated from animals, enjoyed a liberty that agricultural societies, let alone the densely populated commercial society of Rousseau's Europe, had relinquished. Rousseau did not privilege the variable of population in his social critique, but his belief in the tonic freedom of "natural man" is worth noting because Daniel Malthus, Thomas Robert's father, would admire Rousseau greatly.[43]

* * *

The end point of stadial theory was commerce, a terminus on which all theories of population were converging. Reason of state and political arithmetic had defined humans as physical bodies that contributed to commonwealth and empire. The eighteenth-century science of political economy elaborated that definition to specify the economic significance, to nation and to empire, of laboring and consuming bodies. Political economists (most famously Adam Smith) thus defined economic endeavor according to four guiding assumptions. First, national economies were dynamic, no longer describable in terms of stasis, such as a desired balance of trade. Second, economic systems had lawlike properties that could help predict future events. Third, all economic phenomena could be defined in terms of value produced, as represented statistically. Fourth, human economic activities could be categorized as production, consumption, and exchange. All of these features would, by mid-century, invite those who governed nations to think of population in economic terms, either on national or imperial scales. Even so, early political economy represented a philosophical turn that was, for the moment, slightly removed from matters of state. Unlike political arithmeticians, the first generation of political economists were more likely to have connections to universities than to government office. And they still regarded their field as a branch of moral philosophy (if not occasionally theology), the analysis of the best means to achieve happiness, defined as a good life founded on material benefits.[44]

As a branch of moral philosophy, political economy posited that human nature included "moral sentiments," an innate desire to engage with other human beings, a yearning most evident in commercial societies. There, people were liberated from grinding want and could engage in activities that showed their capacity for civility: commerce made the noneconomic possible. That was nowhere more true than in relations among men and women, who, freed from drudgery, were able to regard each other as engagingly sociable beings. Women in commercial society in particular could achieve the highest social refinement, devoted, that is, to activities that brought people into interaction beyond the marketplace. This opinion was critical of the ways in which women in past times and other places might have hard lives, though it continued to assume that there was something "natural" about women that distinguished them from men. Altogether, commercial society was regarded as having a polishing effect on humanity; when different nations connected through trade, their rough edges were smoothed away. So too did people within a commercial nation become polished through social interaction with each other.[45]

There was probably no point at which early political economy did not address questions of population and Atlantic empire. Few agreed with William Petty's conclusion that the Americas drained away Britain's strength. Rather, colonies contributed to the nation's aggregate population and economic power. What remained debatable was *which* colonial people made the largest economic contributions, either as laborers or consumers, with suspicion that non-Europeans were never as valuable as white settlers. In his widely read 1708 assessment of the British Empire, John Oldmixon summarized, " 'Tis said, People are the Wealth of a Nation, and to take away their People is to impoverish them; those that say it, mean only laborious and industrious People." On those grounds, Oldmixon argued, the sugar plantations were the most productive part of the empire, Great Britain included: each Englishman in the Caribbean constituted the economic value of three at home, though this was a measure that rendered African slaves—the real workers—invisible. Colonial ability to consume mattered too. Anyone who earned a surplus was contributing doubly to the economy, first by producing wealth and second by consuming goods. People who were too young, too old, physically disabled, or irrational did not count in the same way. While Oldmixon counted West Indian slaves as consumers, he admitted that they did not constitute as big a resource as free workers. Nor did "savage" people, whose wants were simple. "The *Indians* make the least consumption of our Goods," Oldmixon concluded.[46]

Both the economic assessment of human population and its distanced analysis of colonial scenarios were controversial, as seemingly inhuman if not inhumane visions of humanity. It is intriguing that individuals from the peripheries of the British Empire made the sharpest criticism of the new trends. Two notorious satires are cases in point.

Jonathan Swift's *Modest Proposal for Preventing the Children of Poor People from Being a Burthen to Their Parents, or the Country, and for Making them Beneficial to the Publick* (1729), is the most famous population satire. As William Petty had predicted, and Swift witnessed, English-occupied Ireland's population was rising faster than its food supply. Swift monetized the ensuing misery, calculating, for instance, that the amount a poor woman might make in begging would, by buying her food, subsidize for about a year her production of breast milk for an infant. Feeding the child thereafter was the problem. Swift proposed selling Irish children to the rich, to be slaughtered as meat. To augment this bold critique of British colonialism, Swift made several telling references to the new world. He presented the Irish option of contractingtheir labor to the English and emigrating to Barbados as even worse than butchering children. And he credited a "very knowing American" with information about the succulence of a suckling infant. In this way, he rehearsed the longstanding conviction that native Americans dined on human flesh, and he assessed the trans-Atlantic transfer of labor (whether as servants or slaves) as ethically similar to cannibalism.[47]

Benjamin Franklin had a lighter touch in his "Speech of Miss Polly Baker," written in 1746 and published anonymously in a London newspaper the next year. Miss Baker speaks from a Connecticut courtroom, where she is charged with fornication, again, having just produced her fifth bastard. But Baker protests that she is merely obeying the "command of Nature, and of Nature's God, *Encrease and Multiply*," and that her "steady Performance of which" benefited "a new Country that really wants People." Persuaded, the justices drop all charges and one of Baker's judges offers "to marry her the next day," making an honest woman of the scripturally literal producer of multiple little colonists. The piece was so ably constructed that readers in Europe and America assumed Baker was a real person and her speech an actual event. Only decades later did Franklin confess his authorship. But he never recanted his belief that North America was "a new Country that really wants people," and his assumed low labor-to-land ratio would remain central to debates over new world populations.[48]

* * *

If it was obvious that colonial peoples made significant economic contributions, how best to assess and harness them was not yet clear. This was not a theoretical problem, but one of active governance as war and the threat of war continued to make all aspects of empire into critical issues for Europeans and Americans alike.

No one knew this better than Franklin, who, alongside his satirical pieces, had been making serious claims that American populations were underappreciated imperial assets. He shrewdly offered these statements at hot moments in the Second Hundred Years' War, starting in 1747, during the War of the Austrian Succession (King George's War). Franklin had been reading extensively in both political arithmetic and political economy and in 1751 wrote his most important population analysis, "Observations Concerning the Increase of Mankind," which was to provide Malthus with his own principle of population.

Franklin wrote his essay in the wake of the Iron Act (1750), a measure to support British manufactures by preventing colonial production of iron. He proposed that colonists served the empire much better as producer-consumers when freed from such regulation. But his theoretical contribution was to present American populations as distinctive challenges to metropolitan science. He opened with an attack on political arithmetic's reliance on European bills of mortality. Those records failed to explain North America, where births so outstripped deaths that the settler population "must at least be doubled every 20 Years," the fastest "doubling" estimate yet ventured for such a large population. As Polly Baker had surmised, American fecundity had an agrarian basis: rapid increase resulted from accessibility of land in "a new Country that really wants People." Compared to their European counterparts, American settlers could establish their economic independence, get married sooner, and thus produce larger families. Franklin linked the prospect of rapidly replicating American dyads—myriad Adams, multiple Eves—back to commercial development within Europe's Atlantic society, noting that a greater colonial population in British North American population meant greater consumption of British manufactured goods. Unlike Petty or Oldmixon, Franklin favorably compared the continent's economic contribution to that of the sugar islands, where black slaves, the Caribbean's population majority, barely functioned as consumers.[49]

At this level, Franklin's population analysis was part of an emerging critique of new world slavery, on the grounds that a modern, commercial society needed free workers. The "introduction of Slaves" anywhere, he argued, tended to "diminish" population by edging out white laborers even as the work of slavery (again meaning in the sugar islands) killed slaves faster than they could naturally reproduce, "so that a continual Supply is needed from Africa." While this statement presaged Franklin's eventual humanitarian criticisms of slavery and the slave trade, it was at this point informed by racism. Continental Europeans, he said, "with the English, make the principal Body of White People on the Face of the Earth. I could wish their Numbers were increased." Whatever the value of the sugar and other tropical groceries they grew, slaves were burdens on the freely producing and consuming American societies that were, he contended, the empire's true strength, an important challenge to previous thought.[50]

Franklin drew similar conclusions about America's indigenous populations, partially by using stadial theory. He maintained that American Indians, as migratory hunters and, at best, occasional gardeners, failed to utilize North American land fully. That was prejudicial. All sub-Arctic Indians grew crops. Agriculture was particularly important to the larger populations in the continent's interior. Franklin knew the corn-growing, town-dwelling peoples of the Iroquois Five Nations, for instance, because his colony of Pennsylvania had diplomatic relations with them. In any case, might not Indians become farmers and consumers of manufactures, moving forward through the stages laid out in theory? No: Franklin concurred with the old claims that Indians, compared to colonists, suffered disproportionately from epidemics. He declared that Indian demise was both inevitable and beneficial, given that it would free up yet more land for settlers. In a simultaneous attack on slavery and on non-European peoples, he rejoiced that in the colonies "we have so fair an Opportunity, by excluding all Blacks and Tawneys, of increasing the lovely White and Red" complexion of Europeans.[51]

Franklin's work was, moreover, and despite its formulaic references to Providence, a soundly materialist analysis of human populations as composed of mere bodies. That assumption challenged the natural theology that had been central to population analysis, placing humans above the rest of nature. In contrast, Franklin compared humans to soul-less plants and animals, elaborating in particular a new version of the vegetable imaginary:

There is in short, no Bound to the prolific Nature of Plants or Animals, but what is made by their crowding and interfering with each others Means of Subsistence. Was the Face of the Earth vacant of other Plants, it might be gradually sowed and overspread with one Kind only; as, for Instance, with Fennel; and were it empty of other Inhabitants, it might in a few Ages be replenish'd from one Nation only; as, for Instance, with Englishmen.

The replenishment was well underway. Franklin estimated that from an original 80,000 migrants (mostly English) to North America, there were now over 1 million white colonists. Should they double their numbers within twenty-five years (estimating conservatively), there would be 2 million of them. Franklin thus drew upon long-established arguments for English bodily supremacy and adaptability to new world places. Colonists' fertile bodies held down territory, generated agricultural products, and consumed manufactures. Their virtues stood in contrast to the incapacity, as Franklin saw it, of Indians and of enslaved workers to contribute comparable benefits. His assessment did not so much neutrally describe the peoples of British America as predict the imperial bastion that one population—the settlers—should become.[52]

Franklin's assurance that the million or so colonists resembled Britons, culturally and physically, and that they would cheerfully buy British manufactures if not annoyed by British regulations, were statements of British imperial loyalty. Rejoicing in his proliferating fellow Americans, he wrote: "What an Accession of Power to the British Empire by Sea as well as Land! What Increase of Trade and Navigation!" Such were the glories of new world ghost acres. But Franklin's analysis contained obvious threats about the cost of alienating so many distant British subjects. His intentions were all the clearer in his decision to publish the essay in 1755, one year after skirmishes in the Ohio Valley between French and British colonial military forces would set off the Seven Years' War (1756–1763).[53]

That great imperial conflict represented the apex of the Hundred Years' War. The war began in North America and would be a turning point for the British Empire because it represented a choice between kinds of land and of population. Even before the war ended, Britons understood that the two big prizes would be "Canada" (the northern portion of New France) or Guadeloupe. Acquisition of both seemed unlikely. The choice between them signified competing conceptions of commercial wealth, based either on extensive population and territory or else on intensive cultivation and monoculture, with the former tending toward free labor and the latter toward slavery. Franklin's preferences were clear within his essay, but he heightened them with his decision to publish it, anonymously, in tandem with another man's work on the possible annexation of Canada.

The Treaty of Paris (1763), which ended the war, was Great Britain's clear bid for a continental new world empire. Eschewing Guadeloupe, Britain chose Canada, plus Bengal, both formerly French. The British crowed that they now possessed the largest empire since those of Alexander the Great or Caesar Augustus. But victory cost the victors. Debt from the war meant that Britain's annual payment of interest alone was more than any prewar budget had been. Desperate for revenue, British ministers tried multiple times to tax the American colonists, who firmly rejected that scheme. Their protests against taxation without representation would grow critical in 1765, the year of the Stamp Act, and were barely appeased by the revocation of that act yet simultaneous passage, in 1766 (the year of Malthus's birth), of the Declaratory Act, stating that Parliament had sovereignty over the colonists even if they were not directly represented in that body.

It was at this point that Franklin's essay on population achieved its greatest impact, as a warning of Americans' growing power. Its central claim of North America's settler population doubling every twenty-five if not twenty years (a new benchmark of demographic rapidity on a large geographic scale) implied that British America would soon become the population center of the empire, and perhaps the political center of the English-speaking world once Americans outnumbered Britons. That prophecy revealed the new ambition among colonists that would eventually lead into the revolutionary effort against British imperial authority.

So arresting was Franklin's image of rapid American population growth that it fascinated both American patriots and Britons who were either sympathetic to colonial protests or else apprehensive about a rising American proto-nation. The Reverend Ezra Stiles of Princeton University preached a 1761 sermon in which he referred to Franklin's prediction of a great and greatly populated America, also stating that America's population was doubling every twenty-five years. In 1769 the English clergyman and radical political theorist Richard Price wrote a letter on population to Franklin (a personal friend), later printed in the *Philosophical Transactions* of the Royal Society of London. Price then included the piece in his 1771 book, *Observations on Reversionary Payments*, the payments made when property reverted to a designated recipient, as an annuity to a widow (a classic case in political arithmetic). Referring to claims of Madeira's fast population growth, Price noted to Franklin that "this (as you, Sir, well know) is a very slow increase, compared with that which takes place among our colonies in AMERICA. In the back settlements, where the inhabitants apply themselves entirely to agriculture, and luxury is not known, they double their numbers in 15 years; and all thro' the northern colonies, in 25 years," giving citations to Stiles and to the 1761 edition of Franklin's essay. Price topped it off with the prediction that, within seventy years (the scriptural lifespan), British North Americans would outnumber Britons two to one.[54]

* * *

Even as the multiplying American patriots threatened to reduce the size of the British Empire by declaring independence, Britons had been exploring an extended new world. The conclusion of the Seven Years' War had set off a scramble for new territory, with France in the lead, because motivated to find imperial zones to replace what it had just lost to Great Britain. The Pacific world, only small parts of which had been settled by Spain in the sixteenth century, was the obvious arena of opportunity. From 1764 to 1771, expeditions led by John Byron, Philip Carteret, Samuel Wallis, Louis-Antoine de Bougainville, and James Cook made historic reconnaissance of the interior islands of Polynesia as well as the larger landmasses eventually named New Zealand and Australia.[55]

These significant discoveries were unhappy events for their native populations, who found that they were, among other things, objects of study for population theorists. Expedition leaders and their naturalists were requested to report on these matters. When James Cook sailed into the Pacific in 1769, for example, his initial orders warned him that Tahiti had been described as "populous," which constituted a possible military threat, an impression he was also implicitly invited to confirm or correct. More directly, Cook's secret orders, opened only once he was in the Pacific, instructed him to search for a long-elusive southern continent presumed to exist at the bottom of the globe and, if he found it, "to observe the Genius, Temper, Disposition and Numbers of the Natives, if there be any."[56]

The narrators of the late eighteenth-century Pacific expeditions were right up to date in using stadial theory to describe the newest of worlds. They typically described Pacific peoples as savages, at the earliest or lowest stage of human history. That was not surprising, given that the designation had been bestowed on American Indians even before the development of conjectural history, when "savage" still implied a state of religious oblivion. But by the late eighteenth century, the savage condition was as frequently cor-related with primitive methods of subsistence and lack of recognition of property. The simplicity of savage life could be praised, often when a Eu-ropean observer wanted to stress the natural fecundity of tropical or semi-tropical places, where little labor was needed to get food. Elsewhere, as in Australia, the underdevelopment of natural resources seemed perilous and the obvious reason for a much more thinly settled landscape, compared to parts of Polynesia and New Zealand. Polynesians and Māori were sometimes described as "barbarians" because they kept domesticated livestock (pigs), practiced agriculture, and appeared to have more complex political forma-tions, compared, at least, to Australian Aborigines. If Europeans began to pitch Aborigines as the new exemplar of humanity's lowest, simplest, earli-est social formation, Pacific islanders, particularly on Tahiti, were the newest examples of natural man, noble savages, though the positive and negative valences of these descriptions varied according to the taste and emphasis of the describer.[57]

Concern about food and population extended to interest in marriage cus-toms and the status of women. In the Pacific the absence of legal definitions of property, as Europeans would have recognized them, seemed to include marriage; where no sense of individual ownership existed, monogamy failed. The type specimen for that stereotypic interpretation of Pacific sexuality was Tahiti, where French and British mariners alike remarked on the sexual avail-ability of young women, which resulted neither in marriage nor childbirth. Depending on the commentator, this was either evidence of an Edenic condi-tion—the primal innocence of savage peoples—or else satanic sin and social chaos. Early descriptions of Aboriginal women were if anything even more negative, echoing earlier descriptions of Indian women as woefully exploited by their menfolk, with dire consequences for reproduction.[58]

To a very great extent, these analyses recycled hypotheses that had already been rehearsed in relation to the Americas. Yet again, European observers de-ployed the two extremes of Edenic bliss versus a fallen state to explain non-European societies. And, yet again, they designated the lands of the Pacific as new worlds. The most striking example of this extension of America over and across the Pacific was the early tendency for British observers to use the word *Indian* to name Polynesian, Australian Aboriginal, and New Zealand Māori peoples, as if they were cognates of, or even somehow related to, the peoples of the Americas. *Indian* was the term used, for example, by Joseph Banks (Cook's chief naturalist), to describe people in New Zealand, Tahiti, New Holland, and New Guinea. The result was to connect the new worlds of the Pacific back to those of the Atlantic and to thereby distinguish the Pacific from Asia, as well as from Europe and Africa. If Locke had said that the world had begun as it had once existed in America, that primitive beginning was newly represented to Europeans in the worlds of the Pacific.[59]

* * *

The development of population analyses from the 1760s and 1770s onward took place, therefore, within an expanding global geography understood to be a field for imperial rivalry, if not conflict. With either logic or irony, one of the most aggressively imperial eras in modern history was nonetheless precisely also the time of intense questioning about the morals of imperialism. Guillaume-Thomas-François Raynal (the famous abbé Raynal), in his 1770 *Histoire philosophique et politique des établissemens et du commerce des Européens dans les deux Indes* (Philosophical and Political History of European Settlement and Trade in the East and West Indies), expressed his generation's doubts in his great question: "Has the discovery of America been beneficial or harmful to the human race?" Posed as a moral dilemma about the oldest of new worlds, the abbé Raynal's worry would tinge initial perceptions of the newer versions of them.[60]

Stadial theory and political economy offered efficient ways to make sense of what Edmund Burke called "the Great Map of Mankind," including the renewed possibilities of new worlds as originary points for human societies. By the late 1760s, free British subjects on both sides of the Atlantic were accustomed to marveling at the extent of their nation's empire, if equally likely to worry about its continued state of health. Within political economy, both impulses were expressed as numerical evaluations of colonial economic value. For some theorists, expansion constituted a threat; to others, an intoxicating promise of abundance. Two Britons, in works initially published in 1776, the first year of declared war between the United States and Great Britain, represented the two possible responses; Malthus would later read both.

The historian Edward Gibbon was the decided pessimist. In his *History of the Decline and Fall of the Roman Empire*, the first portion of which appeared in 1776, Gibbon traced the fates of the ancient Romans in what was immediately recognized as a commentary on the modern Britons. With caution about imperial over-reach, as well as warnings against the decadence and luxury that accompanied imperial glory, Gibbon (not unlike Wallace) praised the contrastingly simple virtues of the savage and barbarian peoples who eventually defeated Rome. That had an important dimension in relation to population. It was pastoral nomads who were able to pillage first the out-skirts and then the heart of the Roman Empire. Gibbon resolutely portrayed the forest-dwelling barbarians of ancient northern Europe as few in number and distinguished by their "poverty" (as hunting migrants, they had almost no permanent property), and yet for those reasons enjoyed a "liberty" that the wealthy, trading, town-bound Romans had abdicated. Although Gibbon did not spell out a comparison between the British and the "savage" peoples in British America, readers would have been aware of the comparison, brim-ming with disapproval as it was against their own commercial and imperial statuses.[61]

In contrast, Adam Smith registered optimism over a growing and popu-lous British North America in his *Inquiry into the Nature and Causes of the Wealth of Nations* (1776), an exception to his otherwise skeptical assessment of imperialism. Smith acknowledged the distant glories of ancient empires, and noted the mineral riches of Spanish America, but gave the edge to mod-ern colonies that fostered settlement and settlers. He did not deny that Spain's empire had its strengths, noting that Lima was still larger than any city in British America. Moreover, he concluded of Peru and Mexico that "in spite of the cruel destruction of the natives which followed the conquest, these two great empires are, probably, more populous now than they ever were before: and the people are surely very different; for we must acknowledge ... that the Spanish creoles are in many respects superior to the ancient Indians." But imperial riches were fleeting. Echoing Hume's and Franklin's reservations about slave-generated wealth, Smith wryly proposed that the biggest rev-enues from Britain's Atlantic colonies were founded on human weakness: "Sugar, rum, and tobacco are commodities which are nowhere necessaries of life, which are become objects of almost universal consumption, and which are therefore extremely proper subjects of taxation."[62]

And yet Smith thought some forms of imperialism bore rare fruit: "The colony of a civilised nation which takes possession either of a waste country, or of one so thinly inhabited that the natives easily give place to the new set-tlers, advances more rapidly to wealth and greatness than any other human society." That was quite a claim. "There are no colonies of which the prog-ress has been more rapid," he concluded, "than that of the English in North America." He identified three factors critical to their success: availability of land, technical knowledge among the newcomers of how to cultivate it, and "liberal" institutions that promoted freedom, including free trade with nations other than Great Britain. In consequence, the British colonies had greater social equality among free settlers, plentiful agricultural production,

and therefore incentives to marry. Nature and human nature were beauti-
fully paired.[63]

Certainly, Smith believed that a large and growing population was an
asset to an empire, yet again exemplified in British North America. "The most
decisive mark of the prosperity of any country is the increase of the number
of its inhabitants," he asserted. People in the aggregate made economic contributions, most obviously as producers but also as consumers. Smith flatly
stated that "consumption is the sole end and purpose of all production."
Those whose consumer efforts were constrained—as with slaves or even free
persons restricted by mercantile regulations—could not fully contribute to a
nation's economy. If the British colonies contained less wealth than Britain,
their rapid population growth indicated that the balance might shift. "In
Great Britain, and most other European countries, they are not supposed to
double in less than five hundred years. In the British colonies in North
America, it has been found, that they double in twenty or five-and-twenty
years." Smith's footnote credited Petty's *Political Arithmetick* for the statistic
on Great Britain and Richard Price's *Observations on Reversionary Payments*
for the one on North America, the latter text based on Benjamin Franklin.[64]

Indeed, fascination with Franklin's hypothesis about rapid American population growth ruled the day. Though increasingly divorced from its author,
the thesis that North America's population doubled every twenty or twenty-
five years had a brilliant career, notably in British publications. The *Annual
Register* of 1761 (six London editions) took an "Extract from a piece written
in Pennsylvania in 1751, entitled Observations concerning the Increase of
Mankind," and gave the every-twenty-year estimate of a doubled population.
James Burgh, in his *Political Disquisitions . . .* (1774–1775) cited the calculation without giving a source; Burgh also emphasized that British ministers
would be mad to risk losing such a large consumer population. *The Politician's
Dictionary, or, a Summary of Political Knowledge* (1775) repeated the estimate
without any editorializing.[65]

Franklin's text was in fact the lead essay in an edition of his works published
during the American War for Independence and, astonishingly, in London.
This *Political, Miscellaneous, and Philosophical Pieces* (1779) was edited by an
English friend, Benjamin Vaughan, and published by a noted London bookseller and publisher, Joseph Johnson. Vaughan's choice of publisher advertised the essays as a rebuke to the British ministry, because many of Johnson's
other publications were just that. Johnson was a religious dissenter, raised as
a Baptist, in adult life shifting to Unitarianism, at a time when full participa-
tion in British public life required membership in the Church of England.

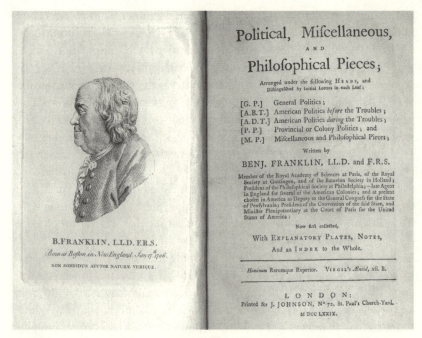

Figure 1.3. Malthus's primary new world source. Benjamin Franklin, *Political, Miscellaneous and Philosophical Pieces* (London: J. Johnson, 1779). Courtesy of the Library Company of Philadelphia.

He had begun his career by publishing fellow religious dissidents, notably Joseph Priestley, another of Franklin's friends. (A surviving letter from Johnson to Franklin, dated 1766, thanks the colonial electrical experimenter for giving, at Priestley's request, a reader's report on Priestley's *History and Present State of Electricity*, which Johnson published the next year.) Johnson also published another of Franklin's radical associates, Richard Price, and his list of critically minded authors would continue to grow until it included T. R. Malthus.[66]

In Johnson's 1779 edition of Franklin, the lead essay on population was accompanied by a 1755 letter to Franklin from "R. J., Esq.," Richard Jackson, a member of Parliament, correspondent, and admirer. Jackson accepted Franklin's point about material circumstances facilitating or inhibiting the growth of population, but his letter otherwise stressed the significance of morals and manners. That was an emphasis on human nature versus nature itself that Franklin would not necessarily have endorsed, at least not at the length and in the detail that Jackson proposed; if he replied to Jackson, the letter has not survived. In any case, Franklin was not in a position to supervise the edition. He was in the US diplomatic service in Paris, part of the Franco-American war against Great Britain.[67]

In 1781, the United States would win that war. Because they did, the Americas, and new worlds beyond them, would undergo important imperial reconfiguration in the 1780s, even as the arguments for political autonomy associated with the growing and confident US population remained divisive. The most direct connection between North America and New Holland, the eastern half of which had been renamed New South Wales by Cook, was in the latter's repurposing as a convict settlement. The British North American colonies had once filled that function. New South Wales would be pressed into service after Britain's recognition of American independence in 1783, and a new colony of settlement in a new world would be born, even as the meanings and value of empire and population remained in dispute, an unresolved problem of the Second Hundred Years' War.

* * *

Here then are the four intellectual strands, sometimes interwoven with each other, that were available to Malthus as he began to consider population. He would have at his disposal a natural theology of life on Earth, an assertion of the value of population to states and empires, a theoretical but also numerical science of political arithmetic, and a political economy of population and empire that assumed that populations could be classed into historic stages of development based on material subsistence, concluding with commercial society. From his familiarity with these intellectual traditions, Malthus would know of the observations that travelers had made of populations beyond Europe and of the information about political arithmetic that creole settlers themselves possessed. He would have been aware of the extraordinary events of the Second Hundred Years' War that gave any observations about population heightened political as well as moral significance, particularly as they commented upon Britain's ability to command imperial zones over new worlds in the Atlantic and the Pacific. From such scraps, the magpie made his marvel.

Chapter 2

Writing the *Essay*

"AN ATTEMPT TO PROVE THE GENERAL UTILITY of colonies to the mother country, after the very recent loss of our settlements in America, may perhaps appear presumptuous," the young man wrote, "yet I persuade myself if the subject be impartially, & not too precipitately judged, it will be found that under proper regulations, they are a source of great strength & power to the country which gave them birth." Given that the legacies of the American Revolution would flow abundantly out of the Atlantic, eventually into the new worlds of the Pacific, it is not surprising that they seeped into the thoughts and writings of schoolboy Thomas Robert Malthus. In a student essay that refers to the "recent loss" of the thirteen North American colonies, as conceded in the Treaty of Paris signed on September 3, 1783, Malthus, still in his teens, made his first foray into the questions of moral philosophy and political economy that would become his life's work. The short piece is unpublished juvenilia, but within it Malthus made two strong statements about new world colonies: they were assets to the nation, not drains upon its resources, but they required "proper regulation" from the imperial center to achieve their maximum benefit.[1]

From these beginnings, during one of the crises that constituted the Second Hundred Years' War, the American Revolution, Malthus came into his maturity as a writer and thinker during a succeeding crisis, the French Revolution. He would publish his central ideas about population in 1798, at a time of renewed war and intense public debate over the fallout of the revolution in France. That itself was a polarizing event, and one that elicited continuing dissent about the nature of the preceding American Revolution and the fate of new world colonies. Malthus would then substantially enlarge his essay on population from 1799 and into the first half of 1803, as Europe and its imperial territories were struggling to achieve a peace settlement.

And yet to live at a particular time in history is not necessarily to accept or absorb all of its consequences. Malthus lived through revolutions but was not a revolutionary, even though he was often surrounded by people who were. Consistently, he was in but not of these radical circles, acquiring, performing, and perfecting an intellectual caution that would characterize his writings, sometimes to the point of outright timidity.

* * *

Do revolutions begin at home? In Thomas Robert Malthus's case, yes and no. He may not consistently have been grateful that his father, strong-charactered Daniel Malthus (1730–1800), possessed radical political sentiments, but these were crucial to his upbringing and indeed success. An admirer of Jean-Jacques Rousseau, Daniel had opened a correspondence with his idol during the Frenchman's sojourn in Britain (1765–1767), on the basis of a brief introduction in Geneva in 1764. (His Rousseau-worship has long been noted, but their correspondence, and first meeting in Geneva, never cited within studies of the famous Malthus son.) Based on that contact, Rousseau had concluded of the senior Malthus, "he seems [a] worthy man to me, and very learned." Rousseau then forgot him. Malthus had to write twice, giving details of their meeting, to convince him that he was not simply a creditor trying to recover a debt. In 1766 Rousseau stayed with his acolyte in Surrey, who wrote him, "I was flattered to have made you spend a few days at least, you and Mlle. Le Vasseur, with my family," which would have included tiny newborn baby Bob, as Robert would be known to family and friends. Daniel Malthus was crushed when Rousseau opted to live at the house of a rival admirer in Derbyshire rather than in Surrey. His pursuit of the Frenchman—professing his admiration, love, and wish to regard him as a father—resulted in the impressive fact that Rousseau, who fell out with just about everyone, maintained cordial terms with his English devotee, declaring of him "you have much [good] sense." And, via Rousseau, Malthus made contact with another philosopher, David Hume.[2]

Some further hints at Malthus family politics lie within a scrapbook now in the Malthus family collection in the Old Library at Jesus College, Cambridge. It is a commonplace book composed of newspaper clippings, with articles ranging in date from 1777 to 1814, some of them annotated. The last one that bears handwriting is marked "1795"; items from after 1797 are not affixed to the book. Although Daniel Malthus claimed he did not follow the news, "living in the countryside, where I but rarely read the public papers," the evidence points to him as at least one of the book's compositors and its probable initiator. The content of the attached clippings indicates an adult with established political leanings, exactly Daniel's status during the scrapbook's generation, from his forties until five years before his death. Although sometimes claimed to be the famous Malthus's work, the handwriting on the early clippings is not young Robert's, and the notes consistently use apostrophic contractions—"appear'd" and "walk'd"—that the older generation favored and which the younger Malthus eventually stopped using. Moreover, the content indicates Wilkite sympathies. The political radical and libertine John Wilkes, who advocated reform of England's constitution in the 1760s and 1770s, was convicted of seditious libel and obscene libel despite considerable popular support and his eventual election to Parliament. Newspaper editors who supported him had faced government investigation and legal penalties. Most of the early articles from the Malthus scrapbook are from just such a paper, the *St. James's Chronicle*. That matched Daniel Malthus's personal acquaintance with Wilkes, which he discussed with Rousseau. The clippings are indeed critical of the British ministry, especially several items of news about the American War for Independence.[3]

If initiated by Daniel Malthus, the scrapbook became a family project, given that it contains loose clippings from well after Daniel Malthus's death. It is possible that the Malthus sons, Robert and his older brother Sydenham (1754–1821), were contributors. The later clippings stray into the youngest Malthus's eventual territory: grain prices, returns of wheat, Corn Laws. It is also possible that Daniel's cousin and legal ward Jane Dalton (1742–1817), helped assemble the book. Dalton was noted (not least by Rousseau) for her botanical expertise—and many news clippings relate to gardening. Dalton was an important if underacknowledged member of the Malthus household, and her influence on Malthus may well have been greater than previously thought. Clearly she was a significant part of the intellectual as well as familial milieu. Indeed, since the famous conversation that sparked the *Essay* would take place at Albury, Surrey, where Dalton lived, it is possible that she was a participant. It is difficult to imagine her *not* discussing Condorcet's recent book with her cousin and his son. She was as familiar as anyone in the household with French intellectual trends. In his 1773 poem on the family, Malthus's first tutor, Richard Graves, reports Dalton as contributing "remarks on books profound, or anecdotes of the gay monde." She continued to bring books from the "gay monde," living in Paris just before the revolution, translating the writer and botanist Jacques Henri Bernardin de Saint-Pierre's novel *Paul et Virginie* (1788) and publishing it in London in 1789, under the title *Paul and Mary* with Daniel Malthus's assistance.[4]

Whoever assembled the scrapbook, it hints at a household with visitors and conversations that were lively if not astonishing. It was the first intellectually radical environment to envelop Malthus, and the first of several he would inhabit but—significantly—dissent from. Given the intellectual caution that would characterize some of his work, it is also possible that he had concluded, from a flow of bold ideas at home, on the safety of timidity.[5]

And yet Robert was prime evidence of the triumph of radical ideas. Born with a disability, a cleft palate, he benefited from new eighteenth-century experiments in education. Traditionally, a boy with a speech impediment would not have been prepared for any kind of public life; all formal education had relied on inflexible modes of intellectual training in any case, and what existed was available only to a few. But educational reformers, including Rousseau, had begun to argue that children needed to find their mental powers on their own terms, even children who had once been considered ineducable. Rousseau's novel *Emile* (1762) preached that gospel. Pedagogical programs that focused on disabled or disadvantaged children (or previously excluded female ones) and the proliferation of new schools likewise manifested this new impulse. As befitted a disciple of Rousseau, Daniel Malthus was atypical in his encouragement of Jane Dalton and in his ambitious plans for his disabled son. Robert received his primary education at home (an important site for new educational programs) and then from 1782 to 1784 at the Warrington Academy, an institution for religious dissenters that had an inventive curriculum. (The academy's emphasis on conversation and drama helps to solve the mystery of how Robert Malthus was eventually able to speak in public.) Many notable individuals passed through Warrington, either as teachers or students. Malthus was instructed by (among others) the Unitarian controversialist Gilbert Wakefield, who became an important contact in his later career.[6]

If his student essay on the loss of the American colonies was composed circa 1783, as he was moving from school to university (and when the Warrington students met in Wakefield's house), it shows that Malthus had imbibed from his father and tutors at least some of their criticism of Britain's ruling establishment, along with ongoing debates over population and empire. "Colonies properly regulated," he stated, "do not tend to weaken the mother country, but only draw off her exuberant population." The value of distant settlements, and the commerce they generated, had been recognized since ancient times. To fear that they could be "the source of gradual depopulation," Malthus continued, misunderstood "of what people colonies are chiefly composed." Any overseas settlement was essentially "a retreat to the unhappy," a place where the bankrupt could repair their fortunes and "a safe refuge" for those uneasy in their natal land, possibly a reference to religious dissent; the word *refugee* had been coined (via French) to describe the

Protestant Huguenots who fled Catholic France for safer places, including America. As the colonies flourished, so would trade, and also the stock of experienced seamen, handy in times of war. But, Malthus warned, "colonies by their nature require ease & freedom." "Sprung from the same stock" as the English, the free population of British America had rightly demanded their "natural rights." A "long & painful war with our fellow countrymen" could have been avoided by granting the colonists their "independance," thus retaining the commercial benefits of colonies without insisting on their political subordination.[7]

In 1784 Robert Malthus entered Jesus College at the University of Cambridge, where the established Church of England dominated. Exposure to varieties of Protestantism would give him a constant religious background, if also awareness that there was more than one Christian faith. Although his father had encouraged Robert to read history seriously while at school, once at Cambridge he was told to pursue science and mathematics, including "Political Arithmetick," as Daniel recommended in a letter of 1786. Those preferences indicated that natural science and the emerging human sciences were regarded as the highest intellectual achievements. "We have some very clever men of our college," Malthus related. "The chief study is mathematics, for all honour in taking a degree depends upon that science." When his attention drifted from mathematics, his father scolded him: "I desir'd to see you a surveyor, a mechanick, a navigator, a financier, a natural philosopher, an astronomer." Malthus insisted that he was in fact notable "in College for talking of what actually exists in nature, or may be put to real practical use," and he promised by the end of his studies "to be a decent natural philosopher."[8]

The life of the mind suited him, and the prestige of knowledge predicated upon natural science definitely attracted him. Malthus acquired a modest talent in mathematics, winning a major Cambridge prize in the subject, as well as excelling in other areas. But outside of his formal studies, the subject that most excited him was stadial theory. Around the time of his graduation, he confessed to his father that he had laid aside his chemistry to read Edward Gibbon, whose *History of the Decline and Fall of the Roman Empire* (1776–1788) was perhaps the most sophisticated rendition of stadial theory. Malthus told his father that his main interest was in Gibbon's analysis of precommercial society: "He gives one some useful information concerning the origin & progress of those nations of barbarians which now form the polished states of Europe; & throws some light upon the beginning of that dark period which so long ovewhelmed the world." Thus Malthus left university equipped with both statistical and theoretical modes of social analysis, plus a curiosity about how other investigators had put them to use.[9]

*   *   *

By the time of his graduation in 1788, Malthus had decided to become a clergyman, a traditional and respectable choice for the meditative younger son of a gentleman. The decision represented a first break with his radical father. Daniel Malthus had had his son baptized but not confirmed—yet more evidence of his household's unorthodoxy. Only with that Christian formality out of the way was Malthus ordained a minister in the Church of England in 1789. He took charge of a parish the same year. Oakwood or Okewood Chapel in Wotton, Surrey, was poor and ranked low within church hierarchy. It was on the other hand conveniently close to Malthus's Surrey family, and family-related patronage had probably helped him secure the post. All the same, the chapel required its incumbent to preach, and Malthus demonstrated considerable resolve in convincing the church authorities that he could do this, despite his cleft palate. His desire for "retired living in the country," he explained to his father in 1786, made the traces of his speech defect not insurmountable for such a position. He took an MA degree from Cambridge in 1791 and was elected a fellow of Jesus College in 1793, a foothold in the world of learning and ideas. His college fellowship gave him a tiny income, so long as he remained unmarried. His decision to write moral philosophy would allow him to draw upon the certainty of numbers as well as to express his sense of duty toward other people, while projecting his career in a more intellectually ambitious direction.[10]

Malthus became a professional Christian in the first year of the French Revolution, which eventually attacked all such people. By 1793, the revolution was undergoing a radical phase often called the Reign of Terror. The king and queen of France were guillotined that year, and the Jacobin leader Maximilien de Robespierre was elected to the Committee of Public Safety. An anticlerical law was passed; clergy who identified themselves as such were subject to an immediate death penalty. At the end of the year and into the next, there were mass arrests and killings, which were effectively purges of sectors of the French population deemed inimical to the revolutionary effort. The 1794 casualties included Antoine Lavoisier, the famous chemical experimenter, and the marquis de Condorcet, mathematician and political philosopher. Robespierre would himself be guillotined toward the end of the year. The revolution had divided Britons even before it became overtly antimonarchical and anticlerical. In 1793 Britain had joined a coalition of European nations that opposed the Republic of France, particularly French attempts to export revolution by military means; in 1798 the Second Coalition was formed to oppose an expansionist French republic led by Napoleon Bonaparte. Opinion was still more sharply divided in the United States. France was that nation's oldest ally, with which it had fought against Great Britain, and its revolution had initially seemed to continue that amity. But Jacobinism alienated many white Americans, who considered Britain, under the circumstances, a safer political partner.

Great Britain's official stance toward France was one of enmity. British subjects could openly debate the political situation, but they were ill advised to express sympathy for the radicals or appeasement toward Bonaparte, let alone suggest that Britons should incite revolution within their own nation or its colonial dependencies. British-occupied Ireland was a particular concern; so were the English working classes, both regarded (with good reason) as reservoirs of discontent. Some of the controversy reflected an unresolved argument over the American Revolution: was the French event its logical continuation? If so, did the new revolution tarnish or add luster to the American cause? Edmund Burke, who had supported the Americans in their revolt, pitched a bomb when he rejected the French revolutionaries in his *Reflections on the Revolution in France* (1790). Nevertheless, several English authors predicted that events in France opened new vistas for humanity. The most radical was Tom Paine, whose *Rights of Man* (1792) argued that the French monarchical state had been illegitimate and its overthrow justified. In the wake of its publication, Britain issued a proclamation against treasonous writings and charged Paine with sedition. He fled to France. Another text from the "Revolution Controversy," this one essential to Malthus's own thought, was William Godwin's *Enquiry Concerning Political Justice, and Its Influence on General Virtue and Happiness* (1793), a utopian and anarchist criticism of conventional law and statecraft, using direct or implied references to revolutionary France. By no means an apologist for the Terror, Godwin instead meant to point a middle way between existing norms and revolutionary excesses. Nevertheless, by positing that the human condition could be perfected, Godwin not only criticized the British status quo but also recommended radical experiments in society in order to perfect human happiness. Widely read and reviewed, Godwin's *Political Justice* was, after Paine's and Burke's assessments of the French Revolution, the most influential at the time.[11]

The controversy was an opportunity for an author to make a mark, as Malthus seems to have realized, however slow he was to enter the fray. In

1796, almost a decade after his graduation, he drafted a now-lost pamphlet. He confided to his father that he hoped it would bring him promotion, perhaps even a "deanery," the level just above a parish church. The contents of Malthus's plainly titled "The Crisis, a View of the Present Interesting State of Great Britain, by a Friend to the Constitution," are known only because two friends who read the work later discussed it in their memoirs—flatteringly, so it is difficult to determine the full scope and critical valence of the piece. The pamphlet, they recalled, warned that the present government was dividing public opinion, advised a path of moderation, and recommended that religious dissenters be accepted into political life. Malthus also addressed the subject of population. He did so to counter opinion that a growing population indicated popular happiness. The growth instead indicated *past* happiness, signifying when people had felt free to add to their families; it could not predict what they would experience going forward. In the end, and to his father's regret, Malthus decided not to subsidize publication of the pamphlet (a common strategy for a first-time author), although his exact reasons are now lost, along with the complete text. Perhaps he feared that his argument was not distinctive enough to stand out; perhaps he worried that, to the contrary, his thoughts would get him into trouble, either with his church superiors for his defense of dissenters, or with political censors for his criticism of the Pitt government, however conciliatory.[12]

His caution was wise. A careful appraisal of the political scene was one thing, and thoughts on reform could be acceptable, but to suggest that Britons take action along anything resembling radical French lines could be deemed treasonous, hinting, as it would have done, that getting rid of king, aristocracy, and clergy might benefit the English. The Pitt government set out multiple restrictions on liberties to speak, print, and assemble (measures now deemed to have been unconstitutional). A wave of trials of authors, agitators, and naval mutineers in the 1790s had traced a line that should not be crossed. Malthus would learn the cost of defiance through the linked experiences of a former tutor from Warrington and of that tutor's publisher, later his own.[13]

The tutor, Gilbert Wakefield, in 1798 crossed the line by publishing *A Reply to Some Parts of the Bishop Llandaff's Address to the People of Great Britain*. The bishop (Richard Watson) had recommended that English taxes be raised to pay for the war against Bonaparte. Wakefield replied that it was unjust to burden the poor, that the elite ought to bear any new financial burdens, if they were necessary. By suggesting that the poor would criticize if not rebel against an expanded and expensive war effort, and by questioning the wisdom of that effort anyway, Wakefield intimated a sense of English plebeian solidarity with radical French opposition to aristocratic and clerical privileges. He was charged with seditious libel, meaning an untruthful statement about a person or class of persons (in this case Britain's political elite) that might incite sedition among those who heard or read it.[14]

The formal charge of seditious libel was also leveled against Joseph Johnson, publisher and bookseller, who had stocked Wakefield's treatise in his London bookshop. It was Johnson who, about a decade earlier, had published the edition of Franklin's political writings that included—indeed, led off with—"Observations Concerning the Increase of Mankind." Because Johnson had published the collection of Franklin's essays in 1779, during America's War for Independence (and while Franklin was rallying French support against Britain), this publication too had suggested that the nation's military effort, in this case against the former British colonists, was, at the very least, of mixed value.

Since that early effort, Johnson had become the most important publisher and bookseller in Britain. He had thereby acquired a role of extraordinary cultural importance, one that is still being explored. His list of authors eventually included (in addition to his early acquisitions, Joseph Priestley and Richard Price), Mary Wollstonecraft, her husband, William Godwin (author of *Political Justice*), the poets William Cowper, Joel Barlow, Anna Letitia Barbauld, Samuel Taylor Coleridge, and William Wordsworth, the naturalist-poet Erasmus Darwin, the novelist Maria Edgworth and, eventually, Thomas Robert Malthus. Several of these authors were Johnson's discoveries, and many would be exclusively published by him. By also commissioning translations (a large part of his business), he introduced the English-speaking world to several continental authors, perhaps most importantly Goethe. He was a friend of writers as well as publisher to them, hosting regular dinners at which his authors consolidated a literary network, lending money (as he did to Godwin), and sheltering homeless protégés, including Wollstonecraft and later the émigré Swiss artist Henry Fuseli. Above all, he ran a business—and it made him rich. While he specialized in religious and political works, he sold a much broader stock, including medical texts and foreign language grammars and dictionaries. From 1770 to 1780 he published an average of thirty-two titles a year; his bookshop offered a new title every week. He had an excellent eye for what might be in demand, both steady sellers and megahits. His profits on Cowper alone have been estimated at £10,000.[15]

Johnson had been careful not to publish exceedingly radical works, but he was known all the same for promoting books that took positions against the great and the good. After initially agreeing to publish Tom Paine's resolutely pro-French *Rights of Man*, he later released Paine to another printing house. His caution revealed how Johnson was a friend of reform, though reluctant to advocate outright revolt. Yet within this careful path, his commitment to American causes was notable. His sympathy for the American Revolution had been clear since he had chosen to publish Franklin in 1779, as well as to continue producing the works of British authors with American connections, such as Priestley and Price. He also supported antislavery, a reform intrinsic to the future character of European empire in the Americas. Johnson's publication or sale of antislavery works (above all *The Interesting Narrative of the Life of Olaudah Equiano*, the 1789 abolitionist memoir of a former slave), as well as other liberationist and politically and religiously dissenting works, clearly marked him as opposed to the British establishment. His patronage of Mary Wollstonecraft, and his publication of Priscilla Wakefield's *Reflection of the Present Condition of the Female Sex; with Suggestions for Improvement* (1798), identified his sympathies for women's rights when that was by no means typical. He made his oppositionist stance even more apparent when he and a business partner launched a periodical, the *Analytical Review; or, History of Literature*, in 1786. The publication was composed only of reviews of recent publications, as with works sympathetic to liberation and radical reform, including abolition of the slave trade and full toleration of religious dissenters. It also introduced authors and topics from Europe that would otherwise have been difficult for British readers to access, and quite often with a slant that hinted at pro-revolutionary sensibilities.[16]

The authorities had probably been awaiting an opportunity to quiet Johnson, which Wakefield's text offered them. An agent had inspected his bookshop almost as soon as the offending book had gone on sale there, and legal charges quickly followed. After a much discussed trial, both Johnson and Wakefield were found guilty of seditious libel. Wakefield served a two-year prison term that ruined his health; he died shortly after release. Johnson was sentenced to a £600 fine and nine months in prison. His wealth guaranteed, however, that the fine was supportable and that he could serve his sentence while renting a luxurious house available to prisoners who could afford it. There he continued to hold his literary dinners, thumbing his nose at his condemners. The penalty of the sentence was in its legal stigma; while he may have appeared to be a martyr to those within his circle, Johnson's anti-Jacobin critics gave him much bad publicity, and he and his partner were forced to cease publishing the *Analytical Review*.[17]

That it was Johnson who published Malthus complicates the received interpretation of the *Essay on the Principle of Population* as an establishmentarian work. To be sure, the *Essay*, which appeared in 1798, the year of Johnson's trial and imprisonment, would be antirevolutionary. And yet note that it did not, in the eyes of the authorities, offset Johnson's more radical offerings. Johnson probably thought Malthus's book would sell, which mattered to him, though not at the risk of appearing to be a friend of the ruling orders, which Malthus—a minister in the Church of England—would on the surface have represented. On the other hand, Malthus knew several of Johnson's other authors, including Wakefield and others with connections to Warrington (as with Joseph Priestley), and discussion at the time of his unpublished pamphlet, critical as it was of the British government in 1798, may have made him seem a plausible ally of Johnson's interests and causes. Without direct correspondence between the two men, it is hard to tell. None of Johnson's existing business letters are addressed to Malthus. It is a systemic problem: Johnson's surviving letterbook is far too small to represent a business of its size; in 1805 the publisher would confess to Priestley, "I seldom copy letters," meaning he sent them without keeping copies, a not uncommon practice. Perhaps Malthus's personal character, reported to have been engaging and sympathetic, convinced Johnson that his new author was not a narrow-minded parson. (Malthus would become an attendee at Johnson's dinners.) Perhaps his politically adventurous relations, Daniel Malthus and Jane Dalton, introduced him to like-minded folk in London; because of her 1789 translation of *Paul et Virginie*, Dalton had connections in London's publishing world. Certainly, Malthus's subject matched the goal of social reform generally defined, which Johnson and the members of his circle would have found compelling enough. So yet again, and as in Daniel Malthus's fascinating household, the younger Malthus became embedded within a radical milieu without being entirely of it.[18]

Indeed, the Wakefield controversy had shown that, circa 1796, producing any political work was dangerous. Malthus acknowledged the hazard in the introduction to his *Essay*. "It has been said," he would report, "that the great question is now at issue, whether man shall henceforth start forwards with accelerated velocity toward illimitable, and hitherto unconceived improvement; or be condemned to a perpetual oscillation between happiness and misery." Out of the ongoing debate on that matter, he had been reading "some of the speculations on the perfectibility of man and of society, with great pleasure." It was a polite way to raise the speculations only to refute them. In his introduction, he singled out two optimists who had predicted human perfection, the recently guillotined Condorcet and the alive (and vivid) Godwin, whose "talents" and "candor" Malthus professed to admire, again a bit of *politesse* that presaged disagreement with the named individuals and disapproval of their use of speculation as bases for recommending a course for humanity. Rather than begin with a statement of conjecture, an accepted strategy within moral philosophy, Malthus proposed instead the examination of "laws."[19]

He meant by this the "fixed laws of our nature," a declaration in favor of the certainty of political economy, founded upon predictable principles. He proposed two laws relevant to the question of human happiness. First, "food is necessary to the existence of man"; second, "the passion between the sexes is necessary, and will remain nearly in its present state." His qualification of the second law, using the word "nearly," indicated some uncertainty as to whether it was as "necessary" as the first. To address that doubt, Malthus firmly stated, "Towards the extinction of the passion between the sexes, no progress whatever has hitherto been made." So the two laws were invariable. Their trajectories were also unbalanced. "Population, when unchecked, increases in a geometrical ratio," he argued, while "subsistence increases only in an arithmetical ratio." It took only "a slight acquaintance with numbers" to "shew the immensity of the first power in comparison of the second." Given these two tendencies, one more powerful than the other—generating a "natural inequality"—there would always tend to be more people than could be fed: "I say, that the power of population is indefinitely greater than the power in the earth to produce subsistence for man." Small wonder that the theorists of human happiness could find plentiful evidence of human misery. But they were wrong to hope that the unhappiness could be erased. Because of "a strong and constantly operating check on population from the difficulty of subsistence," Malthus proposed that "this difficulty must fall somewhere; and must necessarily be severely felt by a large portion of mankind." For that reason, "the argument is conclusive against the perfectibility of the mass of mankind." Two laws, one bitter conclusion.[20]

Although Malthus had directed his rebuke to both Godwin and Condorcet, he dropped the latter thinker after his introduction and focused on what he perceived as the errors of the former, perhaps because he felt it uncharitable to speak ill of the dead (or pointless to address someone who could not answer). It had been Godwin's optimistic (and politically radical) suggestion in his *Enquiry Concerning Political Justice, and Its Influence on General Virtue and Happiness* (1793) that humanity could achieve a utopian state if freed from tyranny. The Malthus-Godwin exchange marked salvos in an ongoing debate—perhaps even a continuing debate—about political revolution's potential to remedy societal evils. It would be simplistic to see the two Englishmen as revolutionary versus reactionary. True, Godwin believed that radical renovation of human society was possible, whereas Malthus cautioned against that expectation. Nor would Godwin's philosophical anarchism have sat comfortably with Malthus's confidence in reforms within a legal structure. But both men utilized arguments about humanity meant to better the human condition, including political arithmetic and political economy; each insisted, with consistency and conviction, that he intended for the best.[21]

Each also wrote in a context of food shortage. Since the 1760s, and increasingly during the American Revolution and Napoleonic Wars, it had become apparent that harvests throughout the Atlantic world were in decline. Reports stretching from Spanish America through Canada confirmed calamity in multiple new world latitudes, and the same was perceived within Europe. Severe famine in British-held Bengal heightened a sense of global imperial crisis. No thinking person could, by the 1790s, pretend that food was not a problem. Ministers, naturalists, advocates of agricultural improvement, imperial schemers and general busybodies recommended various projects to improve the food supply, through the development of new crops, the better mobilization of labor, or the intensified utilization of land. Colonies generally, and new world places specifically, were crucial to the sense of crisis but also solutions to it, especially given that American staples, such as the "white" potato of the Andes, and potential new world ghost acres (perhaps particularly the new expanses of Upper Canada and possibly New South Wales) were figured as promises of plenty. There was slight incoherence amid these multiplying projects, in which new world places might simultaneously need food yet also be possible sources of cheap foodstuffs for the poor or enslaved, as with HMS *Bounty*'s doomed scheme to transfer Tahitian breadfruit to the British West Indies.[22]

Godwin and Malthus were important, as well, in shifting public debate on the best use of natural resources, "nature's government," away from food exclusively and to include sexual reproduction as well. It was not the case that Godwin rejected any natural constraints on human happiness, as if he and Malthus argued from completely divergent starting points. While his main example was revolutionary France, Godwin also referenced the American Revolution as an important event in the improvement of humankind. And he hypothesized "a principle in human society by which population is perpetually kept down to the means of the level of subsistence," citing the "wandering tribes of America" and "the civilized nations of Europe" as evidence. These statements may very well have influenced Malthus's own work. But Godwin had proposed that humanity's ability to control sexual desire was part of this "principle in human society," and that this capacity could be cultivated in order to limit conception, in whatever degree preferred. That self-control was what Malthus found difficult to verify, which was why he took care to deny that passion between the sexes could be modified; no, he insisted, it was as relentless as the need to eat.[23]

In this way, the *Essay on the Principle of Population* was not only a piece of moral philosophy but also, and profoundly, an essay in natural theology, a truth only intermittently acknowledged. Although Malthus did not use the words "original sin" to explain why humanity would always be prone to lust and therefore to misery, his implication was obvious, and as such it rebuked Godwin's secular terms of analysis. The twinned natural laws of Malthus's population principle were the same, moreover, as the curses placed on Adam and Eve: to cultivate the earth and to bring forth children. Malthus explicitly cited divine mandate when he declared that "to furnish the most unremitted excitements of this kind, and to urge man to further the gracious designs of Providence, by the full cultivation of the earth, it has been ordained, that population should increase much faster than food." That statement connected the scriptural mandate to "increase and multiply" with its partner, "subdue the Earth." And Malthus would at the end of his 1798 *Essay* overtly refer to original sin when he said that the problem of population increase was a powerful reason for humans to try to overcome their fallen state: "Evil exists in the world, not to create despair, but activity." The religious valence of these statements is obvious—and interesting. They are quite different from what Robert Wallace, for example, had concluded in his own faith-inflected analysis of population. For Wallace, the production of children maximized the number of souls brought into embodiment, to worship God and (perhaps) achieve salvation. Malthus ignored this orthodox understanding of the scriptural mandate to procreate while maintaining orthodox doubt that human nature could be anything but fallen.[24]

From the initial presentation of his principle of population, in a swift seventeen pages, Malthus moved to a twenty-one page exegesis of the problem on three geographic scales and in three qualitatively different places, beginning with North America. In this way, he transitioned from the natural theology that referenced a lost Eden to the historical discovery of a new world that seemed (to some) to offer a new Eden. Indeed, Malthus's description of the new republic in North America entertained both that possibility as well as the optimism of the revolutionaries that the former British colonies had inaugurated a new order of the ages. "In the United States of America," he began, "where the means of subsistence have been more ample, the manners of the people more pure, and consequently the checks to early marriages fewer, than in any of the modern states of Europe, the population has been found to double itself in twenty-five years." This was a statistic based on "actual experience." But Malthus used that empirical example, adorned with the praise "ample" and "pure," to project the consequences of this population increase for places that lacked North America's material and cultural advantages, where positive descriptions would therefore be impossible.[25]

"Let us now take any spot of earth," he continued, "this Island [of Great Britain] for instance, and see in what ratio the subsistence it affords can be supposed to increase." In this seemingly offhand choice of a small scale of analysis, Malthus established an important contrast. If the case of North America was perfect evidence for the geometrical rapidity of population increase, the case of Great Britain was perfect evidence that improvement in food production would never keep up; that was the point of the contrast between new and old worlds. At best, and even if "every acre of land in the Island [was cultivated] like a garden," the produce of Great Britain could only be doubled in an initial twenty-five-year period, not doubled again over a succeeding quarter century. The most optimal rate of agricultural growth in Britain would therefore be only "equal to what it at present produces," and "this ratio of increase is evidently arithmetical," in contrast to the proven geometrical rates of population increase in the new world. Malthus then took these contrasting rates, from new and old worlds, and projected them over the entire globe, his third and final scale of analysis, in a vision of the future that combined American fecundity of population and British intensity of agriculture. If both trends proceeded to their natural limits, there would still be a gap: "No limits whatever are placed on the productions of the earth . . . yet still the power of population being a power of a superior order," it would take "the constant operation of the strong law of necessity acting as a check upon the greater power."[26]

Malthus turned next to consider "this check," the mechanism that he thought must exist to adjust the naturally occurring gap between human increase and the availability of food, resulting in perpetual oscillation. Plants and animals had no "reasoning" that interrupted their reproduction. They simply proliferated until they and their offspring either starved for lack of nourishment or became "the prey of others." That merciless struggle—Darwinism before Charles Darwin—was the check on unlimited growth in the world of nature. But "the effects of this check on man are more complicated," because humans had reason and therefore the ability to avoid starvation or to become the prey of others. Possession of reason did not always operate to fullest advantage, however. When foresight failed, humans could only resort to "vice," attempts to prevent conception or procure abortion, or else they sank into "misery" as they and their children suffered from want. "The superior power of population cannot be checked," Malthus concluded, "without producing misery or vice, the ample portion of these too bitter ingredients in the cup of human life." Again, the embedded fatalism reflected a sense of God's original curse on humanity.[27]

At this point, Malthus thought it necessary to "examine the different states in which mankind have been known to exist," a bid, yet again, to avoid abstract speculation about the human condition, the error of the optimists. He proceeded historically, and according to stadial theory, by beginning with "the rudest state of mankind, in which hunting is the principal occupation." His prime example of this stage of society, the beginning point of his historical assessment, was "the North American Indians," a choice that showed, yet again, the centrality of new worlds to his analysis. The Indians subsisted by hunting, he claimed, which required them to be spread thin over a large extent of territory—the familiar stadial definition of savagery. While he acknowledged a common opinion that the native American population had remained small due to their lack of sexual passion, Malthus considered this "apathy" beside the point. A hunting way of subsistence was far more likely to impair population, because of its constant toll on human energies without any compensating payoff. As proof of that hazard, Malthus stated that Indians who lived near European settlements, according to a "civilized mode of life," had larger families. Aboriginal social relations could not support a similar increase. "The North American Indians, considered as a people, cannot justly be called free and equal," whatever might have been claimed by their admirers. Rather, women were oppressed and "slavery" flourished. "One half the nation appears to act as Helots to the other half," with consequent "misery" for the subordinated portion. And, Malthus continued, "misery is the check that represses the superior power of population," particularly when it fell on women, whose capacity to bear and rear children was thereby impeded. The physical toll was ingrained, it "is constantly acting now upon all savage nations," and it would operate "a thousand years hence," as if a savage state would exist somewhere on the globe into the distant future, whatever the imperialist spread of commercial societies. Notable here is Malthus's silent rejection of any Rousseauean confidence that savagery might have compensating virtues.[28]

Having begun with aboriginal America, as contemporary evidence of the most primitive stage of human society, the most challenging of circumstances for human increase, Malthus would return to the Americas toward the end of his essay, believing that settler society in North America represented the most optimal circumstances for human increase. By tracing this contrast, Malthus made clear his opinion that it was not America's primal state that offered a glimpse of an Edenic condition but instead its historical development in turning from an aboriginal to a precommercial stage by means of European colonization. "There is not a truer criterion of the happiness and innocence of a people," he concluded, "than the rapidity of their increase." Had Malthus relied only on the "happiness" of a people as his criterion, he would have indicated agreement with Godwin's terms of analysis. Adding the element of "innocence," however, hinted at a moral status that at least approximated the one before the Fall. Thus Malthus continued the tradition of associating the Americas with a prelapsarian condition while rejecting any sentiment that colonizing Europeans had ruined that happy state among the Indians. He repeated that iteration of a partially moral rather than solely physical condition when he concluded that North America had its rapidly increasing settler population both because "the manners of the people [were] more pure" and because they had more land than their counterparts in Europe.[29]

Malthus made a revealing choice, therefore, in selecting evidence from the former British American colonies, now the independent United States, to undermine Godwin's case for that nation's "sister republic" in France. Certainly, any optimism over France's future had dimmed by the late 1790s, particularly since Bonaparte was leading the nation into wars of invasion. Malthus was among an increasing number of Britons who were profoundly sceptical of utopian politics, including those of revolutionary France. All the more striking, therefore, that the new world and not the old was Malthus's immediate example of the natural limits to historical progress, as measured by population. A steady increase in virtue and happiness would be impossible, Malthus countered, if humans' increase outstripped nature's ability to feed them. A number of colonial ventures in the new world had depended on agrarian surpluses that resulted in population growth—the Spanish in Mexico and Peru; the Portuguese in Brazil; the Dutch and the French elsewhere—but the British colonies, now the United States, were the purest specimens.[30]

Malthus's information about rapid population growth in the Americas had a specific origin, Benjamin Franklin, though in 1798 he didn't know it.

In North America specifically, he reported, available land, plus "liberty and equality," meant that "the population was found to double itself in 25 years." Later in his essay, Malthus increased the exponential rate to "every 15 years." He knew he had seen this estimate in a sermon by the American clergyman Ezra Stiles, *A Discourse on the Christian Union* (1761), but not having it "to hand" when he wrote his essay, he cited someone who had cited Stiles, Richard Price, in his *Observations on Reversionary Payments* (1773). Indeed, the surviving volumes of the Malthus family book collection in the library at Jesus College include Price but not Stiles (and the Malthus scrapbook contains a clipping of Price's remarks on the Bishop of London's sermon). Although Price wrote his essay as a letter to Franklin and footnoted Franklin's essay, he did not cite Franklin as author, understandably, because the essay had at that point been published anonymously. Perhaps for that reason, Malthus did not recognize the statistic as Franklin's. Still, his omission is curious, given that his publisher, Joseph Johnson, had in 1779 published Franklin's essay. For whatever reason, and despite his reported habit of giving his authors close readings and detailed notes, Johnson evidently did not advise Malthus of the original source for the statistic, or else Malthus failed to take that fact into account.[31]

The lack of attribution had a serious consequence. Had Malthus read Franklin's essay, he could not have defined his principle of population the way he did, or at least not as easily. Only half of his famous contribution to political arithmetic was based on the American's estimate, the half that referred to humans. In stating that American settlers were doubling in number at least every two decades, Franklin had postulated that human population increased geometrically; that part was true. But the man of science had not claimed that food sources increased merely arithmetically. Far from it: he had explicitly compared humans to plants when he said that the English could fill up territory cleared of other humans just as readily as fennel spread on a patch of cleared land. It is also notable that Franklin used as his example a plant humans could and did eat, which, had Malthus read it, would have queried his assertion that food supply must lag behind population increase, since Franklin had derived no such lesson from the natural world. The scenario that Franklin laid out should have mattered to Malthus. Just as he relied on Franklin's estimate of the doubling of North American settler population—it was essential to his principle of population—Malthus doggedly emphasized the relentless functioning of nature's laws. "Since the world began," he lectured, "the causes of population and depopulation have probably been as constant as any of the laws of nature." But Malthus and his main source did not agree on that central assumption: Franklin had a materialist conception of nature that equated humans and plants; Malthus did not. He could have deduced Franklin's materialism from Godwin, who had cited "the sublime conjecture of Franklin, that mind will one day become omnipotent over matter," conquering even death and denying Christian orthodoxy that souls must return to God. (Godwin had this from Richard Price's nephew; indeed, Franklin privately conjectured about physical immortality.)[32]

Malthus rejected any possibility that mind could conquer matter; he believed that nature had powers that human nature lacked. Although Godwin had gestured only vaguely toward the world's peoples in his comparisons between hunting populations (as in America) and the commercial societies of Europe, Malthus went still further, even in the initial version of his essay, to identify some global populations' capacity to increase so rapidly that they were likely soon, if not already, to run up against a natural limit. True, the older the nation, the more sophisticated its methods of procuring subsistence and the more likely its peoples to increase, as in China and Europe. Newer societies lacked such arts and had to live within starker natural limits. But Malthus concluded, contra Godwin, that productivity was not just a matter of a society's stage of development. When migrants from commercial civilizations settled new worlds, the combination of fresh land and old forms of knowledge guaranteed that population increase would be maximized:

> The happiness of a country does not depend, absolutely, upon its poverty, or its riches, upon its youth, or its age, upon its being thinly, or fully inhabited, but upon the rapidity with which it is increasing, upon the degree in which the yearly increase of food approaches to the yearly increase of an unrestricted population. This approximation is always the nearest in new colonies, where the knowledge and industry of an old State, operate on the fertile unappropriated land of a new one.

But the magical blend of new and old had limits. Richard Price had argued, for example, that the simple, early "stages of civilization" were most favorable to the increase and happiness of humans, as in the American colonies. Malthus retorted that the level of a society could only have the advantage it did when it operated within a "great plenty of fertile uncultivated land"—human nature could never entirely overcome natural limits. It was a considerable adjustment to his youthful confidence, in his student essay, that "colonies properly regulated, do not tend to weaken the mother country, but only draw off her exuberant population." An exuberant population's happiness would expand only so long as its supply of arable land lasted, whether within Europe or in other parts of the world.[33]

Malthus had in the meantime hypothesized that the human capacity for reason or prudence, especially the self-control that could yield a lower birth-rate without resort to vice, was critical to the maintenance of happiness. Godwin had posited that this restraint might itself be perfected and then lead to the general perfection of human society, which in another age would be above mere lust. Malthus looked at humanity's existing record in order to question that prediction: "No move towards the extinction of the passion between the sexes has taken place in the five or six thousand years that the world has existed," he concluded, his estimate of the age of the Earth betraying his religious orthodoxy. (Naturalists had begun to define deep time and a vastly extended chronology for the planet.) And North America was for this reason yet again a key example. He feared that prudence might be most absent there. Savages by Malthus's definition lacked foresight—or considered it a luxury, given the other cares that a hunting existence gave them. New world colonists possessed that quality, in common with their European cousins, but so long as they knew they had lands for the immediate generations, they could reasonably declare themselves independent of the doubts about the material future that might be obvious in older and denser communities. This was another reason why new worlds offered insights into population oscillation that might otherwise be invisible to Europeans.[34]

* * *

Malthus's *Essay* was well received and quickly achieved a place in the public imagination, a boon to any novice and ambitious author. The *Monthly Magazine* declared it, along with another recent work, a triumph over Godwin and utopianism, albeit in Swiftian terms that might have annoyed Malthus. "Mr. Godwin's huge misshapen monster of philosophy ha[s] been deeply pierced by the pigmy lilliputian lance of two separate pamphleteers," the review pronounced. However tiny Malthus's and the other author's pointed weapons, "the giant is now completely slain." More substantively, the reviewer took Malthus's point that "the food that would be necessary" to expand people and happiness could not possibly be counted upon, using "deductions drawn from indisputable data" to make that point. The reviewer of the *New Annual Register*, however, was not quite certain. He (odds are that the reviewer was "he") agreed that Malthus had effectively skewered Godwin and

Condorcet. But he noted that Malthus could not himself resist a touch of the wishfully unworldly, as stated in the religiously orthodox terms that Godwin disdained. Although Malthus posited no utopia on Earth, he promised that those who struggled ignobly with life's material trials would emerge "misshapen," while those who came out in "lovely" form would be "crowned with immortality." The effort was essential. It was the duty of humans "to sublimate the dust of the earth into soul," which was precisely how Malthus had echoed the divine mandate laid down to Adam and his progeny.[35]

Among the most interesting reviews of the *Essay* was the one that appeared in Johnson's own *Analytical Review*, in its final year of publication under Johnson's and his partner's editorship. The reviewer, "S. A.," gave effusive praise to the still-anonymous author, with the encomia for Malthus functioning equally as criticism of Godwin, in precisely the terms that Malthus had defined: hard-headed analysis versus speculative utopianism. The author, the reviewer said, had performed his critique "in the true spirit of candour and philosophy." Godwin could not have been pleased at the review, though it delivered a sting for Malthus too. "Without intending it," the reviewer concluded, "we think the author, in this essay, has furnished the best apology for prostitution, that has ever been written." Indeed, any man seemed "doomed to make his choice between prostitution and infanticide; and the philosophy of Thomas Hobbes thus appears to be established, which states the natural state of man to be a state of warfare. We cannot doubt that this essay will receive much of the public attention." It was a canny review, and canny prediction about the book. With its barbed ending, it avoided being an in-house puff piece and may have soothed one of Johnson's authors, Godwin, by hitting the other, Malthus, where it would hurt most, by suggesting that he advocated immoral practices to control population, and that his frequent references to nature, natural man, and primitive society (above all the Americas) were intended to be Hobbesian. The reverend had avoided using the words "prostitution" and "infanticide," and he may not have wanted to become famous for inviting readers to imagine a Hobbesian war of all against all—men, women, and children—in such vivid language.[36]

By coincidence, the notice in the *Analytical Review* that immediately followed that of Malthus's book was of a work that would be important for the second edition of his *Essay*, and it is possible that it came to his attention this way. David Collins's *Account of the English Colony in New South Wales* (1798) was, the *Analytical Review* judged, a valuable report on a place so remote that most English readers were unlikely to see it. Unlikely, that is, unless they were transported for some crime, the fate of the earliest settlers, most of whom were convicts. As befitted a publication edited by Joseph Johnson, the review pointedly thanked Collins for his critical remarks on how political prisoners had been made to suffer transportation (though it regretted that he did not criticize slavery in Brazil, where Collins's vessel had paused on its way south). And it questioned the wisdom of the antipodean settlement in the first place, noting that the land appeared unlikely ever to support colonists on the basis of settled agriculture. "Famine" ran virtually unchecked, and the desperate convicts appeared unlikely to have any beneficial cultural impact on the Aboriginal inhabitants. These were grounds that Malthus might have appreciated. "It may also be worthy of inquiry, whether it be politic to cultivate the regions of the *antipodes*," the reviewer added, "at a time, when some millions of acres of waste land, and a recent scarcity of bread corn, call aloud for the operations of human industry at home."[37]

*   *   *

It was entirely true, and that criticism of the distant British convict settlement in the newest of new worlds highlighted a sense of crisis that existed within Europe, at a time when Britain wavered between war and peace during this final chapter in the Second Hundred Years' War. Commercial disruptions plus the consignment of young working men to the military had indeed imperiled the British food supply, which would remain problematic until 1802, when the Treaty of Amiens led to a peace, though not one in which most Europeans had confidence. Food shortages (including violent food riots) and debates over investment in new world sites of colonization were therefore the contexts in which Malthus would absorb reactions to his essay and contemplate revisions to it, elaborating, for the first time in modern history, a concept of food security. By this time, British colonial policy had shifted to tighter control over land and labor; the empire's productive ghost acres were not to be imperiled, as they had been with the lost North American colonies, by representative government and autonomy among settlers.[38]

That Malthus did not think his essay was sufficient as it stood is evident in the research into political arithmetic and political economy on which he embarked almost as soon as his *Essay* appeared in 1798. He would later assert that he had written the short, initial version of the treatise in response to Godwin (no mention of Condorcet), "on the spur of the occasion" and armed only with "the few materials which were within my reach in a country situation." These were Hume, Wallace, Smith, and Price. The first two authors had supplied him with temporal coverage (Hume and Wallace, in their debate over the merits of ancient versus modern societies), and the latter some geographic extension, because of their focus on modern Atlantic empires. Although reviewers had not chided him for making a claim about universal laws and principles with so little in the way of evidence, Malthus evidently considered his lack of coverage to be a weakness. In February of 1799 he asked his father to procure for him several works on European political arithmetic, already aware that his examples were far from global. He also ventured abroad to study a part of Europe that was still (unlike the war-torn continent) accessible to British subjects, namely Scandinavia. He entered the kingdom of Denmark-Norway in 1799. There, in territory now in modern Norway, while traveling with university friends, he kept a diary in which he noted the health, number, and plumpness of the people he saw, cross-checked with the availability, quality, and cost of food. Alert to the American hypothesis that a low age at marriage was key to the production of a large population, he duly noted where couples began families early, though Malthus tended to think that large families in Europe were correlated with poverty, contrary to the scenario in North America. Conversely, compulsory Norwegian military service delayed marriage among peasants, "which forms a kind of preventive check to pop[ulatio]n."[39]

His commentary on military service was Malthus's one recognition of the ongoing conflict, which was soon to divide Europe yet again. Britain was growing exasperated over Denmark-Norway's neutrality and in 1801 would lay siege to Copenhagen. Malthus's timing was perfect; private British travelers could not enter Scandinavia again until 1814. In the meantime, however, the Treaty of Amiens between Britain and France opened up the European continent. Malthus, like many other wealthy Englishmen, took the opportunity in 1802 to tour France and Switzerland with part of his family. For five months he rested from his efforts to rework his essay, but he seems to have set at it again on his return in 1803.[40]

The timing of his efforts indicates that he would have been reconsidering his essay at a moment of compelling public debate over the cost of the war. As participants realized, the Napoleonic Wars were vast experiments in statecraft and national mobilization, with serious implications for national food supplies. Within the main combatants, France and Great Britain, military recruitment reached new heights and incited outrage over forced conscription. Keeping the different navies and armies in a deployable condition—fed, clothed, armed, and mobile—required creative finance, not least the imposition of new taxes and the procurement of loans that would at some point need to be paid back, probably through yet more taxation. While France had almost twice the population of Great Britain and a much greater extent of arable land, Britain had better government finances, a stronger navy, and, even at this early date, superior industrial power. Bonaparte's European conquests gave him new territories from which he could harvest matériel and extract money; Britain pursued a comparable strategy at sea, seizing enemy ships (and their contents) to shore up its naval and commercial resources. It was above all obvious that population was essential to the war effort. Just as Renaissance reason-of-state arguments had claimed, more children meant, eventually, more men to be soldiers and sailors, more workers to produce food and matériel, and more women to produce yet more children.[41]

Each participant nation had to look hard, moreover, at commitments to new world dependencies, whose costs were no longer so obviously attractive as longer-term investments at a time when domestic priorities carried such a high price. Even those who hoped that Bonaparte might remain quiet after 1802 would have realized that the disposition of a great deal of territory remained unsettled, including overseas holdings, old and new, that a fresh outbreak of war would put into question. Britain had been determined to establish footholds in the Pacific that would block the French there, and in this way the outcome of the Seven Years' War, with a vanquished France, stripped of Quebec and its other territories in northern New France, was still in lively contention; so too did Britons crave vengeance upon the nation that had aided the rebellious United States. But to persist in extending British naval power to the far side of the globe required significant political will and imagination. Sharp questions about the wisdom of colonizing New South Wales were not unique to the *Analytical Review*'s critical discussion of Collins's 1798 book on the colony there. Colonial holdings in the Americas, even if longer established, also began to seem of debatable value. When a 1791 slave revolt in the French Caribbean colony of St. Domingue grew into a full-scale insurrection and war of liberation, Bonaparte had to choose either to withdraw from the island or fight for it. Either decision would be costly, whether for reasons of finance or of national prestige, particularly because any action would be scrutinized as to the statement it might make about new world slavery, itself contested.[42]

Malthus tackled the domestic dimensions of the crisis first, doing so in a pamphlet of 1800 called *An Investigation of the Cause of the Present High Price of Provisions by the Author of the Essay on the Principle of Population*, again published by Joseph Johnson and again anonymously. In this work, intended to influence Parliament on the question of the availability and price of food,

Malthus wrote "as a lover of truth, and a well-wisher to my country." He argued that the high prices were caused, not by the greedy machinations of commercial agents, but by actual shortages due to lessened production, particularly in 1799. Though Britain had been an exporter of grain as recently as twenty years earlier, the nation was at present growing less than it required for domestic consumption. Importation of grain, particularly to feed the poor, would be inadequate to make up the loss, though Malthus did not explain whether this was because of time, cost, or simple unavailability. Rather, at the end of the essay he argued that the net loss was due to the increase of Britain's population, according to the principle that he had laid out in his earlier work. The essay was evidently read by those in government, just as Malthus had hoped, and it sold well enough to be reprinted later that same year. It represented his first contribution to political economy, distinguished from moral philosophy, as the two fields of inquiry tested their bonds.[43]

The critique was neither terribly sophisticated nor analytically thorough, especially in relation to new worlds. For that, Malthus would have needed to explain more about the dynamics of the international grain trade and to note the effects of the war—and economic development in Britain more generally—on domestic production. North America had been an imperial breadbasket before 1776, and the United States tried during the Napoleonic Wars to maintain neutrality in order to keep the grain trade going. Secretary of State Thomas Jefferson said of his nation versus those in Europe, "Our object is to feed and theirs to fight," and that "we have only to pray their souldiers [sic] may eat a great deal." Indeed, by 1790 flour was the top US export. Most US grain products did not go directly to Europe but instead to European colonies in the West Indies. What Malthus did not recognize, or acknowledge, was the new pressure this placed on British food supplies, some of which would have to be diverted to the sugar islands should Anglo-American relations sour. That was particularly the case as the British economy shifted toward manufacturing and foreign exports. Grain had been so scarce after a poor harvest in 1795 that there was widespread rioting. It was noteworthy that strained relations between the United States and Great Britain did not truly impair the grain trade until the two nations were at war after 1812; Britain imported the greatest amounts of US grain after the harvest failures of 1800, 1801, 1807, and 1809, the first two years being those that concerned Malthus in his pamphlet.[44]

Setting British hunger within the broader network of international trade in food may not have been Malthus's goal, in any case. Given the manner in which he titled and concluded his pamphlet, he (and Johnson) may have intended it mostly as an advertisement for the 1803 edition of his *Essay*. He used the pamphlet to note that "the essay has now been out of print above a year; but I have deferred giving another edition of it in the hope of making it more worthy of the public attention." He would do this, he promised, "by applying the principle [of population] directly and exclusively to the existing state of society, and endeavouring to illustrate the power and universality of its operation from the best authenticated accounts that we have of the state of other countries." Everywhere in the world, he emphasized, population could not grow unimpeded but was always kept in check by the availability of material resources or by apprehension of their limits, which could lead to abortion, infanticide, and abuse of women at childbearing age. *Universality*: it was quite a claim, obviously prompted by widespread interest in the wider world. In the year Malthus had first published his *Essay*, Joseph Johnson had produced a map of the world as augmented by recent European discoveries in the Pacific. (See frontispiece.)

It was this world that Malthus needed to explain. His global aspirations, and his particular attention to new world places, were the analytical frameworks by which he made his principle of population into a universal one for all of humanity.[45]

* * *

Malthus's second edition of his *Essay on the Principle of Population* was a "historical examination of the effects of the principle of population" that would extend over the whole world, past and present. His book of 1803 was described on its title page as "a new edition, very much enlarged." It was indeed much more ambitious, and—at last—published under his name, "T. R. Malthus," which he embellished with his status as the holder of a master's degree and as a fellow of Jesus College, though he decided not to describe himself as a clergyman in the Church of England; he would never be "reverend" on his famous book's first page. (Though he would be in his 1830 *Summary View of the Principle of Population*.) Although he admitted that other authors had preceded him in the task of analyzing population growth, "much, however, remained yet to be done," which was the point of the "new work" that he considered "a whole of itself" and not a mere expansion or emendation of the first edition. While acknowledging the other authors who had considered questions of population, and emphasizing that the issue should get "publick attention," he insisted that his own analysis was singular. Of central importance was "the comparison between the increase of population and food," and so were "the various modes" by which population must necessarily "be kept down to the level of the means of subsistence." For those reasons, "the principle had never been sufficiently pursued to its consequences." Closer attention to the consequences would, he hoped, give the new edition added weight. Whereas the first edition had stated an "abstract truth," that would not itself "tend to promote any practical good," and the doing of benefit was his central concern.[46]

To establish the universality of his principle and its urgent significance to the present and future state of humanity, Malthus added to his analysis a more hopeful "check" on population growth. In his introduction, he still insisted that "vice or misery" were the typical outcomes when population exceeded available food. In that way, he upheld belief in God's curses on Adam and Eve, a decision that paralleled his insistence, in surviving sermon notes from 1789 to 1832, on original sin. But he promised to consider "another check to population possible" in his final section, where once he had placed his insistence that human life on Earth represented struggle, a passage he now omitted. The table of contents indicated the temporal and geographic extent of the work, and it detailed the third and promised check on population. Divided into four books, the work begins with attention to several places and times that fell beyond modern Europe, encompassing "the Checks to Population in the less civilized parts of the world, and in past times," which immediately signaled Malthus's overriding assumption, derived from stadial theory, that contemporary noncommercial societies afforded glimpses into humanity's past. The second book then considers the different modern nations of northern Europe. The third book assesses possible solutions to overpopulation, but the fourth offers what Malthus assumed was the only effective method, "moral restraint," his proposed third check on population and the one that, compared to the other two, vice and misery, was positioned to be much the most attractive. But how powerful did Malthus think it really could be?[47]

The contents of the *Essay* and their organization, plus the background statements that Malthus made in its first two chapters, established three ways in which new worlds were analytically central to his argument, even before he addressed them in the substantive part of his analysis. First, he opened Book I, on "the less civilized parts of the world and in past times," with consideration of the new worlds of the Atlantic and Pacific. Second, his evidence indicated something distinctive about new world populations because he cited settlers as sources of evidence about themselves. Third, Malthus defined an ethical dimension of population growth unique to new world environments, a moral problem that had not troubled him about old world places, or indeed would trouble him about any other part of the world, but which heightened his emphasis on the possibility and necessity of moral restraint.

New worlds led Malthus's exposition literally, as they constituted what were for him the societal forms most unlike those of modern Europe and, by implication, most useful in exposing what was natural to humans as physical creatures that might be concealed by culture elsewhere. By progressing through New South Wales, the Americas, and then the South Seas, he indicated modes of human subsistence that succeeded each other by rough stages, themselves succeeded by societies that better resembled those of the Europe of his day: ancient northern Europe, inhabited by savage and barbarian societies that nevertheless prefigured present-day Europe in ways that new worlds did not; contemporary pastoral societies; Africa, Siberia, Turkey and Persia, and then Asia. Above these examples—more historically advanced than they were—were the ancient Greeks and Romans, the nearest approximates to modern Europeans. (Closer analysis of the new world chapters in Malthus's book will follow in chapters 3 through 5 of this work.) In this way, Malthus established his goal to explicate the world's least and most commercial societies *together*, in order to generate facts that universally supported his principle of population.

If new worlds were characteristic in their stark revelation of population's dependence on material subsistence, European settlers in those places gave equally distinctive information about those conditions. Malthus referred to the "crowd of materials" he had consulted for his new edition, a heavy dose of histories to explicate the long-ago peoples he anatomized, but also travelers' accounts of contemporary places. These were not distinct genres; Malthus used travelers' accounts from past times and histories that discussed relatively recent eras. The variety of sources afforded him examples from as many human groups as possible. The idea of consulting non-European informants was a less-accepted strategy, and Malthus tacitly agreed that accounts from Europeans were paramount. To assess modern Europe, for example, he used his own research notes as a traveler, particularly in Scandinavia. This procedure reinforced his confidence that the mobile western observer was an essential informant on global populations.[48]

But what may be still more significant about his research on new world places is that he included the analysis of those who actually settled there or were descended from such settlers. These people were not travelers in the conventional sense, or at least they lacked that perspective when they

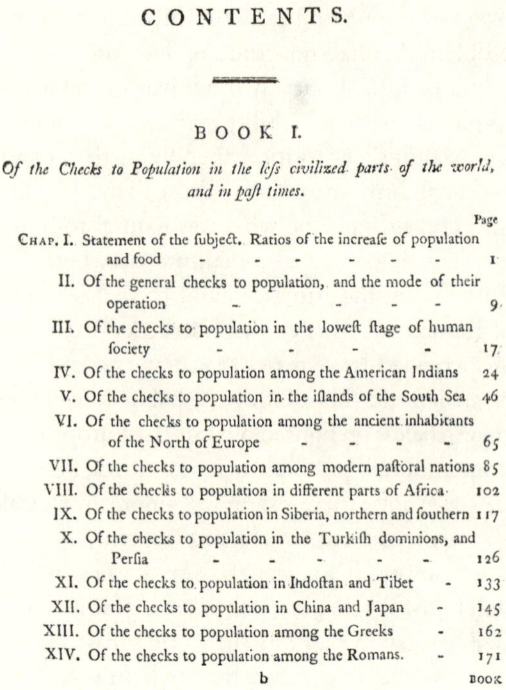

C O N T E N T S.

BOOK I.

Of the Checks to Population in the less civilized parts of the world, and in past times.

Figure 2.1. Analyzing the world, beginning with new worlds. T. R. Malthus, *An Essay on the Principle of Population* (London: J. Johnson, 1803), table of contents. Courtesy of the University of Chicago Library, Crerar Special Collections.

commented on what was or became their home. As colonists, they had knowledge of local population dynamics that trumped that of the passers-by, not least because they themselves embodied colonial population growth through their production of children; they were participant-experts in the history of expanding imperial populations in a way that neither travelers nor indigenes could be. Despite the long tradition of travel accounts as constitutive of early ethnographic analysis, therefore, Malthus's research represented a historically contingent development. Travelers had been prime sources of information about the extra-European world from the 1500s through the 1600s, but from the 1700s onward they began to compete with the authority of people who stayed put. Within an expanding and changing British Empire, the new significance of settler knowledge depended on the increased ability that Britons had to consult the accounts of English-speaking persons who were migrants, or else descendants of emigrants, which really only occurred from the late eighteenth century onward, that is, within Malthus's lifetime. The precondition of that historical development was the existence and extension of settler societies in new worlds—as Robert Boyle had predicted in his 1665 questions for travelers. Malthus understood this. He showcased settler information about new world population dynamics as a distinctive form of modern knowledge, represented nowhere else in the world, at least so far.

Foremost among these settler authorities was Benjamin Franklin, who occupied pride of place at the start of the revised *Essay*'s first chapter. Malthus had discovered that Franklin was the author of the "doubling every twenty years" estimate of American populations, which he had quoted from Richard Price (who himself had quoted Ezra Stiles, whose original had been Franklin's essay). Malthus realized the faulty attribution and carefully followed the intellectual chain back from Price. He requested that his father send him a copy of Stiles's sermon plus "The interest of great Britain considered with regard to her colonies, together with observations concerning the increase of mankind, peopling of countries &c: 2nd edition London 1761," a title that he quoted verbatim from Price's footnote, though again without Franklin's name. He also planned to consult Dr. John Aikin (a Warrington Academy contact), who knew Price and might be able to explain his references. At some point during these researches, Malthus discovered that Franklin's thesis had provided the basis for his original assessment of the fastest known speed of human population growth and duly noted it in the 1803 edition.[49]

Malthus read Franklin's essay as confirmation of his own principle of population, though this required him to ignore some of what his source actually had said. "It is observed by Dr. Franklin," Malthus explained:

> that there is no bound to the prolific nature of plants or animals, but what is made by their crowding and interfering with each others['] means of subsistence. Were the face of the earth, he says, vacant of other plants, it might be gradually sowed and overspread with one kind only; as, for instance, with fennel: and were it empty of other inhabitants, it might in a few ages be replenished from one nation only; as, for instance, with Englishmen.

It was "incontrovertibly true," Malthus stated, again affirming that the principle of population was starkest in new world sites where one population (settlers) appeared to be unimpeded by any other (meaning Indians). The scenario Franklin conjured up had raised British colonial spirits in the 1750s, when he wrote, and definitely encouraged the American patriots and their sympathizers in the 1770s, when the essay had been republished in London. It might have had a similar effect on Britons in the 1800s—to see themselves overspreading the face of the Earth—had not Malthus followed the vegetable imaginary's logic in a direction different from what Franklin (or Botero) had intended. If nature's limits were finite, even the fennel-like Englishmen must confront starvation, and here Malthus explicitly rejected the possibility that plants (and other sources of food) might keep pace with human food; in the end, the fennel would not feed the Englishmen. For that reason, a "strong check on population" must always operate, and its dire effects—"misery, or the fear of misery"—eventually descend on "a large portion of mankind." Malthus restated his claim to a geometrical rate of population increase, doubling every twenty-five years, rather than Franklin's twenty, deliberately choosing the slower conjecture to deflect protest that he was exaggerating.[50]

But why were humans different from plants and, by extension, all other nonhuman parts of nature they might eat? Whereas Franklin had been perfectly comfortable comparing humans to plants, his attitude reflected acceptance of radical Enlightenment materialism, a habit acquired in his youth and never forgotten. That position troubled clergy at the time, unless they themselves were radicals. A case in point was Joseph Priestley, friend of Franklin, ordained minister, instructor (if not during Malthus's time) at the dissenting Warrington Academy, and one of Joseph Johnson's famous authors. In his materialism, Priestley went so far as to interpret the soul as a physical entity, but this was one reason he was deemed unorthodox, if not heretical, and threatened with violence before he fled for Franklin's Pennsylvania. There is no evidence that Malthus entertained similar thoughts about humans as merely material objects, and he surely knew that, as a minister in the Church of England and a fellow of Jesus College, Cambridge, he could not publicly have entertained such sentiments without renouncing his livelihood, his own means of subsistence. Malthus therefore distinguished between the powers of the reproducing dyad and of the vegetable imaginary in a way that neither Giovanni Botero nor Benjamin Franklin had done. His steady distinction between humans and the things they ate reflected his orthodoxy but also made his insistence on arithmetic rates of increase for food and geometrical rates of increase for humans impossible to support with data. It remained an item of faith, quite literally so.[51]

As in the first edition of the *Essay*, Malthus specified that humans differed from other natural beings because they could exercise judgment. This "preventive check," as he put it, "is peculiar to man, and arises from that distinctive superiority in his reasoning faculties, which enables him to calculate distant consequences." Malthus presented this, rather vividly for the time and place, as the series of doubts a married man (specifically) might entertain "if he follow the bent of his inclinations" to have sexual intercourse with his wife, while knowing it might lead to the impoverishment of his household. In a real sense, Malthus presented his treatise as another reason to give an ardent man pause. As he repeatedly warned, the mismatch between rates of increase for human beings and for their subsistence could only be reconciled in three ways, two of them uninviting but the third much more promising: vice, misery, or else moral discipline, as exerted through the delay of marriage and then of any sexual gratification within marriage.[52]

As a case in point, Malthus presented white North Americans as having the least incentive to delay their gratification, a direct challenge to any conception of new worlds as reservoirs of Edenic innocence. He conceded there had never been any "country" where "manners were so pure and simple, and the means of subsistence so abundant, that no check whatever has existed to early marriages." And yet, "in the northern states of America, where the means of subsistence have been more ample, the manners of the people more pure, and the checks to early marriage fewer, than in any of the modern states of Europe, the population was found to double itself for some successive periods every twenty-five years." Malthus added qualifications; mortality in New England towns sometimes exceeded the birth rate, their populations sustained only through migration from the countryside. But in frontier settlements, "where the sole employment was agriculture, and vicious customs and unwholesome occupations were unknown, the population was found to double itself in fifteen years." That example was the closest to a free state of marriage and reproduction than had ever been observed, though "even this extraordinary rate of increase is probably short of the utmost power of population." In new world settlements the manners may have been purer than anywhere else, and subsistence plentiful, but the work of breaking new land and the hazard of attack by Indians would offset those extraordinary conditions to some extent.[53]

By placing this material at the very start of his analysis, Malthus made new world examples, from urban and frontier parts of the United States, function as primary evidence of the capacity of population to increase at its fastest known rate, doubling as quickly as every fifteen years, approaching the theoretical extreme, should humans somehow need no more reason than animals. This analytic conclusion was not necessarily flattering to the western settlers along the US frontier, who were implied to breed almost as indiscriminately as rats. That implication constituted a potential point of criticism about all new world colonists that Malthus would develop later in the book. For the moment, in his introductory material, he moved to examples of places where food production increased least quickly, if at all, in order to give evidence of the other half of his principle of population, thus establishing the contrasting swiftness and slowness that together doomed humanity—again with intimations of the primordial curses on Adam and Eve, if nevertheless with exhortations about how to avoid this fate. He again laid out a hypothetical rate of agricultural growth, at its fastest, only to conclude that it would never keep up with population. "In Europe," he ventured, "there is the fairest chance that human industry may receive its best direction." But it would never force agricultural increase at a geometric rate.[54]

If agriculture could not supply food endlessly to keep up with its eaters, given its only arithmetical rate of increase, this raised an ethical problem about European colonization in the new worlds of the Atlantic and Pacific, the third way in which new worlds were central to Malthus's analysis and his strongest statement about the weakness of human nature, especially when tempted by natural abundance. If settlers in a new land kept reproducing, they would make people faster than their land could make food, even if (as in new world environments) the land had never before been brought into cultivation. Any misery the scarcity might cause their descendents would be a problem, but so too was the misery they meanwhile created for any "new" territory's indigenous inhabitants. "There are many parts of the globe, indeed, hitherto uncultivated, and almost unoccupied; but the right of exterminating, or driving into a corner where they must starve, even the inhabitants of these thinly peopled regions, will be questioned in a moral view." Not only was this usurpation of indigenous peoples immoral, but it would let the settler population live on borrowed time only. "Even where this might take place, as it does sometimes in new colonies, a geometrical ratio increases with such extraordinary rapidity, that the advantage could not last long." Malthus has been thoroughly assessed as to his statement about the moral hazard of the possible increase in the numbers of British poor, yet his parallel claim about the moral hazard of colonial populations increasing in new world environments is equally arresting. And it carries a complex irony: pure manners among humans guaranteed an evil outcome in those contexts, a definite instance of human nature exacerbating rather than compensating for material nature.[55]

Malthus took it as given that noncommercial peoples had much less control over their modes of subsistence. He rejected the possibility that they would quickly adopt the agriculture and commerce of any European settlers among them. "To exterminate the inhabitants of the greatest part of Asia and Africa, is a thought that could not be admitted for a moment," yet "to civilize and direct the industry of the various tribes of Tartars, and Negroes, would certainly be work of considerable time, and of variable and uncertain success." And among the hunting savages of new worlds, "the process of improving their minds and directing their industry, would necessarily be slow." Malthus's analysis of the economics of labor and agricultural production within Europe could not, for that reason, explain other places, least of all new world places, where noncommercial humans would wax and wane according to nature, not culture. "In savage life," he specified, "where there is no regular price of labor, it is little to be doubted that similar oscillations take place." The miseries of war, disease, and famine, plus vicious attempts to prevent conception or promote infanticide, would all take their toll.[56]

After his introductory material, Malthus tackled the primary topic of this first book of the expanded *Essay*, "Of the Checks to Population in the less civilized parts of the world, and in past times." That title implied an investigation of humanity's shared origins, whether historically remote and geographically proximate, or the reverse. Of the chapters on the new worlds, the first addressed New Holland, the second the Americas, and the third the islands of the South Sea or Pacific Ocean. Here the *Essay* became a significant anthropology of indigenous people and history of colonial encounters. It dwelled on the sufferings particular to these configurations of new lands and peoples while using stadial theory to make a case for the universality of the principle of population. Only having done this studied groundwork would Malthus, in later sections of the book, dispute Godwin at greater length than in his edition of 1798 and argue directly against Condorcet for the first time, his point being that theories of human happiness should rely on observations of humans as they were and had been. Throughout he presented the Americas as the metric for all new worlds though also, by implication, for all humanity. And with that, Malthus launched his *Essay* out into an extended analysis of the world, beginning with the new worlds where "savage life" dominated until settler populations arrived and put their fresh lands to the plow, or at least tried to do so.[57]

PART II

New Worlds in the *Essay*, c. 1803

Chapter 3

New Holland

A WHOLE NEW "NEW WORLD" OPENED UP in Malthus's lifetime. He was two years old when James Cook departed Plymouth for the South Sea in 1768, and thirty years later, as a Surrey curate, he read the account of that journey, including descriptions of the thin population of people on the eastern coast of the continent now called Australia, then New Holland. Malthus summarized for his readers claims about "the very small number of inhabitants . . . and the apparent inability of the country, from its desolate state, to support many more." Indeed, Malthus found his own core question already explicitly posed in this account of New Holland: why were numbers so low, and how had they been kept so? He transferred the passage verbatim into his new, long *Essay*:

> "By what means the inhabitants of this country are reduced to such a number as it can subsist, is not perhaps very easy to guess; whether, like the inhabitants of New Zealand, they are destroyed by the hands of each other in contests for food; whether they are swept off by accidental famine; or whether there is any cause that prevents the increase of the species, must be left for future adventurers to determine."[1]

The new world, for Malthus, provided not just data retrospectively to support his thesis, but the question that produced the thesis in the first place. Indeed it was all so much to the point that Malthus quoted this passage not once but twice; in the new chapter on New Holland and in the subsequent chapter on the South Sea islands. The repetition was less about a particular fascination with the Pacific new world than about the scope of the question. What British explorers had asked of Aboriginal Australia and of the South Sea islands, Malthus thought should be rendered universal. "The question, applied generally, appears to me to be highly curious, and to lead to the elucidation of some of the most obscure, yet important points, in the history of human society." He did apply it. Indeed, the long edition of the *Essay on the Principle of Population* might be assessed as one extended response to a question Malthus found retrospectively in the account of Cook's first voyage.[2]

The new edition appeared in 1803 after the great success of the anonymous 1798 pamphlet. Malthus had confided in 1800 that the *Essay* was nowhere to be bought: "This I hope will animate me to proceed in another edition, though to say the truth I feel at present very idle about it."[3] But at some point idleness turned into great activity, and he became committed to the much longer study. Its purpose was to offer empirical material that would demonstrate to his readers just how the principle of population was always and everywhere at work. In two quarto volumes he traveled through time and over space, tracing human societies and their oscillating populations through successive stages of development. His new, long *Essay* took the eighteenth-century "history of mankind" and put population at its center. The first book in volume one concerned people in the "lowest stages and past times," reworking classical authors on Greece and Rome; Scottish writers on European and Asian barbarians; travelers' accounts of China, India, and Africa; and the great proliferation of voyagers' accounts of the Pacific Ocean. With all this detail Malthus substantiated his principle.

The third chapter of the revised *Essay*—"Of the Checks to Population in the lowest Stage of Human Society"—was entirely concerned with the first of the stadial set of four, the "savage" hunter and the gatherer. The "lowest" were not those people who had lived in past historical time, however, as for some earlier theorists in the French and Scottish traditions. Rather, the "lowest" represented a way of organizing knowledge of the world's people living elsewhere in the present, albeit stuck, as it were, in an uncivilized state, in "prehistoric" savagery. And if the work of Scottish and French Enlightenment theorists conventionally discussed American Indians as archetypal and historical savages, the antipodean journeys of Cook and others from the 1760s onwards offered Malthus an entirely new set of information with which to think through population in terms of stadial theory and its links both to colonization and to "civilization." Indeed, in this chapter Malthus eschewed the secondhand accounts offered in the histories by Kames, Condorcet, and a dozen others and drew exclusively, if haphazardly, on the words of those travelers, explorers, and colonists who had witnessed firsthand these faraway people and places.[4]

* * *

Malthus opened his journey through the world's people with "the wretched inhabitants of Terra del Fuego." The Fuegians were "at the bottom of the scale of human beings." In beginning thus, Malthus was also following European mariners to the South Sea. The people who lived at the point where the Atlantic meets the Pacific had been encountered by Portuguese, Spanish, British, and French expeditions for centuries, ever since Magellan sailed his fleet carefully from one ocean into another in 1520. The strait was named for him, the land for them: "Tierra del Fuego," he called it, as he passed the fires at night. Malthus's source of knowledge was much later, Cook's voyages to the South Sea. Unlike Magellan, Cook's fleet had landed at Tierra del Fuego in January 1769, and Malthus read descriptions of local clothing, language, weapons, and the scattered European commodities left by previous visitors: rings, sailcloth, buttons. He read of their lack of government and (importantly for Malthus) about their diet: "We saw no appearance of their having any food but shellfish." They did not, it seemed, harvest the many seals on the shoreline, and so Malthus recounted Tierra del Fuego as a barren land, the people accordingly "half-starved" and filthy, and without "sagacity" to mitigate the effects of such a cold and inhospitable climate.[5]

The account of Cook's first voyage that Malthus read included an illustration of a Fuegian family in front of their hut. It was a dwelling deemed "to stand but for a short time," a sign of the lack of property characteristic of the European category "savage." The engraving was reworked many times from the original watercolor by Buchan (1769), and as art historian Bernard Smith has shown, some versions emphasized primitive brutishness and others noble simplicity. The particular Francesco Bartolozzi engraving that Malthus reviewed portrayed the Fuegian family as considerably more noble and less wretched than earlier versions. The account he read certainly characterized Fuegians as "outcasts of Nature" but hinted at their Rousseauean virtues as well, casting them at times as classically inspired simple societies. Malthus, however, either failed to pick up on the visual clues or deliberately ignored this more sympathetic reading, instead setting out an unequivocal savagery, casting Fuegians as remorselessly miserable.[6]

Malthus cited all of this information as deriving from "Cook's First Voyage." But it was not from Cook's journal as such. It was the second volume of *An Account of the Voyages Undertaken by the Order of His Present Majesty for Making Discoveries in the Southern Hemisphere.* Editor, author, and director of the East India Company John Hawkesworth had been commissioned by the Admiralty to compile an account of several journeys: those of Byron, Wallis, Carteret, and most recently Cook. Hawkesworth's volumes, published in 1773, were immediately attacked, in part for the licentious material on South Sea sexuality that he retained, in part for dubious comments on Providence, and in part for the embellishments from his own pen that immediately

Figure 3.1. The reproductive family in the first stage of stadial theory. The Indians of Tierra del Fuego in their hut. John Hawkesworth, *An Account of the Voyages Undertaken by the Order of His Present Majesty for Making Discoveries in the Southern Hemisphere*, 3 vols. (London: Strahan and Cadell, 1773), vol. 2, facing 55. Reproduced from Jesus College, Old Library, volume of cuts, charts, and maps, by permission of the Master and Fellows of Jesus College, Cambridge.

rendered the veracity of the accounts suspect. Hawkesworth's first-person device seemed dissembling, when he was clearly conflating so many journals and diaries. Malthus knew this, referring pointedly to the "narrator" of Cook's first voyage. Hawkesworth was, and is still, derided (or else analyzed) for intruding his own style into these renditions of the South Sea voyages. But nonetheless they were for many years, and certainly in Malthus's time, the authoritative account. As one of Hawkesworth's later defenders put it, in editorial solidarity, "For a hundred and twenty years, so far as the first voyage was concerned, Hawkesworth was Cook." More important, perhaps, one of Hawkesworth's key contemporary defenders was his good friend and fellow bibliophile Benjamin Franklin (also a friend of their mutual publisher, William Strahan): "It has been a fashion to decry Hawkesworth's book," wrote Franklin in 1773, "but it does not deserve the Treatment it has met with. It acquaints us with new people having new customs; and teaches us a good deal of new knowledge." It was just such new people and new customs that drew Malthus in, when he turned to transform his short 1798 *Essay* into a new kind of universal history.[7]

After visiting Tierra del Fuego with and through Hawkesworth and Cook, Malthus went on his own textual voyage, with passing mention of the natives of Van Diemen's Land as similarly "low." This time he referred to one of Cook's midshipmen made good, George Vancouver, who had just published *A Voyage of Discovery to the North Pacific Ocean, and round the World* (1798). Then, navigating entirely away from the South Sea, Malthus inserted a longer account of another society of savage hunter-gatherers: the Andaman Islanders. For some time, Tierra del Fuegians, Van Diemen's Land Aborigines, and Cape "Hottentots" had figured as the standard ethnographic trio of savagery. In the late eighteenth century and through most of the nineteenth, this became a cluster of four, adding the Andaman Islanders to represent human society in its "lowest stages." Malthus referred to Michael Symes's recently published *Account of an Embassy to the Kingdom of Ava* (1800). Soldier and diplomat with the East India Company, Symes's travel account offered another instance of a society with no civil government apparent to British observers, another instance of a society with no agriculture, no practices of pastoral management of stock, or of settled cultivation.[8]

Symes speculated extensively on the (geographic) origin of the Indian Ocean Andaman Islanders as a "race," engaging with the question of humanity's common or distinct descent in biblical chronology. Just how ancient humans, or humans in earlier stages, had moved across the world and in what time periods deeply engaged earlier stadial theorists as they tried to reconcile Scripture with secular evidence. Johann Friedrich Blumenbach and Georges-Louis Leclerc, comte de Buffon, were monogenists, perceiving all humans to be commonly descended, but having degenerated or advanced in different ways across the globe. Voltaire's polygenism posited different ancestors for different races, a position also argued by Henry Home, Lord Kames, whose *Sketches on the History of Man* Malthus borrowed from Jesus College Library in November 1801, in preparation for his long edition of the *Essay*. This is part of what Symes repeated in his work on the Andamans that Malthus mined. And yet determining human origin was pointedly not the purpose of Malthus's inquiry. He did not engage with the polygenism-versus-monogenism argument that dominated Kames's and others' perspectives as they sought to draw the "history of man." In writing on "the lowest Stage of Human Society," Malthus did not pronounce on lineages or antediluvian connections between peoples. Stadial theory and emerging taxonomies of race were related but were not necessarily the same system for perceiving and evaluating human difference across time and across the globe. Malthus's interest in the so-called savage stage, elaborated in the 1803 edition of the *Essay*, was more socially, ethnographically, and economically classificatory than physically taxonomic. What constituted "savage society" for him was first and foremost a mode of subsistence, a pre- or nonpastoral economy, a gathering and hunting society. He inquired into comparative means of subsistence, detailing the varying customs and manners by which life, death, sex, and food were managed in vastly different climates and cultures the world over, and in the different economies of exchange organized by the four stages. In this way, he was not a theorist of race per se but of economic stages that were nonetheless commonly racialized, and most crudely with the so-called savage.[9]

Malthus may not have been a theorist of racial difference, but he freely repeated derogatory comments that over time turned the meaning of *savage* toward its more nineteenth- and twentieth-century usage, linking it with filth, simplicity, brutishness, and so forth. In doing so, he drew from Lieutenant R. H. Colebrooke's "On the Andaman Islands," published in *Asiatic Researches*. Colebrooke noted that while the islands were circled by countries that had been increasing in population as well as wealth, "having been from time immemorial in a state of tolerable civilization," the Andamans themselves were in a state of nature. And not a good one. "Grossest ignorance and barbarity ... wild appearance ... ferocious disposition." In this piece Malthus read yet another denigrating description of savagery, a literally uncultivated one: "Their mode of life is degrading to human nature, and, like brutes, their whole time is spent in search of food. They have yet made no attempts to cultivate their lands, but live entirely upon what they can pick up, or kill." In all the new world societies he studied, Malthus was interested in food, how people acquired it, and the labor taken to do so. In his short passage on the Andamans, the point was to reveal, again, the gathering practices of a savage economy, the sole preoccupation and activity "climbing the rocks, or roving along the margin of the sea, in search of a precarious meal of fish." Some were observed on the shores, he recounted, "in the last stage of famine."[10]

People on shorelines appear constantly in eighteenth-century accounts of the Pacific, readily perceived and encountered by European maritime travelers Even though Malthus's political economy was fundamentally about land—soil and its improvement—in his early chapters he recapitulated what others had said of the orientation toward the ocean of the Pacific new world.

He had also read some observers' more conceptual and pressing questions about how coastal dwellers' sustenance was related to inland societies. Might people in the interior cultivate land, even if those on the coast did not? If so, what did it mean that this technology had not transferred to people on the shores? As they charted coastlines and wrote up encounters with locals in their journals, some observers occasionally wondered if the lack of cultivation by coastal dwellers meant that there were no inland inhabitants at all.

It was gatherers who populated Malthus's early chapter on Tierra del Fuego, the Andamans, and New Holland. There were few Rousseauean hunters akin to those in his famous deer-hunt passage in *Discourse on Inequality*. Indeed, there is no reference to Rousseau anywhere in the *Essay*. The close family connection makes the absence of Rousseau all the more striking, and clearly the younger Malthus was setting the French philosopher to one side just as strongly as the elder Malthus sought his company and connection. There is a larger point, however, less personal than epistemological and methodological for Malthus. For all his reading on the "histories of man," including Kames's *Sketches*, Condorcet's *Esquisse d'un tableau historique des progrès de l'esprit humain*, and Rousseau's *Discours sur l'origine et les fondements de l'inégalité parmi les homes*, Malthus built his own new stadial history on firsthand, not secondhand, accounts. In the first substantive chapter he relied exclusively on the witness of voyagers, seamen, explorers, and settlers, bringing his work closer to the new world itself than the filtered versions of Scottish and French philosophers and historians. The "savages" who appeared in this chapter were not hypothetical figures (as they were for Adam Smith), or generic "savage nations of the globe" (as they were for Edward Gibbon), or even the geographically scrambled selection that appeared in Kames's *Sketches of the History of Man*. They were very particularly placed, encountered, and represented people, even, in the case of New Holland, individuals.[11]

* * *

Malthus dedicated most of his chapter on people in the "lowest stages" to a detailed case of Aboriginal people of the eastern coast of New Holland. He did so because an observation attributed to Cook had caught his eye: "By what means the inhabitants of this country are reduced to such a number as it can subsist, is not perhaps very easy to guess." Of all the exotic tableaux, florid description, and dashing adventure that made up Hawkesworth's volumes, it is quite clear that this is what grabbed and held Malthus's attention.

He bothered to copy this passage, transfer it into his *Essay* as a direct quotation, and retain it in all editions. Indeed, in the *Summary View of the Principle of Population*, published in 1830, Malthus cast back over his life's major work, and himself characterized the entire project as one long response to "Cook." He had endeavored "to answer the question, generally, which had been applied, particularly, to New Holland by Captain Cook."[12]

The question, however, derived not from Cook at all but from the naturalist on board the *Endeavour*, Joseph Banks. Hawkesworth had acquired Banks's journals as part of the Admiralty-sponsored publication extravaganza, and he tacked the naturalist onto the end of the volumes' long title: *An Account of the Voyages Undertaken by Order of His Present Majesty for Making Discoveries in the Southern Hemisphere, And successively Performed by Commodore Byron, Captain Wallis, Captain Carteret, and Captain Cook, in the Dolphin, the Swallow, and the Endeavour: Drawn up from the Journals which were kept by the Several Commanders, And from the Papers of Joseph Banks, Esq.* Reflecting after thousands of nautical miles, and months of intermittent encounters with Aboriginal people on the eastern coast of New Holland, Banks had written in August 1770: "Whatever may be the reason of this want of People is dificult to guess, unless perhaps the Barreness of the Soil and scarcity of fresh water; but why mankind should not increase here as fast as in other places unless their small tribes have frequent wars in which many are destroyd." This is the sentence, edited and embellished by Hawkesworth, that found its way into the *Essay on the Principle of Population*, capturing for Malthus the very essence of his work.[13]

Unwittingly, then, and despite his own declaration to have been inspired by Captain Cook, Malthus tended to draw into his *Essay* observations that derived more from the naturalist than the navigator aboard the *Endeavour*. It was Banks who keenly detailed human custom and economy, with the interest and skill of a natural historian, and this was the material, via Hawkesworth, that turned up again in the *Essay*. But both Banks and Cook were thinking in terms of population. Cook, indeed, had been officially charged to do so: estimating native numbers was part of his instruction from the Admiralty: "You are likewise to observe the Genius, Temper, Disposition and Number of the Natives." Cook did so, diligently enough.[14]

When Cook charted the eastern coast of New Holland in 1770, there were no European settlements on the continent, although Dutch and French expeditions had intermittently landed on other coasts of the vast continent since 1606, without exception departing quickly. They typically noted the sparse population and arid environment, and Cook's observations confirmed just this: "Neither are they very numerous, they live in small parties along by the Sea Coast, the banks of Lakes, Rivers creeks &C. They seem to have no fix'd habitation but move about from place to place like wild Beasts in search of food, and I beleive depend wholy upon the success of the present day for their subsistance." Cook was very precise about cultivation: "The Land naturly produces hardly anything fit for man to eat and the Natives know nothing of Cultivation." Moving in search of food, not settling and cultivating land, was the key indictor of a savage economy: that was what was significant to Malthus the political economist. But to Cook, as representative of George III, that he "never saw one Inch of Cultivated land in the whole Country" also signaled vacancy. And so from a tiny spot of land called "Possession Island," Cook claimed everything he had seen for the last seven months, and more: "Notwithstand[ing] I had in the Name of His Majesty taken possession of several places upon this coast, I now once more hoisted English Coulers and in the Name of His Majesty King George the Third took possession of the whole Eastern Coast . . . by the name New South Wales, together with all the Bays, Harbours Rivers and Islands situate upon the said coast." This had also formed part of his Secret Instructions from the Admiralty.[15]

Cook and Banks commented repeatedly on the sparse population in New Holland: "thinly inhabited even to admiration, at least that part of it that we saw: we never but once saw so many as thirty Indians together and that was a family," wrote the latter. However, Banks tended to press such observations further than Cook, speculating on causal relations between population and soil, population and food, and even population and government. He wondered, for example, about people in the interior of New Holland, comparing them, as was often the case (and as Malthus was to do), with native Americans:

> The Sea has I beleive been universaly found to be the cheif source of supplys to Indians ignorant of the arts of cultivation: the wild produce of the Land alone seems scarce able to support them at all seasons, at least I do not remember to have read of any inland nation who did not cultivate the ground more or less, even the North Americans who were so well versd in hunting sowd their Maize. But should a people live inland who supported themselves by cultivation these inhabitants of the sea coast must certainly have learn'd to imitate them in some degree at least, otherwise their reason must be supposd to hold a rank little superior to that of monkies.[16]

Cook's observations in 1770 and Banks's commentary on population, soil, and government in New Holland were later key to the British government's decision to establish a new penal colony at Botany Bay. Banks assured the parliamentary committee in 1779 of the low number of natives and also, interestingly, of the possibility of increase:

> there would be little Probability of any Opposition from the Natives, as during his Stay there, in the year 1770, he saw very few, and did not think there would be above Fifty in all the Neighbourhood ... the Proportion of rich Soil was small in Comparison to the barren, but sufficient to support a very large Number of People; ... if the People formed among themselves a Civil Government, they would necessarily increase, and find Occasion for many European Commodities.[17]

Here Banks himself thought and wrote as a theorist of population: civil government itself encouraged population growth, necessarily indeed. It is no wonder that it was Banks's commentary (filtered through Hawkesworth) that made Malthus pause. This was not simply observation of customs, or estimation of numbers, but a more complex musing on the mechanics of population: why and especially how population was sometimes kept low, and might at other times grow, a question that Malthus said could and should be asked of any society. Many in the eighteenth century mused on population growth and decline, but Banks, like Malthus later, wondered "by what means" this came to be. They wondered about the mechanism.

* * *

With the parliamentary intercession of Joseph Banks, the British government sent a fleet of some 1,400 officers, marines, convicts, and a few free settlers to establish a new colony in the antipodes. The British fleet landed in Botany Bay and settled just north in Port Jackson, present-day Sydney, in January 1788. This was the penal colony of New South Wales. The 1798 edition of the *Essay* was thus published just a decade after the British colonized what they thought of as the end of the Earth, but that was in fact the land of the Eora people. The prospect of a new penal colony itself did not raise much popular interest in Britain, since that had been done before, and on several different continents. But this particular "thief colony" was impossibly far away, and it was this almost other worldliness that garnered attention from an astonished public. Might a route through the center of the Earth be proposed as a short cut to Botany Bay, quipped one commentator in the *St. James's Chronicle*, the triweekly evening paper from which at least one member of the Malthus family habitually took clippings. "Botany Bay" was certainly a talking point for Londoners in the 1780s, after the idea was proposed by Banks, and remained so through the 1790s, as multiple accounts of the earliest years of the New South Wales colony, especially of the encounters with local Aboriginal people, went to press.[18]

Population was to prove important to the new colony from the beginning. "The natives are far more numerous than they were supposed to be," reported the first governor, Arthur Phillip. He reckoned more than 1,500 in the local coastal region, about as many souls as had been in his charge on the long voyage from Portsmouth to Botany Bay. And there were certainly "inhabitants in the interior parts of the country," he reported back in early dispatches. This was all a response to Banks, who had speculated at one point that the inland was uninhabited. "We saw indeed only the sea coast: what the immense tract of inland countrey may produce is to us totaly unknown: we may have liberty to conjecture however that they are totaly uninhabited."[19]

None of this made its way into the first edition of the *Essay*: neither New Holland nor New South Wales was mentioned. By 1803, when Malthus turned to look at New South Wales, it was a fifteen-year-old experiment in colonization, penal authority, and the difficulties of antipodean agriculture. The colony had moved through three governors, each of whom had to rule on, and manage—insofar as they could—relations between the British and indigenous people. But Malthus was not interested in New South Wales as a colony. He did not envisage the antipodes as a place where great swathes of land might come under cultivation, and where settler populations might double, Franklin style (though in the 1820s he was to do so). In other words, for the purposes of his *Essay*, and in contrast to his following chapter on the Americas, Malthus was only interested in Aboriginal people, not the British colonists or the process of colonization itself. Nonetheless, the new chapter came about only because of British colonization, its antecedent maritime exploration of the South Sea, and the great publishing appetite in Britain and Europe for firsthand accounts of late-eighteenth-century new worlds.

If Malthus's core question derived from Banks's observation of Aboriginal people, material for his answer was offered by a slightly later British observer, Lieutenant David Collins. Sailing with the founding fleet of marines, convicts, and officers from Portsmouth to Sydney to start a settlement from scratch, Collins was judge advocate and secretary to the governor. His account of the English colony in New South Wales was published in 1798, too late for the first edition of the *Essay*, although there is no evidence that Malthus was looking for Pacific material at that point. But it offered perfect material for the second edition of the *Essay* in 1803: detailed, systematic, and just the kind of firsthand witness of Aboriginal society that Malthus favored. Indeed, much of Malthus's new chapter *was* David Collins; whole paragraphs were directly quoted and meticulously cited.[20]

There were any number of lengthy accounts of the new colony from which Malthus might have drawn detail on Aboriginal life and economy. Colonists of all ranks published and thus gained from the adventure. All the government dispatches and multiple public accounts of the new colony that were published over the 1790s dealt with Aboriginal population and culture, one way or another. He could have drawn his material from the detail offered by marine Watkin Tench's *Complete Account of the Settlement at Port Jackson* (1793) or from the official account, *The Voyage of Governor Phillip to Botany Bay: with an Account of the Establishment of the Colonies of Port Jackson and Norfolk Islands* (1789). The Malthus family library held George Barrington's more romping version of events, *Voyage to New South Wales, with a Description of the Country; the Manner, Customs, Religion, &c, of the Natives, in the Vicinity of Botany Bay* (1795), although that author—already an infamous Irish pickpocket and serial transportee—was hardly likely to be perceived as authoritative. Barrington was transported first to the American colonies for theft in 1773 and then, in 1791, to the Australian colonies. In any case, there is no evidence that Malthus researched especially widely for this chapter. It seems that once he had located Collins's book—either already in his father's library or acquired for this purpose—it more than served. He went no further.[21]

Whereas other accounts interspersed encounters with Aboriginal people among detail of British colonization, settlement, cultivation, and exploration, Collins systematically sequestered his observations on Aborigines into lengthy appendices, usefully organized by topic: Government and Religion; Stature and Appearance; Habitations; Mode of Living; Courtship and Marriage; Customs and Manners; Superstition; Diseases; Property; Dispositions; Funeral Ceremonies; Language. Collins taught Malthus about Aboriginal capacity to reason (defined as awareness of right and wrong), and, importantly, about Aboriginal "real estates" and hereditary property. Malthus had certainly chosen his source and intermediary well, for Collins was a phenomenal observer, his volume carefully recounting detail from ceremonies to conversations, everyday encounters to devastating events. Everything that Malthus wanted to know about Aboriginal systems in relation to food, reproduction, labor, health, death, culture, and ritual was neatly arranged. And the volume drew from sympathetic, close personal engagement, knowledge, observation, and information. Collins was deeply involved in negotiations with local people, in equal measure intricate, difficult, and fascinating. He came to know many of them well and individually, over time counting particular

Aboriginal people as friends, reciprocally so, it seems. His account built on nearly nine years' experience in the fledgling colony, offering Malthus an entirely different basis for claims about Aboriginal life than did those who had watched from ships' decks or assessed on the basis of intermittent beach-based encounters. Unlike the work of voyagers—Cook, Banks, Vancouver, or La Pérouse—Collins's account was the work of a settler.[22]

For Malthus, New South Wales Aborigines were exemplars of "savage" hunter-gatherers; the most important fact for him was that this society did not cultivate land. The availability of food, the nature of diet, and the economy of exchange were each important for Malthus to establish in his foundational chapter. He wanted to demonstrate the relation between food scarcity and low population density, as well as to suggest some of the means by which that density was kept low. The chapter thus served to illustrate how the Aboriginal population was limited by various checks: those relating to birth, death, and sustenance. Via Collins he brought remarkable detail into the *Essay*, documenting coastal-dwellers' seafood diets and comparing it to inland natives' more difficult hunting of small animals, "the flying squirrel and the opossum." This cast back to Banks's question about knowledge transfers between territorial and coastal communities. Inland Aboriginal people climbed tall trees for honey, notched up to eighty feet, Malthus recounted, emphasizing the labor expended more than any ingenuity or dexterity— very little reward for "so much toil." The "woods" afforded some berries, yam, fern root, and the flowers of the Banksia, the small bushes named for Joseph Banks. This made up the "vegetable catalogue." Malthus could have detailed the hunting of large game when he turned to the animal diet of New Holland Aborigines, but instead he focused upon gathering: grubs, worms, ants, and pastes made from fern root and insect eggs. Animal and vegetable food was so scanty and the labor to acquire it so intensive that "the population must be very thinly scattered in proportion to the territory," he concluded. It was necessarily so, according to Malthus, the "must" in this sentence indicating the principle that all this detail was intended to both illustrate and substantiate.[23]

Malthus then turned to explain the culture, rather than the nature, that led to such a thin population. Any reader of Malthus's major work, in any edition, was told firmly at the outset that human societies had the potential to reproduce very rapidly (like Franklin's fennel), but the real point was that they rarely did so. The 1798 edition had established that this potential would always be checked in some way, eventually restrained by varying availability of room and nourishment. The 1803 edition laid down all of this in its opening paragraphs, the first footnote of the new edition referring to Franklin's pamphlet: it was foundational. In these chapters on savage societies, Malthus was showing just why and how the vast continent of New Holland, far from being overrun with humans as this potential would imply, in fact had relatively few. Fertility and mortality were moderated by natural checks but also by all kinds of human interventions, all kinds of reason and custom.

Culture, for Malthus, was invariably about gender. What interested Malthus in the case of New South Wales Aborigines was the reported low fertility, rather than high mortality. Collins had told him of the violence to which women were subject, detailing how they were bashed and dragged from their families as a means of becoming "wife," permanently scarred with the "traces of the superiority of the males." He surmised that miscarriages must be common in this violent context, exacerbated by the difficulties of wandering and gathering. This, plus the abuse of very young girls, likely resulted in Aboriginal women's low fertility, he thought. In many ways, Malthus selected the worst that Collins's book had to offer, and in the end he painted a far grimmer overall picture than the firsthand *Account of the English Colony in New South Wales*. He noted that men could and did have more than one wife but found it "extraordinary" that only the first wife, it seemed, bore children. "A great part of the women are without children," Collins had claimed, and other women appeared to have only a singleton. Some of the local people had told Collins (relayed Malthus), that the first wife "claimed an exclusive right to the conjugal embrace." Malthus himself thought this unlikely, supposing that the second wife, rather, "might not be allowed to rear her offspring." It is not quite clear what Malthus meant here, though it would seem a reference to infanticide. Malthus himself commented that it was hard to know precisely how fertility was reduced: all kinds of customs may not have been disclosed to Mr Collins.[24]

Many contemporary histories of humankind assessed the treatment of women as an index of savagery or civilization; gender was part of stadial theory's core business. The kind of brutality that Malthus documented was certainly intended to signal the lowest state of savagery, and to distinguish British men of honor from such violence. Malthus quoted David Collins's "feeling" response, his almost Romantic sensibilities: " 'The condition of these women is so wretched, that I have often, on seeing a female child borne on its mother's shoulders, anticipated the miseries to which it was born, and thought it would be a mercy to destroy it.' " It was a curious selection from the sentimental Collins, since endorsed infanticide—merciful or otherwise—was a clear sign of savagery, as well as sinfulness. And indeed in this chapter, and each that followed, Malthus addressed infanticide directly. Exposing and thus killing infants was one clear means by which populations were kept low, according to Malthus, and he recounted Collins's description of the Aboriginal practice of burying live infants with their dead mothers. This is what Malthus read in Collins's account:

> When the body was placed in the grave, the bye-standers were amazed to see the father himself place the living child in it with the mother. Having laid the child down, he threw upon it a large stone, and the grave was instantly filled in by the other natives. The whole business was so momentary, that our people had not time or presence of mind sufficient to prevent it; and on speaking about it to Cole-be, so far from thinking it inhuman, justified the extraordinary act by assuring us that as no woman could be found to nurse the child it must die a much worse death than that to which he had put it. As a similar circumstance occurred a short time after, we have every reason to suppose the custom always prevails among them.

The practice was another of the parallels Malthus was to draw in the following chapter between Aboriginal people in New Holland and native Americans. In such ways, Malthus found Collins himself intrigued by population, the long local tradition received from Banks: "This may in some degree," wrote Collins, "account for the thinness of population which has been observed among the natives of the country." The accumulation of such habits of life and death, Malthus considered, "forcibly repress the rising generation."[25]

Malthus also considered epidemic disease in his chapter on New South Wales, a further check that limited population numbers overall, but that also contributed to an oscillating pattern. He recounted the terrible epidemic of smallpox over 1789 that followed the arrival of the British in January 1788. It was a tragic instance of new world depopulation, perhaps 50 percent of the local population dead. "The desolation that it occasioned was almost incredible," Malthus stated correctly. When tribes almost disappeared, those who were left united with other tribes "to prevent their utter extinction." This, too, was correct, from all accounts.[26]

Importantly, however, Malthus did not link massive Aboriginal mortality in 1789 from smallpox to the arrival of the British the year before, or to the visits of French ships, which is what Governor Arthur Phillip thought might be the case. Instead, Malthus drew attention to habits of living: "the smoke and filth of their miserable habitations" produced "loathsome cutaneous disorders, and above all, a dreadful epidemic like the small-pox." In assessing the dreadful epidemic thus, Malthus took liberties with Collins's account, actively ignoring the wide speculation about British responsibility in this episode. Collins himself neither blamed the British for introducing smallpox nor the locals for bringing it upon themselves. But he did make a point of explaining that not one of the colonial children or infants died of smallpox that terrible year, the adults being immune from exposure to endemic smallpox in Britain itself. This is also what Governor Phillip dispatched home. It is still unclear whether the British infants had been inoculated or if vials of smallpox matter intended for British inoculation had been released knowingly or unknowingly into the Aboriginal community. Indeed, some historians argue that smallpox predated the arrival of the British entirely and had traveled south from Australia's northern borders with South East Asia.[27]

Collins himself had witnessed the American smallpox epidemic in Boston in 1775–76, when he had been a British officer in the revolutionary war. In that context, smallpox was experienced on all sides of the conflict—among the British, the French, and the revolutionary colonists—either as an offensive or else a terrible military setback. He would have known of the mortality within Indian societies across that continent. And so, among the great dying in Port Jackson in 1789, and in the context of the unexplained healthiness of the British children, he made a point of noting that the only non-Aboriginal death was that of "a North-American Indian, a sailor belonging to Captain Ball's vessel, the Supply, [who] sickened of it and died." This was Joseph Jefferies, who had joined HMS *Supply* at Rio in August 1787.[28]

For Collins, smallpox was certainly part of the encounter between the old world and the new, whether or not he understood it as a tragic consequence of British presence. For Malthus, however, the smallpox episode in 1789 was nothing of the sort. Rather, it served as evidence of positive checks—epidemics that naturally (though just as tragically for Malthus), operated when population levels pressed against subsistence levels. If for later observers the smallpox epidemic served as evidence of the fatal impact of colonialism, just as surely, in Malthus's view, it served as evidence of the permanent oscillation and regulation of population vis-à-vis resources. This conclusion entailed some crude exclusions and blatantly expedient selections from Collins's account. But for Malthus, it was the principle of population, not the principle of colonialism, that was in operation.[29]

* * *

In drawing from David Collins in such a detailed way over so many matters, Malthus was operating as vicarious ethnographer. Malthus's *Essay* thus

became a text in which fleeting first meetings between the English and Aboriginal people at the end of the Earth could be witnessed. He recounted one
such episode: "A native with his child, surprised on the banks of the Hawks-
bury river by some of our colonists, launched his canoe in a hurry, and left
behind him a specimen of his food." Even local Aboriginal words were included in the *Essay*. "These worms, in the language of the country, are called
cah-bro," reported Malthus. And so, the tribe of natives who lived inland and
ate them "is named Cah-brogal." Collins was not just a participant-observer,
or a colonial acquaintance, but clearly a friend of any number of Aborigines
in early New South Wales. Through him, Malthus was textually introduced
to dozens of individuals: Go-roo-bar-roo-bool-lo, "the daughter of an old
man named Met-ty," Ca-ru-ey, "a youth of about sixteen or seventeen years of
age," War-re-weer, Yel-lo-way, Wat-te-wal, and more.[30]

It was thus that two Aboriginal men came to be named in the *Essay on
the Principle of Population*: Bennelong and Colbee, for Malthus exemplars of
new world savagery. It so happened, however, that the former had journeyed
across the world in 1793, from the apparent lowest stage of civilization to
the center of civilization. Bennelong spent two years in and around London,
enjoying the hospitality of, among others, Lord Sydney, after whom his land
and waters had come to be named. Thus, during the years in which Malthus
became a fellow of Jesus College and curate of Okewood, Surrey, in which he
wrote his first (unpublished) pamphlet, Bennelong of New South Wales trod
Malthus's local paths. There is no evidence that Malthus and Bennelong met,
but we know that the political economist did ponder the portrait of "Georgian" Bennelong that graced the pages of Collins's 1798 volume.

By the time Malthus wrote his *Essay*, there was already a long tradition
of new world people visiting the old world, even as the savagery of stadial
theory itself was in the process of invention. Bennelong was one of a line
of visitors who graced London tables and then return to their homelands,
or else died in the metropolis from homesickness or old world diseases. A
sequence of native Americans had arrived over the seventeenth and eighteenth centuries, their visits framed in diplomatic and ambassadorial terms,
signaling the extent to which they perceived themselves, and were perceived
by the British, to be representatives of independent nations. This was not
how Bennelong was received, however, notwithstanding his connection to
Lord Sydney. Rather, London's public sphere announced him in the manner
that Malthus was a decade later to portray him: as an uncivilized savage. Indeed, in the London press there was a signal distaste that betrayed an offence
at Bennelong's civil pretensions. The *London Packet (New Lloyd's Evening*

Figure 3.2. Portrait of Bennelong. Engraving by James Neagle in David Collins, *Account of the English Colony in New South Wales . . .* (London: T. Cadell and W. Davies, 1798), 439. Reproduced by permission of Cambridge University Library.

Post) announced Bennelong and his people as being "totally incapable of civilisation" and "from a lower order of the human race." No inducement, it was said, can draw the natives of New South Wales "from a state of nature." Anticipating Malthus's claims that food and sex were the two fundamental needs, it was the basics of human life that were reported. Londoners read that Bennelong and his people fished, trapped kangaroos, and voraciously ate the whales that were "cast on their coast." And as for sex: "That instinct which teaches to propagate and preserve the species, they possess in common with the beasts of the field." Neither in the London press, nor slightly later for Malthus, did Bennelong serve as interlocutor, as aspiring native, or even as noble savage. All he stood for was prepastoral savagery.[31]

On the ground in Sydney, however, Bennelong had represented for colonists the possibility of civilizational improvement. Collins wrote (and Malthus read) that "friendly intercourse with the natives which had been so earnestly desired was at length established . . . acquiring our language;

readily falling in with our manners and customs; enjoying the comforts of our clothing, and relishing the variety of our food." In this way, Bennelong had become a valued friend of Governor Arthur Phillip, with whom he sailed to London in 1793. But their relationship began inauspiciously, barbarically: Phillip had ordered Bennelong's capture in 1789, a traumatic episode involving betrayal of trust, shackles, and firearms, all in a bid to find and secure a local man for more concerted cross-cultural communication. The notorious episode had also caused Bennelong's captors pain of a different sort, their late eighteenth-century antislavery sentiments deeply challenged. Bennelong did become a major interlocutor and cross-cultural mediator. In Sydney, in the early years of the British settlement, Bennelong enjoyed the governor's table, his specially built hut, and his tailored garments. And in London, Bennelong had all civilization at his disposal, and at considerable expense. This Aboriginal man, named in the *Essay* as exemplar of the savage stage, lived near Grosvenor Square, toured London sites, attended theatre at Sadler's Wells, Drury Lane, and Covent Garden, and studied with his reading and writing tutor. Multiple and elaborate outfits were tailored for him. He visited Parkinson's curio museum that displayed, amongst other things, artefacts and human remains from Cook's voyages, a macabre mirror for the Aboriginal visitor. He visited Lord Sydney, secretary for home affairs, while staying in Eltham, and he witnessed the peculiarities of British justice at the sensational trial of Warren Hastings.[32]

But civilization was not easy for the Eora man. His young countryman, Yemmerrawanie, who had traveled with him (and who did not have the dubious distinction of appearing in Malthus's *Essay*), died and was buried at Eltham. Bennelong himself longed for home and sickened progressively in an era when homesickness—"nostalgia"—was real in the sense of a medical diagnosis and was considered deadly, made all the more so by the knowledge of great distance. The sailors on Cook's voyage had felt something like it, Banks noting in September 1770 that they "were now pretty far gone with the longing for home which the Physicians have gone so far as to esteem a disease under the name of Nostalgia." Homesickness and the traumas of separation and departure affected all of the humans at this point in the world's history, when a whole quarter of the globe opened up to more frequent and far longer oceanic voyaging. Collins wrote that when the Aboriginal men had left Sydney, they had to endure "at the moment of their departure the united distress of their wives, and the dismal lamentations of their friends."[33]

The years that Bennelong was in London are the years about which least is known of Malthus's movements, but it is known that he was then composing his first but unpublished essay. One of the extant fragments is a lengthy musing on the significance of home in the context of migration. Malthus wondered what could possibly induce familial separation, except extreme distress. Observing the rural poor around him, he wondered "what is there to attach them to life, but their evening fire-side with their families ... surely no wise legislature would discourage these sentiments, and endeavour to weaken his attachment to home, unless indeed it were intended to destroy all thought and feeling among the common people, to break their spirit, and prepare them to submit patiently to any yoke that might be imposed upon them." During his years in London, Bennelong was immeasurably better off in material terms than the poor of Okewood, of whom Malthus wrote. But his tailored outfits, doctors' attention, tutor's guidance, and plays in town proved a pale substitute for evening fireside on the shore of Sydney's harbor. When he did return to his own shores, Bennelong himself wrote back to his English hosts: "Not me go to England no more. I am at home now."[34]

Everything about Bennelong would seem to confound stadial theory. Yet versions of this idea—reinforced and retold in the early nineteenth century, precisely in such influential texts as Malthus's *Essay*—came to shape Bennelong's life and his death. On the one hand, experience (rather than theory) of "savages" did make the British wonder about their own civilization. Collins, for one, demurred on the superiority of British civility. But what more typically bemused and troubled colonists was the tendency for Bennelong (and others in his bicultural situation) to drop into and out of "civilization," more or less at will. One colonist wrote: "The Natives of this country are more & more Savage though Some of them have been quite Civilized they prefer wandering stark naked in the bush living on worms insects &c this is the case with Bennelong who was in England. He visits the settlements now and then, is very polite, begs a loaf and departs." It was the seeming preference for their original life and custom that troubled such observers in the colonies, although sometimes—perhaps more often—this preference was represented as a kind of instinct. Another colonist wrote, again of Bennelong: "Upon his return to the Colony he fell off spontaneously into his early habits, and in spite of everything that could be done to him in the order of civilization, he took to the bush, and only occasionally visited Government House." Bennelong's assimilation to civilization remained a matter of colonial speculation and comment. His local obituary in 1813 was ungenerous: "In fact, he was a thorough savage, not to be warped from the form and character that nature gave him by all the efforts that mankind could use." In death, Bennelong was caught by a concept of nature that was increasingly fixed, separable from, and as this colonist would have it, trumped culture. This was a far cry from Rousseau's natural man, and closer to the image of the almost unchangeable savage drawn in the *Essay*'s chapter, although Malthus typically stressed great lengths of time required for change, rather than total incommensurability.[35]

It was just after Bennelong's return from London to his homeland in 1795, that Collins produced his account of New South Wales, the engraving was reproduced, and Malthus thus wrote him into his long *Essay*. Yet Malthus nonetheless portrayed Bennelong as entirely removed from Britain, as if he had never been there, and as if Aboriginal society was untouched by the colonists. Clearly, by 1803 the implications of British occupation for Aboriginal people in Bennelong's land were already as dire as they were permanent. And it seemed not to occur to Malthus—though he must have known of Bennelong's time in London—that the Aboriginal man had enjoyed at least three of the plays at Covent Garden that season, that Malthus, a great devotee of theater, knew from his father's library and likely saw himself. It was a willful blindness. Collins's account explicitly detailed Bennelong's departure to England, reports of his conduct in London, and his fortunes and manners on return to his native land:[36]

> Bennillong had certainly not been an inattentive observer of the manners of the people among whom he had lived; he conducted himself with the greatest propriety at table, particularly in the observance of those attentions which are chiefly requisite in the presence of women. His dress appeared to be an object of no small concern with him; and every one who knew him before he left the country, and who saw him now, pronounced without hesitation that Bennillong had not any desire to renounce the habits and comforts of the civilized life which he appeared so readily and so successfully to adopt.

Indeed on the very pages that Malthus copied into his own *Essay*, he read in so many words that Bennelong was "the native who was some time in England." Looking at the engraving of Bennelong, in other words, Malthus actively ignored the unmistakable signifiers of civilization that were foregrounded in the central portrait, and wrote solely about the frame—the artefacts of hunting and war, the signifiers of savagery.[37]

In such interpretive and textual acts, as well as in the direct encounters that Bennelong experienced across supposedly savage and civilized worlds, the paradox of the invention and discovery of "savagery" that J. G. A. Pocock has nominated is both heightened and dispelled. Pocock has detailed in *Barbarians, Savages and Empires* (2005) the peculiar eighteenth-century circumstance in which the "savage," meant to be ancient, was discovered in the modern world. And savages invented in the old world were encountered in the new. While historians and anthropologists have sometimes written of this period as one that developed an increasingly deep time in which to consider the history of humankind (although Malthus only accepted biblical time), the presence in the present of Bennelong and other antipodean and South Sea inhabitants is also striking. The reciprocal visits, if one can equate them, of the British to Botany Bay and of Bennelong to London confounded the element of time and sequence in the Scottish stadial theories that Malthus recapitulated for the early nineteenth-century world. Bennelong was not "ancient," but in this respect his journey did involve a kind of time travel.[38]

Malthus himself undertook none of this cultural journeying; he just read, thought, and wrote about it, like so many political economists and historians of his generation and milieu. His own life, after all, was not a daring one. He traveled to town to the theater. He traveled through Scandinavia with his college friends, took a riding tour of the Lakes, went once to Ireland, and when international relations permitted, traveled comfortably to the continent with family. Indeed, in later life he resolved "not to make distant excursions more than once a year," declining an invitation from his friend David Ricardo to stay at Gatcomb Park, Gloucestershire, for example: "that part of the world" was simply too far away.[39] His knowledge of the rest of the world was vicarious, as he dipped into his father's library, and those of his Cambridge college, his club, and his friends, to read accounts of exotic new world people and how they lived, died, ate, and reproduced. In all, he was nowhere near as cosmopolitan as Bennelong—or, for that matter, as David Collins.

* * *

Soon after Bennelong returned across the globe to Sydney, and in the year that Malthus was busy reading James Cook and David Collins so as to incorporate the Pacific new world into his next edition, the British government decided to establish another colony in New South Wales, a satellite far south of Sydney. It was Collins himself who was charged to set up a whole new settlement from scratch, from a state of nature, we might say. It was another of the profound exchanges that characterized imperialism in the Pacific new world. If savage Bennelong went to London's civilization, civilized Collins went to Bennelong's "nature," where for a time at least, he would have fared rather better if he had been a hunter or a gatherer, rather than a cultivator. Colonial encounter on the ground was completely different from stadial theorizing in books.

By 1803 Collins was very experienced in multiple colonial contexts—he had fought against the American revolutionaries at Bunker Hill, lived in Novia Scotia, and helped shape the new colony in Sydney for the best part of a decade from January 1788, not returning to London until June 1797. Collins set sail again, reluctantly, in April 1803, charged to set up a new society in Port Phillip Bay, near present-day Melbourne. He brought 402 people into Port Phillip Bay in October and set to clearing land for a garden, as a first task for this new society on new shores. The process of cultivation brought the hungry group into a state where they might feed themselves and simultaneously enact that mixing of land and labor so symbolically central to civilization and effective occupation. Collins was introducing cultivation, the lack of which had rendered the continent available to the British, or so his law reasoned. But they failed. The soil, he wrote "is light & mixed considerably with Sand: even the few Patches of Black Vegetable Mould, which here and there have been met with, abound therewith. I have nevertheless penned 2 Acres of Ground for a Garden, and am preparing 5 Acres for Indian Corn. Of the success of the latter I do not entertain much hope, but I find in it some employment for my people." Successful cultivation and agriculture—so central to Malthus's political economy–was essential for that small new society: without a crop they considered themselves unviable. Collins's charges—convict and free—were getting both hungry and discontented. The British colonists themselves were experiencing scarcity firsthand, and the four stages of stadial theory in practice were rapidly unraveling on the distant shores. Ironically, the British seemed doomed precisely because they were not hunter-gatherers.[40]

Collins removed his community and sailed further south to Van Diemen's Land, there to establish a far more viable settlement in Hobart. The French were also busy that year in Van Diemen's Land, coming and going on their scientific expeditions. But it was the British who settled. Indeed, Collins was to serve as lieutenant governor of this new colony until 1810, unaware that in the meantime his early observations on Aboriginal society were being widely read, less through the sales of his own book—popular enough—but more through its repetition in Thomas Robert Malthus's famous *Essay*.[41] The soil and climate proved responsive to British seeds and plants that Collins had brought with him, and acres of grain did grow. In the unequal exchange that was the constant companion to colonial ventures, Collins began to extract and send local specimens back to Joseph Banks, bio-prospecting that had potential for production of even greater British wealth.

And so, while Malthus's second edition ran off the press in St. Paul's Churchyard, London, the Van Diemen's Land Aborigines identified by

Malthus as "lowest," along with Andaman Islanders and Fuegians, watched gardens cleared, huts built, and stock proliferate on their land, all under the direction of David Collins. True to Benjamin Franklin's predictions from another time and place, this race of Englishmen doubled and tripled with astonishing rapidity, and like fennel replacing all other plants, came to displace and then replace, almost entirely, the Aboriginal people. But none of this unfolded passively or inevitably. By the time the final edition of the *Essay on the Principle of Population* was printed in 1826, the savage and the civilized that stadial theorists such as Malthus so naïvely imagined as separated by time and space, were in a state of war. In Van Diemen's Land that year, the *Colonial Times* expressed the views of some colonists that "self defence is the first law of nature. The government must remove the natives—if not, they will be hunted down like wild beasts, and destroyed!" They should be removed to an island, there to be civilized: "Let them be compelled to grow potatoes, wheat, &c, catch seals and fish, and by degrees, they will lose their roving disposition and acquire some slight habits of industry, which is the first step of civilization."[42] Tasmanian Aborigines eventually yielded to just such a plan—one that saw their demise—but not before a major escalation of conflict and the declaration of martial law.

Malthus was very much alert—in theory—to the generic problem of Aboriginal people's removal, and he was troubled by it. "There are many parts of the globe, indeed, hitherto uncultivated, and almost unoccupied; but the right of exterminating, or driving into a corner where they must starve, even the inhabitants of these thinly-peopled regions, will be questioned in a moral view." And yet in his *Essay* Van Diemen's Land and New South Wales Aborigines continued to stand as exemplars of savagery, as if none of these well-known events were taking place. Malthus wrote about Australian Aborigines in the present tense, even naming individuals, but such was the power of the stadial idea that it could still seem as if they existed outside time. Malthus needed "pure" savages for his first substantive chapter. It was to be about hunter-gatherers, not the process of colonization or civilization, and thus stadial theory trumped current events, both Bennelong's residency in London and, later, the frontier wars and Aboriginal removals in Van Diemen's Land.[43]

Despite all these events playing at the end of the eighteenth century and into the early nineteenth, in Malthus's book antipodean natives remained as unchanged as his own chapter. In all six editions, his assessment of "the lowest stages" of humanity remained unedited. In the fifth edition (1817), he briefly returned to what he still called New Holland, in a new Appendix.

The "natives of New Holland" there exemplified his basic point that any improvements in food production would always be far slower ("the most remote relation imaginable") than the power of unchecked ("unrestricted") reproduction. The "natives" might acquire some knowledge and industry to increase the yield of their natural resources, but this would be slow and quite possibly "ineffectual." By contrast, reproduction of the population continued apace: "The passions which prompt to the increase of population are always in full vigour, and are ready to produce their full effect even in a state of the most helpless ignorance and barbarism." In Malthus's view, the misery and vice there witnessed was evidence of his enduring principle: the mismatched pace of the production of food and the production of humans.[44]

Yet Malthus, this time, missed both the irony and the history. The very process and effect of colonization in Van Diemen's Land and New South Wales meant that the already comparatively "thin" population found itself in an entirely unprecedented context, and it was getting sparser by the month. Food proved even harder to find, given settler incursions and disruptions; disease meant mortality rates increased, and fertility rates plummeted; and killings amplified both. Even with seemingly humanitarian solutions—removal to safe islands, away from violence, where food and shelter was provided—it was not possible in some cases, and barely possible in others, for "the passions which prompt to the increase of population" to replace precolonial numbers. Malthus did perceive generically that "war and extermination" problematically followed the mass movement of British colonists to new worlds.[45] Of the British in New South Wales and Van Diemen's Land, however, Malthus never quite said that colonization itself was the great check, causing the war and extermination that was unfolding over the very years in which he wrote, and rewrote, his famous book.

Chapter 4

The Americas

WHILE NEW HOLLAND MAY, FOR MALTHUS, have represented the earliest stages of human society and the beginnings too of another chapter in the history of European settlement in a world new to them, the Americas (before the ne plus ultra of Tierra del Fuego) represented both indigenous peoples at a slightly later stage of history and current European settlement there. By opening his book's substantial sections with the antipodes and then moving to the Americas, Malthus not only began his analysis with a part of the world newly interesting to British readers but also reinforced his stadial analysis, moving forward through analysis of sequentially different forms of primitivism. But he was meanwhile working backward through the history of colonized landscapes, from the Pacific back to the Atlantic, a counterchronological presentation that masked the fact that his central assumptions about preagricultural societies had been initially formed in relation to North America, still his central example of a forebodingly maximized rate of human reproduction. North America had supplied his earliest case study of new world society, dating from the 1798 edition of his *Essay*, in which he had introduced America as a part of the world where the principle of population was most starkly apparent, ever present in the form of oscillation if not extinction.

That new world extremity of circumstance was what he would develop, dramatically, in his 1803 chapter, "Of the Checks to Population among the American Indians," in which, with repeated use of verbs that represented destruction, he portrayed the indigenous populations of North America in terms of a war of all against all. His implication was that the indigenes were predators who, accustomed to hunt animals (which he regarded as their dominant mode of subsistence), preyed upon each other in the same way. That was the logical outcome of a population so dependent on a migratory, preagricultural way of life. But Malthus also warned that a more lasting extinction of Indians, as an entire "race," might result from the introduction of agriculture, should a settler population contrastingly flourish in a natural world that had never been developed in such a manner. His conjecture was that colonists' expansion in extent and numbers could only occur as the

Indians themselves declined, when constantly driven from available territory for hunting.

To some extent, Malthus had already applied these insights to the newer worlds of the greater Pacific, as if those places were bound to recapitulate the earlier experience, amply described by earlier generations of analysts. Throughout his chapter on America, Malthus, like many commentators before him, had in each measured detail of his principle of population a selective vision of the indigenous peoples of the Americas: he was highly reliant on theories of racial and cultural differentiation that had been in gestation since the 1500s.

Malthus had, of course, even earlier presented his central point about what he regarded as the inevitable outcome of the settlement of America (and of new world places generally), within the first ten pages of his revised edition. "The right of exterminating, or driving into a corner where they must starve, even the inhabitants of these thinly peopled regions, will be questioned in a moral view." In this way, the sharply contrasting trends in population, settler versus native, were matters of fact but also of morals, and here the situation in North America, with its well-established and rapidly increasing settler population, was far more likely to pose an ethical dilemma than would be the case in New South Wales for decades. Although Malthus would later be understood as an apologist for genocide, this misreads his text. He was in fact critical of the displacement of natives, the clearance of people that accompanied the clearing of new world land for the plow. And yet he adjusted the ethical valence of that statement by suggesting, as well, that there were reasons for native American population decline that were not due to settler intrusion but to indigenous weakness. Those suggestions did not criticize settler action but instead adopted long-standing arguments as to the innate bodily inferiority of American Indians. He linked this to observations, as he saw the case, that Indians were unlikely to adapt to settler society. In his images of destruction, therefore, Malthus naturalized native population decline, making it seem inevitable, however unfortunate, and this exposed his underlying racist assumptions.[1]

His two impulses, moreover, to protest displacement of Indians yet portray them as doomed, did not entirely match. He may not have intended them to. Yet again too timid to make any full-throated criticism, his goal seems instead to have been to analyze North America, specifically, as the land of two type specimens: of a (native) population inclined toward extinction and of a (settler) population inclined toward rapid increase. The two populations did not differ because of what nature offered them—the American environment was the constant variable—but because of the different ways in which human nature could be developed: positively, in the case of the English settlers of North America. This was therefore not so much a history of a new world as an ahistoric and moralizing abstraction of part of it, one that used elements of stadial history to propose historical stasis, the inability of savages to become anything else, even as settlers could become paragons of virtue. The typology permitted little complexity, and it portrayed the Americas, oddly, as places somehow lacking in material productivity, which was by 1803 far from the case.

* * *

No manuscript draft of Malthus's 1803 *Essay* has come to light, and there are few pieces of correspondence about it, but an excellent guide to his intellectual priorities does exist: his cited sources. The authorities he chose to cite and his pattern of citation have never been examined fully, particularly in relation to the Americas. Such an analysis is therefore an important opportunity to orient the facts Malthus believed he was imparting in his *Essay on the Principle of Population* in relation to the opinions about the first new worlds that had been circulating for several centuries.[2]

The very first footnote in his chapter on American Indians refers to William Robertson, *The History of America*, third edition, published in 1780, with eight books in three volumes; the second is to Benjamin Franklin's "Observations Concerning the Increase of Mankind" in the 1779 compendium of Franklin's writings published by Joseph Johnson. Malthus in this way gave credit where it was most due: to Franklin as the intellectual origin of his principle of population, excavated from the series of citations that had led Malthus backward from Richard Price's work on reversionary payments to the original text, and to Robertson as his major source for a stadial interpretation of the Americas, as well as other primary sources that could provide greater detail about American population and subsistence. Malthus had already acknowledged Franklin in the very first note to the 1803 *Essay*, in its opening chapter. His footnote to Robertson nicely acknowledged, as well, how that historian was praised for his own scrupulous analysis of sources, with his book representing a milestone in the history of the modern apparatus of scholarly citation, a mode of establishing intellectual authority and credentials. Malthus emulated that example, unambiguously disclosing his desire to be seen as a modern authority on history and society. As he put it in a note on the second page of his chapter on Indians, "I often give the same references as Robertson;

but never, without having examined and verified them myself. Where I have not had an opportunity of doing this, I refer to Robertson alone."[3]

Malthus had not cited Robertson in his first edition of 1798, but his subsequent discovery of him built on his earlier enthusiasm for Gibbon and stadial theory more generally. Robertson (1721–1793) had also been a clergyman, though in the Church of Scotland rather than in Malthus's Church of England. He had been one of George II's chaplains and principal of the University of Edinburgh. A contemporary of Adam Smith, David Hume, and Gibbon (he counted the latter two as friends), he turned to writing history and was considered one of the finest interpreters of the histories of Spain and of Scotland, and of the more recent history of European colonization of the Americas. Using stadial theory, Robertson assessed the Americas as historically distinctive sites where polished, commercial societies had interacted (if not collided) with the pastoral economies of the South American highlands and the hunter-warrior cultures of the North American forests. The printed result was extolled as a sophisticated investigation of the human past, one that explicated several centuries' worth of firsthand European testimony (including documents Robertson had identified for the first time and surveys that he solicited) about the social and physical natures of the new world. His work also represented an important counterblast to the Black Legend. Robertson believed that "Spain, with an excess of caution, has uniformly thrown a veil over her transactions in America." Were the truth known, the nation and its empire would look different, with a greater harmony between colonizers and colonized, and a prosperity and population vigor that Great Britain should emulate for its empire.[4]

Malthus leaned hard on Robertson's work in the fourth chapter of his 1803 edition—it makes thirty-six appearances in his footnotes, whereas the average number of citations he gave to any given source from his whole set was only 7.3 (see table 4.1). However belated his discovery of the book, the first volumes of which were published in 1777, his preference for it is unsurprising. It was one of the two most important synthetic histories of the Americas that had been produced up to that point. The other synthesis, Guillaume-Thomas-François Raynal's *Histoire philosophique et politique des établissemens et du commerce des Européens dans les deux Indes* (1770), ran through far more editions than Robertson, attracting attention, as it did, for its blistering criticism of European imperialism, very much in sympathy with Rousseau's reservations about human life removed from its natural condition of equality. Malthus preferred Robertson's cooler assessment, though it is curious he did not cite the full edition of Robertson's history, with two additional books, which were

TABLE 4.1. TEXTS CITED IN MALTHUS, *ESSAY* (1803), CHAPTER 4, "AMERICA"
Average number of citations per title: 7.3; total titles = 20; total citations = 146

(Listed in order of first citation.)

Robertson: 36
Franklin, *Misc.*: 1
Burke's *America*: 5
Charlevoix, *Histoire de la Nouvelle France*: 16
Lafitau, *Moeurs des Sauvages*: 5
Travels to Discover the Source of the Nile: 1
Voyage dans l'Intérieur de l'Afrique: 1
[Jesuit] *Lettres Edif. et Curieuses*: 37
Hennepin, *Moeurs des Sauvages*: 2
Voyage de la Perouse: 4
Major Rogers' North America: 3
Ducreux, *Hist. Canad*: 3
Raynal, *Histoire des Indes*: 4
Ellis, *Voyages*: 3
Voyage d'Ulloa: 5
Cook, *Second Voyage*: 1
Cook, *Third Voyage*: 6
Vancouver, *Voyage*: 6
Meares, *Voyage*: 6
Kames, *Sketches of the History of Man*: 1

published in 1796 after the author's death; the 1780 edition, which Malthus used, was essentially a reprint of the 1777 incomplete first edition, in which Robertson had deferred discussion of the English-speaking colonies because of their state of war with Britain and unresolved status. Most of his other cited titles were drawn from Robertson's own notes, which makes Malthus's intellectual preferences obvious; he plucked certain titles from Robertson and ignored others, and the resulting patterns are intriguing. Above all, his initial footnote was acknowledgement of his continued confidence in stadial theory.[5]

But perhaps because of his intellectual debt to a book first published in 1777, the rest of Malthus's cited sources on the Americas are somewhat elderly for a work published in 1803. (See table 4.2.) Leaving aside two titles on Africa, the remaining twenty-three about the Americas (including Franklin and Robertson) have an average year of initial publication of 1755. Two of the works, on New France, date from the seventeenth century, representing early

TABLE 4.2. AVERAGE DATE OF TEXTS CITED IN MALTHUS, *ESSAY* (1803),
CHAPTERS 1, 2, 4 (CITATIONS REFERRING TO THE AMERICAS)

Average date of initial publication: 1755.26 (total titles = 23)

Travel accounts, single-authored and compendia (12), avg. date: 1752.92

Lafitau	1724
Hennepin	1683
Charlevoix	1744
La Pérouse	1797
Ellis	1748
Ulloa (Pacific)	1752
Cook (2nd voyage)	1777
Cook (3rd voyage)	1782
Vancouver	1798
Meares (Pacific NW)	1790
Ducreux	1664
Jesuit letters	1776

Philosophic/Historic (9), avg. date: 1769.5

Robertson	1777
Burke	1757
Raynal	1770
Kames	1774
Price	1771
Petty	1711
Steuart	1767
Hume	1741
Montesquieu	1748

Settler account (2), avg. date: 1760.0

Franklin	1755
Rogers	1765

Jesuit dominance in accounts of the northern regions of North America, early modern attempts at comparative ethnography, though not quite the latest in such efforts. Another work, a compendium of Jesuit *Lettres*—the famous "Jesuit Relations"—published in several volumes from 1702 to 1776, also reflects that earlier history, despite its more recent date of printing; Malthus cited it thirty-eight times. The implied geographic extent of European knowledge about America, circa 1753, is, therefore, that of the time of the Seven Years' War, the era when Franklin had written, and not that of 1803, midway through the Napoleonic Wars, when Malthus published his work, at a point when European knowledge of the Americas penetrated further into the interiors of the continents, and more Indian populations had accordingly been exposed to a white settler presence.[6]

Still other patterns among these works establish that Malthus relied mostly on the accounts of people who did not settle permanently in the Americas, and that his sources for the part of the new world he would discuss most extensively, the northeastern coast of North America, were oldest of all. Twelve of his fourteen first-person accounts, a clear majority, were written by travelers or at least those (including missionaries) who did not stay in the Americas; two of these were compendia of travel accounts. Works in these categories had an average initial date of publication of 1753. There are two works by creoles, individuals born in North America (Benjamin Franklin and Robert Rogers), with an average first date of publication of 1760. Finally, philosophical or historical works, including Robertson's, by authors who never went to America (a total of four works) had an average date of 1769. Separating the cited accounts of the eastern part of the Americas from those that treated its Pacific edge reveals a chronological distinction as well. The seven texts on Atlantic America have an average date of 1730, while the average for the seven that focus on the Pacific coast is 1778. The time spread indicates that Malthus' more recent sources (Cook, Vancouver, and so on) had assimilated their new discoveries in the Pacific to old conclusions about population decline among the indigenous peoples of the new world, an assimilation that Malthus himself then accepted.

Perhaps most indicative of his selectivity, he cited only one author on Spanish America and his choice, of Francisco Noguerol de Ulloa, who explored Baja California and the Pacific in the sixteenth century, is highly eccentric, maybe a consequence of his ignorance of Spanish and unwillingness to go beyond Robertson's citations. Missing are all the important and widely reprinted accounts of Iberian America, from Christopher Columbus onward, including a great many important examples that Robertson had cited. Despite his statement about delving into what Robertson had cited, Malthus usually accepted Robertson as the dominant authority on Spanish America, rarely reexamining the relevant sources.[7]

The resulting picture very much privileges British and French accounts of North America and focuses on experiences when the two imperial powers were vying for power within the new world midway through the Second Hundred Years' War: they do not convey a larger and more complex image of all of the Americas. For that reason, and whatever its dependence on Robertson,

Malthus's *Essay* is very unlike its Scottish source, the greatest part of which concentrated on Spain's new world empire. (The book is still mostly studied in relation to Latin America.) Malthus had quite obviously made a choice: to look at the parts of the Americas of greatest significance for the history of Britain and of its empire, including the former continental colonies that had separated from Great Britain but also the land gained from France in the Seven Years' War, which had remained in the empire and was now called Canada. But above all he was interested in the colonies that had become the United States. He would acknowledge this decision in the sixth and final edition of the *Essay* (1826), when at several points he substituted "United States" for "America." The full name of the republic appeared only four times in the 1803 edition, but it would feature thirteen times in that of 1826.[8]

* * *

Malthus made several other decisions that further narrowed his focus on North America rather than extending it over all of the Atlantic new world. First, he considered the Americas (south, north, and central) as one uniform entity. He referred to it in the singular as "the vast continent of America," described it as covered with one form of nature ("an almost universal forest" with "few of those fruits and esculent vegetables which grow in such profusion in the islands of the South Sea"), and presented it as having one societal form, the small nation based on mobile hunting and warfare. These emphases again reflected his selection of British and French accounts on North America; it is an old view of the new world, formed in relation to the forested regions of North America that were first colonized in the seventeenth and early eighteenth centuries (though again, leaving aside the areas farther to the south whose Spanish colonial origins were at least a century older). "The greatest part of" America, he summarized, "was found to be inhabited by small independent tribes of savages, subsisting nearly in a similar manner to the natives of New Holland," and "principally by hunting and fishing." That statement again connected the different parts of the new world, this time in terms of their material subsistence. As his references to abundant forests and lack of "esculent" fruits and vegetables indicate, Malthus was ignoring tropical or semitropical regions of the Americas. Only briefly, and toward the end of the chapter on American Indians, did he acknowledge the great civilizations of Central and South America, which he nevertheless said had been frequently unable to feed any extra persons, as the invading Spaniards discovered early in the sixteenth century. And only fleetingly did he admit the possibility of other large Indian populations, which however he described in the past tense: "the villages here *were* large," he said of the southeastern corner of North America, and their urbanized societal elaboration meant that "distinction of ranks *prevailed*."[9]

Why the past tense? Malthus indicated several reasons for the historical decline in native American populations. He reiterated the gist of the Black Legend, which he might have absorbed from Robertson (though indeed a great many other sources), to the effect that early Spanish atrocities against Indians in the Caribbean and Central America had nearly obliterated certain native populations. Spanish conquest of the Americas, he related, in one of his very few references to the Iberian colonies, had generated incidents that "make humanity shudder." He emphasized that the sleepy condition of the Spanish Monarchy in his day should not in any way disguise the original ferocity of that nation's imperialism. "Whatever may be the character of the Spanish inhabitants of Mexico and Peru at the present moment," he said, "we cannot read the accounts of the first conquests of these countries, without feeling strongly, that the race destroyed, was, in moral worth, as well as members, highly superior to the race of their destroyers." This was an overt expression of sympathy if not admiration for the conquered Indians, registering a black mark against other Europeans, Christians soi-disant. And yet Malthus used language that firmly situated the population glories of the indigenous Americans in the past, never to be recovered. That was obvious in Malthus's three devastating words about the great civilizations of the Inca and Mexica: "the race destroyed." As far as he was concerned, no other part of the Americas had ever had comparable size and density, nor would any American region or people ever achieve it.[10]

Malthus clearly considered that a hunting economy, which he thought the primary mode of subsistence for any native Americans who lived beyond the "destroyed" race of Inca and Aztec, would never maintain population of any great size, and he exhibited again his characteristic impatience with the glorification of savagery. Of hunting he said, "the narrow limits to this mode of subsistence are obvious" and the "improvident savage" could never manage to save much of what he caught. Thus far, Malthus considered his observations a mere truism, "that population cannot increase without the food to support it"—a central tenet of stadial theory. "But the interesting part of the inquiry," he continued, "to which I would wish particularly to draw the attention of the reader, is, the mode by which the population is kept down to the level of this scanty supply," the mechanics of oscillation that the stadial historians had not supplied. Here he thought the story was even worse than the simple case of "famine." Yet more "permanent forms of "distress" arose from "certain customs, which operate sometimes with greater force in the suppression of a rising population, than in its subsequent destruction." The abortive or infanticidal means by which Indians reacted to the prospect of births, that is, fell very much into Malthus's categories of vice and misery, if with characteristics specific to a hunting stage of society that existed within a forested environment.[11]

Natural constraints on this way of life led to a brutal existence prone to conflict and disintegration, not Edenic serenity. While Malthus again noted the long tradition of regarding Indian men as lacking sexual ardor for their female partners, he did not accept that this was something distinctive to the Indian "character" or indeed to any form of savagery. Lack of procreative function was a feature of all "barbarous nations, whose food is poor and insufficient." In this instance, at least, Malthus firmly rejected any racialization of Indian bodies; Indians had no "constitutional defect" in regard to sexual activity, merely a reduced passion that any adult would experience if deprived of food. Among Indians who lived in places with a ready supply of fish, for example, men and women indulged their desire, and if anything, "the dissolution of their manners is sometimes excessive." But almost everywhere, Malthus thought, Indian women led a degraded existence. He continued the long tradition of comparing Indian wives to slaves and an almost equally long exposition of this as characteristic of people who lived in "a savage state," as Robertson had "finely observed." The typical female experience of "depression and constant labor" made it difficult if not heroic for women to endure pregnancy and childbirth and to raise up small children. Malthus pointed to other customs that were likely to inhibit procreation: "libertinage" among women before they married, abandonment of deformed newborns, and infanticide of those whose mothers had died.[12]

This description of female Indian degradation was quite conventional. What should be remarked, however, is that not even Malthus, with his emphasis on food and population, thought to reconcile the long-standing inconsistency within these remarks: Indians lived improvidently by hunting, the concern of men who were otherwise lazy and careless about finding provisions, even as native American women were somehow incredibly busy to the point of perpetual exhaustion. But busy with what? Some European commentators had made the additional point that it was the women in native American societies who grew crops, principally corn.

Figure 4.1. Native American women making maple sugar and growing maize. Joseph François Lafitau, *Moeurs des sauvages ameriquains* . . . (1724), vol. 2. Courtesy of the John Carter Brown Library at Brown University.

And yet *maize*, the English word that would have described Indian corn in Malthus's England, goes entirely unmentioned in his text. In contrast, Robertson had referred to maize thirteen times, not a generous measure, but an acknowledgement of Indian agriculture, at least. And other sources on which Malthus relied, for example, Joseph François Lafitau's *Moeurs des sauvages ameriquains* (1724), described and illustrated women's work at getting food. The fact that Indians cultivated the soil, which would have complicated Malthus's picture of savage life, including the life it gave to women (and their potential children), is therefore omitted. The result is a misleading emphasis on a pure form of a hunting "savagery" amid forests inhabited by wild animals, unbroken with any land cleared for agriculture. Malthus did mention that "the fertile provinces of the South" afforded greater subsistence, but this is a rare notation of diversity among native American habitats and societies, and he gave no supporting detail about how and why the subsistence might be better in warmer places, whether, that is to say, it was because of a natural abundance only or because the natives had developed technologies to use that abundance better, as through agriculture.[13]

It was because of their materially pinched existence that Indian nations, whose members knew that they could not expand in size and power without greater territory for their subsistence, made constant war upon each other as a matter of foreign policy. More food was always needed, which made the temptation to stray into another nation's territory extreme. And yet because "it is of the utmost consequence to prevent others from destroying the game in their hunting grounds, they guard this national property with a jealous attention." Conflict was the result; "neighbouring nations live in a perpetual state of hostility with each other." In consequence, population was always in decline due to loss of life, which Malthus presented very much as a Hobbesian war of all against all; each Indian sought to preserve himself, sacrificing even family members if necessary. Malthus also stressed the materialist goals and context of Indian warfare, as if the participants were governed purely by laws of nature, in a scenario where total destruction was the frequent outcome. Any military conflict continued, for example, "either till the equilibrium is restored by mutual losses, or till the weaker party is exterminated, or driven from its country." That image of physical extinction was echoed in a subsequent statement, that "in this manner whole tribes are frequently extinguished."[14]

This war of all against all was what made American savagery truly distinctive in Malthus's analysis and for him made American Indians more like animals than might have been the case in other hunting societies. Among the Iroquois, he said, a declaration of war took the form of the phrase "'Let us go and eat that nation.'" It was as if Indians resembled the creatures they hunted, indeed, were habitual carnivores who ate any flesh, including that of their own kind. To make this point, Malthus concluded that explorers' and travelers' rumors of Indian cannibalism had described subsistence strategies, notwithstanding other contemporary interpretations that, if such customs existed, they were ritualistic, deplorably pagan but nothing to do with quotidian food. On this issue, Malthus parted ways even with William Robertson. "Contrary to the opinion of Dr. Robertson," he lamented of Indians' cannibalism, "I cannot but think that it must have had its origin in extreme want," although it might have been continued for the other reasons that some commentators had cited. If anything, Malthus thought it better that the practice had its origins in "necessity," not "malignant passions," as that would slightly modify the disapproval that could be expressed for the action; subsistence cannibalism was, under carefully defined circumstances, an accepted part of British maritime custom, for example, and not contrary to British law.[15]

All the same, American Indians seemed to seek opportunities to turn their enemies into meat, and that was Malthus's point. "Their object in battle is not conquest, but destruction," he explained, in a direct paraphrase of Robertson's own statement: "they fight not to conquer, but to destroy." Malthus thus differentiated between the wars to acquire territory that might preoccupy agricultural and commercial societies (as in the Napoleonic Wars that had until recently preoccupied Great Britain) and the battles among hunter-warriors who simply wanted to kill each other, like animals, and to eat each other, like animals. That this distinction had been Robertson's point, as well, showed how Britons were registering a sense of distance from savage societies, even as "total war" had become, particularly under Napoleon's wars of expansion, a dominant form of European conflict. It also registered another of Malthus's firm rejections of the Rousseauean (and anti-Hobbesian) view of natural peoples. Contrast it for instance to Thomas Paine's insistence, in *Common Sense* (1776), that "even brutes do not devour their young, nor savages make war upon their families."[16]

The Malthusian image was dire, and intended to be, meant to dampen any reader's enthusiasm over the potential nobility of savagery or the lingering hope of finding a paradise among America's original inhabitants. Perhaps because faith in humanity's natural state had been especially marked in the philosophic writings of Rousseau, Daniel Malthus's friend and idol, Thomas Robert Malthus did not attack Rousseau directly; family members certainly would have seen that as lacking in filial respect. But Malthus marked his distance from all things Rousseauean by taking on another French defender of primitive life, the abbé Raynal, whose question about whether the discovery of the Americas had been "beneficial or harmful to the human race" implied that European empires might have obliterated rather than fostered felicity. Malthus was skeptical of that skepticism. "The Abbe Raynal," he wrote, "is continually reasoning most inconsistently in his comparison of savage and civilized life." On the one hand, the French author praised "the savage as morally sure of a competent subsistence" but then would admit that the natives of Canada, living amidst at least some degree of natural bounty, were routinely destroyed by "famine." Even if Raynal could argue that savages were not prone to vice, meaning practices that depressed the birth rate, he had nevertheless admitted that they suffered from Malthus's other universal human condition, misery. By scorning Raynal, Malthus again made very clear his non-Edenic reading of the new world, his insistence on humanity's utterly and universally fallen state.[17]

* * *

Because of his consistent emphasis on the oscillation of Indian populations in relation to natural resources, over which they had to fight to the death, it is doubtful that Malthus had intended to write a full account of all native inhabitants of the Americas. Rather, he used some of them selectively in order to construct an abstract type of population dynamic, a form more ideal than real. Certainly, he finished out his chapter on American Indians with an assessment of how they could sometimes increase the sizes of their populations, and had done so, though never without damage to their neighbors. He cited the example of some Paraguayan Guaraní who had migrated to Peru, where they flourished by making war on the longer-settled tribes there. Because they "gradually exterminated" these other people, they were able to grow from a mere three to four thousand migrants to a group thirty thousand strong. Their example proved that Indians were capable of impressive growth under the right conditions, though the instance cited was also a perfect example of the way in which migratory savages exemplified the toll that humanity exacted from the rest of nature, including other humans, which might be harder to detect in agricultural and commercial societies that did not exterminate their competitors quite so openly. So too were Indian populations larger wherever the means of subsistence was easier, as near bodies of water that contained fish, including the Great Lakes, the banks of the Mississippi River, Louisiana, and parts of South America.[18]

That state of plenty, in warm places with stocks of freshwater fish, existed in contrast to regions where subsistence was scarcer. In the southwestern part of North America, for example, the desertlike physical conditions resembled those in the interior of New South Wales, where food had to be painstakingly gathered from the creeping and the small. Indians were driven to eat insects, worms, and the powdered bones of snakes. Population in this place was in consequence drastically smaller, and woe betide the colonists who strayed there. The resulting picture was one in which "the population seems to have been spread over the surface very nearly in proportion to the quantity of food." So too did regions far to the north have quite limited natural resources. One explorer of the area around Hudson Bay described it as a place so cold and lacking in available food that its inhabitants were sometimes driven to eat the leather they had made into clothing, the animal pelts they had gathered to sell to European traders, and even, on occasion, their own children.[19]

But those exceptional zones within North America showed by way of contrast how most of the Americas were unlike New South Wales. The forested environment with which Malthus endowed the greater part of the Americas provided a greater array of wild game than in New South Wales. The natural abundance in the Americas allowed a somewhat better life, though not the greater comfort agriculture afforded. Here is where Malthus again admitted that some Indians did cultivate the land, but he insisted that they could not rely on that for their entire subsistence and that the natural world of the Americas could not in its wild state feed a very large population. The Caribbean islands, for example, "rich as they appeared to be," had been peopled up to their maximum capacity before Europeans arrived with better modes of cultivation. Even within the forests where they hunted, the Iroquois had been sometimes forced to eat their shoes, the bark of trees, and their companions. Accounts of the Pacific Northwest (including those by Vancouver and La Pérouse) had indicated that fishing from the sea was a similarly uncertain method of gathering food, particularly during harsh winters. Descriptions of famine in Nootka Sound during the winter of 1786–1787, when stocks of dried fish had given out, "would shock any mind tinctured with humanity." In another bad year, inhabitants of another Pacific fishing community resorted to a paste made from pine bark and cockles. Even within the most promising parts of the Americas, therefore, conditions were perfect for tensions among competing populations whose male members were superbly trained to practice the violent chase either of animals or of other human beings—all in all, a combination guaranteed to produce misery for someone, if not destruction of everyone.[20]

*   *   *

Because of his emphasis on how Indians lived in an aboriginal state, in wild dependence on hunting, Malthus did not give many specific examples of their adaptation to the presence of European settlers and their creole descendants, though these alterations had been occurring (depending on the place) for up to three hundred years. The longest-settled part of North America, Florida, had had a steady and growing European presence since the sixteenth century. Moreover, there had been persistent evidence within Britain itself of acculturated Indians in the form of native embassies that had been arriving since Pocahontas's celebrated 1616 to 1617 tour of London with her English husband, John Rolfe, in the wake of her well-publicized conversion to Christianity. And yet English observers of her and other native visitors had tended to regard them as unconvertible savages. The "Four Indian Kings" who were ushered around London during Queen Anne's War (1702–1713) were highly familiar with English language, clothing, religion, and customs. As representatives of important indigenous allies (Mohawk and Mahican), they were presented at court, attended plays, toured the observatory at Greenwich, and acted as intelligent and dignified ambassadors. Yet they were treated in contemporary popular culture as wild Mohawks, evidently inspiring London street ruffians to call themselves just that, in emulation of a people that most Britons deemed to be permanently beyond the civilized pale. Indian diplomatic visits to Britain would continue. Desperate to secure support against the first and then the independent United States, the Mohawk diplomat Joseph Brant visited London twice, from 1775 to 1776 and then in 1785, both times within Malthus's lifetime. But the negative response to native Americans would also continue and condition later English perceptions of colonized peoples who voyaged to Britain.[21]

In any case, Malthus did not think that Indians, if they passed into a non-hunting form of society, would in future be released from pressures on population. Their progress into pastoralism or agriculture—or whatever arts of food procurement might be best suited to the Americas—would simply bring them into a stage of development prone to different material difficulties. As evidence, Malthus observed that the Indian nations with larger populations also had greater social inequality, in notable contrast to the rough social parity that characterized migratory bands of hunters. Here, at least, he agreed with the Rousseauean admirers of savage life—up to a point. The greater the degree of social inequality, the more likely that an oppressed underclass existed, and it was this class that suffered first and worst whenever food was scarce. "The positive checks to population would act almost exclusively on this part of the community," but the total effect on the population would be the same: an oscillation in numbers in order to adjust to the failure of the food supply, the pattern that was, at this point in Europe's history, the default.[22]

Moreover, Malthus accepted with neither hesitation nor commentary the long-standing argument that American environments fostered epidemics to which Indians had little bodily resistance, a corporeal defect that resulted in a fatal corrosion of indigenous population that was either tragic or convenient, depending on the observer's perspective. Hot regions in the Americas, he said, generated "dreadful epidemics" and "contagious distempers." Equally virulent maladies could be found in cooler, northern climates, as George Vancouver had recently described for the Pacific Northwest. There the inhabitants had been decimated, and survivors bore scars showing that "the small-pox appears to be common and fatal." Native preferences to live in close proximity with each other and in "filth" were surely contributing causes of their recurring demise: "Under such circumstances, it may be easily imagined what a dreadful havoc an epidemic must make." Vancouver, as many before him, failed to note that earlier European contacts might have introduced smallpox and other contagious diseases. (The western coast of North America had been repeatedly visited since the 1500s, and Spanish missions and Russian trading posts had proliferated in Alta California and Unalaska in the 1770s and 1780s.) Instead, and as in New South Wales, the European consensus was that Indians' bodily weakness and lack of cultural adaptation to serious illness were a deadly combination. The Indians in South America were said, for example, to be "subject to perpetual diseases for which they know no remedy."[23]

Although Malthus did not see settlers' malign influence in relation to contagious epidemic disease, he did worry that settler and Indian populations were unlikely to coexist for other reasons. He assented to another long tradition of commentary by claiming an Indian propensity toward drunkenness, "an insatiable fondness" or uncontrollable "rage" for alcohol. This habit weakened their health, including their ability to procreate, while increasing their violent tendencies. Given that extreme drunkenness itself could impair population replacement, violent quarrels and warfare were sadly adequate in erasing whatever small increases might still occur. Although Malthus fit this malady into his overarching category of "vice," as one of the many ways in which humans everywhere made fatal, nonrational adjustments to their superabundant populations, it is not clear whether he meant that Indians' use of alcohol was a universal feature of human existence. His brief and noncritical adoption of a long-standing racialized interpretation of Indian bodies was another way in which his principle of population operated according to criteria that were not geographically and culturally universal. Malthus concluded that all the reasons for Indian population decline he had identified could be relegated into "the three great checks to population that have been stated," while admitting that these conditions of vice, misery, and presence or absence of moral discipline were, among the Indians, so marked as to be "more powerful even than the principle of increase."[24]

Moreover, not even the good lessons that settlers might impart to native populations would offset any indigenous or adopted vice. Instead, "almost everywhere the connexion of the Indians with Europeans, has tended to break their spirit" and "to diminish the sources of subsistence." Indeed, Malthus presented the modern period of colonization as one of notable declension in the Americas, indicating several points at which white settlers had initiated the damaging trends. In regions where they had introduced trade for animal pelts, for instance, the commerce had directed Indians' energies away from gaining food and toward getting alcohol. In Peru and Chile "the forced industry of the natives was fatally directed to the digging into the bowels of the earth, instead of cultivating its surface." Although attention to agriculture might have benefited from the presence of Europeans, it had instead been "everywhere slackened." Meanwhile, "the general introduction of fire-arms among the Indians, has probably greatly contributed to the diminution of the wild animals," a calamitous consequence of encounter between hunting and commercial peoples. A natural imbalance between indigenous people and available food had therefore continued, even as the Indian population had declined. "In spite of all the powerful causes of destruction that have been mentioned," Malthus concluded, "the average population of the American nations is, with few exceptions, on a level with the average quantity of food, which in the present state of their industry they can obtain."[25]

Because Malthus questioned the morality of pushing Indians out of their homelands, it is surprising that he otherwise consistently adopted prejudices about them that made their extinction seem inevitable. It is all the more apparent that he avoided the overt criticisms of imperialism in the Americas that were not uncommon, as in Raynal's *Histoire des deux Indes*. Such sentiments were not unknown in the new United States, where Indian policies remained controversial and native peoples had allies in some quarters. (That could be seen in Benjamin Franklin's late-life, culturally relativistic "Remarks Concerning the Savages of North America": "Savages we call them, because their Manners differ from ours, which we think the Perfection of Civility. They think the same of theirs.") Malthus above all insisted that, whatever the elements of destruction that assailed Indians, their perpetually diminished population was "on a level with the average quantity of food" they were likely to procure, such was their stunted capacity for subsistence.[26]

Malthus reflected an anti-Indian bias, as well, in ignoring the larger indigenous populations of the Americas, even within North America. For example, he referred to the Iroquois only twice, once in a vignette on their propensity to kill each other in war and again in a reference to how hunger drove them to cannibalism—descriptions unlikely to make the Five (later Six) Nations seem like a significant demographic presence. And Malthus either did not know of the southern counterparts to the Iroquois, especially the Cherokee, one of the larger nations that practiced large-scale agriculture and settled in towns, or he simply left them out. It is notable, for example, that neither his citations nor his family's surviving book collection in the library at Jesus College include Cadwallader Colden's *History of the Five Indian Nations Depending on the Province of New-York in America* (1727), a well-known text on the Iroquois that Malthus's main source, Robertson, had himself cited at several points. While Colden's analysis of the Iroquois had definitely stressed their excellence as warriors and propensity to warfare, he, unlike Robertson and Malthus, also made the points that their populations were large and that their military engagements had been influenced by conflict among the rival European powers vying to control territory in the eastern part of North America. Colden thus gave Iroquois warfare a historical context, and he interpreted their society as capable of population growth. Robertson's interpretation shifted away from those emphases; Malthus's text continued the slant of that reading without acknowledging the continuing presence of the Iroquois in British imperial diplomacy, as initiated by Joseph Brant within his lifetime.[27]

Nor did Malthus betray any knowledge of William Bartram's *Travels through North & South Carolina, Georgia, East & West Florida, the Cherokee Country, the Extensive Territories of the Muscogulges, or Creek Confederacy, and the Country of the Chactaws* (1791), which was reviewed and read widely in Europe. This book likewise represented Indian populations as considerable and, in contrast to Colden's interpretation of the Iroquois, presented them as peaceful, though rightfully defensive against mistreatment by white settlers. It is especially surprising that the book eluded Malthus's attention given that its many British reviews included an extensive one in the December 1792 issue of the *Analytical Review*, the journal founded by his publisher, Joseph Johnson. The unnamed reviewer noted in particular Bartram's favorable representation of the Indian nations of the lands just south of the United States, which still belonged to competing European powers, including Britain. (Panton, Leslie and Company held a monopoly on British trade in the area.) Bartram's account included details about the southern Indian nations' extended populations, large towns, practice of agriculture, and adoption of European domestic animals. His vision of peaceful southern Indian nations served as inspiration for at least two of Joseph Johnson's other authors, William Wordsworth and Samuel Taylor Coleridge; the latter author's Xanadu, it has been noted, resembles the natural Eden of Bartram's Creek, Cherokee, and Choctaw.[28]

Finally, Malthus never betrayed awareness that military conflict in the Americas resulted from European or colonial antagonisms, a big reason to suspect that not all population decline among native populations had endogenous causes. As a reading of Colden would have established, Indians did not only fight against each other in a continuing expression of pre-Columbian antagonisms. In North America, and since the seventeenth century, their enmities had instead been exacerbated if not incited by imperial and colonial ambitions. By the time of the Seven Years' War—the immediate context for Robertson as he wrote his *History of America*—the clash of empires had been the major invitation for Indian warriors to enter battle, typically as allies either directed by white military leaders or else as subcontracted military units. Although enslavement of defeated Indians, often for use on southern and Caribbean plantations, had ceased to be a routine outcome of military co-optation, the recruitment of Indian men as military allies had a constantly corrosive effect on native populations, only partly offset by the complicated (and effective) Indian strategy to play the European powers against each other. The significance of Britain's hybrid military empire in North America was apparent even in the heart of London. In Westminster Abbey a monument to Roger Townshend, designed by Robert Adam and completed in 1761, features a sarcophagus for Townshend, slain in the Seven Years' War, held up by myrmidons in the form of stone Iroquois warriors perpetually loyal to a fallen commander. Significantly, the carved figures have native American garb yet modern weapons; both have powder horns and one carries a musket.[29]

The United States was continuing a strategy of divide and rule over native Americans, along with the expectation that most Indian populations would diminish and be displaced by white farmers. The new settler assumption was that any military services native men might yield were temporary, unnecessary once territories had been secured from imperial rivalries. That was possible because the field of European competitors within North America was shrinking. After US victory in the War for Independence, Great Britain had ceased to be as powerful a potential ally for any eastern Indians who had welcomed its role as counterweight. The United States had, accordingly, used military force in the 1790s to extract land from Indian nations united in a Northwest Confederacy within a region bounded by the Ohio River, the Great Lakes, and the Mississippi River. US forces would defeat the Indian confederacy in the Battle of Fallen Timbers (1794). In 1795, in the Treaty of Greenville, members of the confederacy were forced to cede most of what would become the state of Ohio. Distant though the Ohio region may have been from Malthus's England, news of the battles had been covered there, not least because Great Britain had been in alliance with some of the Indians who fought against the United States. That open expression of antagonism against the former colonies had been an irritant for the young republic, one that played into the escalating ill will between Britain and the United States that would climax in the War of 1812, the final North American chapter in the Napoleonic Wars.[30]

Malthus's warning about the moral hazard of settler population growth, the questionable right to exterminate native peoples or drive them from their land, however sympathetic to those peoples, must therefore be read in relation to the racist pro-settler discourse that coexisted alongside it. By leaving these competing assessments of humanity within his analysis, he suggested that there were natural reasons for indigenous population decline beyond his principle of population. In that way, he made the decline particular to some new world populations, even as he tried to integrate an analysis of Indian mortality into a universal set of laws. Just as Protestant propagandists of the Black Legend of Spanish imperialism had done before him, he might have been emphasizing American Indians' weakness because he wanted to heighten the fatal impact of European settlement on such a delicate population, in order to cast moral blame on the colonizers.

But the net effect was rather odd, given that Malthus used stadial theory to emphasize a static condition, the lack of historic progress among American Indians. They were, he said, mostly incapable of any cultural change, unlikely to progress through the transformations that would lead from a hunting stage of subsistence toward pastoralism and agriculture. He stated this explicitly in his argument with Henry Home, Lord Kames, who had conjectured the possibility of Indians' evolution from hunters to pastoral herders. Kames had posited this against the French naturalist Buffon, who had marveled that Indians, surrounded by wild animals, had not managed to domesticate them, with a few exceptions "among the polished people of Mexico and Peru. Is this not a proof, that man, in his savage state, is but a sort of brute animal?" Kames countered with a climatic interpretation: hunting was to cold climates as agriculture was to warm ones, according to natural distributions of animals versus plants. It was an argument based on plenitude, entirely of a piece with Kames's other statements of religious faith, though in its proposal that human societies must move through successive stages of material development adapted to natural situations, it was equally grounded in stadial theory. Thus Kames thought that people in cold climates were fully capable of becoming shepherds, though he questioned their ability to turn their surroundings into cultivated land.[31]

Nonsense, Malthus responded. At this point in his text, at the end of his chapter on American Indians, he took care to refute any suggestion that their level of population might have a future different from its past: "It is not, therefore, as Lord Kaimes imagines, that the American tribes have never increased sufficiently to render the pastoral or agricultural state necessary to them; but, from some cause or other, they have not adopted in any great degree these more plentiful modes of procuring subsistence, and therefore, cannot have increased so as to become populous." Malthus was not concluding that native populations could never increase (he had already admitted they could, as with the marauding migrants into Peru). But he was saying that the ultimate circumstances under which it might happen were mysterious, and to have staying power would have to be autochthonous. Under Jesuit tutelage, he related, some Indians in Paraguay had begun to grow crops and keep domestic animals, but when drought killed their cattle and spoiled their grain, famine resumed. Nor had mere hunger ever been enough to prompt new customs. "Some fortunate train of circumstances, in addition to this stimulus, is necessary for this purpose." What those circumstances were Malthus could not say, but he did express confidence that "the inventive powers of the human mind" in America, no less than anywhere else, would be used to develop food-getting strategies "in those spots that are best suited to them."[32]

It seemed unlikely, however, that the pace of any transformation would match the swiftness with which white farmers could appropriate Indians' land. For that reason, American Indians were doomed to be replaced. "If America continue increasing, which she certainly will do," projected Malthus, "the Indians will be driven further and further back into the country, till the whole race is ultimately exterminated." In the 1817 edition of his *Essay*, he would anticipate Frederick Jackson Turner in prophesying the closing of the frontier: "and the territory is incapable of further extension." His phrasing indicated criticism of settler actions and policy, but it redeployed the terms by which he had described Indians as predators on each other, each seeking the other's extinction. Yet again, he had stated a central ethical difficulty in timid terms, reluctant to draw the radical implications that another critic—certainly Rousseau, Raynal, or Bartram—would have done. Malthus's statement that edging the Indians into an unlivable situation "will be questioned in a moral view" showed that his intentions were good. But the overwhelming implication was that Indians had somehow always failed to thrive and that they might easily fail to survive, unless they received special assistance.[33]

This was predictive rather than descriptive, and the ongoing politics of empire gave the prediction a doomful power that even its author may not entirely have welcomed. Malthus's 1803 edition of his *Essay* appeared in June, not two months after Napoleon Bonaparte had agreed to sell France's remaining North American territory to the United States on April 30, in what is now called the Louisiana Purchase. The idyllic and autonomous Indian nations that William Bartram had described were now under the dominion of the aggressively expansive US republic. (President Thomas Jefferson, who had eagerly brokered the sale, requested his team of exploration, headed by Meriwether Lewis and William Clark, to document the sizes and characters of Indian populations.) It is unlikely, given the close timing, that the vast land sale affected Malthus's composition. But his lament over native propensity to recede and dwindle before the ranks of white settlers uncannily matched the expectation of US citizens—including Jefferson—that Indians must adapt, migrate, or die. The similarity between Malthus and Jefferson seems to have been unconscious, a case of parallel development rather than intellectual connection. Although the Malthus family collection at Jesus College includes a copy of Jefferson's *Notes on the State of Virginia*, and although Jefferson's surviving papers record that he ordered "Malthus on population" in 1807, neither man ever cited the other.[34]

* * *

The antithesis to Indian population decline was settler increase, and Malthus knew he needed to explain why the latter had ultimately been successful. He was careful to emphasize that material conditions were only part of the story—the moral state of the Europeans had been crucial. Having avoided any such conclusion earlier, he seems to have felt comfortable adding it to his 1803 edition, perhaps because it matched his fourth admonition about population dynamics: that they were subject to individuals' moral force. So although he related the difficulties of the early English settlements in America (paralleled by those of other nations there too), he did not conclude that such efforts were always doomed.[35]

The secret of success was moral steadfastness and hard work. Malthus extolled English colonists for their effort in spreading civilization and cultivating the earth, but he warned of the exceptional character necessary to undertake these tasks. In New England the puritan settlers, overjoyed at their freedom from old England's religious tyranny, "reduced this savage country, by degrees, to yield them a comfortable subsistence." The statement echoed all the earlier claims as to the "pure manners" of North American colonists (and restated Malthus's sympathy for dissenters), while warning that few other groups of would-be new world settlers would share what Malthus called "their energy of character." This point strengthened his emphasis on moral discipline as an important factor in population dynamics. For the most part, he cautioned that lack of discipline would slide a population into misery and vice. But in positive terms, "energy of character" could foster reproduction where there was land still in plentiful stock:

> It has been justly observed, by a correspondent of Dr. Franklin, that one of the reasons why we have seen so many fruitless attempts to settle colonies at an immense publick and private expense, by several of the powers of Europe, is, that the moral and mechanical habits adapted to the mother country are frequently not so, to the new-settled one ... it is to be remarked, that none of the English colonies became any way considerable, till the necessary manners were born and grew up in the country.

Yet again, North America was a distinctive type-specimen, powerful mostly as a counterexample for the rest of the world, an evidentiary case with which Malthus softened his otherwise orthodox definition of human nature in a postlapsarian state.[36]

Malthus likewise warned against enthusiasm over the prospects of American settler population growth and, by implication, displacement of Indians, based on confidence that ghost acres would feed old world populations, including the people of the United Kingdom. In his chapter "Of Bounties in the Exporation of Corn," he continued the analysis of Britain's grain production and its Corn Laws that he had begun in his pamphlet *An Investigation of the Cause of the Present High Price of Provisions.* He remained steadfast in his admonition that imports of grain were stopgaps, not real solutions to any shortfalls in the nation's food supply. Although British outposts in Upper Canada would not produce steady surpluses—and exports—of grain until the 1830s, the United States continued to export both maize and wheat. (The center of production was moving into the continent, out of the mid-Atlantic region and toward the Midwest.) US free trade policy meant that the American grain was technically available to Britons.[37]

In fact, Malthus issued his cautions against faith in American food imports even as trade policies were being discussed in the wake of the Treaty of Amiens. Concern was all the keener because of continuing declines or failures in domestic production. A severe shortfall had occurred in early 1800, relieved only by a good harvest in late 1801. In the 1803 edition of his *Essay*, Malthus continued his discussion of grain within Britain, praising the laws that encouraged its production and offered bounties for its export. Only in passing did he address the existence of grain imports, identifying their sources in the Baltic and in America. In those two places, he stated, farmers were not, unlike their British counterparts, burdened by the high cost of land and by the high taxes on consumer goods—hence their advantage, hence the need for continued British bounties to encourage domestic grain production and duties to discourage its export. To this extent, Malthus represented a critical response to free trade interpretations of British grain production, including that of Adam Smith (the primary object of his extended refutation.) He scored an excellent point, in the delicate state of peace after the 1802 peace treaty, by observing that British dependence on foreign grain was poor policy. Should imports continue their upward trend, foreign grain would soon be feeding over 2 million Britons. Were there any dispute with the seller nations, and 2 million people to feed, "with what a weight of power they would negotiate!" The British ministry agreed. The 1803 Corn Laws set into place the strictest prohibitions on grain imports yet.[38]

In the fifth edition of his *Essay*, published in 1817, Malthus would be even firmer, adding a separate chapter, "Of Corn-Laws. Restrictions upon Importation," that again argued for such a policy. He began by admitting good reasons for a nation to import grain; labor might be more efficiently deployed in other economic sectors, for example. And yet a nation should still have, as a policy, the need "to procure and maintain an independent supply." Malthus would reuse that statement, variously phrased, throughout the chapter, in order to make apparent that he thought that any growth of national population resulting from food imports might give a false sense of national strength, if the additional subjects or citizens would go hungry or actually starve when the imports stopped, even temporarily.[39]

Whatever Malthus contended, the Americas in truth constituted for British consumers millions of crucial ghost acres. He in fact admitted the economic significance of these distant lands—just not for food. In the 1817 edition of the *Essay*, Malthus wrote of "the cotton trade of this country." Though he did not specify the source of the raw cotton, vanishingly small numbers of his readers would not have known that it came principally from the southern parts of the United States. The total of those American imports, Malthus explained, "has extended itself so wonderfully during the last twenty-five years" in the absence of "foreign competition." Meanwhile, "domestic competition" in manufacturing the raw cotton into thread and the thread into cloth had driven down prices and created a glut on the market. Advances in mechanization had also leveled off wages; reforms had made it more humane for children to work in cotton mills, which itself depressed wages. (Adults had to be paid more.) Altogether, "the country has ... been very greatly benefitted" from the expansion of the cotton trade, by the provision of good, cheap clothing for all and the generation of capital for some. Malthus's implication was that cotton imports did not represent the dangerous dependence that grain imports did. Great Britain and the United States were at peace by 1817, when Malthus discussed cotton manufacturing. Even were the peace to be disrupted, the English could shiver in worn-out clothing more easily than they could do without bread.[40]

Grain and cotton were, however, not the full story. The Caribbean was the much more important contemporary example of American ghost acreage. Whatever the disruptions of the Second Hundred Years' War, the sugar islands of the West Indies remained within the British Empire, and commentators had been remarking on the rising quantity of sugar consumed in Britain, both in absolute terms and per capita, since the seventeenth century. So too was there a strong sense that sugar was replacing more traditional ways of eating. The anthropologist Sidney Mintz, in his deeply important book *Sweetness and Power: The Place of Sugar in Modern History* (1985), has pointed out that sugar was the primordial food of modern capitalism and of modern empire, connecting old and new worlds as it functioned in this manner, because it simultaneously extracted labor from black workers in the greater Caribbean, did the same to the working poor in jam factories in England, and then fed those workers with cheap quasi-foods (sugar in tea; jam on bread) in place of the beer and plain bread that had been the domestically produced mainstays of the everyday English diet, from the Middle Ages into Malthus's boyhood.[41]

All the more remarkable, and especially given Malthus's concern elsewhere over his nation's food supply, that Caribbean ghost acreage plays such a tiny role in Malthus's assessment of the foods available to the English poor. This is immediately obvious in the fact that the word "sugar" never appears, not once, in the *Essay* of 1803, despite the fact that sugar was the most important edible new world product imported into Great Britain at precisely that time, and that it played what can be described, in nutritional terms, an important caloric function. That this verbal omission was no casual oversight becomes apparent in the invisibility of other words relevant to the islands where sugar was produced by slaves for British consumption (and profit): "Caribbean," "West Indies," and "West Indian" never appear in the text either. It is an incredible performance of blindness, if an unconvincing one. To be sure, Benjamin Franklin and Adam Smith had earlier questioned the benefits of slave-driven plantation economies. But they at least acknowledged their existence—in order to criticize them. As multiple scholars have established, the sugar islands of the West Indies were centrally visible within British society as sources of national and personal wealth. Malthus had to have known this, as the analysis of his family's holdings in Jamaica, in chapter 6, will make clear. For Malthus to ignore the Caribbean was to ignore the central place of a new world food within everyday British diet, and the way in which the ghost acres of empire therefore complicated the relationship between a nation's population and its material resources.[42]

There is a greater problem here: in relation to America, Malthus had a misleadingly narrow definition of who should be regarded as economically important within and to a population and why. Like Franklin and Smith before him, he assumed free white settlers were the population that counted (and should be counted). That rejected an older tradition, going back to early modern reason-of-state arguments, that slaves counted too; it exposed his assumption that certain economic activities were more moral than others. His silence about sugar matched his insistence that Indians were by nature subsistence hunters of meat. He ignored how Indian hunters were in truth the major and commercially oriented contributors to the lucrative fur trade, providing tens of thousands of animal pelts to British merchants per year and generating dividends for the Hudson's Bay Company that, despite war, held between 5 and 8 percent. By concealing the economic activities of slaves and Indians who lived within the British Empire, he implied that they were not subjects. But they were. Through a series of legal determinations in the latter half of the eighteenth century, they had been formally constituted under just that heading. Further, Malthus did not admit that US citizens were economically valuable to Great Britain as consumers. That fact had been discussed for about a century; Franklin had made it part of a claim for creoles' autonomy yet also their continuing value to the British Empire.[43]

Malthus's silence on this dimension of commercial economies again shows his ongoing decision to focus merely on land and agriculture as the sole bases for human livelihood and happiness. (It is notable, in this regard, that he also ignored the significant extraction of wood from North American forests.) Within these selective terms, Indians as hunters versus settlers as agricultural-ists are typologically important for his principle of population. But as types of new world denizens, they are constructs, and by 1803 no longer entirely accurate ones, as Malthus's elision of commercial production of furs, sugar, and grain, as well as lumbering, makes clear, along with his blithe description of the benefits of US cotton, grown primarily (he did not explain) by slaves. In a sense, he was deferring hard questions about the ethical hazards of new world colonies that would come back to haunt him in ongoing debates about emigration and antislavery.

This is not to say that Malthus could not have refuted any suggestion that ghost acres represented a constantly expanding set of edible resources, a prom-ise of future food (as with future clothing) that might have questioned his central warning about the principle of population. His point about nature's incapacity to keep up with human reproduction would have been consistent across global geography, whatever the momentary advantages that imperial territories might offer. But it is odd that he did not address the potential ob-jection himself. It gives his analysis a simplistic cast, as if he were avoiding complex realities that might have questioned his conclusions. That he ignored both North American grain and Caribbean sugar indicate how he wanted to avoid the whole subject of new world foods, lest readers wander away from his line of analysis. Should they do so, they might expect too many miracles from America. They would put their faith in cornucopias that were distant, tempo-rary, and ultimately false.

* * *

It was in his depiction of North America as a land of antithetical popula-tion type specimens that Malthus achieved his most dramatic point about new world places, however selective he may have been. At every step of his analysis, he simplified things. The Americas were one continent. Most of it was covered with arboreal forest. Its native populations were migratory, de-pendent on animal flesh brought down by male hunters. Competition for hunting grounds was the main source of tension among Indian nations, who fought to the death and consumed the bodies of slain enemies. Indians had a distinctive propensity to foster and suffer from epidemic disease; they drank to medical excess. English settlers, but above all New England puritans, had a contrasting ability to thrive. The natives were probably going to be destroyed, one way or another. Exceptions to these patterns were just that, blips that confirmed the general trend. And yet none of Malthus's assertions was wholly true; many are damagingly misleading. The result is a set of stripped-down analytics about human social types rather than a full relation of the cultural and historical complexities of actual human beings: corn-growing Indian women, warmongering imperial officials, children in the teeming families of Mexico, and so on. The half truths may represent an end stage within stadial theorizing. Malthus's criteria moved the theories away from the first stadial historians' attempt to criticize or even satirize the earlier historical narratives that had accepted received wisdom and toward a more forthright (if not yet entirely convincing) method of social science analysis, yet with a use of categorical constructs that themselves seem parodic.[44]

In a related way, Malthus had, between the 1798 and 1803 editions of his *Essay*, profoundly changed his discussion of how human beings could cease to exist. In the first edition, he had used the word "annihilation" in its theological sense, to indicate the utter destruction of lost souls, which is what he thought Godwin's and Condorcet's indifference to spiritual salvation implied. He omitted that phrase in the second edition. He never again used any form of *to annihilate*, even as similar verbs proliferated. Variations on *extinct*, *extirpate*, and *exterminate* abound in the 1803 *Essay*, though *destroy* is the most frequently used, a distressing fifty-three times. Not all of these instances describe the fate of humans, as with the "race destroyed" in Spanish America. But many do, and their frequency compared to that within the 1798 edition (a mere eight times) hints at an adjustment of emphasis: away from the spiritual annihilation falsely preached by two individuals, Godwin and Condorcet, and toward the physical destruction actually experienced by thousands of indigenes at the hands of thousands of settlers. This is not so much a shift from religious to secular terms as a more precise reckoning of moral and ethical faults.

Malthus used the "Americas" as a warning, as a demonstration of the moral hazards embedded in the primordial new world scenario. True, he displayed prejudices about Indians that most Europeans of his generation may have had; he was no worse than his white contemporaries. But he was not like the vast majority of his contemporaries: he exercised greater cultural and intellectual authority than they did. By placing predictions of Indian extinction so centrally within his principle of population, he gave new life to old ideas about Indian death, recycling some of the worst suppositions about new world peoples that had been generated since the sixteenth century. Without addressing his father's friend Rousseau directly, he nevertheless thoroughly attacked Rousseauean conceptions of humanity's natural virtues, crafting one of the most inventive rebuttals of the concept of an Edenic new world, and therefore a powerful reminder of humanity's fallen condition.

Chapter 5

The South Sea

THERE WAS A STEADY STREAM OF NEW WORLD VISITORS to London over the seventeenth and eighteenth centuries, anticipating Bennelong's visit in the mid-1790s. One of them arrived to particular acclaim: a Ra'iatean man—Mai, called Omai by the English—passed momentarily but with great impact through London society in the mid-1770s. Kept carefully and proudly under the wing and watch of Sir Joseph Banks, Mai was celebrated within the circle that was just beyond the reach of wealthy but rural Daniel Malthus and his family. Mai's diplomatic encounter took its cue from earlier visits of native Americans, but its timing meant that he engaged with metropolitan culture at the height of British Rousseaueans' interest in "man in the state of nature." Mai's apparent natural civility made him a great object lesson for those inclined toward British self-critique. He countered European civilization, showing instead its decadence and degeneration: ignoble civilization.[1]

South Sea islanders had fairly quickly secured themselves a favored place in European visions of the global order of things. Malthus recognized this structurally, dealing with Mai's Polynesia in his third "stadial" chapter, "Of the Checks to Population in the Islands of the South Sea," pointedly placed after the Americas. Substantively, however, Malthus challenged rather more than he extended the great popular interest in South Sea islanders' civility. Except for attention to the hierarchical nature of Polynesian society, the civility that Mai had so famously embodied, at least in British primitivists' eyes, was barely discernible in Malthus's *Essay*. South Sea islanders appeared in the chapter as both higher up the stadial scale on an economic and political measure and uncivilized on a cultural measure: some of them sacrificed humans and endorsed infanticide, Malthus documented, while others ate human flesh, the ultimate marker of the new world savage. Naturally he stated his moral objection, but he was nonetheless relatively dispassionate about such practices, assessing them rather more as manifestations of his principle of population in those particular societies than as outrages.

The South Sea chapter of the *Essay* distilled information from voyage accounts on the one hand and French and Scottish histories of humankind on the other. Malthus thus received a double dose of stadial theory, since so many of the South Sea voyagers were self-consciously offering up material for the stadial scholarly tradition.[2] The celebrated French and British journeys through Oceania that had accelerated from the 1760s offered Malthus extremely useful cases through which to demonstrate to his readers the oscillation of population over time and in limited spaces, and the range of checks that effected this oscillation in different locations and societies. He redeployed for his purposes accounts of the journeys of Bougainville, La Pérouse, Vancouver, and especially Cook, his main source. Having relied extensively on the Hawkesworth account of Cook's first voyage in his chapter on New Holland, in this chapter Malthus mined publications from the second and third voyages as well. His reliance on the accounts of Cook's three voyages is important, certainly for our understanding of Malthus's thesis, but also for ongoing assessment of the navigator's influence. This reworking by a key political economist casts the nomination of Cook as "Adam Smith's first and perhaps greatest global agent" in a whole new light.[3]

It is surprising that scholars have not put Cook and Malthus together before, but it is equally unsurprising that Malthus found so much that was useful in Cook's accounts. Counting locals, as we have seen, formed part of Cook's specific instruction from the Admiralty, and it engaged any number of naturalists and surgeons on board, as with Banks on the first voyage and, on the second and third, Edinburgh-educated surgeon William Anderson, whose accuracy of observation Malthus specifically endorsed as "of the first authority." It was early in the South Sea chapter that Malthus again quoted the core question on population that he had come across in the account of Cook's first voyage: "By what means the inhabitants of this country are reduced to such a number as it can subsist." It was one thing, he said, to apply this to thinly populated New Holland, but it was especially telling to consider the far more populous islands in these terms. It was here, at the beginning of the chapter on the islands of the South Sea, that Malthus revealed the whole aim of the first book of his new, long *Essay* to be an answer to that antipodean-derived problem; it was "an endeavour to answer this question so applied."[4]

* * *

From Thomas More's *Utopia* (1516) to Francis Bacon's *New Atlantis* (1627), islands had long functioned as allegories of British society, French society, the perfect society, or world society. The factual new world inspired and enabled any number of fictional islands. Defoe located *Robinson Crusoe* (1719) "in an un-inhabited Island on the Coast of America, near the Mouth of the Great River of Oroonoque." And a few years later Swift had Gulliver travel to Lilliput and Blefuscu, situated somewhere near Van Diemen's Land (1726). Deserted islands were tabula rasa on which social theories could be freely illustrated. Thus Adam Smith began his description of stadial theory with a hypothetical island—"If we should suppose 10 or 12 persons of different sexes settled in an uninhabited island"—and proceeded to describe the progression that would then unfold from hunting and gathering, to the emergence of concepts of property in the shepherd state, to ownership in the agricultural state and the beginning of the division of labor that he argued made food surplus possible. Islands could be Edens, where Adam and Eve prospered and then fell.[5]

When British and French mariners encountered new islands and islanders in the South Sea in the middle of the eighteenth century, their accounts were grafted onto this strong tradition of insular ficto-politics, as well as a tradition in which natural history was turning into commercial bioprospecting. Isolated islands were inspiring places where Europeans fashioned their own visions of untainted nature, including human nature. Islands and islanders were a measure of themselves. Seeking to understand "savage" societies, French and Scottish stadial theorists were thus already primed to think about islands, even before the great rush of South Sea expeditions in the 1760s that centered on Tahiti. Certainly, by the time Malthus turned to consider that part of the world at the turn of the century, Pacific islanders had been strongly integrated into French natural and universal histories. Indeed, the *philosophes* had to some degree prompted those journeys in the first place. Malthus made considerable use of *Histoire des navigations aux terres Australes* (1756) by Charles de Brosses, for example, volumes that consolidated knowledge of South Sea societies known by Europeans up to that point. De Brosses strongly called for more (French) exploratory journeys, more firsthand knowledge that could contribute to the intellectual project of the history of all humankind. This information flow between stay-at-home stadial theorists and explorers was reversed as well. The writings of the *philosophes* were sometimes extensions of the writing of Pacific explorers, most notably in Denis Diderot's *Supplément au voyage de Bougainville* (1772), in which a dialogue between a Tahitian and "Bougainville" was a device for Diderot to consider nature, culture, colonization, slavery, and citizenship.[6]

Scottish texts written in the 1770s and '80s tended to retain the convention of representing native Americans as quintessential hunters and gatherers, or else to present "savages" hypothetically and generically. Henry Home, Lord Kames, did integrate the Pacific into his history of man, however. Indeed, he commissioned James Lind, surgeon on Cook's second expedition, to gather information that might verify his polygenist theories. *Sketches of the History of Man* included Tahiti, but Kames's key instance was an older Pacific, a Spanish domain in the Philippines, where the colonists drove the natives from the coast to inland mountains, there to live by gathering fruits. Malthus absorbed Kames thoroughly, especially the chapter that directly addressed his own concerns, "Progress of men with respect to Food and Population." He read Kames's classic iteration of islands as places of tantalizing purity, perfect instances of original society now available for Scottish, English, or French assessment. "Nations are for the most part so blended by war, by commerce, or by other means, that vain would be the attempt to trace out an original character in any cultivated nation," Kames wrote. "But there are savage tribes, which, so far as can be discovered, continue to this day pure without mixture.... The nations that may be the most relied on for an original character, are islanders at a distance from the continent and from each other." While the Pacific generally played a more marginal role in the Scottish than the French histories, Malthus's chapter fully combined Scottish stadial theory with French and British mariners' and naturalists' travel accounts of the South Sea.[7]

Some of the traffic between French and British ideas on Enlightenment islands was facilitated in the Malthus family home. The English translation of Bernardin de Saint-Pierre's *Paul et Virginie* is often attributed to Daniel Malthus. The book is a novel set in Île-de-France, now Mauritius, the plot driven by the malign influence of French civilization on the Mauritians, and their fall from a state of simple, natural, and harmonious equality. Paul and Virginie were a thwarted breeding pair. The book was an enormously popular novel that very obviously fictionalized Rousseau's philosophies on "natural man." The assertion that Daniel Malthus was the translator endured after being noted in his obituary. But his second son, Thomas Robert, firmly denied this, clearly offended that his father be remembered merely as a translator (which begs the unanswered question of what Daniel Malthus actually did write and publish): "The turn of his mind very little disposed him to imitation, or to the copying, in any way, the work of others." It was not Daniel Malthus who translated and anonymously published this English translation in 1789, however, but his cousin, ward, and companion, the learned Jane Dalton. She had lived in Paris in late 1788, an acquaintance of Jacques Henri Bernardin de Saint-Pierre, writer and director of the Paris Botanical Gardens. Five of her letters to Bernardin de Saint-Pierre survive, dated 1788 and 1789, from what seems to have been a larger correspondence. She called the English translation *Paul and Mary: An Indian Story*, and while the novel's *tableau de la nature* was Île-de-France, Jane Dalton clarified in her English edition's preface that this island resembled those in the South Sea. She added the latitude and longitude of Île-de-France, clarifying its colonial history— discovery by the Portuguese, possession by the Dutch and then the French— and of the island wrote, "It seems, by the accounts of the Abbé de la Caille, and M. de Bougainville, to resemble Otaheite, and other islands in the Pacific Ocean." Dalton also added the Linnaean names of animals and plants as footnotes "where it seemed requisite, and it could be done with tolerable certainty." She enjoyed a strong interest in botany alongside Daniel Malthus. For his part, the elder Malthus clearly felt that his connection to botany (and Rousseau) was more meaningfully shared with Dalton than with any other member of his family—more so, even, than his well-educated sons, as they learned on the execution of his will: "To Mrs Jane Dalton all my Botanical Books in which the Name of Rousseau is written, likewise a Box of Plants given me by Monsr. Rousseau." Many of Dalton's books are extant in the Malthus Collection at Jesus College, Cambridge. The box of specimens has been lost.[8]

Thomas Robert Malthus's interest in and deployment of the South Sea was an extension into the early nineteenth century of the early modern convention of islands as allegory for the world, combined with the empirical material on actual Pacific islands that had entered the Enlightenment canon. Yet island spaces and populations had a special significance for the British, irrespective of the vogue for the exotic Pacific. Britain was routinely conceptualized by philosophers and political economists as a small island, the British an "island race," as Kathleen Wilson has shown. Certainly, when Malthus sat down to talk through the first *Essay* one summer morning in 1798, his companion was suddenly compelled by the insular geography in which they lived. "In our conversation this morning I omitted the most material part of the subject, the most striking view in which it may be placed," William Godwin wrote to Malthus, excited enough to underscore his thoughts. "*Myriads of centuries*, for ought I know, *of still increasing population* may occur, before the island of Great Britain shall contain all the population it is capable of subsisting." We are inclined to think of Malthus and Godwin as rivals and forget that they lived in the same worlds and talked through their work occasionally in person. Godwin here saw more or less limitless capacity to cultivate and improve land on their island home, while Malthus saw a quickly diminishing return. Nineteenth-century commentators were later to suggest that Malthus's heightened awareness of the relation between population and space was a particular product of British geographical sensibilities. He certainly wrote about Britain as an island repeatedly through all editions of the *Essay*.[9]

When Malthus turned to construct his chapter on the South Sea, he began with the abbé Raynal's *Histoire philosophique des deux Indes* (1770). All islanders, wrote Raynal and his collaborators, including Diderot, adopted strange customs for the limitation of fertility and, sometimes, for the acceleration of death: male castration, female infibulation, late marriages, the consecration of virginity, the approbation of celibacy, anthropophagy—the practice of eating human flesh. Malthus brought all of this into his *Essay*. But Raynal was not just writing about the South Sea. "All islanders" for him included the ancient inhabitants of the British Isles, a fact that Malthus made a point of repeating in his opening to this chapter. Raynal himself had put these kinds of practices down to insular population pressure. Malthus concurred but went further: this was applicable to societies on continents as well, since they were also, ultimately, islands. Raynal seemed not to understand, wrote Malthus, that societies besieged or hemmed in in any way, whether "savage" Americans and islanders, or "civilized" Europeans, were essentially in the same situation. And since the "whole Earth," too, was a bounded space, it was necessary to think through whether and how this situation was in fact a universal principle. In this way, the South Sea islanders stood in for the world, for humanity.[10]

* * *

Malthus's study of Tahiti lies in the tradition of island studies that stretched back to the early modern period and forward to biogeography. "Otaheite" became the talk of Enlightenment Europe after Samuel Wallis's one-month sojourn in 1767. Bougainville followed one year later. And James Cook based his fleet in Tahiti for long stays in 1769, returning in 1773 and 1777. Suddenly the British and French discovered Tahiti and Tahitians. Conversely, "Tahiti" invaded Europe's republic of letters. All the accounts Malthus read of the island centered on the two abiding human "wants" that he had set out as his original postulata: food and sex. The culture and nature of food and sex in Tahiti positively consumed eighteenth-century British and French observers. Joseph Banks was equally interested in cultivating both. His documentation of Tahitian sexual cultures and practices was only matched by his eagerness for promoting oceanic botanical exchange, especially the possibilities of Tahitian breadfruit for the economic sustenance of West Indian slaves. For Malthus,

Tahiti was a particularly important case in his three new chapters, providing evidence of a population living within clearly demarcated insular space but somehow managing to keep numbers down more or less to a subsistence level.

Part of the reason Malthus was writing about the South Sea islands at all was the already conventional commentary on their varied fertility, mortality, and population density. Tahiti served Malthus's thesis well, first because it was routinely observed as populous, even crowded, unlike sparsely populated New Holland. Cook, Banks, and Bougainville all made a point of noting the great number of Tahitians, but more precisely tied to the principle of population was Malthus's own extrapolation from the observations of those three that there were cycles of population growth and decline, a response to changing prosperity. It is unlikely, he proposed, that Tahiti's population had always been the same—stationary—or that it had been constantly increasing, however slowly. Rather, it oscillated: overpopulation would lead to war; this would lead to deprivation and, over time (after war had been forgotten), population increase. Then, unfavorable seasons would bring about a society "pressing hard against the limits of its food," and that would prompt more war or more infanticide, a process of depopulation that would continue longer than the famine itself. A "change of habits" then, produced by the availability of food, would "restore the population." And so on. It was the oscillation between scarcity and living just on or over subsistence that Malthus noted from the Tahitian case, empirical evidence of his principle, and he made a point of saying so: "This is exactly what we should suppose from theory." From such statements it is clear that Malthus saw his work as extending conjectural history into a wholly new domain of evidence. His book substantiated a universal principle that was observable and demonstrable; he delivered empirical material that illustrated a law of population at work.[11]

Malthus had a considerable amount of population data on Tahiti at hand. Indeed, notwithstanding its exotic culture, remote placement, and the intermittent reliability of English and French accounts, Tahiti's population was arguably better documented than that of his own British Isles. It was Cook's Pacific estimates—in Van Diemen's Land, Tahiti, New Holland, and elsewhere—that consistently served as the baseline from which later voyagers calibrated their numbers. Malthus cited Cook's reckoning in the first instance, for both total population estimates and for area (and therefore density). The island that Cook circumnavigated and charted was around forty leagues in circuit, with an estimated 204,000 people.

But *how* were these population estimates made? On what basis and through what methods? Eighteenth- and nineteenth-century censuses some-

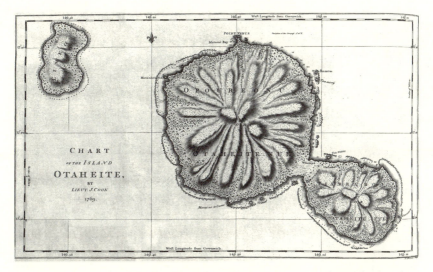

Figure 5.1. Chart of the island Otaheite by Lieutenant James Cook, in John Hawkesworth, *An Account of the Voyages Undertaken by the Order of His Present Majesty for Making Discoveries in the Southern Hemisphere*. 3 vols. (London: W. Strahan and T. Cadell, 1773), vol. 2, facing 79. Reproduced from Jesus College, Old Library, volume of cuts, charts, and maps, by permission of the Master and Fellows of Jesus College, Cambridge.

times enumerated people individually. In Europe early censuses tended to estimate by household, by "hearth." Occasionally they worked from the number of men in the military and from that base estimated numbers of women and children, and thus a total population. Malthus himself at one point worked through the common calculation that the proportion of European men capable of bearing arms was one-fourth of the entire population of that country. The navigator Tupaia was the source for a Pacific rendition of a similar method. While still in Tahiti, Cook wrote that "Tupia [sic] informs us that . . . the whole Island can muster 6780 Fighting Men, by which some Judgment can be form'd of the number of inhabitants. Each district furnishes a certain number which the Chief is obliged to bring into the Field when summoned by the Eare de hi, or King of the Island, either to make War or repell an invasion." Another Pacific version of a census was to estimate population by canoe. Witnessing preparations for a great naval expedition on Cook's second voyage in 1774, naturalist Johann Reinhold Forster recounted his own method for population estimates. Forster (who had taught at the Warrington

Figure 5.2. Counting population by canoe. A war canoe of New Zealand, with a view of Gable End Foreland in John Hawkesworth, *An Account of the Voyages Undertaken by the Order of His Present Majesty for Making Discoveries in the Southern Hemisphere.* 3 vols. (London: W. Strahan and T. Cadell, 1773), vol. 3, facing 463. Reproduced from Jesus College, Old Library, volume of cuts, charts and maps, cut no. 16, by permission of the Master and Fellows of Jesus College, Cambridge.

Academy, though before Malthus's time) counted the number of men in each canoe and the number of canoes: "Let us further suppose each of these men to be married to a woman, and to have one child, and in this case, we shall have the number of 81,000 persons. Everyone will allow, that this is the very lowest computation that can be made, and that the number of living inhabitants of T-Obreonoo must be at double that number." Forster, like many, had been struck by the populousness of Tahiti: "Wherever we walked, we found the roads lined with natives, and not one of the houses was empty, though we had left the shores opposite the ship, crowded with people." He concluded there to be an "extraordinary population in this queen of tropical isles." But more than this, Forster wondered, rather like Malthus, how many people *could* subsist there. "Though we found population to be very great in proportion to the extent of country, yet we were led to believe that a much greater number of inhabitants might be supported on these islands, and in ages to come might be found there," Forster speculating that this would be a great number "unless such manners and regulations should be introduced as tend to check or stop the progress of population." In this respect, Forster anticipated Malthus's ideas very directly indeed.[12]

Malthus's assessment of new world societies was shaped strongly by the peculiar mid-eighteenth-century mix of Enlightenment universal histories and these remarkable travel accounts. This is what he inherited, intellectually. But unfolding around him was a new kind of engagement with antipodean societies, envisaged to be permanent, not passing. An evangelical humanitarianism centered on slavery began to cast its efforts in new directions. In 1795 the nondemonimational but nonconformist-inclined Missionary Society was founded, and by 1797 thirty missionaries had landed in Tahiti, inspired by Cook and instructed by Banks. The account of their earliest venture, a text on which Malthus strongly relied and cited simply as the "Missionary Voyage," was published in 1799. In the very years that Malthus's first *Essay* was being written and read, the missionaries in Tahiti, like Joseph Banks and Johann Forster before them, were not just wondering about but actively hypothesizing on the means by which island populations expanded and diminished in relation to interventions into both birth and death. They had been charged to save the heathens but to count them too. With rather more time on their hands than did captains, lieutenants, naturalists, or marines, the missionaries diligently estimated Tahitian numbers, documenting the process and the results in their "Survey to ascertain the Population of the Island." Initial estimates were in the neighborhood of 50,000, far less than Cook's overblown calculation. Still, the missionaries thought even this number too great, and so a dedicated and systematic regional circuit of the island was made. From household numbers, they aimed to estimate the population in each district and to tally a total. This South Pacific "national" census thus anticipated the first national census of the United Kingdom (1801) by several years, but both proceeded in methodologically similar ways. With intermediary beachcomber "Peter the Swede," the missionaries quickly learned the local units by which calculations were to be made:

> He said that in Whyripoo there were four matteynas, and to each matteyna there were ten tees; and by these he estimated the number of men, women, and children, to be about two hundred and fifty. I desired him to explain what a matteyna was, and what was a tee. The former, he said, was a principal house, distinguished either by a degree of rank in its ancient or present owner, or by a portion of land being attached to it . . . in some matteynas there are eight or nine persons in the family, in others but two or three . . . [from] what I afterwards saw of the thin population, I allow but six persons to each matteyna, and the same to a tee.

264 souls were counted in that district, 186 for another region, and so forth until they had circled and crossed the island and tallied 16,050 people. The missionary-statistician thought this a thin population, especially in the light of received wisdom of Tahiti's populousness, and certainly a small number compared with Cook and Corner's estimate. But he had been diligent, he

Diftricts.	Prefiding Chiefs.	Matt.	Tees.	Numb. of Souls
1 Whyripoo . . .	Inna Madúa . .	4	6	264
2 Whapiawno . . .	Wytouah . .	28	238	1596
3 Wharoomy . . .	Wyreede Aowh .	1	9	60
4 Hewow . . .	Mánne Manne .	2	11	78
5 Hahbahboonea . .	Otoo . . .	1	8	54
6 Honoowhyah . .	Ditto . . .	3	28	186
7 Nahnu Nahnoo . .	Pomárre . .	3	18	126
8 Ot-yayree . . .	Noe Noe . .	2	22	144
9 Wha-ah-heinah . .	Roorah and three more	4	53	342
10 Hedeah . . .	Inna Madúa . .	42	167	1254
11 Part of Terrawow on this fide the ifthmus uninhabited.				
12 Wy-eree . . .	Maahe-hanoo (female)	32	42	444
13 Wyooreede . . .	Tayreede (wife of Temárre)	13	161	1044
14 Attemonoo . . .	Ditto . . .	2	24	156
15 Pappará . . .	Ditto . . .	17	157	1044
16 Ahaheinah . . .	Ditto : . .	8	105	678
17 Attahooroo . . .	Ditto . . .	25	243	1608
18 Tettaha . . .	Pomárre . .	12	130	852
19 Opárre . . .	Ditto . . .	16	199	1290
20 Matavái . . .	Miffionaries . .	27	110	822

Total of men, women, and children, in Otaheite		12,042
Ditto in Tiaraboo		4,008
Total on the whole ifland		16,050

Figure 5.3. The Missionary census, Tahiti, 1797, in *A Missionary Voyage to the Southern Pacific Ocean, Performed in the Years 1796, 1797, 1798 ...* (London: T. Chapman, 1799), 215. Reproduced by permission of Cambridge University Library.

said, and had paid every attention. Even so, the missionary documented his inclination that even "this small number exceeds the truth."[13]

Malthus nonetheless took that number, considered the area of the island itself from Cook's charts, and thought through the possibilities, or more to the point the impossibility, of population growth. He applied Franklin to the South Sea. Supposing that Tahiti's population might double in twenty-five years, it would reach three million within a single century. Malthus suggested a revision of Franklin, however, suspecting that without checks, the potential to double was even faster, perhaps less than fifteen years and thus, he made a point of noting, rather more like William Petty's earlier estimate. But where could such a population go? "Where could they be disposed?" asked Malthus. Vague and thoughtless "solutions" to the problem, including the possibility of emigration or more intense cultivation, were simply inadequate. "The usual" he dismissed, clearly reminded of the responses to his own writing on the British Isles. Even if there was some movement between the islands, "effectual emigration" was in no sense a possibility. The improvement of cultivation sufficient to feed this population, which in theory (that is, without checks) could be three million within a century, would be equally impossible, an explanation "glaringly inadequate."[14]

Thus, Tahiti was for Malthus *the* case that all but proved the principle of population: that checks are always in operation. It was so clear, he wrote, that the evidence "must stare us in the face, that the people on this group of islands could not continue to double their numbers every twenty-five years." Unless the women became somehow miraculously barren ("a perpetual miracle"), something else perpetual was going on. This was proven especially forcefully for Malthus precisely because of the fecund potential of Tahiti's environment, its "delightful climate" and its "exuberant plenty." That "something" was the principle of population, the functioning of checks of various kinds, in this case less natural than the "very powerful checks to population in the habits of the people."[15]

One of these checks was the war and civil strife documented closely by Cook, Bougainville, and Vancouver. Not only were significant numbers of people killed, their means of subsistence were also destroyed. Previously productive environments were laid waste. "Most of the animals, plants, and herbs, which Captain Cook had left, had been destroyed by the ravages of war," Malthus noted. He ran through other checks in Tahiti as well. Human sacrifices took place, and although deemed insignificant in population terms, he made a point of noting this as a Tahitian barbarism. Malthus also foregrounded the relation between a particular sexual culture and infanticide as a major population check. From Cook, from Cook's surgeon Anderson, from Bougainville, and from the accounts of the London missionaries, Malthus described the "Eareeoie" society, the religious section of Tahitian society that traveled, performed ceremonies, and lived in a kind of sexual freedom. He clearly expected his readers to be familiar with the Arreoy or Arioi, "they have been so often described." It was less promiscuous intercourse, than infanticide, however, that he thought important, though he made a point of linking these two practices, which he named as Tahitian "fundamental laws." Any child born to an Arreoy woman was suffocated at birth, Malthus recounted. Cook himself had observed that this prevented the increase of "the superior classes," an antipodean counter-eugenics before its time. But Malthus thought that infanticide was practiced in Tahiti beyond the Arreoy classes, including the lower classes; that it had no "imputation of poverty" (presumably thinking about his own society), and that among Tahitians infanticide held no moral censure. A man, he reported, might kill a newborn if he did not intend to "marry" the woman/mother. And he inferred from evidence presented in the missionaries' account about the small numbers of women that female infanticide had been practiced in particular.[16]

At this point in his chapter, Malthus introduced David Hume and his essay "On the Populousness of Ancient Nations" (1752). Hume had also been interested in infanticide and had nominated China as the only nation still publicly condoning the exposure of infants. Yet he had linked contemporary China to one of the great ethical failings of the Greek and Roman ancients: even the humane and good-natured Plutarch thought infanticide a virtue, Hume had exclaimed. Though "cruel," infanticide was not just a marker of savagery but also a "barbarous practice of the ancients," as Hume had put it. But neither Hume nor Malthus concluded that infanticide necessarily diminished population numbers. Indeed, Malthus agreed with Hume that infanticide could just as easily lead to an increase in population, arguing that it gave license for people to marry younger, momentarily unburdened by the prospect of supporting infants, but in the long run the more years married, the more children would be born. He thought that Tahitian society was an exception, however: infanticide seemed to license promiscuous sex more than marriage, thus acting as an effective check that limited Tahitian population to its available resources, which were, on the face of it, plentiful. In other words, in an environment and climate marked by "the most exuberant plenty," occasional infanticide alone might be sufficient to keep population growth in check.[17]

Of course both Malthus and Hume knew that infanticide was common, if not condoned, in their own period and place, an indicator of British poverty in Hume's time that had become more visible and discussed by the turn of the century. Indeed, discussion of infanticide approached something like standard fare for eighteenth-century political economists and stadial theorists. Malthus nonetheless assured readers that he was describing such preventive checks as they *did* function, not as he thought they *ought* to function or would ideally function. "A cause which may prevent any particular evil may be beyond all comparison worse than the evil itself." Malthus implored his readers not to misunderstand him, and perhaps more privately he hoped that they remembered the "is/ought" distinction as first set out by his father's acquaintance, and known as Hume's Law.[18]

Disease also figured in this third new world chapter, but curiously and differently to those that had come before. Tahiti was the one new world instance in which Malthus indicated a European responsibility for diseases. He called them "European diseases," but even so he was reluctant to attribute any great population significance in terms of mortality, with a note to Cook's Third Voyage: "The diseases, though they have been dreadfully increased by European contact, were before peculiarly lenient; and even for some time afterwards, were not marked by any extraordinary fatality." Once again Malthus wanted to understand disease as a universal check, coming and going in all societies no matter how isolated, not a happenstance effect of maritime exploration or colonization. And again he actively set aside material before him that did not fit this thesis. The London missionaries, for example, tended to point to European diseases having a great impact and linked venereal diseases to the depopulation that they immediately noted: "On landing among these islanders, our compassions were more powerfully excited to find their population greatly diminished, and, through the prevalence of vice, tending to utter extinction." Already in 1799 they hoped to save the islanders in ways more than spiritual, "to rescue from destruction of body and soul a gentle race of fellow-men."[19]

The missionaries were the main source for Malthus's claims about female infanticide in Tahiti: "As no odium whatever is attached to this unnatural deed, many hundreds born into the world are never suffered to see the light."[20] But they had in their own account offered a few further practices to explain Tahiti's limits on reproduction, observations on nonreproductive sex that Malthus stopped short of recapitulating. There was "onanism," which they understood as causally related to the lack of women. There was the class of "mawhoo," men who dressed as and otherwise "mimicked" women. And finally, there were "other practices too horrible to mention," over which the missionaries felt obliged to draw a veil and which Malthus totally ignored.

Food and famine years were more of a problem than would be expected, given Tahiti's reputation for abundance, Malthus explained. He drew this from Anderson, and noted that it was contradicted by the missionaries' 1799 account, which detailed famine in the Friendly Islands and the Marquesas, but not in Tahiti. In fact, Malthus claimed confidently, plenty and scarcity in Tahiti were less about sufficiency of food for all than about unequal distribution across Tahiti's strict social hierarchies and distinctions of rank. Chiefs enjoyed life in plenty; their vassals were pinched with want.[21]

* * *

When he departed Plymouth, James Cook had been given a sealed package that contained orders for the second part of his journey and instruction from the Admiralty to open this only after he had completed the first task, observing the transit of Venus from Tahiti. He was to sail south and west, sweeping through the ocean in search of the large continent known to exist in the

Southern Hemisphere. He did so, accompanied by Tupaia, the Ra'iatean navigator and priest. In October 1769 the coast of New Zealand was sighted, some of the crew exclaiming that they had finally found *terra Australis incognita*, others, including Cook, more reticent. In reading through the Hawkesworth version of these remarkable events, Malthus was far less interested in the exploration of new seas than in the discovery of new people. The inhabitants of New Zealand served nicely as another focused case in his consideration of South Sea populations.

Malthus read how the Englishmen's initial encounter with the local Māori was violent and deadly. When Cook, Banks, and Daniel Solander landed, four Māori armed with "long lances" rushed at their boat, the cockswain fired two warnings, and then shot one of the "Indians" through the heart. The body was dragged some distance by the surviving Māori, dropped and left on the ground. In Hawkesworth's account, the Englishmen then turned seamlessly from armed invaders into ethnographers. They inspected the dead man, noting skin color, the design of facial tattoos, the fine nature of the cloth he wore. The next day Cook landed again, this time with Banks, Solander, and Tupaia, and the second encounter unfolded just as violently: "we had not proceeded many paces before they all started up ... Tupia called to them in the language of Otaheite; but they answered only by flourishing their weapons, and making signs to us to depart; a musquet was then fired wide of them." On Cook's instructions, Tupaia warned them again in his own language that the English would be obliged to kill them, if there was any further violence. And indeed another man was shot that morning, wounded first by Banks and then killed by Monkhouse.[22]

In distilling information on New Zealand for the *Essay*, Malthus looked wholly past the violence of the first encounter between English and locals and instead offered his views on Māori violence toward each other. This was not violence by men against women, as in the New Holland case, but between men. Writing himself in the middle of a European war that had spread to several continents, Malthus attributed mortality among the islanders to their more or less constant state of warfare. That was, for him, the significant element of a local population story that he was weaving into one that was universal.

Malthus told his readers that he could not locate from accounts of New Zealand much information on Māori women, fertility, sex, or infanticide, comparable to that he had found useful in David Collins's account of New South Wales. His pages were far less about relations between men and women, or familial and reproductive patterns, and more an account of relations between men. In a self-serving argument he speculated that given death rates from warfare, the regulation of women's fertility was perhaps a less significant factor in minimizing population numbers in the New Zealand case than it was in New Holland.[23]

Just where did New Zealand sit for Malthus as he built up his stages of development centered on population dynamics? Cook's accounts provided evidence for him of pastoralism in the North Island of New Zealand, the voyagers at one point perceiving fenced hills and headlands, which they presumed were for the enclosure of sheep, oxen, or deer. Malthus read of cultivation too. More than New Holland (where he noted the cultivation of soil to be entirely absent) and the Americas (where he considered cultivation to be occasional), Malthus detailed the successful cultivation of vegetables in New Zealand: in the North Island fern roots, yams, and potatoes were grown, as were "clams," an assertion that both reflected an idea that shellfish were a kind of plant (an interpretation that went back to classical Antiquity) and a knowledge that they could be cultivated. Malthus also claimed, after Banks and Cook, that there was no evidence of agriculture on the South Island. Indeed, Banks had originally thought it uninhabited, recounting that the fleet sailed for four days without seeing a soul on the coast. But then "an immence fire on the side of a hill . . . this is the only sign of people we have seen yet I think it must be an indisputable proof that there are inhabitants, tho probably very thinly scattrd over the face of this very large countrey." Population density in any new world environment was always base knowledge for Banks the naturalist, as well as Cook the representative of the Crown, instructed to take possession.[24]

If cultivation in New Zealand meant for Malthus that the locals were not simply hunters and gatherers, their claim to have risen beyond "the lowest stage" was compromised by the anthropophagy observed in successive Cook journeys and journals. Malthus dwelt on their consumption of human flesh, transferring a long quote from Cook's third voyage into his *Essay*: "'When the massacre is completed, they either feast and gorge themselves on the spot, or carry off as many of the dead bodies as they can, and devour them at home with acts of brutality too shocking to be described.'" And yet it is notable that Malthus explained, even if he did not excuse, both violence and anthropophagy by the great distress brought by hunger. Like the multiple eighteenth-century South Sea voyagers themselves, Malthus perceived marked variation among societies and among islands, and he summarized their distinctions: some ate human flesh and some did not. He read of it practiced in New Zealand but not elsewhere. According to David Collins, for example, the natives of New South Wales recoiled with horror at the idea, and said it was "*wee-re* [bad: wrong]."[25]

These were not generic but highly distinct societies, and to some extent Malthus's *Essay* reflected that variety and scope. His point was, clearly, to show that checks worked perpetually to keep numbers down. But in describing the powers for "the prevention or destruction of life"—setting down evidence for it—he identified locally specific dynamics and circumstances. In New Holland women's low fertility was due to their violent treatment by men; in Tahiti it was familial, sexual, and reproductive customs; in New Zealand the main check was war between men. He extended this to other Pacific islands too, although not all of them. Endemic violence characterized societies in New Guinea, New Britain, New Caledonia, and the New Hebrides, drawing on de Brosses, *Histoires des navigations aux terres Australes* (1756), for information on indigenous people on the Melanesian islands. Malthus conceded that little was actually known compared with the detail on Polynesia that had been disseminated by Wallis, Bougainville, Cook, and Banks.

In this chapter on the South Sea, Malthus ranged as widely as the voyagers' accounts themselves. He wrote briefly about Easter Island—Rapanui—in terms of its disproportion of women to men, also resulting from female infanticide. And like Tahiti it seemed to have a fluctuating population, he thought, neither steady nor steadily growing. It was an interesting case for Malthus because, unlike Tahiti, it had had very limited intercourse with Europeans. Again he scoured the eighteenth-century accounts for numbers, noting Cook's estimate that six to seven hundred people lived on Easter Island. La Pérouse, however, had estimated two thousand and thought numbers were increasing. Malthus also mentioned the Marianna Islands, where sexual cultures held a particular place for young unmarried men, something like Tahitian practices. And he reported that women in Formosa could not bear children before the age of thirty-five and had abortions if they were pregnant before that time.[26] In all this detail, Malthus aimed to show the principle of population in constant and universal operation but also manifesting in different ways, in different contexts.

* * *

For Malthus, as for British and French observers on the ground, the complex hierarchical and ranked social and political societies through all of the South Sea islands set them quite apart from native societies in New Holland or in the Americas. Its placement third in the series, after America but before "the ancient inhabitants of the North of Europe," structurally mirrored stadial theory. But the South Sea islands confounded stadial theory too. Malthus slipped from "savage" to "barbarian" when he discussed Tahiti, for example. More notably, at one point he described islander society as "feudal," bringing islanders curiously inside European historical time, and certainly beyond savage, barbarian, or even pastoral stages in terms of stadial theory. Not that this was any compliment, because by "feudal" he meant "tyrannical." Most of the islanders, but especially those in the Friendly Islands (Tonga) and the Sandwich Islands (Hawai'i), dealt with turbulent "feudal" disputes, compounded by, even caused by, "the unchecked power of the chiefs over the 'degraded' lower orders." Cook (or really Hawkesworth) had termed it a "despotic" power. The power of the king in the Friendly Islands "was said to be unlimited, and the life and property of the subject at his disposal." The "inferior people" belonged to their chiefs as "property" and were beaten "most unmercifully" (said Cook, according to Malthus). This was a description of slavery, except that the Polynesian chiefs seemed to think the lowest "as absolutely of no value," not a society based on their labor, apparently. Thus, for Malthus, the common people (of the Sandwich Isles, for example) were servile and utterly obedient "debasing both their minds and bodies."[27]

It had become conventional by Malthus's time to compare if not equate the upper ranks of Tahitian society with European society, to construct a comparable Island monarchy, to receive Mai, for example, as a representative of South Sea nobility. By contrast, Malthus himself was eager to consider and compare the lowest ranked Tahitians with the lowest classes in England, and claimed that the former were "in a state of comparative degradation much below what is known in civilized nations."[28]

Tahiti's ranked social organization and governance had long been assessed by voyagers and Enlightenment scholars alike as a sign of their comparative civilization. Focusing on the lowest was thus not conventional "Tahiti." It was, however, conventional Malthus. He characteristically turned to consider the state of the poorest, perceiving that the principle of population was most acute among those closest to or on the line where lack of food first manifested. He was quite clear in his first edition: "The distress arising from a scarcity of provisions, must fall hardest upon the least fortunate members of the society." In his own society, he saw this as the "redundant" population, those out of work. In the case of New Holland Aboriginal societies he saw it as women. In the South Sea islands he saw it as the quasi-slaves who labored and provided luxuries for a rank of tyrants.[29]

Malthus styled the British in the South Sea as potential liberators of the savage poor, less because they brought Christianity than because they brought civilized political organization. Indeed, it is notable that even though Malthus came to be strongly involved in the controversial British and Foreign Bible Society, Christian mission was absent from this section of the *Essay*: he deployed the missionary account strictly ethnographically and, as it were, demographically. Population was a political and economic matter, and Malthus considered the poorest in Tahiti in the same way that he observed poor families in Lancashire or Surrey. The degradation of islanders by their overlords was as unwelcome and loathsome to him as the degradation of Irish Catholics by the English, which he was strongly to condemn some years later. It was not, after all, Christianity that was going to mitigate poverty in England or Ireland, it was (for Malthus) proper civil government that would begin by doing away with a Poor Law in England, doing away with the Catholic Codes in Ireland, and by educating people to plan ahead, aspire to something more, marry later, and have fewer offspring. Ultimately, for Malthus, civilization was aspirational: the "civilized man hopes to enjoy, the savage expects only to suffer." Educating people out of the expectation of degradation was Malthus's version of improvement, but for him this would both signal and require their movement out of a low stage of civilization. Stadial theory here met the political economy of poor relief, both in the context of colonial and humanitarian improvement. The single advantage of savage life, he decided, was the greater degree of leisure for the lowest, compared to the "incessant toil" of the lower classes of society in agricultural economies, in England for example. But he thought this South Sea advantage was entirely offset by the great tyranny of many of the island chiefs and lords.[30]

In ranging over so many different societies in preparation for his long edition, Malthus was constantly looking in voyagers' accounts and within existing histories for evidence of what happened to the "least fortunate." But he found his sources insufficient in this respect, repeatedly critiquing existing "histories of mankind," the tradition in which he was himself writing. Quite simply, he wrote, the lower classes were far too often ignored; "the misfortune of all history," he called it, meaning the misfortune of all history-writing. "The histories of mankind that we possess, are histories only of the higher classes. We have but few accounts that can be depended upon of the manners and customs of that part of mankind, where these retrograde and progressive movements [that is, the oscillation of population] chiefly take place." And elsewhere, he regretted that the histories of princes and leaders neglected to examine the motives of "willing followers." It is no wonder that Malthus was at least as much ethnographer as he was historian. But this was also consistent with his efforts to analytically privilege the aggregate over the single unit, population over the individual. His argument for the abolition of the Poor Law, for example, he regretted as difficult for individual families, but ultimately better economic policy for the whole. Private and public interest were not necessarily the same.[31]

This attention to the least powerful occasionally turned Malthus's history of man into a history of woman. At one level this was of a piece with Enlightenment histories, the indexing of civilization through gendered violence standard in stadial theory. But this was not the extent of Malthus's interest. Instead he looked for, and made strong claims about, the effects of different modes for the production of food on women's reproduction. For Malthus the new arts and technologies that enabled settlement after roaming, and then tillage after pasturage, had particular impacts on women's fertility, a causative relation. Population could increase in a shepherd society, for example, *because* "women live in greater ease than among nations of hunters." Aboriginal population was sparse *because* it was difficult for women to gather food effectively when roaming with more than one infant, and *because* such activity would be more likely to cause miscarriages. Like all stadial theorists Malthus pointed broadly to "want" and "the strong goad of necessity" that produced a distinct "spirit of enterprize," and that moved societies on from one stage to the next. This was what launched the northern Europeans out of savagery and into pastoral economies, at some point in history. But whereas most stadial theorists saw population increase as causing the transition from one mode of subsistence to another, Malthus tended to see it as a result of that change.[32]

*   *   *

Malthus's new "Book I" that so lengthened and conceptually expanded the substance of his original edition extended beyond the new world on both temporal and geographical axes. Fourteen chapters in all made up this section of the new *Essay*, including reflections on the principle of population in Africa, Siberia, the Turkish dominions, Persia, India, Tibet, China, and Japan. But this required a structural decision on how to reconcile ascending "civilization" and progressive historical time. In his own part of the world, progress from pastoral to agricultural and commercial stages *was* conventional history. Two chapters on the "modern pastoral nations"—on the ancient barbarians and on their Tatar and Mogul Eurasian descendants—directly followed Malthus's account of the new world, a progression from hunter-gatherers to "shepherds." And he concluded this book with chapters on classical Greece and Rome, including the barbarians who had brought about their downfall, received largely from Edward Gibbon's *History of the Decline and Fall of the Roman Empire*, in which he had delighted as a Cambridge student. Thus, for Malthus, "Past Times" in the title of his Book I meant Antiquity, considered immediately before his treatment of population in the states of modern Europe, considered in Book II.[33]

The peculiarities of late eighteenth-century stadial theory were thus built into the structure as well as the substance of this first book, geography and history divided in his title—"the Checks to Population in the less civilized parts of the world, and in past times." Malthus was writing a history that was as all-encompassing as he could possibly make it, but different geographies raised different temporalities. All the universal histories of civilization had to twist and turn in order to tell the story of successive economic stages over time and place. The "discovery" and observations of Pacific "savages" had vastly complicated the time and space of universal history, even as the voyagers themselves were clearly writing their accounts specifically within, and as contributions to, the "history of man" genre. Savages who had generically come to be written about in the past were now firmly back in the global present.[34]

In Malthus's history this difficulty was betrayed by his constantly alternating tenses. Some of Malthus's new world savages lived in the past, in historic time, and some in the present. Malthus tended to write about Native Americans in the past tense precisely because they were connected to the history of European expansion. Yet, ironically, this recognition of historical status therefore relegated them only to history, as belonging to the past, not the present. The Fuegians, Andaman Islanders, and Australian Aborigines, by contrast, were only written about in the present tense. The time being constructed was also a "dimension of power," as Johannes Fabian noted of all early anthropology. New world "savages" were placed outside civilization in a different way, located in a permanent prehistory. The generation after Malthus was to render antipodean "savages" into vestiges of an increasingly remote past: evolutionary time. Charles Darwin began to do so, when he read the *Essay on the Principle of Population*, importantly in its long edition. For Malthus, however, antipodean natives were rather more like Rousseau's infants or youths, living in a species that was old. They all existed in the *Essay's* present, but at the same time they were often rendered strangely separated from the actual process of European exploration and colonization that delivered up this information to Malthus in the first place. Such real and textual encounters make up part of the history of time itself.[35]

Pacific islanders—third in Malthus's series—occupied a different space again. He certainly used the present tense. New Zealand, for example, "contains some of the darkest shades that are anywhere to be met with in the history of human nature." The Polynesian "national" diaspora that Cook early remarked upon was especially brought into the "history of mankind" as an already historicized society, a society with its own past. Polynesian cyclical history was observable (or so the voyagers thought) in the comparative decline of Rapanui's population and Tahiti's crowded progress, for example. This was the historicity and variability of the Pacific Islands that Malthus himself repeated in the *Essay*, the cases that rounded out his suite of chapters on the new world.[36]

Twisting the neoclassical comparison between noble savages and worthy ancients, Malthus's unexpected final word in his chapter on the South Sea was not about the Pacific at all but about Sparta, a coda enabled by the complexity and confusions of stadial theory that characteristically leaped across global time and space. There was little nobility in the islands for Malthus, no Spartan simplicity to which Europeans should aspire. And even so, Malthus was not in the least beholden to the Rousseauean idea that the simplicity of the ancients was admirable. Indeed, he wrote entirely against it, calling the traditional admiration for Spartans absurd and the system of Spartan discipline preposterous; the tendency to inflate this characteristic to a worthy patriotism should be punctured. Instead, Malthus wrote, it was simply another response to perpetual want. Sparta was in fact miserable and in an "almost savage state." Far from an intellectual loyalty to his familial Rousseauean roots, this was more like David Hume's positioning of the ancients as a barbaric stage between agriculture and commerce.[37]

Successive chronology in Malthus's *Essay* functioned on yet another axis altogether: biblical time. Malthus's account of the ancient inhabitants of northern Europe that immediately followed the chapter on the South Sea served to illustrate the relation between population pressure and human migration, and it began with Genesis. Abram and Lot's land, "we are told," was insufficient for their two herds of cattle. Abram's response to the circumstance, his proposal to Lot that they separate and disperse in different directions, was for Malthus an early and simple version of what was in fact a perpetual response, the "great spring of action which overspread the whole earth with people." Continual pressure to migrate dispersed people over the globe "to seek a scanty subsistence in the burning deserts of Asia and Africa, and the frozen regions of Siberia and North America." Here, the phenomena of global human origin, migration, and difference were retold by Malthus in a way that stitched the biblical convention onto an Enlightenment history of humanity. Kames the polygenist had focused on the Tower of Babel episode to explain plural global difference. Malthus reintroduced a kind of diffusionism, though his attempt to reconcile his work with Scripture was passing, at best. Abram and Lot's dispersal became a history of Eurasia, in which North America was momentarily included as a continental extension, not as a new world across the ocean. He perhaps received this from William Robertson, who held to the thesis that American Indians were descended from the Tatars, having migrated across northern Asia. Accordingly, North America was included in this rendition of global migration, while the people Malthus had just detailed, the Pacific islanders, were not.[38]

Such inconsistencies abounded in the strange scholarly tradition of eighteenth-century historiography. Malthus, for example, seemed to move effortlessly between the biblical truth of Abram and Lot's dispersal and the account of the shepherds in the "middle latitudes of Europe and Asia," as told by Thucydides. And he read Arabic scholarship too. The genealogical history of the "great Tartar nation" came to him through translation of the seventeenth-century histories by Abū-al Ghāzī Bahādur. Through this work, Malthus claimed that the territory spreading from China to the Baltic was peopled by enterprising and warring barbarians, pressing in on "settled Governments" in China, Persia, Egypt, and Italy.[39]

This fluid movement across time and between tenses had to be shoehorned into an already complicated chronology that rendered Antiquity, Eurasian barbarity, prehistory, and biblical history part of one world historical story. Read together, then, these chapters shifted from an ethnography of antipodean savages in a permanent present, to North American Indian societies grafted onto European history and therefore, ironically, given the privilege of a past tense, to the present of Polynesia with its own distinct historicity, back to biblical time, and then to classic European history from Antiquity, to barbarians, and onwards to modern Europe. For all the differences between societies over time and place, Malthus thought that all "stages"—the lowest and the highest, the first and the last—were governed by the same principle of population. Thus, even though this edition of the *Essay* was driven structurally and conceptually by stadial theory that emphasized difference, human society was fundamentally one. What distinguished savage from civilized society was the means by which the negative checks on population (mortality through disease, famine, war) and immoral checks on fertility (infanticide, abortion) were mitigated and replaced by moral positive checks to population (management of fertility through later marriage). Differences across human societies were not irreconcilable, and this meant, in effect, that the savage could in theory become civilized. But as Malthus and others framed the situation, this would only materialize with the assistance, tolerance, and benevolence of those already civil. That was when antipodean "savages" turned into "natives," people to be managed by colonists and colonial governments.

PART III

Malthus and the New World, 1803–1834

Chapter 6

Slavery and Abolition

SOMETIME ON FEBRUARY 23, 1807, Malthus rushed, "distressed," to intercept William Wilberforce before the abolitionist leader entered the House of Commons. The West Indies planting and trading lobby had been citing the *Essay on the Principle of Population* in their support and claiming Malthus himself as "a friend to the Slave Trade." This had to be put right and in the most powerful of public spheres possible. Wilberforce proceeded to do so and later claimed Malthus as a convert to his cause. The eagerness with which Malthus sought to extricate his name and his theory from use by slave traders would seem to align with his Whig politics, his association with the abolitionist *Edinburgh Review*, his acquaintance with the Clapham group, and his dissenting education. Malthus had recently added a hurried footnote to his 1806 edition of the *Essay*, countering the arguments of British merchants and slave traders who had been deploying his work in their cause. But his statement gave hostages to fortune. "As long as the nations of Europe continue barbarous enough to purchase slaves in Africa," he wrote, "we may be quite sure that Africa will continue barbarous enough to supply them." Supporters of abolition would have welcomed the first clause; those on the opposite side could take refuge in the second.[1]

On closer inspection, Malthus's statement was more an ex post facto personal disclaimer than a principled attempt to further the abolitionist cause. Indeed, it is the absence of analysis of the West Indies and Atlantic slavery in the *Essay*, not its presence, that is striking and requires explanation. With the exception of the rushed, if lengthy, footnote, the British slave trade, slavery in North America, and the West Indian plantations barely featured in the *Essay* in any edition. Malthus did not pursue the extensive mid-eighteenth-century debates on slave versus free labor, nor, perhaps more surprisingly, did he squarely enter the extensive discussion on population and the slave trade, one of the major axes on which the whole abolition question turned. In his sweep across the globe in the long edition of the *Essay*, one part of the world that escaped treatment almost entirely was the West Indies, a neglect that extended to all other parts of the new world that had plantation economies that depended on slave labor.

This was not an innocent omission, given the very public nature of the debate on the slave trade and the vast wealth produced by slave labor in the British sugar colonies in those very years. It was not despite the controversial topicality of abolition, but because of it, that West Indian plantations and the contemporary slave trade made such brief appearances in the *Essay*. There was a private story too that at the very least contextualizes Malthus's clipped treatment but that may partially explain it as well. The Malthus family was involved in litigation over the inheritance of Jamaican plantation wealth, a matter unfolding over the years in which Malthus was revising his *Essay*, indeed, just when the abolitionist debate itself was reaching its apex. After the abolition of the slave trade (1807) and into the decades when antislavery reformers argued for emancipation, Malthus himself intermittently dealt with these family disputes over the division of profits from the annual sale of Jamaican crops. Thus, while historian of slavery and abolition Seymour Drescher suggests that "Malthus had no interest in slavery as a transatlantic phenomenon," when viewed in terms of his immediate family's legal business, perhaps Malthus had too much interest in the West Indies. The sugar islands might have been all too close to home.[2]

If Malthus's grandfather's and father's lifespans had coincided with the eighteenth-century upswing of West Indian planting and the slave trade that enabled it, Malthus's own life coincided with its apogee: it has been estimated that in the fifty years after 1775 British slave plantations in the Caribbean expanded tenfold. The slave trade itself peaked in the first years of the nineteenth century—just when Malthus was reworking his *Essay*. Although slave traders were in this case responding at least partly to accelerating abolitionist activity, they were also servicing an expanded geography for sugar planting, as new soils in Demerera and Trinidad, for example, came into cultivation: slavery was growing along with calls for its demise. When Malthus was still at Jesus College, Cambridge, the Society for Effecting the Abolition of the Slave Trade was established in London, and the first bill to abolish the slave trade was introduced into the House of Commons, in May 1788. With a great mobilization of petitions, the parliamentary process was repeated unsuccessfully in the 1790s, the years in which Malthus's dissenting tutor, Gilbert Wakefield, also took up the cause. The revolution in Saint Domingue that ended with Haitian independence in 1804, along with William Pitt the Younger's second ministry that year, changed the political landscape again, encouraging Wilberforce to introduce another unsuccessful bill to abolish the slave trade. It all came to pass in the early months of 1807. After Pitt's death, Lord Grenville introduced the Slave Trade Abolition Bill into the House of Lords on January 2, 1807. It came to the Commons on February 10, passed on February 23, returned for a further reading on March 16, and was assented on March 25, 1807. Either Malthus himself or his principle of population were present at each point in the parliamentary process. And while Wilberforce's defense of Malthus was part of the triumphant debate on February 23 that closed down British slave trading, the curious fact is that both opponents and proponents of the slave trade thought the principle of population useful.[3]

That is interesting in and of itself, but it is all the more so because few historians have noticed the role of Malthusian theories and Malthus himself within the story of the battle over abolition. His place there is primary evidence of the uncertainty of the battle against new world chattel slavery. Though the ending of slavery would seem inevitable, a part of the unfolding history of modernity in the West, that only appears to be the case in hindsight. Historically, the story was messy, nonlinear, and littered with ironies. Malthus's tentative disapproval of the slave trade, yet ultimate silence on the standing institution of slavery, could be taken as typical of a stage of reform, led by planters, that has been labeled *ameliorist*, an attempt to improve the lives of West Indian slaves without freeing them. And the fact that Malthusianism could support arguments either for or against slave trading powerfully demonstrates that even thinkers who have been categorized as supremely modern, perhaps especially those who wrote political economy, nevertheless could be perfectly useful to slaveholders and slave traders.[4]

* * *

Historical interpretations of the origins of antislavery have been typically sorted into two camps: humanitarian and economic. The humanitarian thesis emphasizes both the Christian desire (particularly among Evangelical Protestants) to prove the full value of the gospel through acts of liberation, as well as the secular reforms in human relations often put under the Enlightenment label. The traditional Christian doctrine of "one blood" explained why small groups of dissenters, notably Quakers from the Society of Friends, began to doubt the morality of slave ownership, let alone slave trading. So too did eighteenth-century *philosophes*, including Raynal and Franklin, begin to label slavery as barbaric and unjust. Other scholars, however, have emphasized the new awareness, especially during the eighteenth century, that neither the slave trade nor the slave-operated sugar plantations of the Caribbean were as good economic prospects as they had once been perceived to be. Most recent attempts to explain antislavery have used elements from each camp, as captured in the title (and analysis) of Christopher Leslie Brown's *Moral Capital* (2006). Still other scholars have warned, however, that many statements critical of slavery were intended to reform rather than dismantle it; slaveholders might therefore seem to be in accord with abolitionists, though in fact they were talking straight past them.[5]

Certainly attention to the political economy of slavery has brought the history of the Americas into a close Atlantic conversation with that of Great Britain. It was the Trinidad scholar Eric Williams who, in his *Capitalism and Slavery* (1944), suggested that sugar planting, however geographically remote from Great Britain, was the foundation of modern British society, funding everything from the eventual industrial revolution to hallowed sites of cultural prestige, including All Souls College, Oxford. Whether or not subsequent scholars have sought directly to vindicate the Williams "thesis," they have amply demonstrated two recurring phenomena. First, that in demographic terms, sugar was a matter of death more than life. In comparison to slaves on the North American continent, those in the Caribbean died at rates faster than they reproduced: mortality was the central characteristic of the West Indies. Second, people at the time knew it, which meant that analyses of the cost of death—in terms of insurance, losses from production, and cost of continued importation of laborers from Africa—were all heavily scrutinized matters. The pivotal *Zong* incident of 1781, in which a slave ship's captain flung at least 132 sickened slaves to their deaths in the sea, rather than face insurance losses on the "cargo," had galvanized contemporary attention to the value of slaves as individuals and as populations.[6]

To a very great extent, the antislavery debate was a transatlantic one, and it often generated statements (if not propaganda) championing national prestige. Citizens of the United States proclaimed that their republic stood for liberty, that their Constitution of 1789 (ratified the following year) had gloriously set a termination date (1808) for the slave trade, and that many of its states were in the process of emancipating slaves. Revolutionaries in France made similar claims, even as many of these promises were later rescinded, as with Napoleon's punitive invasion of revolutionary Haiti. British leaders and indeed even ordinary citizens felt obliged to respond to these international prompts, at the very least by addressing the worst abuses of chattel slaves, then perhaps with attention to abolishing the slave trade, with a smaller and more radical group venturing on to suggest emancipating slaves. The American Revolution galvanized British antislavery opinion twice over, first in its anti-British propaganda and again with the negative impact the war (and its aftermaths in the Napoleonic Wars) had on the trade in North American foodstuffs to hungry slaves in the sugar islands.[7]

These developments structured public debate during Malthus's life as an adult. He was fifteen in the year of the *Zong* massacre, twenty-four when the US Constitution was ratified, and he would be thirty eight in 1804, when Haiti declared its independence. In some ways he would seem to have been a logical enthusiast for these events. His publisher's circle included several antislavery authors; the Church of England was under pressure from reformers to declare its opposition to the slave trade. And yet there were countervailing influences. The Church of England had been active in upholding slavery, with its missionary body, the Society for the Propagation of the Gospel in Foreign Parts, actually a slaveholding entity with financial interests and property in the West Indies, if also with promises to set a model for humane and Christian treatment of chattels. It is little wonder that Malthus felt torn, given the division within the national institution that gave him faith, status, and livelihood.[8]

* * *

Slavery was notable for its absence in the first *Essay* of 1798. This is immediately surprising, given the long-established place of the subject in population theories, beginning with the reason-of-state texts of Bodin and Botero, which insisted that slaves, as members of polities and empires, must count and be counted. But Malthus only mentioned slavery twice, both times evading altogether its contemporary significance for Africa, Britain, the West Indies, the United States, and the rest of the Americas. Malthus described women in savage nations to be in a state of slavery: "much more completely in a state of slavery to the men, than the poor are to the rich in civilized countries." And second, he argued that barbarians often pursued the possibility of selling their own children into slavery in extreme circumstances, in times of famine, for example. In the 1803 edition, slavery in the United States was not discussed directly at all, while seventeenth-century Barbados was mentioned once in the context of the difficulty of colonization: "Even the plantation of Barbadoes, which increased afterwards with such extraordinary rapidity, had at first to contend with a country utterly desolate, an extreme want of provisions, a difficulty in clearing the ground unusually great, from the uncommon size and hardness of the trees, a most disheartening scantiness and poverty in their first crops, and a slow and precarious supply of provisions from England." Malthus thus sidestepped the West Indies geographically and contemporary slave labor substantively.[9]

This is not to say that slavery was absent from the *Essay*. Malthus dealt with the political economy of slavery at two points, first in a chapter on Africa and second in a chapter on Rome. Malthus's analysis of Africa is particularly important because it became a reference point at the height of the abolitionist debate in 1807. He relied heavily on two sources: Mungo Park's recently published, and highly celebrated, *Travels in the Interior Districts of Africa* (1799), which he used as the authority on West Africa; and James Bruce's *Travels to Discover the Source of the Nile* (1790), which he questioned more strongly but nonetheless mined for information on the north of the continent. Toward the end of the chapter, Malthus briefly considered Egypt through the work of Constantin François de Chassebœuf, comte de Volney, and although in an earlier chapter on America he had cited François Le Vaillant, *Voyage dans l'intérieur de l'Afrique, par le Cap de Bonne-Esperance* (1795), he did not refer back to this book in his chapter on Africa itself. And he did not utilize the extensive contemporary discussion on the recent colony of Sierra Leone at all. Indeed, all accounts of Africa from this era were deeply implicated in contemporary arguments over slavery and empire.[10]

Malthus's sources chronologically paralleled the travelers' accounts on which he relied for his Pacific chapter. Bruce (exploring North Africa while Cook sailed in the South Sea) and Park (struggling in West Africa while the London missionaries arrived in Tahiti) were both Edinburgh-educated explorers and travel-writers. They linked the Scottish Enlightenment with the London-based Association for Promoting the Discovery of the Interior Parts of Africa, founded in 1788 in the light of Bruce's journeys, and with strong direction from Joseph Banks. But unlike the Admiralty's extravaganzas in the Pacific in the 1770s, or the Missionary Society's plan to settle a community of Christians in Tahiti in the 1790s, Bruce and Park's journeys, and their accounts (which Malthus read), were those of the lone traveler, the sole observer, the model of travels within the Americas, as in William Bartram's 1791 account of his inland voyage of the southeastern corner of North America.

Edinburgh physician Mungo Park's journey inland via the Gambia and Niger rivers in 1795 was epic by any measure. Imprisonment and illness dogged his attempts to navigate West Africa, and returning to Scotland in

December 1797, he put it all down as *Travels in the Interior Districts of Africa*, published in 1799. Malthus opened his chapter on Africa with Park's observations that the regions through which he had traveled were neither well cultivated nor well peopled. Yet Park (and so Malthus) observed that while some areas were sparsely peopled and even deserted because they were "unhealthy," other parts were filled with potential for population and cultivation, though were neglected not by virtue of nature, but by virtue of "the general habits of the negroe nations." The demographic and economic situation was at least as much an effect of poor governance as poor climate, according to Malthus. Multiple small states warring constantly led to chronic insecurity of property. This in turn disinclined societies to "industry" and "improvement," by which Malthus meant cultivation beyond subsistence: the production of a surplus that could be traded was rare in this part of the world, he claimed. For Malthus, the African problem was insecurity of property in the first instance, not the lack of people per se. Without security of property, additional people in West Africa would only exacerbate distress. Critically for the uptake of his work in the abolitionist debate, Malthus emphasized incessant war, relying on Bruce: "For the last four hundred years . . . it has never ceased to lay desolate this unhappy country." This was not a useful statement for abolitionists, who generally charged slave traders with responsibility for African discontent. Indeed, it was a statement to be turned to some use by West Indian merchants, planters, and slave traders.[11]

The phenomenon of famine years in Africa was itself evidence that the total population was intermittently increasing "beyond the means of subsistence." From Park's account and *L'Histoire naturelle, générale et particulière* by Georges-Louis Leclerc, comte de Buffon, Malthus commented on the short life-spans of Africans: "longevity is rare." And—unusually, because he often disputed Montesquieu's climate-related arguments—Malthus thought that heat might be responsible for this fact: people in hotter climates were thought to reach maturity earlier, and so it made some sense that they might die younger. Whereas Buffon considered African women "prolific," Park noted that each woman had few children and that they nursed them for up to three years. Both Park and, in turn, Malthus put this period of infertility down to the diversion of the husband's sexual attention to other wives, not to any physiological effect of breastfeeding. In all, Malthus was comfortable claiming that at least those African societies described by Park were not increasing in numbers.[12]

Malthus repeated the claim that slavery was common in West Africa, as set out in Park's chapter "Observations on the State and Sources of Slavery in Africa." According to the Scottish traveler, there were three slaves for every one free man, at least in the regions he had visited. He reported strict protocols on slave trading among African communities. Neither domestic slaves, nor those born in the master's household, could be sold, except in extreme circumstances—such as famine times—to spare the life and health of a slave-owner's wife or children. Malthus speculated that this was incentive to limit the number of slaves both purchased and reproduced within any given household to the amount of labor—"employment"—available. With Park in hand, Malthus considered African slavery mainly in the light of food production. In famine years, the number of slaves would increase dramatically, Malthus recounting that even free men would sell themselves: "many free-men came, and begged with great earnestness, to be put upon his slave chain to save them from perishing with hunger." In other cases Park reported, mothers sold their sons in times of famine. And from Bruce, Malthus offered the following: "In Dixan . . . the only trade is that of selling children. Five hundred are exported annually to Arabia; and in times of scarcity, Bruce observes, four times that number." For Malthus, this was all at least as much evidence for famine as it was evidence for slavery. And although much of this chapter went on to deal with polygamy and reproduction, Malthus was at pains to ensure that his readers realized that population trends were a result of food availability to a far greater extent than of human fertility: "how little population depends on the birth of children, in comparison of the production of food, and of those circumstances of natural and political situation which influence this produce."[13]

The net rise or fall of the African population was an old question, and by addressing it Malthus lent his name, the most important within political arithmetic at the time, to an ongoing debate over whether the slave trade had any negative demographic impact. "Africa has been at all times the principal mart of slaves," he admitted. And he claimed that the continent had experienced a relatively constant drain of population due to a slave trade, but more so "since their introduction into the European colonies." This was one of the very few references to new world slavery in the 1803 edition. Here Malthus touched on a major line of eighteenth-century inquiry. Robert Wallace's argument in *A Dissertation of the Numbers of Mankind in Ancient and Modern Times* (1753) had been that population had decreased over time, including statements that the slave trade had depopulated Africa. On the other hand, Malthus read Hume's and Kames's counterclaims. Kames had written "that Negroland is well peopled is past doubt, considering the great annual draughts from the country to America, without any apparent diminution of numbers." And Hume's critique of slavery in "On the Populousness of Ancient Nations" had also been framed by discussion of numbers of people, arguing that part of the reason the population had in fact increased over time was that the practice of slavery (meaning villeinage) had declined early, so it had been absent in Europe for centuries.[14]

For Hume, modern liberty was defined against ancient slavery, and he articulated a traditional argument that the slave owner exercised tyrannical power on a local scale. Like Montesquieu and Franklin, Hume considered waged labor to be more productive than slave labor. Adam Smith had later famously honed the economic argument against slavery in favor of free labor, although as Drescher stresses, "political economy's second generation did not elaborate on Smith's potentially potent thesis." This is significant, not least since Malthus was to teach the *Wealth of Nations* to East India College students year in, year out, for decades.[15]

A more thorough discussion of the political economy of slavery appeared in Malthus's chapter on the Romans that concluded Book 1 of all post-1798 editions of the *Essay*. He explained that normally—"in modern states"—those who have no land and no means to support themselves would sell their labor to the rich in order to prevent their own and their family's starvation. But in ancient Rome that work had been performed by slaves: the wealthier Rome became, the more slaves there were, filling up "every employment both in agriculture and manufactures." This was, perhaps, an oblique reference to the debate on free versus slave labor, but Malthus connected it immediately to poor relief, on which he was always willing to speak publicly. In a major error of classic public welfare policy, at least in Malthus's view, the free poor were only able to exist because of Rome's custom of distributing free grain.[16]

Malthus's commentary on Roman slavery was not mere antiquarianism. Rome was both a comparative reference point and an object lesson, a classic example in stadial theory and therefore cited by both critics and supporters of modern slavery. In one of his abolitionist speeches in the House of Commons, for example, Henry Thornton referred to Gibbon, "to shew that, when the sources of procuring slaves were cut off by the union of Asia and Africa with the Roman empire, the Romans obtained them by the more tedious method of propagation, which was promoted by mild treatment, and encouraging marriage." Malthus would have been quite aware of the possible significance of the classical case for the West Indies. But (for once) he was not drawn into a discussion of his favored Gibbon.[17]

He did, however, develop Wallace and Hume's well-known comparison between the keeping of slaves and the keeping of cattle and in this way identified himself with the ameliorationist debate over humane treatment of slaves. Wallace, Malthus explained, had drawn this comparison to show that it would be in the interest of masters to take care of their reproducing slaves. Hume, by contrast, argued through the same analogy that it would be in the interests of masters to prevent, not encourage, their reproduction. Malthus thought Hume correct: it would be cheaper to buy more labor (more slaves) than to raise them. In general, Malthus conceded that slave populations did not reproduce strongly, for one reason or another. Later (in 1806), he was to note briefly that slave populations in the West Indies did not increase naturally because of their ill treatment. But given this line of argument on slavery in Rome, it is little wonder that the slave-trade defenders thought Malthus rather more in their corner than that of the abolitionists.[18]

In applying Hume and Wallace to ancient Rome and not the West Indies, Malthus was evading the immediate political context. It is notable, to say the least, that Malthus's treatment of slavery was sectioned off geographically and temporally to Africa on the one hand, and ancient Rome on the other, with some short analysis of slavery in China as well. Malthus thus managed in his first and second editions to cleave slavery from the Americas almost entirely. That was a feat in itself. And it was at sharp variance with his acknowledged source Benjamin Franklin, who had, a half-century earlier, openly questioned whether sugar and slaves represented tangible benefits to the British Empire, using sophisticated analysis of their (small) contribution to the consumer economy—and supplying relevant statistics. Malthus's silence on the Caribbean islands is also at odds with his interest, elsewhere, in islands as sites of production and reproduction; thus had he analyzed England and Tahiti. But what makes this silence on the sugar islands even more striking is the fact that the public debate on slavery, the slave trade, and abolition had been shot through with talk of population for over a generation.

Shelves of publications on West Indian and African population were readily available to Malthus, from small pamphlets to multivolume works, every one of which he set aside. He did not, for example, cite Lord Muncaster's *Historical Sketches of the Slave Trade, and of its Effects in Africa* (1792) or Gilbert Francklyn's *Observations: Occasioned by the Attempts Made in England to Affect the Abolition of the Slave Trade; shewing, the Manner in which Negroes are Treated in the West-Indies* (1789), books easily accessible in his cousin Jane Dalton's library, if not his father's, one of whom also kept Hannah More's *Slavery,*

A Poem (1788). Someone in the Malthus family bothered to clip a series of articles on the slave trade for the commonplace scrapbook, and the family collection now in the Jesus College Old Library contains early nineteenth-century pamphlets on the West Indies, which were bound together with Malthus's reviews of books on Ireland, published in 1808. This included Joseph Lowe's "Inquiry in the State of the British West Indies" (1807), a defense of planters. Nor did Malthus refer to abolitionist or antislavery works published or sold by Joseph Johnson, including the powerfully influential *Interesting Narrative of the Life of Olaudah Equiano* (1789). And he ignored the vast amount of statistical material on West Indian births and deaths that had been compiled and argued over for decades. Malthus thus also pointedly ignored population data from colonial returns referenced extensively in parliamentary debate and readily available as published speeches. In short, the famous political economist of population was failing to engage with major population data which everyone else was routinely consuming and assessing.[19]

The demographic effect of the trade on African societies had been part of the public discussion from the earliest abolitionist mobilization in the 1780s. As Drescher notes, abolitionists themselves had firmly reoriented the terms of debate "from production to reproduction and from economics to demography," hoping to avoid discussion of the wealth produced by West Indian trade, since it was so very great and so very important to national revenue. Indeed, the fertility and mortality of slave populations in the Caribbean have constituted strong lines of inquiry ever since. The questions have remained more or less the same, even if available data, demographic method, and the politics behind investigations have changed. What was the rate of natural increase among slave populations? Did deaths exceed births, and if so why? And thus: was the slave trade necessary to maintain the population, or even to expand it so that more land could be freshly cleared and planted by slave labor? Abolitionists argued that African population was steadily diminishing due to the slave trade and that the importation of new slaves was unnecessary in the West Indies: natural increase, slowly recovering, was sufficient for the plantations. Planters argued routinely on a demographic basis too, for the slave trade to be sustained. Low fertility and high mortality demonstrated the demand for new slaves from Africa; and a greater aggregate population was needed in any case to augment clearance and cultivation in the sugar colonies. Political arithmetic somewhat later than theology, but certainly alongside ethics and economy, had been a persistent mode of argumentation in the debate on abolition, long before Malthus was drawn into the discussion—indeed, long before he even contemplated a principle of population.[20]

Thomas Cooper, for example, had early published a statistical supplement to his *Letters on the African Slave Trade* (1787), which set out the figures and calculations leading to the claim that Africa lost 510,000 souls annually. This was a convoluted and difficult abolitionist argument because it suggested a robust replacement of that lost population within Africa. Nonetheless, versions of it endured into the next century. The Edinburgh reviewer of Brougham's *A Concise Statement of the Question regarding the Abolition of the Slave Trade* (1804), for example, claimed that the traffic "condemns a whole quarter of the world to unceasing and ferocious warfare—which annually exterminates more men than fall during the bloodiest campaign of European hostility." Equally, years before Malthus's *Essay*, Pitt the Younger had framed the discussion squarely in terms of births and deaths in slave populations in the West Indies, calculating that the excess of deaths over births was diminishing. Wilberforce used Pitt's data in 1791: "The natural progress of population" was returning to the West Indies, with births almost equalling deaths, and this trend indicated both that importation was no longer required and that it would, of itself, consolidate that trend toward greater natural fertility, "propagation" as Wilberforce put it. Despite such optimistic forecasts, it was generally accepted that deaths exceeded births in most if not all Caribbean populations, and long-term growth of the slave population, including the more acute expansion immediately before abolition, was due to the importation of slaves, not their natural increase. This is the more recent consensus as well, that the Caribbean was the "Reaper's Garden," in a reference to death personified.[21]

In such ways, a great many planters and abolitionists, politicians and merchants, all thought of Atlantic slavery in terms of population. As Malthus put his research on slavery in Africa and Rome to paper, slavery in the West Indies was daily news. His silence on the West Indies and on contemporary slavery more generally (as with production of cotton in the United States) was an act of avoidance. It is difficult to say precisely why Malthus set aside all of this available material on fertility and mortality in slave societies either in the West Indies or anywhere else in the Americas, foregoing an extraordinary opportunity to analyze closely documented population changes. Perhaps he considered abolitionist and antiabolitionist material too partisan, too political for his empirical purposes. Perhaps he considered plantations as altogether exceptional circumstances (he was to claim this obliquely in the 1806 edition).

Perhaps there were additional private reasons, since the Malthus family was just then becoming embroiled in financial claims on a Jamaican plantation.

* * *

Like many men of his generation and class, Thomas Robert Malthus was connected to the African slave trade, slavery in the West Indies, and the wealth derived from sugar plantations. Some of the Malthus family's considerable wealth had been acquired through investment in slave-trading companies, helping to lift the late eighteenth-century generation from a line of lawyers and apothecaries (albeit royal apothecaries) to country gentlemen able to botanize and write books. His father's uncle, James Eckersall, had speculated in the Royal African Company (1660–1752), which was originally granted a monopoly on all English trade to West Africa, and Eckersall documented the movement of slaves in his journals. In 1740 he noted the company's contract to supply four hundred slaves in January and another two hundred in May, detailing three ships newly fitted for the Cape Coast, their "cargo" valued at £2,500 each. The family also invested in the South Sea Company (established 1711), the joint stock company (and eventually notorious financial "bubble") that commanded the *asiento*, the monopoly to supply slaves and other trade items to Spanish America. The company's business also shipped slaves to Jamaica. An earlier Sydenham Malthus (who had, as they all seemed to do, married a cousin, a Dalton) was a director of the company in the early 1750s.[22]

In Malthus's generation the family connection with slavery, plantations, and the West Indies became far more direct. In 1783 his cousin Mariana (or Marianna) Georgina Ryves (1766–1830) shocked the family by eloping with William Leigh Symes, marrying when they were both only seventeen, she likely pregnant. At that young age, Symes became far more than a remote speculator in the slave trade, inheriting (also in 1783) the Oxford Estate in St. Mary Parish, Jamaica. This was a substantial plantation of about a thousand acres, and it was where William Leigh Symes died in 1796. An inventory taken on his death valued the estate possessions at £19,880. His widow remarried, but this time back into her own family, as if to redeem herself. In 1799 (or 1798, according to some sources) she married Sydenham Malthus, Robert's older brother. Mariana Georgina Malthus, née Symes, thus became Thomas Robert's sister-in-law as well as cousin. They were exact contemporaries, born in the same year.[23]

This marriage back into the family rendered Symes family business that of the Malthus family as well. As was the case with all absentee sugar planters, they operated their business through agents and, in this case, a most untrustworthy trustee. Symes had appointed his brother-in-law Henry Swann, later Tory MP, trustee of the estate along with its "negros and slaves," and in his will required that Mariana Georgina be paid £500 per year for the rest of her life. Swann was also made guardian of six surviving Symes children, who now lived in the Malthus circle in Surrey, the oldest (Robert) fourteen, the youngest (George Frederick) four. Both Symes's will and papers in Jamaica clearly recorded that the Oxford Estate was the "property of the heirs of Symes," but Swann managed to hold onto the plantation until his death in 1824. By 1819 the Jamaican Crop Accounts described the estate as "the property of Henry Swann" and its produce—that year 181 hogsheads of sugar and 101 puncheons of rum—were also consigned to Henry Swann.[24] He did well from the plantation, managed intermittently by his brother and a succession of overseers, although it slowly decreased in size. In 1807 the Oxford Estate was 840 acres, and by 1819 the Tory MP "owned" 195 slaves.[25]

This possession was disputed all along in the Court of Chancery. Apart from the question of ownership of the estate, Swann was neither paying Mariana Georgina an annual jointure of £500 nor other debts incurred to the estate after Symes's death. One major unsettled debt was to the Hibbert family. In May 1804, West Indian merchants Hibbert and Purrier lodged a bill of complaint as creditors to the late William Leigh Symes, a debt now accruing to Swann. City merchants, the Hibberts for many years shipped Oxford plantation sugar and rum to London's docks. The Hibbert family covered the two ends of Jamaican planting and commerce profitably: Thomas Hibbert had been a planter in Jamaica since 1734, and his set of estates reached three thousand acres and included nine hundred slaves by the end of the century; meanwhile, nephew George Hibbert traded from London and was a principal of the company that opened the new West India docks in 1800. Hibbert was to become agent-general for Jamaica in 1812 and, as we shall see, directly implicated Malthus in parliamentary debate on the slave trade. In August 1804 Swann answered the powerful Hibberts that he had not sufficient income from the Jamaican estate either to pay their debt or the jointure due to Mariana Georgina Malthus. Sydenham Malthus himself pursued the matter in January 1805, charging the Oxford plantation with the jointure, monies owed to his stepchildren, plus a claim on an estate at Esher, Surrey, that had belonged to William Leigh Symes. By May 1806, Sydenham and Mariana Malthus were seeking £4,500 (nine years' unpaid jointure), which Swann still refused to pay. Significantly, their complaint also sought new managers to run the Jamaican Oxford Estate.[26]

At that point, Mariana Georgina's oldest son, Robert Symes, turned twenty-one (in December 1806) and began to pursue Henry Swann on his own behalf, submitting that Henry Swann possessed sufficient funds from the Estate's profits to pay Symes's debt to the Hibberts, monies owed to his mother (Mariana Malthus), and to the younger Symes children. Finally, Robert Symes claimed the Oxford Estate in Jamaica itself, arguing that Swann had taken improper possession of the plantation and "has enjoyed the rents, profits, negros, slaves, cattle, plantation stock belonging to Robert Symes." He itemized his claim to goods, humans, and real estate, listing storehouses, millhouses, sugarhouses, boiling houses, burning houses, kilns, "negros and other slaves . . . together with the increase and progeny . . . and also all horses and mules, cows, oxen, sheep and other cattle and all plantation tools, implements, good, chattels."[27] Over 1807, then, Malthus's step-nephew, who had lived with his brother and the wider Malthus family in Surrey for nearly ten years, had come of age and was claiming possession of a sugar plantation in Jamaica and ownership of that estate's slaves and their offspring. It was an unsuccessful bid, though Robert continued to pursue his claim to the Estate itself into the mid 1820s.[28] After the Slavery Abolition Act (1833) 169 slaves on the Oxford Estate were emancipated, and compensation for this "loss" went neither to the Swanns nor to the Symes/Malthus family. It was in fact John Gladstone, father of William Ewart Gladstone, who was awarded £3059 in 1835 as the new owner-in-fee of the disputed Oxford Estate.[29]

The extended saga, with overtones of the famous Jarndyce versus Jarndyce case in Chancery that runs, comically and tragically, through Charles Dickens's *Bleak House*, amply demonstrates how slaves were conspicuous by their presence in British society, even if they were physically absent from Britain. This was because slaves' labor was commodified and then financially abstracted, whether through mortgage, jointure, or absentee ownership. Plantation proceeds were thus fluid and highly mobile. A person did not have to own slaves to reap the profits, and British law protected those profits.

On behalf of his brother, Thomas Robert Malthus acted directly and personally in the long-running Jamaican matters. Often absent in Geneva and in Rome, Sydenham Malthus left Robert with power of attorney over much of his business, including "money . . . out of the Jamaica Estate." And when Sydenham Malthus died in 1821, it fell to Robert as executor to sort out the remaining mess as best he could (complicated by a new claim, from someone who appears to have been an illegitimate daughter of William Leigh

Symes), and to pursue the entitlements for Mariana Georgina, his cousin turned sister-in-law. By that point, the question circled around whether her jointure might be paid in Jamaica, claimed directly from estate managers, rather than in Britain, claimed from the elusive Swann. She was reassured that "you are entitled to the money as it becomes due, without waiting for the Sale of the Crop." William Bray, family lawyer, advised that she discuss the matter with her famous brother-in-law, since he was entirely familiar with the case, "acquainted with Mr Swann [and can] say what will be best to be done." She did so, and with Malthus's help Mariana Georgina Malthus eventually received the jointure owed to her. This meant that until her death in Albury, Surrey, in 1830, the family was benefiting from the wealth that the Oxford Estate slaves were producing.[30]

In the meantime, Thomas Robert Malthus's direct role also intensified through a connection with the youngest Symes, nephew George Frederick. Having entered the East India Company's military in 1813, Symes was posted across the subcontinent, and it was his uncle who took responsibility in London for his claims on the Oxford Estate. Symes instructed Malthus at one point thus: "If Mr Swann pays the whole or part of his Fortune on demand he should like to have £200 or £300 remitted to him." Malthus continued to manage matters for his Indian-based step-nephew into the 1820s, in part because in 1824 Symes also married back into the family (to a cousin, Katherine Ryves). Through family solicitors, Bray and Warren, Thomas Robert Malthus engaged in intricate business for several years, concerning, for example, "who should be employed in Jamaica." Swann, needless to say, continued to prevaricate at every turn, right up until his death.[31]

This family story of inheritance, annuities, marriage, remarriage, illegitimate claimants, and endless dispute over property was quotidian for Malthus's milieu. Cousins married constantly in order to keep wealth within familial bounds or to bring it back into the family, as in this case, and the Malthus tribe outdid itself in this respect. Even the fact that West Indian plantation and slave-derived wealth was implicated was more common than uncommon for Malthus's class. Yet there are several elements to this family history that make it pertinent context, at the very least, for Thomas Robert Malthus's reluctance to engage in robust public discussion on the political economy (and demography) of the slave trade and slavery.

First, these were not temporally remote matters; they were coincident. The years in which the matter arose for the Malthus family (1799), was pursued (1803–1804), and reached Court of Chancery (1806–1807) accounted for not just the period in which Malthus was writing and rewriting his *Essay* but included the very months when the abolitionist debate was at its height in the House of Commons and the House of Lords. (Interestingly, old radical Daniel Malthus, who died in 1800, was not on hand for the majority of this period to offer his opinions about slavery.) Second, two actors involved in the Oxford Estate dispute both happened to be members of Parliament in those very years. Henry Swann was member for Yarmouth in 1803–1804 and for Penryn from 1806 until his death in 1824 (with the notable exception of a period in Marshalsea prison in 1819, for corruption), while George Hibbert was elected member for Seaford from 1806 to 1812. They were both participants in, and profiteers from, the slave trade, just when it was under strongest attack, and witnessed its round defeat in the Commons in February 1807. Finally, in his own parliamentary speeches opposing abolition, George Hibbert himself invoked Malthus's principle of population. This was the proximate cause for Malthus's late and reluctant public statement against the slave trade. Lines of connection—familial, commercial, political, legal—crossed, as public and private worlds folded into one another.

For centuries, wealth from the production and consumption of slave-produced goods had pervaded private and familial spaces in Britain, just as it shaped public endeavors. Edward Said's famous observation about the ubiquity of the West Indies in Jane Austen's novels, and the subsequent identification of West Indian interests in the Austen family, have been the most famous example of Britons' profound, quotidian dependence on the fortunes of sugar, legacies of which continue even today. Abolitionists of Malthus's generation politicized the intricate connection between private and public domains, urging their fellow subjects to reconsider every act of domestic consumption in terms of the moral cost of purchasing slave-produced commodities, thereby diminishing demand for them. The cause thus entered and implicated homes and families. Malthus, it seems, worked hard to keep the private versus public considerations of a slave economy firmly separate, just as he was trying to keep the West Indies and slavery apart in his otherwise expansive history of the economic world. And yet he could not sustain this separation of matters. In the end, it was not because of his family's involvement in Jamaica that Malthus was forced to take a public position, but simply because "population" ran so deeply through the abolitionist debate.[32]

* * *

Malthus very much wanted to attend the critical slave-trade debate in the House of Commons on February 23, 1807, but was not quite organized enough to make it. Or at least so he told his Jesus College friend and traveling companion, now professor of mineralogy, Edward Clarke: "I went to town ... but was too late." This is just when he intercepted Wilberforce, however, and furnished him with information and argument to counter the public statements that had recently connected him to the slave trade. Malthus expressed abhorrence for the traffic in humans, but the real urgency seems to have been a concern about his reputation. He himself said the intervention was about rescuing his character. "I would have been much distressed if the accusation had been made without being contradicted." After so much studied avoidance in the *Essay*, Malthus offered himself—more or less reluctantly—to the public sphere on abolition.[33]

Given the standard demographic mode of argumentation on both sides, it would be surprising if Malthus and his suddenly famous book had not become implicated in the debate. This was first done publicly in the February 16, 1805 issue of pro-slave-trade William Cobbett's new *Political Register*, the weekly précis and commentary on parliamentary debate that was later sold to the printer, Thomas Curson Hansard. Perhaps to heighten the shock of a Malthusian interpretation, Cobbett made an awkward reference to homosexuality: "*celibacy*, and other circumstances therewith connected" were pertinent, he thought, in the context of slave populations' failure to naturally increase by procreation. Cobbett ventured that even Wilberforce would not want to open that field for discussion, but if he did, he might wish to refer "to the profound work of Mr Malthus, who has not scrupled to recommend *checks to population*, as conducive to the *good* of mankind." Close to a year later, on January 18, 1806, *Cobbett's Weekly Political Register* included a long pro-slave-trade piece that began with the claim that Malthus's principle of population offered much-needed clarity of reason among so much excitement. Cobbett much later was to attack Malthus in his *Advice to Young Men* (1829), but at this point he glowed, freely claiming Malthus's principle of population in the anti-abolitionist cause: it offered a "luminous principle" that entirely undid, according to Cobbett, the "hypocritical humanity" of the abolitionists. It so happens that Cobbett had been introduced to Malthus's argument by West Indian trader George Hibbert: "The application of Malthus's doctrine (a doctrine which never can be shaken) is most happy," wrote Cobbett to Hibbert. "I have to thank you for pointing out to me so able a supporter. Malthus is becoming, with regard to this subject, what Newton is with regard to Astronomy. He will be found a most powerful supporter of our opinions. Indeed, after having read his book, the visionary nonsense about the population of Africa slides gently and imperceptibly out of the mind." Their correspondence reveals just how unequivocally Malthus's work could be claimed as pro slave trade.[34]

In that issue, Cobbett's correspondent, "Senex," wanted to dismiss the claim that incessant war in Africa was an effect of the slave trade, and, unhappily for Malthus, the *Essay on the Principle of Population* (1803) was his key authority. Over multiple columns, the first three pages of Malthus's African chapter were reprinted verbatim. The intention was to persuade the reader that wars in Africa were more or less permanent, that they antedated the European slave trade, and thus (the writer argued) abolition of the trade would have no particular impact. Malthus's reliance on Park was what mattered.

> The statement of Mr Malthus (connected as it is with the well known fact, that the wars which Park declares to be the primary cause of Slavery in Africa, are at this day neither more frequent, more atrocious, nor more lightly undertaken than they were in the same districts three or four hundred years ago), seems to me to lead to a conviction that the abandonment of the Slave Trade would, under such circumstances, no more benefit Africa than the drawing an impenetrable line of circumvallation around it, would benefit a garrisoned town, already overstocked with inhabitants.[35]

So much of the *Essay* was reprinted in the widely read *Political Register*, and in a letter that was so determinedly pro slave trade, that Malthus had to respond. He was bound to act.

Yet Malthus's treatment of the West Indian slave trade—at last—was indirect. The intervention came not in the body of the *Essay* but in a last-minute final footnote to the appendix of the 1806 edition that appeared in March. Malthus rushed his footnote addition over "while the last sheet of this Appendix was printing." It is an important supplement to the *Essay*, precisely because the West Indian colonies were nowhere else treated, and yet its add-on status betrays avoidance as much as afterthought.[36]

Malthus offered a convoluted self-defense. He explained that if the abolitionist position rested on the argument that the slave trade depopulated Africa, his principle of population would have countered that concern. But, he said, he was not aware of that argument ever being put forward as a ground for abolition. Instead, he nominated the two common arguments for abolition of the trade: first that the trade itself and the treatment of slaves in the West Indies "is productive of so much human misery, and that its continuance is disgraceful to us as men and as Christians"; and second that the West Indies' plantations could viably continue without the further importation of slaves. But these were the classic abolitionist arguments, not necessarily Malthus's own. He then went on to explain (in contradistinction to his second point) that the fact that continual importation of new slaves from Africa seemed to be necessary to keep up the population in the West Indies indicated some kind of excessive check to the natural increase in the islands themselves. That is, the power of reproduction would—ordinarily—be so great that natural increase should return a population to a level equal with subsistence. If this was not happening, some "*excessive* and *unusual*" check, force, or action was necessarily in play, words that Malthus had the poor typesetter put in italics three times. The West Indies were exceptional. The very fact that the population was maintained *only* by importation was for Malthus evidence that the conditions were "most wretched, and that the representations of the friends of the abolition cannot easily be exaggerated." If, he went on, the abolition of the slave trade improved even marginally the treatment and condition of slaves already in the West Indies, the population would increase proportionally by procreation alone, to meet the demand for labor. Even in the worst-governed countries of the world, he said, populations did so. Thus he wound his way finally to an abolitionist position, though not an emancipationist one, in contrast to other public figures at the time, and here again his overall effort was congruent with planters' efforts simply to reform the worst abuses of the Atlantic system rather than annul it entirely.[37]

Malthus also explained his statements on Africa. He asked the reader to understand that in describing population trends in that continent he was not intending to assess the question of the slave trade. To do so, he dissembled, would lead him into "too long a digression." But since he had now been brought into that discussion by others (he seemed to imply), he was perfectly happy to state that the facts he had gathered, mainly from Park, strongly suggested that wars in Africa were indeed compounded by the trade: "excited and aggravated by the traffic on the coast." The problem was that the trade made capturing and selling slaves more lucrative than agricultural or manufacturing labor. Slave trading may well have been ancient in Africa, he admitted, but the European traffic nonetheless continued to grant it significant additional value— and, problematically, value over and above agricultural work.[38]

As Drescher has noted, the abolitionists "were not particularly happy with Malthus's link between slavery and population in Africa." Malthus—who had not looked at the data, even though slave populations in West Indies were perhaps the most studied, calculated, and recalculated population of all—ended up offering a less than useful "abolitionist" argument. Whether or not abolitionists believed that slave populations maintained themselves by natural increase (which would render trade in new slaves from Africa unnecessary as well as immoral), they expediently made this claim. Indeed, as the slave trade debate entered the houses in Westminster in 1807—as it turned out for the last time—abolitionist parliamentarians clearly felt they had to refer to the new "principle of population" because so much of the debate was about just that. And yet in doing so, they often found they had to explain Malthus's own "abolitionist" argument away.[39]

Key among the parliamentarians was the Whig Lord Grenville, who had a long and fractious relationship with Malthus. They exchanged public verbal blows in 1813 and 1817 over the East India Company College.[40] Grenville referred to the principle of population when introducing the abolitionist bill to the House of Lords on February 5, 1807. In doing so, he had to undo some of Malthus's own arguments to make the principle of population work in and for the abolitionist cause. He raised the political arithmetic of slave trading that he had himself pursued with Pitt the Younger, who had died in January 1806 and whom he had recently succeeded. Some arguments, he explained, held that the population of the islands could not be maintained without "fresh importations." But then (and this was a reference to Malthus's recent footnote) "[we are] told that that law of nature, which has hitherto been considered as universal, meets with an exception in the West Indies, and that there alone the increase and multiplication of the human species does not take place." Grenville wished to take issue with both of these positions. His abolitionist argument was that in fact the much-cited excess of deaths over births (the supposed great mortality in the West Indies that justified continuing slave importations or in Malthus's instance indicated excessive check) was itself an error. With Pitt, he claimed that he had calculated deaths and births from 1730 to 1800. This showed "that the population of the island is perfectly competent to support itself." In the same session in the Lords, February 5, 1807, Thomas Douglas, Earl of Selkirk, mentioned Malthus by name but similarly avoided Malthus's own "abolitionist" argument about excessive deaths. Rather, Selkirk explained the principle of population working thus: "In countries where the means of human subsistence were proportionate to the number of inhabitants, the increase of population had always been found progressive. This principle had been acknowledged by all writers on the subject, and had been unanswerably explained in the able work of Mr Malthus upon population." Selkirk was just then deeply involved in a different kind of population movement in those years: clearance evictions in Scotland and the colonization of Upper Canada with emigrant Highlanders. In that capacity he was immersed in Malthus's work, planning and prospecting for new colonial settlements.[41]

Thus, when the abolition bill came to the Commons on February 23, 1807, population, the "principle of population," and Malthus himself, were each firmly part of the debate. Population was introduced first by the Whig

Lord Howick, later Earl Grey, and then secretary of state for foreign affairs. Those opposed to abolition, he said, stressed the incapacity of the West Indian slave population to replace itself, the excess of deaths over births. Howick reiterated Pitt's demographic work yet again, which countered these claims: they showed, he stressed, that the "number of births was increasing, and the number of deaths diminishing." The balance was currently nearly equal in Jamaica, he claimed, and indeed in Dominica, the Bermudas, and Bahamas births exceeded deaths. "When the causes were considered that checked the population of the West Indies, there was reason to believe that, by the regulations which the abolition would produce, nature would there, as in other countries, accomplish her own ends, and that the population would maintain itself." Early in the famous debate, then, Lord Howick drew on Malthus's terms directly—the "principle of population" and "checks" to population—but toward a different line of argument, or at least a different emphasis, than Malthus's own with respect to the West Indies. Indeed, Howick ignored Malthus on the West Indies altogether—the 1806 footnote that had stressed the great mortality—while still putting Malthus's general theory to work: "According to the principle of population confirmed by experience, the numbers would increase, unless checked by some powerful cause." This natural increase, Howick claimed, was evident in St. Helena after abolition, and even in Bencoolen, "the most unhealthy place in the world." It was also evident in the slave population in North America, where they "double their number in twenty years." Howick thus incorporated evidence of slave population growth in the United States, the data that Malthus consistently failed to use. The increase of the slave population in the West Indian colonies was not dependent on continued traffic, he argued; rather, it could and should be remedied by the planters themselves: population increased with good treatment and improvement of moral and physical conditions.[42]

This was in fact also Malthus's position. Lord Mahon concurred that the population would increase as an effect of abolition. Abolitionists insisted that the natural increase of slaves already in the West Indies was, in essence, a positive outcome, while at the same time condemning the traffic itself: as Lord Mahon put it, "a system which would disgrace times and countries the most barbarous and uncivilized." The bitter irony was that this particular argument for abolition of the slave trade rested on an increasing number of slaves, and it again matched the ameliorist program to avert attacks on slaveholding itself.[43]

As we have seen, Malthus wanted to sit in the gallery to witness the Commons debate on February 23, 1807 but had arrived too late, or at least so he told Edward Clarke. The next day, he must have read the *Times* account with some anxiety, given his family's business in Jamaica, but also, perhaps, with some relief up to that point, since "his" principle of population was now invoked in the abolitionist cause, albeit not consistently with his own argument. But then, surely, his heart sank. Malthus's name was next introduced into the Commons debate, not by an abolitionist but by George Hibbert, West India merchant and member of the well-known Jamaican planting and trading family, who had been shipping consigned sugar and rum from the Oxford Estate to the London docks for years. This was the very complainant then pursuing Henry Swann (also MP) for debts incurred by William Leigh Symes, business that Sydenham Malthus and Mariana Georgina Malthus were also just then answering in the Court of Chancery. Thus, while Wilberforce's and Howick's deployment of Malthus is important and interesting, perhaps more significant—certainly more unexpected and less noted—was George Hibbert's. Hibbert was elected to the Commons on February 10, 1807, not two weeks before the Abolition Bill debate. His speech unequivocally opposed abolition.[44]

One of London's great bibliophiles, Hibbert brought his faith in books to the House; he favored old books, whose age rendered them not outdated but, in Hibbert's view, especially authoritative. He told the Commons that he had Leo Africanus's writing in his hand, which described Africa as it had been witnessed in the sixteenth century, including the perpetual wars and incursions, tyranny, and slavery in "the different districts of Negro Land." Those nations, he claimed, would be no better off if the slave trade was abandoned. Bringing the House up to the minute, as he saw it, Hibbert then stated that this was all supported by Malthus's new book on population. He owned the *Essay*'s 1798 edition, the 1807 edition, and, later, a three volume gilt-leaved 1817 edition, as well as Malthus's *Principles of Political Economy* (1820). He was, perhaps, puzzled to see West Indian trade so little treated in the *Essay*, but he nonetheless used Malthus's chapter on Africa in defense of his business. Hibbert made a point of indicating that he did not know with any certainty "the sentiments of Mr Malthus upon the subject of the slave trade," but from reading the book itself, he claimed that one could "gather no hopes of accomplishing a salutary revolution in the state of society in Africa by the operation of this bill." Hibbert could have been reading the 1803 edition, which included the chapter on Africa but not the abolitionist footnote in the appendix. Or, if he had access to the 1806 edition, he might not have read the footnote at the end of the book, and indeed later he claimed this to have been the case. It is clear that he was not simply relying on Cobbett's *Political Register*, which had reprinted much of the 1803 Africa chapter; as we have seen, Cobbett himself thanked Hibbert in late 1805 for introducing him to

Malthus's arguments, which the political printer thought complemented his own antiabolitionist position.[45]

In any case, William Wilberforce must have listened with delight as novice member George Hibbert introduced Malthus's *Essay* in this manner. It was a small act of parliamentary self-destruction. Wilberforce struck: "Pliny, and Park, and Malthus, and many other authors, had been quoted as friends to the Slave Trade." But this was not so:

> Now it happened that he had a conversation, not ten minutes before he entered the House, with Mr Malthus, who was distressed extremely that any part of his work should have been so misunderstood, as to have it supposed that he was a friend to slavery. He had drawn up a short Appendix to his work, merely to explain his ideas on that subject. As one of their authorities, he positively disclaimed the opinion imputed to him.[46]

Even after the bill was passed, and he had been curtly corrected by Wilberforce, Hibbert continued to attach Malthus's *Essay* to his argument for the slave trade, though he never made public mention of their connected private proceedings. Again in the House of Commons on March 16, 1807, Hibbert opposed the claim of abolitionists that the wars and miseries besetting Africa were caused by the European slave trade, this time clarifying that whatever Malthus professed politically and personally, his *Essay* and the principle of population stood in support of, not against, the trade.

> When, in a former debate, I connected the statements of Parke with the comment with which Mr. Malthus has accompanied them, I expressly said (not knowing then that Mr. Malthus had published any opinion about the Slave Trade) that I was not able to say whether that gentleman was or was not a friend to abolition; but the principle he has advanced, and the reasoning he has introduced on this subject, remain unaltered; and when he states that the population of Africa is continually passing beyond the means of its subsistence, and that the condition of the negro nations will experience no amelioration until industry and security of property be introduced among them, these circumstances appear to me to bear strongly upon this question.[47]

Not to be put off, Hibbert published his speeches in 1807, including the two speeches that had mentioned Malthus in the Commons. He presented Malthus as impartial, much as Cobbett had: "a writer, whose deep and careful investigation of the interesting subject of population has excited general attention and approbation." Unfortunately for Malthus, the pamphlet ended with a long extract from the *Essay*—the section drawn from Mungo Park that Cobbett had also printed—selected to support Hibbert's disposal of the abolitionist argument that the slave trade caused misery and war in Africa. This sat alongside extracts from Alvise Cadamosto's account of his fifteenth-century travels in Africa (a French edition of 1556) and Leo Africanus's description of Africa in Latin (c. 1556).[48]

When William Cobbett digested all of this debate for his *Political Register*, he was as surprised as Hibbert that Malthus supported the abolitionists. He confessed to having always considered Malthus—"the check-population philosopher," he called him—"a defender of negro-slavery." Cobbett more or less accused him of expedient indecision, speculating that Malthus might justify his change of mind thus: "'when I wrote my book the ministry were opposed to the abolition of the slave trade; now the ministry are for the abolition; and, if Pliny were here, and wanted a snug place or pension, he would be for the abolition too.'" It was a cutting remark, but Cobbett correctly isolated Malthus's dissembling approach to, if not indecision over, public statements on abolition.[49]

Malthus had (and has) a reputation for mild evenhandedness, for middle-ground argument,[50] but on some matters he was fierce, and publicly so. Unsurprisingly, he had no compunction disavowing French revolutionary politics as debased and barbaric. More surprisingly, he raged against British colonization in Ireland and the oppression of Irish Catholics, in terms almost as strong. His condemnation of the slave trade, by comparison, was so contained as to be ineffectual. It was, at best, reluctant, matching his equally tentative defense of indigenous populations and indicating a consistently specific timidity on matters of race. It would scarcely have been possible for Malthus—as a man educated by dissenters and as a Whig associated with the new *Edinburgh Review* and thus with Henry Brougham, Francis Horner, Francis Jeffreys, and to some extent the salon at Holland House—to support the slave trade in the very early nineteenth century. But like many men of his age in the Church of England, he had not finally assimilated the invitation to regard slave trading as un-Christian. And like many men of property—including Whig members of parliament—Malthus had to reconcile his family connections to Jamaica, and to slave-produced wealth, with the abolitionist debate. He was hardly unique in that respect. Lord Holland, to take just one example, supported abolition, but like the Malthus family, he had acquired plantations and plantation wealth through marriage.

Yet it was Thomas Robert Malthus alone who assumed the new professional title "professor of history and political economy" on the back of the success of the *Essay on the Principle of Population*, thus assuming a public responsibility for thinking through relations between land, crops, commodities, and labor for British wealth and for British poverty. To do so without addressing the economy of the British slave trade, without addressing the pressing questions of land and labor in the West Indian colonies, without discussing the origin of the cotton imported to British manufacturers, represents a remarkable evasion, even on an empirical level. In the absence of additional private correspondence, and lacking any private journal, it is difficult to say why, and yet his indecision and unwillingness to tackle the issue in the public sphere, until absolutely pressed, is quite clear. Moreover, if Malthus was reluctant to go on public record in opposition to the slave trade, he never did so at all with respect to the abolition of slavery itself.[51]

* * *

It was over the years of intense public debate about the West Indies that Malthus accepted his position for the East Indies. In July 1805 he became professor of general history, politics, commerce, and finance at the East India College, for life as it turned out. In the 1806 edition of the *Essay*, the first to be published from this new institutional base, Malthus contracted his title to "professor of history and political economy." He took up the post at a time when India, in contrast to Britain's old empire, was supposed to represent imperial government that would be better regulated, a financial and moral improvement on the Atlantic colonies that were perceived to have grown by accretion and despite lax supervision.[52]

Geographically separate, the West Indies and the East Indies were nonetheless routinely joined in public debate, as in economy. With great wartime expenditures, Britain needed to look both to the East and the West for wealth, noted one member in the parliamentary slave trade debates.[53] At the same time, Jamaican planters often complained that government preference was given to the produce of the East India Company. For its part, the abolitionist campaign promoted the purchase of East Indies over West Indies sugar, thus boycotting the products of slave labor in favor of free (Indian) labor: "By six families using East India instead of West India Sugar one less slave is required. Surely to release a fellow-creature from a state of cruel bondage and misery, by so small a sacrifice, is worthy the attention of all." Comparison of sugar production in the East Indies and West Indies, as a way to demonstrate the profitability of free over slave labor, had been one line of abolitionist argument since Thomas Clarkson's early pamphlets (reprinted in 1823), a position later repeated in the debate on abolition of slavery itself, for example in Zachary Macaulay's *East and West India Sugar; or, a Refutation of the Claims of the West India Colonists to a Protecting Duty on East India Sugar*. Whatever the intentions of the advocates of Indian sugar, they were naive as to the nature of South Asian labor systems, for which coercion was common.[54]

The appointment to the East India Company College proved significant for Malthus for many reasons, but in the context of the slave trade debates, it is important to recognize that the position brought him close to Charles Grant, driving force of the East India Company and member of the Clapham evangelicals. Chair of the Court of Directors, Grant appointed Malthus to his position with the company's new college, and it was Grant to whom the economist wrote his letter of acceptance. Scottish-born Charles Grant had made Indian fortunes several times over since 1767. His religious conversion profoundly reshaped his work in India, in Britain, and within the company, and so his appointment of a clergyman to teach history and economics very much suited. An active humanitarianism meant that Christian mission came to be added to the company's ambitions, accompanying Grant's personal commitment to the abolition of the slave trade and slavery. With Wilberforce, Grant had attempted to have missionaries formally recognized by and integrated into the structure and culture of the company in 1793, a bid finally successful in 1813. This Christian humanitarianism materialized domestically too, in such initiatives as the British and Foreign Bible Society, in which Grant had a strong hand. Malthus was a member of this society, participating in its publishing and organizational activity. In doing so, he reasserted his occasional inclination to press the edges of the established Church of England. The society was formed as nondenominational, but it therefore sanctioned cooperation with nonconformists and was surrounded by controversy for many years.[55]

Among his multiple projects and activities, Grant was the great advocate and promoter of a new path for training young men for civilian positions within the East India Company. The college to which Malthus was appointed was originally located at Hertford Castle, but soon after a wholly new establishment was quickly designed and built: the grand college at Haileybury where Malthus spent the rest of his life. The purpose of the college was to educate young men (age sixteen to eighteen) whose families sought positions within the civilian arm of the East India Company. As a "writer," a younger son secured a position that bestowed a valuable lifelong attachment to the company. Other young men secured positions with the military of the company, as did George Frederick Symes (1794–1851), youngest son of Mariana Georgina Malthus and her Jamaican planter first husband, and who joined the artillery in 1813; he was commissioned as first lieutenant in 1818 and as captain and commissary of stores in 1825.[56]

Charles Grant and Malthus had drawn up the Convention of the Principal and Professors, a code of regulations for the college, as well as a prospectus. Malthus's contribution to the curriculum was a course in "general History, and on the History and Statistics of the Modern Nations of Europe" and "a course of lectures on Political Oeconomy." One set of examination questions Malthus assigned perhaps had as much private as pedagogical significance, given the exasperating unfolding of William Leigh Symes's Jamaican will: "What is necessary to make a good will, to devise real property?" And: "What interest has the executor of a will?" Another he set that year, under "Moral and Legal Questions," was "What degrees of kindred are prohibited to intermarry, and how are degrees of kindred reckoned?" Malthus had recently done that reckoning himself, marrying his cousin, Harriet Eckersall, in March 1804. They would have three children, and they lived at Haileybury from 1809 until Malthus's death in 1834.

Malthus also examined his students on the political economy of colonies: "What are the principal causes of the prosperity and rapid increase of New Colonies?" And: "In what manner do the State and People of Great Britain derive a revenue from India? And in what form is it transmitted?" There was no such question for the West Indies, however. Malthus expected his students to answer these questions in the light of his instruction on Adam Smith's *Wealth of Nations*, which comprised the core text of his curriculum. But this meant that they read Smith's chapter "On Colonies," learning that "in all European colonies the culture of the sugar-cane is carried on by negro slaves. The constitution of those who have been born in the temperate climate of Europe could not, it is supposed, support the labour of digging the ground under the burning sun of the West Indies."[57] Malthus's students thus had a view on plantation slavery from 1776 before them. However, if they sought their teacher's own early nineteenth-century views, either on West Indian commerce or on slavery or on the slave trade, they would have had to look very hard indeed.

Despite or perhaps because of the connection often drawn between sugar production in the West Indies and the East Indies, the Caribbean colonies remained as excised from Malthus's publications as from his examinations. The West Indies and Africa were both absent from his long *Principles of Political Economy*, neither appearing in the first edition (1820) or the posthumous second edition (1836). Sugar, on the other hand, was examined often enough, a commodity as critical as tea, coffee, indigo, silk, and cotton. Reading the

Principles of Political Economy sugar would seem to arrive at the docks, magically processed from nowhere and grown and harvested by no one. In the editions of the *Essay* produced in his years at the East India Company College, the West Indies, plantations, and slave labor were as minimally treated as they had been in the early editions of his *Essay*. The slave trade he transferred from the appendix into the Africa chapter in the 1826 edition, still a footnote, however. It stated that the desirable population increase in Africa, and concomitant security of property and industry, could not exist alongside a traffic in slaves. "Were this traffic at an end, we might rationally hope that, before the lapse of any long period, future travellers would be able to give us a more favourable picture of the state of society among the African nations, than that drawn by Park." Here Malthus continued to refer to slave trading among Africans, as much as to the market still operated by Europeans, and he did not take the opportunity to note the abolition of the trade by British merchants and shipowners.[58]

Over the years in which the abolition of the slave trade turned into public debate about the abolition of slavery, Malthus's principle of population was redeployed in another round of demographic arguments. Abolitionist Fowell Buxton, for example, used population returns from the colonies to present his case for emancipation to parliament, mining material that Malthus had pointedly not, but nonetheless rehearsing Malthus's argument that diminishing slave populations signaled their suffering and ill treatment, since populations would normally increase: "It was an arithmetical proposition." Zachary Macaulay's son, MP Thomas Macaulay, also used the substance of Malthus's "anti-slavery" footnote: "In the West-India colonies alone was found a society in which the number of human beings was continually decreasing without the surviving labourers obtaining any advantages. In the West-India Colonies a state of society existed unparalleled in the history of the world." And yet Malthus himself remained publicly silent on the matter. We know that he discussed the abolition of slavery privately, taking part in the proposition debated at the Political Economy Club on June 7, 1824: "Would the proprietors of estates in the West Indies sustain any pecuniary loss by the enfranchisement of their Negro Slaves?" It was hardly theoretical for Malthus, since that was the year in which, on Henry Swann's death, the Oxford Estate business reached another round of disputes, and he had recently been pursuing money still owed to India-based George Frederick Symes. There is no record of the position he took among his colleagues at the Political Economy Club.[59]

One of Malthus's eulogies proclaimed him to be "a consistent good Whig," although his failure to support the abolition of slavery over the 1820s and

1830s, or the slave trade before that, would qualify this claim.[60] He was perhaps too taken up with the Poor Law debates in the early 1830s to deal with abolition as well. He may have remained wary from the first round, when it became clear that his principle could be deployed any number of ways with regard to slave populations, and therefore could be, and was, taken up by both abolitionists and antiabolitionists. It may have been because the East India Company itself was implicated in the business of the Abolition Act (1833), passed the year before Malthus's death. Slavery was abolished across the British Empire, with three geographical and administrative exceptions: Ceylon, St. Helena, and the possessions of the East India Company. Slavery persisted in multiple other zones, including the United States, Brazil, and Cuba.[61]

Simply put, Malthus failed to engage with slavery in his political arithmetic and political economy, and his failure indicates how those fields of inquiry, however modern, remained for the moment shackled to economic formations of the past. Hence the massive commercial enterprise of plantation slavery, the system of agricultural production and exchange, labor, and land use that raised theological, moral, economic, and the demographic questions at the very core of Malthus's inquiry, are systematically underplayed in central texts of political economy. Slavery in the new world was a starkly meaningful omission in what was intended to be an embracing economic history of new worlds and old in the *Essay on the Principle of Population.* It is not at all obvious that Malthus was, as is often implied, indifferent to the plight of the English poor; it is sadly likely, however, that the most famous figure in modern population analysis was indifferent to the exploitation of slaves in Atlantic new worlds, whatever his timely opposition to the slave trade. Moreover, his readers, including those who actively supported the continued existence of slavery, recognized him as an ally, if only through his sins of omission.

Chapter 7

Colonization and Emigration

As a moral philosopher, Malthus often relied on hypothetical scenarios. What if the island of Great Britain doubled on itself, he asked in a new chapter on emigration published in the 1803 edition of his *Essay on the Principle of Population*. "If a tract of rich land as large as this island were suddenly annexed to it, and sold in small lots, or let out in small farms . . . the amelioration of the state of the common people would be sudden and striking." He was describing the fantastic transformation of ghost acres into contiguous acres. But Malthus's point was that such a benefit could only be a passing one. This additional "Britain" would be tilled and filled, people would be fed, and the price of labor, momentarily rising, would mitigate some poverty and then make it worse. The population would grow and then be limited again, necessarily. Land constraint was Malthus's bottom line, even if Britain were doubled. As with any island, there were always shoreline limits.[1]

Malthus well knew that North America *was* the "tract of rich land" that had been annexed, in effect doubling the size of Britain and much more, at least until the American War. And he knew that significant grain was still returning from America, as well as the Baltic, anticipating it shortly to be enough to support about two million Britons. Reliance on imported grain would increase the prosperity of the exporting country, and diminish Britain's "riches, and her power." He worried about North American acres, precisely because the most productive ones were no longer British. Rather, they produced grain that an independent United States could decide to export or withhold. The United States of America was not the straightforward "doubled" Britain at all. Surplus agricultural produce from Britain itself, he considered, was the source of its own future wealth, and at the very end of the *Essay* he argued for Corn Laws to protect just that.[2]

Still, there was land in North America beyond that claimed, or even desired by, the United States. Great swathes of forest and woodland seemed available for the taking in Upper Canada. Indeed, to settle this land would be to secure it for the British, in the light of the perceived threat from United

States expansion into the Northwest Territories. The War of 1812 between the United States and Britain was in large part fought over this region. With the settlement of borders that year, and with the peace after the Napoleonic Wars in 1815, the need to secure Upper Canada through clearing land, creating gardens and fields, planting stock, and building new settlements was on the public agenda.

At the same time, British economists, statesmen, speculators, and colonial reformers began to look afresh at the antipodean penal colonies: New South Wales and Van Diemen's Land. Might wholly new settlement projects be established on the vast continent that was still known as New Holland? As events unfolded, the Swan River Colony in Western Australia was established in 1829, an enterprise beleaguered by difficulties of cultivation, hunger, and, if anything, too much land. The South Australia Colonisation Act passed in the year of Malthus's death, 1834, ushered in a more successful and liberal endeavor that dictated a society of free settlers only. Indeed any number of new settlement schemes in Upper Canada, Nova Scotia, the South African Cape, South and Western Australia, and slightly later New Zealand, were all outcomes of intense postwar political economy and public policy talk about colonization and emigration. Some thought that state-backed and -funded emigration programs would benefit Britain economically, relieving payments to the poor, creating additional overseas markets, and securing colonial territories for good measure by bringing "waste land" into cultivation. As one of Malthus's discussants put it, "These are questions in the science of public economy, which must be speedily decided." In each case, the amount of territory vis-à-vis the number of people and the value of land vis-à-vis the value of labor—the staples of political economy—were core principles to be argued over in theory, as on the colonial ground. For James Mill, John Ramsay McCulloch, Jeremy Bentham, Nassau Senior, Thomas Robert Malthus, and a score of younger commentators on political economy— Robert Torrens, Edward Gibbon Wakefield, Robert Gouger—colonization and emigration were perennial themes after the Napoleonic Wars, effectively exporting and internationalizing the third great British problem of the era: the Poor Law.[3]

Since settler colonialism and political economy were powerfully fused in these population-driven emigration schemes, it is unsurprising that Malthus's principle was invoked readily and regularly. He was wary of that in 1803, but over the 1820s he became more inclined to support emigration as beneficial for Britain, in political economy terms. Typically, he was too measured, too undecided, and in a plain way too distracted with East India College business (as well as college scandals), to embark on any political lobbying himself, for or against the multiple emigration schemes that circulated over that decade. That was done by others, who used his work, his words, his principle, and his reputation to some considerable effect. Equally, those who objected to the "redundant population" rationale for emigration, especially colonists themselves, constantly used his name to sully any given scheme. Toward the end of his life, for better or worse, "Malthus" was already a brand. But his role involved far more than "theorization and representation" of the British efforts to colonize the Pacific new world, as his interest has been characterized. Malthus was directly involved in inquiries about emigration and the new colonies.[4]

Indeed, Malthus thought that all these schemes, and all this human movement, constituted an "age of emigration." His commentary and involvement connects him not just to a fresh round of settler colonialism but also to its implications for indigenous people. In 1803 he had not yet imagined continental Australia as the vast new territory available for British settlement that it would become; rather, it had figured for him as a place where savage societies lived in his present. Over the 1820s, however, when he was drawn into debate on emigration and colonization, he became so inclined. That was the decade when pastoral expansion into Aboriginal lands in New South Wales and Van Diemen's Land suddenly accelerated. This involved "clearing" both native land and native people, a process directly related to the Scottish and Irish clearances that in part produced the very populations destined for the Pacific new world. In his *Summary View on the Principle of Population* (1830), Malthus himself identified the local impact when emigrants from the "improved parts of the world" moved to those unimproved: "It is obvious that it must involve much war and extermination."[5]

* * *

Schemes for colonization that emerged in the early 1820s did so in a very different domestic and international context from Malthus's first foray into the political economy of colonies composed twenty years earlier. In 1803 Malthus had dedicated a chapter of the new *Essay*, "Of Emigration," to the question of colonization. It began with the common perception that emigration of redundant population was a remedy, where "redundant" for Malthus, like most political economists, signaled able-bodied male laborers who were out of work. It seemed "natural and obvious" that removing people from cultivated parts of the world to uncultivated and sparsely peopled regions would be beneficial. But in fact, and by experience, he argued in 1803, peopling new countries was little more than "a very weak palliative."[6]

In his chapter "Of Emigration," the very places that had served as backdrops for his stadial sweep across "savage" societies were revisited, this time as colonial ventures. But Malthus was no straightforward advocate of settler colonialism. Indeed, he took some trouble in his *Essay* to talk down colonial enterprises and to compose a history that detailed their difficulties rather more than their possibilities. At least for first settlers, conditions of living were typically worse than the circumstances they had left.

He began with the Americas. After damning the Spanish for their treatment, indeed "destruction" of the original "race" of inhabitants, he turned to seventeenth-century English colonization in Virginia, absolved of such destruction in Malthus's eyes because the indigenous population was far sparser than in Mexico and Peru. Still, the early settlement of Virginia was miserable— "three attempts completely failed," he took pains to explain—relying upon Burke and Robertson:

> Nearly half of the first colony was destroyed by the savages, and the rest consumed and worn down by fatigue and famine, deserted the country, and returned home in despair. The second colony was cut off to a man, in a manner unknown; but they were supposed to be destroyed by the Indians. The third experienced the same dismal fate; and the remains of the fourth, after it had been reduced by famine and disease, in the course of six months from 500 to 60 persons, were returning in a famishing and desperate condition to England, when they were met in the mouth of the Chesapeak bay, by Lord Delaware, with a squadron loaded with provisions, and every thing for their relief and defence.

As for the puritans in New England, there was no Lord Delaware either to rescue or support them, dependent as they were on "private funds." Malthus called the few settlers "an infant people," subject to an extreme climate, perishing from scurvy, famine, and cold. Yet they overcame the elements "by their energy of character, and the satisfaction of finding themselves out of the reach of the spiritual arm." Religious liberty was economically enabling, a claim that betrayed Malthus's liberal position on religious toleration. In the early New England case, Malthus recounted, after Burke, that energy and character were enough slowly to extract a subsistence and to make the land yield. Or, as he put it, the settlers invested a spirit and effort that slowly "reduced this savage country."[7]

The French in Guiana in 1663 met equally tough circumstances. Citing Raynal, Malthus recounted a massive instance of depopulation, this time of the colonizers. Twelve thousand men were reduced to two thousand, and the attempt at colonization was aborted completely, 25 million livres wasted in the attempt. Given that government-assisted emigration was already part of British public discourse, it was likely the fiscal as much as the human cost of this venture that was salutary to Malthus and his British readers. Similarly, the more recent settlement at Port Jackson in New Holland was a "melancholy and affecting picture," in which extreme hardships had been suffered. The character of the settlers did not help: convicts were the antithesis to the enterprising New Englanders. (Malthus never acknowledged the sizable presence of convicts, as forced laborers, in the American colonies.) Crops failed; land was unhealthy. Eventually the New South Wales colony's "produce was equal to its support," but not before great resources had been expended in the latest "colonization of savage countries."[8]

Colonial ventures presented in the *Essay* were not limited to European maritime empires. Malthus detailed the same problems that Empress Catherine of Russia seemed to be having, settling people near the Volga. He recounted a resettlement scheme whereby 75,000 Christians were "obliged by Russia" to emigrate to the country abandoned by the "Nogai Tatars" but again climate and environment rendered them into savages, sheltering in "holes dug in the ground" and perishing, the population reducing to 7,000.[9]

This was a history of early settler colonialism that sometimes failed outright, and at other times reduced civilized colonists to barbarians and savages. At the very least, new colonies were expensive. Those that succeeded were propped up with supplies from the home country until they could produce for their own needs, according to the greater or lesser limits of their immediate environment. Settler colonialism too, it turns out, was claimed by Malthus as an empirical instance of his principle of population. Settler populations would reduce in number to match scanty original resources, and increase only when soil was cultivated to produce enough food locally to support more families and settlers. "The frequent failures in the establishment of new colonies tend strongly to show the order of precedence between food and population." A form of acclimatization was required. What Malthus called "moral and mechanical habits" had to readapt from the mother country to the newly settled one. Manners needed to be naturalized, "born and grew up in the country," as he put it.[10]

The question for Malthus, and for others in the public debate about emigration, was the extent to which additional and expensive support for new colonies could or should be provided by government. How could Britain avoid wasting the equivalent of the lost 25,000 livres in Guiana? In what sense, he asked, is funding emigration and colonies incumbent upon any government? Clearly thinking of his own, he concluded that "perhaps it is too much to expect, that except where any particular colonial advantages are proposed, emigration should be actively assisted." Support offered by individuals or private companies was another matter, and Malthus always thought that this should not be hindered.[11]

These were old questions, inherited from centuries of debate about the value of colonialism and plantations in Ireland, in America, and in the Caribbean, staples of classical political economy as it had developed over Malthus's lifetime. Malthus himself thought that before the War of Independence, the American new world had offered "unusually great" advantages, and it was a happy circumstance that Britain had "so comfortable an asylum" for its redundant or surplus population. During the American crisis itself, however, Adam Smith had argued strongly and famously against the possession of colonies, against British commercial monopoly, and for the benefits of free trade. He asked pressing questions about the cost of the colonies, especially the cost of their defense. What, precisely, were the economic benefits? In short, were the American colonies worth it? Unequivocally, he nominated "the futility of all distant dominions" as an answer to this. Malthus pressed his East India College students on this matter in the early nineteenth century: "Why ought Colonies to be considered in the same light as Provinces of the Empire? And if they may be so considered what difference will this view of the subject make in the reasonings of Dr Smith on Colonial Trade?" And: "How does it appear, that most of the arguments which Dr Smith uses against the Exclusive Trade of the Colonies, would apply, with almost equal force, to a Free Trade?"[12]

Jeremy Bentham had also stressed the costs of maintaining, and in particular defending, colonies. He thought the penal colony of New South Wales absurdly costly for British public coffers, attacking the scheme in *Panopticon versus New South Wales* (1812). A classic in penology, Donald Winch has suggested that this pamphlet had a broader anticolonial message and sentiment. But if that is the case, it is clear also that Bentham's anticolonialism tempered over time. Bentham's weakening resolve seems to have been grounded, at least in part, in his assessment of population growth in Britain. In 1801, for example, he projected a future in which British domestic soil could not sustain an increasing population and that therefore the colonization of "fresh lands" was both possible and beneficial. This demographic rationale that made colonization a different prospect was new to Bentham's writing on colonies, according to Philip Schofield, a response "perhaps" to Malthus's *Essay*. As much nineteenth-century as eighteenth-century political economists, near contemporaries Malthus and Bentham lived in a very different world to that of Adam Smith.[13]

Malthus was also to become increasingly undecided about state-sponsored emigration schemes. In 1803 he conceded that the emigration of a surplus ("redundant") population was of momentary benefit to Britain. There was even a concession that emigration—colonization—was good so far as it went, in the medium term, with a nod to providential replenishing ("as a partial and temporary expedient, and with a view to the more general cultivation of the earth, and the wider spread of civilization, it seems to be both useful and proper.")[14] But then what? Colonies were palliatives, at best, for domestic (British) poverty; the problem always seemed to return. Despite all this colonial venturing, poverty at home had continued apace, he wrote in 1803. In the periods of great emigration to the new world, had distress in Britain been relieved? "The answer, I fear, could not be in the affirmative."[15]

In a sentimental paragraph, Malthus wrote emotively of a kind of immigrant experience. Working against emigration and even against "the great plan of providence" was strength of attachment to native soil, to love of parents, kith and kin. Emigration would "snap these cords which nature has wound in close and intricate folds round the human heart." It is hardly the fault of individuals if they fail to seize the opportunities of emigration to better their circumstances, he implied. Malthus felt keenly and emotionally— perhaps one might say Romantically—about hearth and home, and still more so about the separation of emigrants to distant lands: "The sea which they are to pass, appears to them like the separation of death from all their former connexions." This was followed by lines from *Hamlet*, Act III, Scene 1: "Make them rather bear the ills they suffer/Than fly to others which they know not of." Historian Eric Richards has written of Malthus's social psychology of emigration. But there was, perhaps, an individual psychology as well, in which such a separation seemed almost incomprehensible, a projection of Malthus's own attachment to family and home.[16]

In the end, in his 1803 edition, Malthus seemed torn on the question of emigration and colonization. With respect to poverty at home, he was clear that it was an inadequate solution in the long run, no matter how vast the new world was. Neither colonies nor, famously, the Poor Law was Malthus's remedy for domestic poverty. And yet colonization had other purposes and effects, of which Malthus took some account. It assisted a providential cultivation of the earth, and in the process it spread civilization. In this sense, colonization was "both useful and proper" and governments should never actively prevent it, he pronounced. Malthus was ultimately so unsure as to contradict himself. If wages for labor kept people in "tolerable comfort," they would be very unlikely to emigrate. Indeed, he was certain that attachment to home was so strong that emigration would only be prompted by extreme poverty or marked political discontent. However, if wages were too low for comfort, the lower classes should not be prevented from emigrating: "it is cruelty and injustice to detain them." This would likely be to their own advantage but also "for the advantage of their country." Here it seems that Malthus conceded the economic benefits of emigration. But he implied emigration of a privately funded kind: it could not be strongly argued, he wrote in 1803, that governments should actively encourage emigration or financially assist it. This ambiguity, evident in Malthus's earliest views on emigration, endured over the next two decades, as discussion about emigration and pauperism escalated in the public sphere.[17]

* * *

With the end of the Napoleonic Wars, and over the years in which Malthus revised his population treatise, 1817–1826, population, pauperism, and colonization were a constant triad in the republic of letters that made up political economy. Plans for the removal of unproductive Britons to other shores broadened from the criminal justice system that had dominated policy and thinking in the 1780s and 1790s, to the poor relief system, which was stretched to breaking point. The decade after 1815 was economically difficult, to say the least. The national debt after the war was astronomical; harvests were poor in 1816 and 1819; 300,000 soldiers and sailors were demobilized, more or less simultaneously, returning to a population that had increased dramatically; the war had lasted long enough for infants born at its outset to now be both entering labor markets and themselves reproducing more laborers. Wages were low, and parish Poor Law expenses were ever greater. "Redundant" and "surplus" population meant, quite strictly, able-bodied laborers out of work. There were too many of them.

In this context there was renewed debate on the Poor Law in the light of population and colonization. Might emigration mitigate parochial costs? Might this make government assistance for emigrant passages to the new world fiscally worthwhile? Might more colonial lands–in Australia and in Canada—be freshly tilled by imported labor? And in the process, might new markets be created for British-produced goods? In the 1817 edition of the *Essay*, Malthus took account of the extraordinary postwar circumstances, adding a lengthy final paragraph to his chapter on emigration. While fluctuations in population are responses to surfeit or deficit of labor, the response also necessarily lags: "Some time is required to bring more labour into the market . . . and some time to check the supply." Mostly, he claimed, this was a "natural sort of oscillation noticed in an early part of this work . . . a part of the usual course of things." Sometimes, however, circumstances arise that suddenly stimulate population for a decade or so (referring implicitly to the recent war), and then, equally suddenly cease, resulting in a rapid flow of labor into the market that cannot sustain, employ and pay it. Such extraordinary circumstances justified a one-off intervention. "The only real relief in such a case is emigration; and the subject at the present moment is well worthy the attention of the government, both as a matter of humanity and policy." That was Britain's situation in 1816 when Malthus was revising for the 1817 edition. By the time of his final edition, 1826, Malthus saw no reason to amend this statement to his chapter on emigration. Indeed, by that year it had all become formal government business.[18]

In 1826 a select committee was called to hear evidence on emigration, poor relief, and economic policy. It was the work of Robert Wilmot Horton, Derbyshire landowner and under-secretary of state for war and the colonies between 1821 and 1828. Wilmot Horton explained to Malthus that he had begun to think through the connection between emigration and poor relief in 1819, opposing radical William Cobbett's proposition that "all the Evils of our Population would cease" with parliamentary reform. Not reform of Parliament, but of the Poor Laws, was needed, argued Wilmot Horton, followed by a "System of Emigration . . . *to our own colonies*." He outlined to Malthus that it was his experience in the Colonial Department that persuaded him to reverse this formula and to foreground colonization and emigration over Poor Law reform itself.[19] As under-secretary of state he had learned that the "improvement" and "development" of the colonies was retarded because of the thin British population: plenty of land but few hands to work it, and not enough capital for feasible development.[20] In that capacity he was intricately engaged with colonists at all levels; in day-to-day work, Malthus's correspondent was almost as close to the colonial ground as he was to his own Derbyshire estate, negotiating land sales, agricultural charters, and the formation of new colonial companies.[21] In doing so, Wilmot Horton complained to Malthus that he had to battle domestic views that removing ablebodied men, even if they were paupers, entailed removing potential wealth:

"the opinion that Population is wealth." But in fact—as if Malthus needed persuading on the matter—"population in excess is weakness and poverty." The substantial correspondence between Malthus and Wilmot Horton over the 1820s offers valuable insight into just how intimately British political economy was tied to new world colonization and emigration.[22]

Wilmot Horton consistently hoped to persuade everyone in his political and social sphere that the cost of removal (emigration) of people who were consuming but not producing was over time lower than the cost of maintaining them parochially. He had a working definition of "pauper" that ran through his multiple schemes, and he took time to spell this out specifically in letters to Malthus: "such poor persons as being physically capable of labour, are willing to labour, but can find no possessor of property willing to exchange against their labour, wages sufficient to procure them the average means of subsistence, such possessor being influenced in such exchange, not by charity, but by a sense of his own interest."[23] His claims were not modest, writing to Malthus in 1828: "I believe that an insular Country, with a redundant population and extensive colonial possessions, may, by a proper system of National Emigration, effectually prevent the existence of poverty altogether."[24] He sought the opinions and advice of all the major political economists—Mill, Torrens, Senior, McCulloch, Ricardo, as well as Malthus—and they discussed his schemes with each other. Many were members of the Political Economy Club, founded in 1821, one of the venues in which Malthus and Wilmot Horton met and talked.[25]

In 1823 Wilmot Horton took the liberty of sending both Malthus and Ricardo his newly printed *Outline of a Plan of Emigration to Upper Canada*, which had been appended to the *Report of the Parliamentary Select Committee on the Employment of the Poor in Ireland*. Here Wilmot Horton set out the initial rendition of a scheme that he was to refine and lobby for over the next decade and on which Malthus commented closely. It entailed able-bodied pauper families receiving free passage, grants of colonial land, and tools and initial provisions for one year, in exchange for any future claim on parish assistance: that is, rights to parish benefits for themselves and their children would be permanently forfeited. The cost of passage and settlement in the colonies would be paid by parishes, the funds loaned from the government on security of a mortgage on the poor rates. In this initial rendition, and in multiple later versions, Wilmot Horton detailed the proposed conditions of loans to parishes, expenses of emigration, and evidence concerning the feasibility and benefits of clearing and settling land, not only but mainly in Upper Canada.[26] Horton's *Outline* followed a similar pamphlet by a Scottish colonist in Upper Canada, Robert Gourlay (1822), in which the seemingly endless lands of British North America were still a prize to be won by the British, notwithstanding the already rapid expansion of the United States. "The vision of quickly and thickly peopling the earth with our species, brightens in my imagination day after day," wrote Gourlay floridly. Wilmot Horton was more measured. Providential arguments about replenishing the Earth had great purchase emotionally, spiritually, and theologically, but did they work politically and economically? By the 1820s it had become routine for theorists of colonization and colonists themselves to refer to Malthus on population and land. Gourlay, for example, declared himself to be "a steady disciple of Mr Malthus."[27]

For his part, Wilmot Horton had engaged in correspondence with Malthus since 1823. In their early conversation, Malthus simply repeated to Wilmot Horton what he had set out in his 1803 chapter: "I have always thought it very unjust on the part of Governments, to prohibit, or impede emigration; but I have doubted whether they could reasonably be expected so to promote it." Still, he confessed this to be a doubt rather than a decided opinion. In line with the revisions for his 1817 edition he told Wilmot Horton that "the peculiar circumstances of the times" were beginning to incline him toward a warmer reception of proposals for government assistance for emigration. Indeed, in 1823 he considered Wilmot Horton's plan a reasonable one, even a scheme that held out many advantages. The calculations of expenses he thought sound. Malthus's chief worry was the type, or character, of person most likely to be selected by parishes. Why, he asked, would they send their most able men? The redundant population would not make the most efficient settlers, partly because the "indolence" they had learned from parish assistance may well be carried to the new settlement. In the event, what Malthus called "the present crisis" meant that the benefits of emigration to all parties (parishes, the government, the British economy, the colonies, the emigrants) outweighed any objections, even if momentarily so.[28]

Wilmot Horton successfully persuaded Parliament that the whole matter, including his own plan, would benefit from the careful scrutiny of formal evidence, and he chaired the Select Committee on Emigration over 1826 and 1827. All the major political economists were asked for their views and, if possible, for their evidence at the inquiry. It took some persuasion to extract a reluctant and disorganized Malthus from duties at the East India College. Perhaps he was disinclined, having sat fairly recently on the Select Committee on Artizans and Machinery. That Committee had considered, among other matters, the laws preventing the emigration of artisans, and some of those men returned to give evidence to the Select Committee on Emigration. Their presence reveals that pressure to design and implement assisted emigration schemes in these years did not come just from landowners and statesmen such as Wilmot Horton, or from agricultural laborers turned paupers, but also from out-of-work artisans. Communities in Scotland had formed their own emigration societies to press their case. Indeed, the first witness that Wilmot Horton brought before his 1827 select sommittee spoke for the Glasgow Emigration Society. Operative weaver Joseph Foster explained that about twelve anxious families had turned their attention to emigration to the "North American Provinces." They had petitioned—without success—the secretary of state for a grant of land in Canada, requesting that "their deep distress may be taken in favourable consideration; that they are starving, and will be ejected from their dwellings in a few days." They were looking, in part, at the emigration experiments that Wilmot Horton had helped implement earlier in the 1820s, when he first became under-secretary.[29]

All of Malthus's work concerned the value of land relative to the value of labor, and this was precisely what was under discussion in the mechanics of settler colonialism. Wilmot Horton's *Outline of a Plan of Emigration to Upper Canada* appended, for example, a detailed report from Colonel Thomas Talbot, younger son of an Irish baron, who had been granted five thousand Canadian acres in 1803 on the shores of Lake Erie. From 1809 Talbot himself granted land to settlers, acres that had until that time "appeared an impenetrable wilderness." Wilmot Horton tabled material that itemized the intricate political economy of clearing: brushwood was cut first and piled, and young trees were cut into short lengths and piled atop the brushwood; large trees were to be cut at five feet from the root and then stems cut into lengths of eleven feet. Piles were then dried—taking perhaps a fortnight—and burned. If a potash work was nearby, this might cover the expense of clearing. Logging then took place, with a yoke of oxen, after which the land was ready for fencing and then sowing. All of this labor, Talbot made sure to emphasize, was performed on Crown land granted in perpetuity to the settler. "His labour, therefore, is wholly expended upon his own property." Likewise, the appendix of the 1826 report to which Malthus provided evidence included summary tables for calculating labor required for clearing land in New South Wales (for which convict labor proved useful): the felling of forty trees in one acre took one week of one man's labor; the burning of eighty perches (the antique unit for height and volume still in occasional use) took one man one week; and so on for hoeing and breaking up new land, for planting, reaping, and fencing; and for raising new dwellings—sawing, shingling, brickmaking. This was the work of colonial clearance.[30]

Letters from settlers were reprinted in parliamentary documents, perhaps the best propaganda possible to support Wilmot Horton's schemes. Everything in Upper Canada seemed to be turning from waste into produce. Andrew Angus wrote to his parents that after they felled the woods, his new land in Upper Canada grew potatoes well, in addition to Indian corn and wheat. Although the land had been settled for little more than three years, and although many families had left Scotland with nothing, he recounted that they now had up to eighteen head of cattle, besides sheep and hogs.[31] Unhappily for Malthus, this settler was insistent that the larger the emigrant family, the more chance they had of doing well. This was also something that had been stressed in Wilmot Horton's 1822 *Outline*, which Malthus read and commented on. Large families of children were not a burden, the report from Upper Canada had stated, but contributed greatly in the process of clearing and cultivation. And with that, advancement of a settlement was demographically and agriculturally rapid; the Talbot Settlement on Lake Erie had collected 12,000 souls over ten years. They arrived as "persons of the very poorest description" and they were now "as independent, as contented, and as happy a body of yeomanry, as any in the world." That was the demographic news from the ground in those new world places in Upper Canada, now called Lanark or Dalhousie or Port Talbot.[32]

Other settlements were explicitly based on Malthus's evidence that new world populations increased rapidly. Thomas Douglas, Earl of Selkirk (who introduced Malthus to the parliamentary abolition debate), had successfully negotiated to send 800 Scottish highlanders to Prince Edward Island in 1803. The next year he settled 102 Scottish men and women near Windsor, Upper Canada, to prepare an estate for sheep breeding, but between malaria and war, that colony crumbled. Later Selkirk attempted colonization of Red River in western Canada. Throughout all of these ventures, he relied explicitly on Malthus's principle to justify his own settlement and colonization plans:

> From the principles so clearly laid down by Mr. Malthus, it will be easily understood that in a Colony where an original nucleus of population has been planted, that population increasing at a certain rate, will be capable of carrying forward the improvement of the country with a proportional degree of rapidity—a rapidity increasing like the population in a geometrical proportion.[33]

Indeed, colonizers and speculators used Malthus's material on new world population growth constantly in support of their ventures. They did so even when they recognized that Malthus was not a straightforward supporter of emigration, and even in places located outside the British Empire. Settlers in Sydney, for example, read that even though Malthus did not approve of

emigration in general, he nonetheless endorsed "the more general cultivation of the earth and the wider extension of civilization" as "both useful and
proper." Why not consider the colonization of the extensive and fertile island
of Borneo alongside the new colonization plans for Canada, the Cape, and
New Holland?[34]

Wilmot Horton himself insisted that his scheme was applicable to any
colony. The first report of his select committee included detailed papers on
various plans for emigration to New South Wales and the Cape of Good
Hope, as well as British North America. Papers submitted by New South
Wales colonists announced—ambitiously—that every able-bodied pauper
in England "may be established as an independent free-holder." The soil of
New South Wales was so rich that crops of wheat, maize, and barley had been
continuous for thirty years in some cases, "without manure and without rest."
The climate of New South Wales was so health-inducing that "not one single
case" of smallpox was known, ignoring the 1789 epidemic among Aboriginal
people about which Malthus and a hundred others had written. Finally, tens
of thousands of convict laborers, and more each year, stood ready to clear
land for settlers at government expense. This would offset the common
problem that pauper (but free) emigrants lacked the capacity to buy enough
labor to clear land, when their own labor was insufficient. Indeed the evidence tabled by this colonist was so optimistic as to be irresponsible. Colonizing the antipodes might extinguish not just pauperism but the poor rate
itself, and that "at no very distant period." On the face of it, it was easy to
render colonies into solutions to multiple problems in both the old world
and new. The devil was in the detail.[35]

* * *

Although many of the early schemes involved Scottish emigration, Wilmot
Horton's plans were almost obsessively about Ireland, and had long been so.
It is unsurprising, then, that when he sat down to preside over the Select
Committee on Emigration on Saturday, May 5, 1827, his opening question
was to ask his star political economy witness whether he had ever been to
Ireland. A short visit in 1817, witness Malthus replied. Ireland was distinct
in the population-emigration complex that was under discussion after the
Napoleonic Wars, in part because there was no parish poor relief, no poor
law equivalent to that of England and Wales. (This also meant, Malthus noted
with regret in his *Essay*, no parochial records to speak of that could help with
mortality, birth, and marriage rates.) Wilmot Horton had an Ireland-specific

variation on his emigration scheme, proposing that government loans could be secured by private subscription fund, rather than by parishes, as was his English plan.[36] In the case of the Irish laborer, he explained in a letter to Malthus, "colonization is entirely a gratuitous benefit," while in the case of the English pauper it was an "exchange," settlement in a colony in lieu of settlement in an English parish.[37]

Ireland was also distinct because of its demographic circumstances. As Malthus and Wilmot Horton spoke, the population of Scotland was about 2 million, England and Wales, about 13.3 million. But it was Irish population that was most troubling, because of its rate of increase. Malthus had been thinking about this in recent years. Perhaps prompted by his discussion with Wilmot Horton, he added a short section to the 1826 edition of the *Essay* on Irish numbers. While in 1821 it was counted at 6,801,827, in 1695 it had only been 1,034,000. This was the most rapid increase anywhere in Europe, a claim he repeated at the Select Committee on Emigration.[38] At that point, 1827, he estimated 7.5 million Irish, calculating the rate of increase from Beaufort's baseline in 1792 (which Malthus reported to the Committee was 4,680,000), against the census undertaken in 1821.[39] Malthus projected a doubling of the Irish population in about forty years, more rapid than the forty-eight-year doubling noted in the 1826 edition of the *Essay*. Yet the report produced by the select committee suggested an even more alarming rate, in the light of Sir Henry Parnell's evidence: the Irish population may well have doubled in the preceding thirty years. In both the *Essay* and his evidence, Malthus was eager to record that the Irish circumstance was unique, not just because of the rate of increase but because that increase had been so sustained. Where other European populations might grow over one or two generations, and then become stationary or even decline, the Irish seemed to have been increasing steadily since South's first population estimates in 1695.[40]

Rapidly doubling populations in the new world were one thing. In old world Ireland it was quite another, compounding distress and poverty, according to Malthus, and unless mitigated leading toward a crisis-level "check." The whole circumstance was of some interest to Malthus theoretically. *Why* was population increasing so rapidly, and in such a sustained way? Wilmot Horton also wondered aloud to Malthus why the Irish population, already in such distress, was still increasing its numbers. Deploying Malthus's own principle, why had not the population become stationary if resources were so thin? Ireland was no ordinary case. Malthus was not alone in suggesting that part of the problem was reliance on a peculiar staple, the potato. Able to be grown in small plots of land, any surplus had almost no value. Potatoes could not be exchanged for anything.[41]

Malthus had insisted in his *Essay* that population growth typically accompanied the availability of fresh land with a good dose of "liberty": the American case. While there was precious little liberty in Ireland—a problem for Malthus, as we shall see—there was some "waste land." Malthus thought that population was increasing because there were still parts of Ireland to be freshly cultivated, but he also thought that as a response there would eventually, even soon, manifest as a great increase in what he called premature mortality. Thus, while some in the 1820s recommended that Ireland's "redundant"—out-of-work—population be relocated onto the island's wastelands, Malthus himself considered that a shortsighted policy: one or two generations later the population will have grown and there would be even greater "redundancy of population than before." Better to remove the out-of-work population, introduce changes in land and estate management, and inculcate prudence among laborers through education "and better habits of respecting themselves."[42]

Ireland was, in many senses, the actual "doubled" Britain with which Malthus opened his chapter on emigration. The Acts of Union in 1801 had made it so, forming the new United Kingdom of Great Britain and Ireland. But what a precarious union it was. The proximate cause—the 1798 uprising of Irish republicans with the support of French troops—followed several centuries of colonization bedded down by a suite of sectarian laws, the Catholic Code or the Penal Code. By the time Malthus wrote his *Essay* at the end of the eighteenth century, Catholic ownership of land had dropped to about 5 percent. It had been 20 percent a hundred years earlier, and 90 percent in 1603. For many years the Penal Code excluded Catholic merchants from local government, disqualified Catholics from voting (until 1793), and from sitting in Parliament (until Catholic Emancipation in 1829). The laws dictated that Catholic estates be divided among all sons, unless a son converted, in which case he would inherit the whole estate. For Irish peasants, the tithes collected on small potato fields were a grievance raised again and again in Parliament, without resolution.[43]

English and Irish commentators at the time assessed the Union as unashamed colonial rule. In 1829 Malthus read Parnell's fierce statements on English colonialism in Ireland: "We dispose of the lives of brutes, and the liberty of negroes, with very little compunction; it was in the same spirit that it was lawful to kill a wild Irishman; and that neither his property, nor his person, was thought worthy of the protection of the common law." It is no wonder that Irish political agitators and disaffected laborers looked to France, and even to Napoleon, for liberation, if not liberty. Malthus himself thought as much and, quite remarkably, said so in 1808, even as the British were fighting Napoleon's army in Spain and Portugal.[44]

The Union meant that one hundred representatives of Ireland now sat in Westminster. They were all Protestant. Partly because of this stark fact, Catholic emancipation was high on political agendas, not least for the Whigs, with whom Malthus associated and identified. The memory of both Irish republicanism and the recent war was still fresh, still playing out; the Union needed to be secured. Ireland needed to be brought into the fold, but poverty and disaffection made that difficult, and this was the important context for the suite of select committees and inquiries into Irish poverty, as well as emigration and poor laws, that peppered the decades after 1815. Malthus contributed in person to some of these, while all of them mentioned his principle of population, one way or another. The aspiration to what Wilmot Horton called "tranquillity and security" in Ireland was directly connected to population, emigration, and colonization.[45]

Malthus worried to Wilmot Horton that plans to send Scottish and English laborers to the new world would simply result in an influx of labor from Dublin to Liverpool, undermining all potential benefits.[46] Malthus was unequivocal: population increase in Ireland would be "most fatal to the happiness of the labouring classes in England," since increasing emigration from Ireland to England would lower wages for labor. Thus, ongoing emigration across the Irish Sea would undermine "the good effects arising from the superior prudence of the labouring classes in this country"—clearly a matter close to Malthus's heart. It would have the net effect of increasing the number of English paupers.[47] He wrote to Wilmot Horton in 1827 that diminishing—or even possibly preventing—movement from Ireland to England and Scotland would be an "incalculable" advantage to both.[48] Wilmot Horton worried back to Malthus about his "deepest conviction": whatever else happened, there would be no advantage unless the out-of-work Irish poor found an outlet other than England or Scotland. If not, the laboring class across Great Britain would be brought "to a uniform state of degradation and misery."[49]

They spoke with one voice on Ireland. "The focus of mischief, in every point of view, is there,"[50] wrote Malthus to Wilmot Horton in 1827, a sentiment repeated in the select committee's second report:

> The great increase of population in Ireland has so much outrun the increase in the funds for employing it, as to occasion the almost universal prevalence of the most squalid and abject poverty, and to justify an opinion, that a check to the further progress of population has begun to have operation by emigrations to Great Britain, and by increased mortality, arising from the inability of the people to obtain such supplies of the coarsest and cheapest food as are necessary to support their existence.

The "mischief" that concerned them was both the actual distress in Ireland and the emigration to England and Scotland that that distress created. Ireland continually threatened to export its poverty, as far as Malthus and Wilmot Horton were concerned.[51]

Prompted by strong and leading questions from Wilmot Horton, Malthus was clear in the select committee that a one-off large-scale emigration would bring about a beneficial change in the demographic and economic future of Ireland, and that the dividend justified a "great pecuniary sacrifice" on the part of government, as an emergency measure. He was equally sure that emigration needed to be accompanied by sustained reform of Irish estates, the only way to effect permanent relief. Malthus thought that any emigration scheme—from Ireland, Scotland, or England—needed to be accompanied by measures that would prevent the vacuum left behind from simply refilling. Farms that had been cleared of people, as leases ended, should stay cleared. How? The cottages of departed Irish emigrants might be pulled down. Destroying cottages was at one level a symbolic response, since the process of enumeration in Ireland (and elsewhere) had long been pursued by "hearth"; population was estimated as much in stone fireplaces as in people. It is as if, by obliterating domestic spaces the negative pressure of the vacuum would be minimized, but at the same time agricultural space would still remain void and vacant, to be populated not with people but with stock.[52]

The measure was a harsh response for a people already living in great poverty. It may come as a surprise, then, that Malthus had earlier pronounced himself a fierce critic of oppressive English laws and strongly in favor of Irish Catholic emancipation. In 1808 and 1809 he wrote two articles for the *Edinburgh Review*, nominally assessing three recent publications on Ireland, but actually using the opportunity to put down his thoughts on just how and why English oppression had produced Irish distress. Malthus's contribution was prompted by contact with the *Edinburgh Review*'s founder Francis Horner, who had earlier discarded his own plan to write a book about population after reading Malthus's *Essay* ("the new world which *Malthus* has discovered," resentment betrayed, perhaps, by his emphasis). Endlessly procrastinating, Horner dropped his plan to write even a review of the *Essay* (the editor writing to Horner in 1804, "for our sake, for my sake, for your own sake, and for God's sake, do set about Malthus immediately"). The connection with Horner signals Malthus's political alignment, including his broad commitment to religious toleration, of both Catholics and dissenters.[53]

Malthus had written very little indeed on Ireland in his revised *Essay*, but he made a point of noting just this in his anonymous review. Commenting on "the doctrines which Mr. Malthus has advanced in his late Essay on Population," he feigned surprise that "he did not enter into it more in detail." John Pullen has suggested that in these articles Malthus showed "sympathy for the plight of the Irish, and argued strongly for Irish emancipation." But this is an understatement. Malthus's 1808 articles displayed less sympathy than outrage. If the strength of the written word is our measure, Malthus was more resolute about Catholic emancipation, including its effect on Irish laborers, than any other political matter.[54]

The Catholic Code was his target, "the disgraceful code under which the Catholics had been so long oppressed." Those who did not consider Irish Catholics as "fellow Christians worshipping the same God, and fellow subjects entitled to the same civil privileges," were both bigoted and ignorant, the terms he used in 1808. They "are not only violating the genuine spirit of Christianity, but blindly endangering their own security, and risking the subjugation or dismemberment of the empire." Malthus meant the Union of Great Britain and Ireland, Ireland being "the fourth part of the empire." At one level Malthus wrote of a kind of imperial federation. At another level he saw colonization manifesting as the Irish "oppressed," his own word. Civil distinctions between Catholics and Protestants had to be disbanded by the legislature, thereby removing the cause of Catholic disaffection; diminishing argument and agitation toward the political separation of Ireland; and, especially, removing any attraction for Bonapartist rule that would only seem attractive or possible to Irish Catholics if the British retained civil distinctions.[55]

Thus, while population in Ireland was an interesting economic case, that was nowhere near the extent of Malthus's interest. Population growth there was also a political and security problem, one that Malthus thought would be ignored at the peril of the Union. The rapid increase of population was disproportionately Catholic (four to one, he thought), and thus constituted a growing "physical force." "Every year fifty thousand youths rise to the military age in Ireland," a number certainly not offset by men growing old or dying. But his point was that a contest of numbers and force needed to be exchanged for a process of conciliation. Thus, he was forthright in 1808: while Croker's *Sketch of the State of Ireland* (which he was nominally reviewing), located "Irish misery" with the ignorance and poverty of the laborers, Malthus thought it sprang first and foremost from the penal code. Anti-Catholic laws were not incidentally problematic for Malthus; he claimed they had *produced* the "political debasement of the inferior orders" and "the present moral and political degradation of the mass of the Irish poor."[56]

It is important to stress this because Malthus's principle of population is often interpreted as having naturalized the phenomenon of distress, of poverty, and even of famine. Patrick Brantlinger, for example, understands Malthus's comments on Irish distress in the *Essay* as evidence of "divine wisdom expressed through nature's laws." Others see his work as setting in place the idea that poverty and distress were somehow biologically determined, prefacing the mid-nineteenth-century uptake of Malthus by Wallace and Darwin and onward to eugenics. But Malthus's whole point in this focused piece on Ireland written at the beginning of the century was to insist on a political cause that required a political response. The poverty of the Irish was an "evil," the remedy for which ("the only possible relief") was the abolition of the Catholic code.[57]

Malthus's detailed consideration of Ireland in these two articles contained no mention of emigration as a source of relief. The articles did, however, enumerate the numbers of Irish who had annually departed for America, averaging four thousand per year over the last half of the eighteenth century.[58] His passing point was that such emigrations added to the habit of early marriages. Twenty years later, emigration was the precise context within which he was asked for his views on the Irish poor. Something of the substance but little of the outrage emerged in his evidence. In 1827 Malthus was still directly critical of the government of Ireland—"it has tended to degrade the general mass of the people"—and this oppression inculcated nothing other than an expectation of a very low standard of living, "the very lowest degree of comfort." One of Ireland's greatest faults, he concluded, was that the laboring classes were treated "as if they were a degraded people." Living thus, Irish laborers and families married early, reproduced rapidly, and on the whole expected little more than "being able to get potatoes for themselves and their children." Such circumstances prevented them "looking forward and acquiring habits of prudence." This would and should change, Malthus commented. The poor in Ireland needed to be treated with greater respect by their superiors. With the introduction of civil and political liberties, and especially with education, people who respected themselves more and expected higher comforts for themselves and their children would marry later. Ireland, then, was the first case of what came to be termed *development*.[59]

Patricia James wondered in her biography how Malthus's Evangelical friends and acquaintances among the Clapham sect might have assessed his forthright views on Catholic emancipation and his statements about augmenting Catholic population in Ireland. They were less religiously tolerant than the Whigs in Holland House, certainly less tolerant than Malthus. Nonetheless, there is a link between Malthus's views on conciliating Irish Catholics and his views on religious toleration in general. Malthus's unpublished pamphlet, "The Crisis" (1796), had dealt in part with "the policy of religious exclusions." Problematically, nonconformists had been rendered more or less "professed enemies to the State as well as the Church," despite their historical connection to the constitution. But if, historically, the tests had been removed and nonconformists had been treated as civically equivalent—had they been drawn in and not excluded—they "should never have seen the present violent opposition from them to the established government." Malthus's logic was conciliatory, but it was also assimilationist. The "slight shades of difference in their religious tenets" should have been tolerated because soon enough they would have been absorbed by the dominant view and, indeed, eliminated: since politics and religion is not innate (not "born with men"), "the next generation . . . would quickly be lost and undistinguished in the great mass of the community." Malthus never suggested or sought the conversion and assimilation of Catholics in this way, but he was writing within a tradition of demographic-assimilative thought on Ireland. Political union could sometimes be effected by reproductive union. Soon enough just this kind of intergenerational assimilation would become Aboriginal policy in the Canadian and Australian colonies.[60]

Malthus's ideas on Irish conciliation and intergenerational assimilation may well have their source with his seventeenth-century predecessor, William Petty. Petty's famous *Political Arithemitick* stemmed from work in and on Ireland; the Down survey, and his *Political Anatomy of Ireland*, was a thesis on Irish plantation. The books that Malthus reviewed in 1808—Newenham and Croker—had their intellectual and political provenance here. Petty aired plans for resolving not just English-Irish differences but actual difference, not by force but by intermarriage. "Declining all Military means of settling and securing *Ireland* in peace and plenty, what we offer shall tend to the transmuting one people into the other, and the thorough union of Interests upon natural and lasting Principles." The union between England and Ireland that Malthus's seventeenth-century predecessor had dreamed of was certainly political, but the key was a union of the population, a "transmutation" of the Irish into English custom, economy, and improvement, if not religion, building from the elements of domestic economy. Unmarried English women would be transplanted to Ireland, there to marry local men and raise children in English customs in English-like households. In Petty's plan, 200,000 Irish men might be brought to England, dispersed, and absorbed. The exchange of population, writes Ted McCormick, "would transmute Irish society from within." Petty, like Malthus, imagined a neutralization of Irish political agitation and disaffection less through the expectation of religious conversion than through a combination of religious tolerance and cultural assimilation. Political arithmetic, Ted McCormick has written, "turned government into a kind of demographic alchemy."[61]

If contact with native Americans offered "savagery" to stadial theory, it was the history of colonialism in Ireland that offered instances of contemporary "barbarity." Gaelic land, property, and inheritance practices did not naturally incline to improvement; Ireland was marked by its lack of commerce. But Petty and his intellectual successors in political arithmetic tended to comprehend Irish "barbarism" as reformable rather than fixed. Hence the possibility of "transmutation." This in many ways characterized the possibility of civilization in stadial theory and in Malthus's expectation that different cultures might adapt, improve, progress; that they might civilize in economic terms. For the Irish, Malthus thought, like Petty, this did not necessarily require conversion. Quite the contrary, productive union required religious tolerance on the part of the English. The problem for Malthus was the time that this would take, and the demographics of decline (in numbers) against which gradual "improvement" was pitted.

* * *

In writing up his reports from the Select Committee on Emigration in 1826–1827, Wilmot Horton used the authority of Malthus's name at every opportunity. He made it clear that the testimony of multiple "practical witnesses" was confirmed by his star theoretical witness and, conversely, that Malthus's principles aligned with the facts and evidence brought before the committee by men on the ground. It was with reference to Malthus specifically that assurances were given that removing laborers who were out of work was not a loss to the wealth of the home country, despite common perceptions; on the contrary, such redundant laborers are a "tax upon the community." Therefore, "Mr. Malthus admits that if it can be shown that the

expense of removing such labourers by Emigration is less than that of maintaining them at home, no doubt can exist of the expediency of so removing
them." Malthus, the committee's final report pronounced, thought that the
increase in Irish population was a dire problem not just for the starving Irish
but also for English and Scottish laborers, whose wages would decrease with
Irish immigration to their shores. Malthus's evidence was repeated verbatim.
And he was directly deployed in the report to affirm the connection between
redundant population, colonization, and the wealth of the British Empire.[62]
In writing Malthus so strongly into the final report, Wilmot Horton went to
the trouble of checking Malthus's evidence with other political economists,
Thomas Tooke, Thomas Chalmers, Robert Torrens. He did so because the
"queries put to Mr Malthus embrace the whole principle of the Reports."
Torrens corrected Malthus on some matters but overall lent his endorsement
to Wilmot Horton's plans: "It is morally and physically certain, that unless
an Extensive plan of Emigration be carried into effect, the labouring classes
in England must become what in Ireland they are." Chalmers, by contrast,
thought emigration plans a misplaced solution to pauperism, but that did
not deter Wilmot Horton. Speaking to the extended Enquiry on Emigration in Parliament in 1827, Wilmot Horton again authorized it all via Malthus: "Mr. Malthus was of opinion, that unless emigration was extensively
resorted to, an alteration of the poor-laws would speedily be found necessary.
The opinions held by Mr. Malthus on the subject of emigration were, he was
happy to find, adopted by many persons in this country, and in the colonies
themselves."[63]

As a way of wrapping up the whole issue of colonization and prosperity,
Wilmot Horton curiously underscored Malthus's assessment of colonization
and emigration with that of William Penn's *Benefit of Plantations or Colonies*,
signaling the longevity of the significance of new world land for British populations: "'I deny the vulgar opinion against plantations, that they weaken
England; they have manifestly enriched, and so strengthened her, which I
briefly evidence thus: *those that go into a foreign plantation, their industry there
is worth more than if they staid at home.*'" It was a peculiar bid to authorize his
schemes for colonization, an antiquated instance from another economic
and political world. Nonetheless, Wilmot Horton announced that his own
proposition, that of his select committee, was "precisely similar": that a laborer out of work in Great Britain was more valuable in work in the colonies.
This was the justification for appropriating public funds for emigration.[64]
Wilmot Horton was looking back to the early modern new world just when
others were looking forward to colonial reform. It was a sign, perhaps, that

he had had his day. Fresh plans to put old world populations and new world land together were engaging public and government attention, plans that developed from Wilmot Horton's Malthus-inspired lobbying decade but departed from it as well.

* * *

In the new decade, February 1830, Malthus asked Wilmot Horton if he had heard anything about the new plans for emigration to Australasia. He was referring either (or possibly both) to Edward Gibbon Wakefield's anonymous *Sketch of a Proposal for Colonizing Australasia* (1829) or, more likely, the version of it that was published as *A Letter from Sydney, the Principal Town of Australasia, together with the outline of a system of colonization*. The so-called *Letter from Sydney* (Wakefield was in fact in Newgate prison, having abducted a fifteen-year-old heiress) had appeared in the *Morning Chronicle* and in this new pamphlet format was compiled and published as edited by Robert Gouger, the philanthropically interested son of a prosperous city merchant, soon to drive plans for a South Australian colony and eventually to become its colonial secretary. Wakefield, born in 1796, and Gouger, born in 1802, were young and energetic, with a suite of new ideas. They were talking to a middle-aged Wilmot Horton (born 1784), who was about to become governor of Ceylon, and an even older Malthus (born 1766), who was not aging particularly well. Wakefield and Gouger left the eighteenth century, and for that matter William Penn's seventeenth century, well and truly behind.[65]

The new proposal for colonizing Australasia was inspired, Wakefield said, both by Wilmot Horton's *Reports on Emigration* and by Malthus's general theory that lay behind it. Both Ireland and economy ran in Wakefield's blood. His father, Edward Wakefield, had written *Ireland, Statistical and Political* (1812), another tract in the Petty tradition. His Quaker grandmother, Priscilla Wakefield, had deployed Adam Smith to write her *Reflection on the Present Condition of the Female Sex, with Suggestions for its Improvement*, another of the radical publications that ran off Joseph Johnson's press in 1798. Cousin of another Quaker activist, Elizabeth Fry, Edward Gibbon Wakefield was surrounded by both theorists and practitioners of political and moral reform.[66]

The Australasian plans that alerted Malthus started with population, prompted by an article, "On the State and Prospects of the Country," in the *Quarterly Review*: "Population has, for at least fifteen or twenty years, been increasing at a rate for which no improvement in agriculture or manufactures could afford employment." Like the "excess" barbarians of Europe's past who

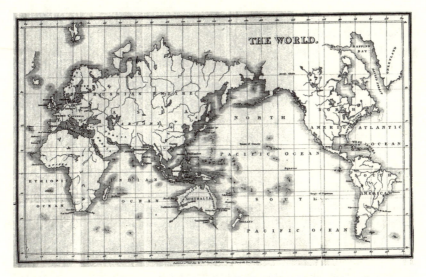

Figure 7.1. Map showing the world c. 1829, including New Holland (west), Australia and New South Wales (east), United States (east), North America, and Owhyee in the Pacific Ocean. Unattributed, from Robert Gouger (ed.), *A Letter from Sydney, the Principal Town of Australasia, together with the Outline of a System of Colonization*, (London: J. Cross, 1829). Reproduced by permission of the Master and Fellows of Trinity College, Cambridge.

swarmed south, England's population should travel over the seas, to the great land in the south, the western half of which Wakefield and Gouger still called New Holland. New South Wales was the eastern half of the continent, while by "Australasia" they meant the surrounding large and small islands, including Van Diemen's Land.[67]

The younger men doffed their hats to their elders, in discursive moves that at once acknowledged and dismissed them. For example, if an Englishman ("Mr Wilmot Horton, for instance") were offered one wish to bring about the greatest good for the country, for what would he ask? The destruction of his natural enemy, the French? For an earthquake to swallow up troublesome Ireland? No. He would wish for "the power to increase the territory of Britain according to the wants of the people." "Behold your wish accomplished!" the writers continued, inviting readers to imagine the wasteland of South Africa or Australasia removed and attached to the coast of Britain. Readers, of course, had been asked to imagine just this by Malthus, thirty years earlier. Gouger and Wakefield, like Wilmot Horton and Malthus, thought the mother country might well think of the colonies "as so many extensions of her own territory." But what value would that land acquire? What role should government play in creating that value? And what was the value of labor in such a colonial extension of territory? Wakefield and Gouger's point was to suggest that this land, like the colonial wastelands that were the property of the Crown, should not be given away, but sold to the highest bidder. The first point of political economy that the fictional writer of the "letter from Sydney" made was that thousands of acres could be purchased for very little but were accordingly hard to sell. Its value was low: "There are millions upon millions of acres, as fertile as mine, to be had for nothing." Labor, on the other hand, scarce in the colonies, was worth a lot—enough to create entirely different social orders, upside down and back to front, in that antipodean way. Agricultural laborers were of more value than "literary men," for example. "Sir Walter Scott, Sir Humphry Davy, and Mr Malthus, would not earn as much in this colony as three brawny experienced ploughmen." The generational dismissal was as clear as the new assessment of the value of land and labor in the colonies.[68]

It is not apparent whether Malthus met Wakefield, but Malthus and Gouger certainly became acquainted, and between February and August 1830 talked over colonization and emigration in some detail. Malthus was not enough persuaded to respond to Gouger's announcement in April 1830 of a public meeting to establish what was to be called the National Colonization Society. Wilmot Horton, by contrast, chaired the meeting that successfully formed the society in June of that year.[69] In the committee room in the British Coffee House, Cockspur Street, Gouger had prepared the *Statement of the Principles and Objects of a Proposed National Society for the Cure and Prevention of Pauperism, by Means of Systematic Colonization*. It acknowledged Wilmot Horton by name and Malthus by principle:

> From the moment when, in consequence of the zealous exertions of Mr Wilmot Horton, emigration was seriously contemplated with a view to the cure and prevention of pauperism in Britain, philosophers and statesmen have acknowledged the importance of the question; but those, almost without exception, who have carefully examined the whole subject, insist on two *conditions* as indispensable to any good practical measure . . . 1st. That the vacuum created by emigration, should not be filled up by an increase of people, arising from that tendency of population to increase beyond the means of subsistence, which, alone, class for emigration. 2ndly, That the cost of emigration should *inevitably*, be less than that of maintaining the excess of people.[70]

What was Wakefield and Gouger's "systematic colonization," and how did it differ from Wilmot Horton's plan? The architects worked from a definition of "colonization" where implicitly unoccupied land was the first principle: "the creation of everything but land where nothing but land exists." With this definition in mind, he claimed that "the North Americans are the most extensive *colonizers* (in the strict and proper sense of the word) that ever existed." First, then, this Crown-owned land would be bought for cash, without exception, not granted free ("for the execution of this provision, the *mode* of selling waste land in North America would furnish a useful model"). Second, rent from land would be taxed, and the proceeds of that tax, together with sales of land, would form an emigration fund to bring British laborers, free of cost, to the colony. Third, the specific emigration of young couples was sought: "an absolute preference be given to young persons, and that no excess of males be conveyed to the colony free of cost." And finally, they sought a concentration of settlement, not its dispersal. This would be effected by keeping the price of land high enough that emigrants could not purchase it immediately, thus retaining a labor force for some time, in closer settlements in which there would, additionally, be some division of labor.[71]

"Concentration" was Wakefield and Gouger's signature argument. Dispersed populations brought no particular value; dense colonial populations did. America was very much their key instance here as well. They looked historically, like Malthus, to early colonial ventures. The pamphlet described the Dutch colonization of New York where settlers were profitably hemmed in, kept dense. In the Dutch Cape Colony, by comparison, early settlers dispersed "and, by degrees, they became half savages." According to this view, too much land with too few people was a problem, the downfall of the precarious Swan River Colony in Western Australia (1829). Concentration of people *is* civilization in this account, recalling Malthus's stadial theory that aligned density with economic development, thinness with native economies in New Holland and North America, and higher density with agriculture and commerce. Over 1831, Gouger and Robert Torrens developed a plan to request a charter similar to seventeenth-century North American charters, in the name of the South Australian Land Company. Put to the Colonial Office in July 1832, this initial version of a newly planned antipodean colony was rejected.[72]

This new world lesson of concentration was quite different from Wilmot Horton's aspirations for British North America, something he discussed with Malthus. The great advantage of North America, he wrote, was the easy diffusion of people right across it—"population can spread itself . . .

the excess would always be drained off imperceptibly"—and into the long-distant future. No one ever complained of excess population in the United States, agreed Wilmot Horton, but who does not complain of it in the United Kingdom? In America, if population presses on subsistence, it has "nothing to do but to retire to the outer circle of present civilization, and to form a circle of still larger area, which the unlimited extension of territory renders possible and easy." For insular Britain, there was nowhere to go, and the lower classes inevitably suffered—unless, of course, the colonies themselves were considered Britain's larger area. In comparing America and Britain, Wilmot-Horton parroted Malthus's own ideas back to him.[73]

Malthus responded that British colonists might just as easily flow from Canada to the United States; in fact, "there is a considerable chance of its being taken by the 'United States'," an entity he still put in inverted commas.[74] Malthus had warned that this was one risk in contemplating expensive government-assisted schemes. Indeed, in their conversation at the Select Committee on Emigration, Malthus agreed that while accession of population to British North America would turn land currently "in a state of desert" into fertile land, the fact remained that that land may not always belong to the British Empire. Why so, asked Wilmot Horton? Why would they want to separate? "There might not," Malthus responded, "be a particular wish on the part of the colonies to separate; but they may be conquered by the United States." Both men agreed that the greater the British emigrant population in British North America, the more secure the colonies would be against such an outcome.[75]

America was always the key instance, always the benchmark for the possibilities and pitfalls of colonization, even for the new generation of colonial reformers who still saw wealth in terms of relations between humans and land, even if much of the produce was returning to Lancashire cotton mills. Indeed, *England and America* (1833) was Wakefield's next major publication.[76] One curious element of Wakefield's work that distinguished it from Malthus's was its forthright treatment of slavery. An economic advantage of slavery, Wakefield wrote, was that it kept people in one concentrated spot and efficiently divided labor to produce exchangeable commodities. "If there were no slaves in America, if slaves were allowed to appropriate and exhaust new land, every one of them doing almost everything for himself, who would produce those exchangeable commodities?" Gouger and Wakefield did not want to "dwell on the advantages, not to mention the terrible evils, which America has derived from slavery." (And, in another register, they stated that slave labor is less profitable than free labor). But they did want to ask, "What might Washington and Jefferson have been, if their father had not been slave owners?—a sort of wild men of the woods!" The slavery analysis in these documents is little remarked upon but is quite remarkable, not least because Britain's Slavery Abolition Act was just around the corner, 1833. Slavery, for Gouger and Wakefield, was a historical object lesson in the benefits of concentration and accumulation. In colonial circumstances where colonists and laborers were dispersed over free or cheap land, "the want of power to accumulate soon removes the desire whereby civilized men are converted into semi-barbarians." This was the unfortunate, degenerate fate of the French in Lower Canada and the Spanish in Buenos Aires.[77]

Malthus considered the work of the National Colonization Society and the plans for systematic colonization closely, in correspondence with Wilmot Horton. He had a few difficulties with it. Malthus explained that his inclination toward the Wakefield-Gouger scheme was precisely because—in theory—it was not going to cost the British government anything and therefore might be attempted with little risk.[78] But he was not convinced that funds could be raised for emigration solely by the sale of land by the New South Wales government. He did not think that young couples would volunteer to emigrate if the price of land was high "such as would render an independent settlement comparatively difficult . . . particularly if they could obtain greater advantages by the higher wages of labour and the greater facility of settling in the Canadas or the United States." And then Malthus offered not a principle of population but a "principle of colonization": that multiple settlements were needed, not just one "concentration around a single town," so that new markets for produce could emerge. "There is certainly danger of defeating the great object of colonization by prematurely forcing concentration." While he agreed that "artificial concentration" of population has its advantages, the means for effecting this—through the price of land—should be kept as low as possible. "I always also expressed my opinion that the lowest price of land talked of was too high rather than too low." In fact, the upper limit of the price of land should be that which "*would not prevent the greatest possible increase of people.*" In the manner of his principle of population, this principle might derive from observation of "long experience." Running counter to its own deployment of US history, the National Colonization Society would do well here to observe the great experience of the United States that had not forced concentrations. In the end, Malthus saw the new systematic colonization plans as vainly attempting to combine irreconcilable elements, and he described them to Gouger thus: "namely the advantages of cultivating a new and fertile territory involving a very high reward for labour, and a constant succession of settlers from the labouring classes, with the advantages derived from a concentrated population, cheaper labour, and the employment of capitals of a more mercantile character." [79]

They discussed it all in the context of a detailed emigration bill that Wilmot Horton had written and was—still—gathering information and opinions on. Nassau Senior was asked for extensive commentary that Wilmot Horton, typically, was to publish in his endless round of consultation. Malthus returned forensically detailed and itemized responses, both to Wilmot Horton's plan and Senior's view of it. [80] He took a draft away with him to Great Malvern, on a short tour in June 1830 "by way of change of air," since both he and his wife were unwell. [81] From the Malvern Hills he still pressed his concerns that the vacuum produced by emigration would simply be filled. How could sufficient numbers be removed to prevent or offset this? "It would be a contradiction to all theory and all past experience to deny the strong tendency of population to recover lost numbers." They talked over all the elements again: Ireland, redundance, potatoes, labor, voids, wages, and the cost of colonization. In the end, he "quite approve[d]" of the Bill. But Malthus also brought Wilmot Horton back to the core agenda: relief for the poor. "I think you have not dwelt sufficiently on the duty of the higher classes to make every exertion that is likely to be effectual to improve the physical conditions and moral habits of the labouring classes. . . . We are bound to remedy as far as we can the evil we have inflicted." And then, signaling final persuasion after years of discussion: "Unquestionably the best first step is a plan of emigration." [82] Again, on August 23 Malthus affirmed Wilmot Horton. "I am convinced that it is emigration alone which, in the present state of things, can present any fair prospect of an essential improvement in the condition of the labouring classes, consistently with humanity and good policy. And should it be determined by Parliament to introduce Poor Laws into Ireland, it appears to me, I own, that a large previous emigration would be absolutely necessary as a preliminary step." [83] Such a statement shows how Malthus had rethought his own position on emigration over a thirty-year period.

The intricate discussion between aging men was poignant, however. As events turned out, the House of Commons had heard enough from the endlessly consulting Wilmot Horton, and for too long. The session closed for the summer of 1830 without even discussing the matter. Over the next few years it was not Wilmot Horton's emigration bill but the energetic new systematic colonization that garnered attention.

Wilmot Horton's reports on emigration nonetheless prompted responses from many different quarters, and often because they featured Malthus's contribution. The first and longest came from Thomas Sadler, Tory MP. Quick off the mark, he attacked Malthus's views on Irish emigration in an anonymous pamphlet, *Ireland: Its Evils and their Remedies, being a refutation of the errors of the Emigration Committee and others.* But that was not all. He prefaced his commentary on Ireland with a synopsis of "an original treatise about to be published in the Law of Population developing the real principle on which it is universally regulated." It was an attack on Malthus that was soon after boldly published in long version, announcing not merely a *principle,* but a *Law of Population* (1830). A "strange work," Malthus called it, privately, a restrained assessment since in public Sadler had called Malthus's principle an "utter fallacy," "pernicious dogmas," a "false theory," "an indelible disgrace to the age," and "equally injurious to man and derogatory to his Maker." Sadler's work prompted a long response from Wilmot Horton on which both Senior and Malthus commented. More importantly, it was reason for Malthus to publish his own *Summary View of the Principle of Population*, a reprint of the earlier entry on population in the *Encyclopaedia Britannica*. Appearing in 1830, this was his final attempt to clarify his principle and to clear up long-accumulating misunderstandings. The new 1830 preface to this pamphlet suggested that misinterpretations had arisen from people pronouncing on the *Essay* without having read it but also that the quarto edition was less available than it should have been because of its length, size, and therefore its expense. Something shorter was warranted.[84]

And there was the new world again, driving Malthus's central proposition. His whole endeavor was "to answer the question, generally, which had been applied, particularly, to New Holland by Captain Cook, namely, 'By what means is the population of this country kept down to the number which it can subsist?'" The clearest question to which his principle was an answer, came by Malthus's own admission not from his own pen, but from that of Cook.[85]

By the time Malthus rewrote his *Summary View* he was an old hand at deflecting criticism. There was a lot of it. One of the predictable responses to his work was that it ignored vast parts of the world still uninhabited and uncultivated; that he underplayed how much of the Earth remained to be claimed and peopled. "This is unquestionably true," he conceded. Many parts of the Earth were "very thinly peopled." There might in theory be population growth for a time, enabled by a great increase in the cultivation of that part of the Earth. But, he asked himself as much as the reader, how could this cultivation be put fully into operation? How was civilization and improvement—economically considered—to be brought to thinly peopled regions? One option was for local—indigenous—economies and societies to develop new methods and means of cultivation. "If it is to be accomplished by the improvement of the actual inhabitants of the different parts of the earth in knowledge, in government, in industry, in arts, and in morals, it is scarcely possible to say how it ought to be commenced with the best prospect of success, or to form a conjecture as to the time which it could be effected." Malthus simply did not know how this indigenous improvement might happen. On the other hand, improvement might be effected by emigration from the already-improved parts of the world. This also had Malthus puzzling: new settlements had always been attended with great difficulties; people were always unwilling to leave their own country. And what happened to the indigenous people driven back? This would entail either war or extermination, or both, he wrote in his *Summary View*.[86]

* * *

Over the 1820s and early 1830s, when Malthus was so engaged with the questions of emigration, a number of new antipodean agricultural and colonization companies were chartered. The Van Diemen's Land Company, the South Australian Company, and, slightly later, the Wakefield-inspired New Zealand Land Company. These were decades of significant territorial expansion in the colonies, as previously coastal maritime entrepôts became bases for a commercial pastoral economy. The new agricultural companies explored, surveyed, and cleared great new regions of Aboriginal land that had previously been left more or less alone. As significant in terms of impact on Aboriginal people in New South Wales were the so-called squatters, who neither bought nor were granted land that lay beyond the formal limits of settlement but who nevertheless moved their stock and their laborers onto it. They simply took it. Many were soon to become very wealthy indeed, benefiting from the displacement of locals. In this process of land taking, both within and without British law, Aboriginal inhabitants were sometimes moved on, sometimes incorporated into the pastoral and agricultural industries, and sometimes killed. In short, these were crisis years.

When Malthus nominated war as one outcome of British effort to improve the unimproved land of the world, he may well have had Van Diemen's Land in mind; it is not entirely clear. What was called at the time the Black War was waged between Aborigines and British settlers between 1824 and 1831, later labeled by Tasmanian historian N. J. B. Plomley a "Seven Years War." Major new agricultural ventures saw first surveyors, then sheep and shepherds, and then settlers and convicts move onto land that Aboriginal groups traditionally crossed seasonally. Aboriginal people resisted this rapid change, raiding settlements, stealing stock, wounding and killing settlers. Hostilities escalated dramatically, on both sides, from 1824. Huts were burned, convict laborers and settlers were speared, sheep were stolen, Aboriginal men, women, and children killed in reprisal attacks. "All is terror and dismay in this part of the Colony," wrote one colonist in 1831.[87]

The sudden change in the mid-1820s from relatively peaceful to warring relations between Indigenous people and British settlers was partly at the hand of Robert Wilmot Horton. On behalf of Secretary of State Bathurst, Wilmot Horton directly negotiated the formation of the Van Diemen's Land Company, which was granted (and indeed still holds) much of the northwestern portion of the island. It was Van Diemen's Land Company laborers who carried out some of the most notorious killings on some of the most contested ground and whose actions were later subject to official inquiry.[88]

The company was formed "for the cultivation and improvement of waste lands in His Majesty's island of Van Diemen's Land." But did this "waste land" belong to the Crown in the first place? Clearly Aboriginal people did not think so. The claim that it was "His Majesty's Island," to be surveyed, distributed, improved, sold, and settled was in dispute. Unlike a small number of instances in the history of North American colonization, there had been no official treating in New South Wales or Van Diemen's Land. This was unusual, and even by its own measure British sovereignty over Aboriginal land and people was by no means a settled matter. This war raised the very question of British right of occupation, something that David Collins had simply presumed on his arrival in 1804 but that had become increasingly scrutinized by the Colonial Office. To the Aboriginal people in Van Diemen's Land, the British were invaders, outsiders in law and custom. But it was not only Aboriginal people who thought this, one settler observing, as the violence escalated, "We are at war with them; they look upon us as enemies—as invaders as their oppressors and persecutors—they resist our invasion." Wilmot Horton's own Colonial Department issued instructions to the governor about how Aborigines were to be treated when they attacked British property, stock, and people: "When such disturbances cannot be presented or allayed by less vigorous measures, to oppose force by force, and to repel such Aggressions in the same manner, as if they proceeded from subjects of any accredited State." Troops were mobilized, and, albeit reluctantly, the governor proclaimed that Aborigines who attacked the British were to be treated "as open Enemies." Action against the Aborigines was unequivocally military, as indicated in the 1831 House of Commons paper, *Military Operations lately carried on against the Aboriginal Inhabitants of Van Diemen's Land.* There was, indeed, a war over the land that Wilmot Horton and Malthus agreed should be settled, cultivated, and improved with British capital and British public funds for the benefit of redundant Irish, Scottish, and English paupers.[89]

None of this was immaterial to British political economy. Two of Malthus's circle—Robert Torrens and Robert Gouger—were as wholly embroiled in the question of land, colonization, and indigenous sovereignty as it was possible to be. Torrens in particular, who had founded the Political Economy Club with Malthus and others, was deeply engaged in debate with the Colonial Office over the relationship between land, Aboriginal people, and the proposed new settlement in South Australia. George Grey wrote to Torrens questioning the Colonisation Commission's plans, asking him to remember that "numerous tribes of people whose proprietary title to the soil we have not the slightest ground for disputing." And: "Before His Majesty can be advised to transfer to his subjects the property of the land of Australia he must have at least some reasonable assurance that he is not about to sanction any act of injustice towards the Aboriginal natives of that part of the globe." Nobody wanted in South Australia the kind of war with Aborigines that had been going on in Van Diemen's Land since the mid-1820s. Some of those who wanted war least were political economists in Malthus's club who doubled as colonial speculators.[90]

In 1830, then, Malthus nominated both "war and extermination" as an effect of emigration and colonization, developing his longstanding anxiety about natives being removed, driven into a corner. That year the so-called Black Line in Van Diemen's Land was executed. One colonist called it "a war of extermination," using Malthus's own terms. The governor organized a military operation, enlisting civilian men, convict and free, as well as his troops, to sweep across the settled districts of the island as a human chain, aiming to drive the remaining Aboriginal tribes into the southeastern corner, across a narrow isthmus and onto a peninsula that would be reserved for them and where they would be theoretically free from settler violence. The expensive manoeuvre failed, however, and the governor turned to more diplomatic efforts, eventually persuading Aboriginal people to surrender and to relocate to a protected reserve. In 1834, the year Malthus died, 134 Aboriginal people were removed to Flinders Island in the Bass Strait, where government hoped they would be civilized and christianized. It was a humanitarian response to just the kind of anxiety about extermination that Malthus himself had expressed, one that was shortly to take institutional form as the Aborigines Protection Society. The moral implication of "driving natives into a corner where they might starve" was perhaps solved by protecting them in that corner and supplying food and good shelter. A decade later, however, only 47 people survived. The survivors of the Black War did starve, less from hunger—they were amply provided with food—than from the dispossession of life-giving land. That same land gave life, and more, to the rapidly doubling population of settlers.[91]

The two related meanings of extermination were thus playing out. "Extermination" meant removal to another place, an older, spatial meaning closer to the Latin root. It is to the point—if ironically so—that the word was sometimes used in this period to describe the removal of Scottish Highlanders. In 1820, for example, the *Scotsman* described a "system of extermination": "nearly 600 souls to be removed, without a place of residence provided for one of them—not knowing under the canopy of heaven where to go." The second sense of extermination—utter destruction or elimination—was also current in the early nineteenth century. One use, for example, was the Jennerian Society for the Extermination of the Small-pox, established in 1803, a context in which Malthus also used the term. There was thus an ambiguous or perhaps double sense in which Malthus described what might happen to native people driven into a corner. One kind of extermination became another, and the removal of Van Diemen's Land Aborigines was the most precise, and already famous, contemporary instance.[92]

Over a thirty-year period—just over one generation after David Collins's original settlement—the indigenous population had been reduced by an estimated 90 percent. During the warring 1820s, the British population grew from only 5,400 in 1820 to 24,000 in 1830. While the numbers of Aboriginal people are unknown in 1820, by the end of the Black War they were enumerated precisely: 350 in 1831. As a colonist later observed in a statement that had Franklin and Malthus's work behind it, "A change so rapid in the relations of a people to the soil, will scarcely find a parallel in this world's history." This colonist was certainly not alone in noting the depopulation of one people and the rapid repopulation by another. Just two years after Malthus's death, the young Charles Darwin visited Van Diemen's Land, taking note in his diary: "The Aboriginal blacks are all removed & kept (in reality as prisoners) in a Promontory, the neck of which is guarded. I believe it was not possible to avoid this cruel step; although without doubt the misconduct of the Whites first led to the Necessity." He speculated on the reproduction of human populations, Franklin style: "Thirty years is a short period, in which to have banished the last aboriginal from his native island,—and that island nearly as large as Ireland. I do not know a more striking instance of the comparative rate of increase of a civilized over a savage people." Darwin shared Malthus's misgivings: "I fear from what I heard at Hobart Town, that they are very far from being contented: some even think the race will soon become extinct." This was not, ultimately, the case. Nonetheless, it was certainly the case that British population increase over the nineteenth century was very largely enabled by what was grown on new world land; "ghost acres" that were never ghostly to start with.[93]

The removal of the Irish and Scottish poor with which Malthus was so engaged, their transformation into "emigrants" and "colonists" and "settlers," connected old world clearances with new world clearances of both land and people. These Scots and Irish even became landowners themselves, an outcome inconceivable in their old world context. The Irish and Scottish "clearances" that so exercised Malthus are thus profitably brought into the same frame as the simultaneous (indeed, in some ways the consequential) colonial clearances in the Australian colonies. The very emigration, agricultural, and pastoral endeavors that Wilmot Horton's Colonial Office and the colonial reformers proposed *were* the reason indigenous occupants were being removed, "exterminated," and with some vigor in the 1820s and 1830s. Malthus's *Essay*, so fundamentally concerned with land improvement across the globe, serves to highlight this truth of settler colonialism, at once connecting land and people (depopulating the Aboriginal estate, to enlarge the settler farm and agricultural company) and connecting old world clearance of people and land, with a different order of new world clearances, so as to turn seeming wastelands into something apparently more productive. This "age of emigration," as Malthus called it, was one in which the old world and the new clashed violently.[94]

Chapter 8

The *Essay* in New Worlds

THOMAS ROBERT MALTHUS'S *Essay on the Principle of Population* belonged to new worlds not only in its inception but in its reception. Even in Malthus's lifetime, his work was read, reviewed, reprinted, translated, discussed, and appropriated in the very places he had identified as central to his population principle. Those repeated analyses demonstrate that, alongside their criticism of Malthus over intra-European concerns (most apparently with poor relief), his contemporaries understood that his argument had always, and fundamentally, been formulated in relation to the Americas and then extended to the new worlds of the Pacific Ocean. But the chronology of the new world discussion was crucial to its impact; Malthus's text achieved international and trans-oceanic discussion at a time of mounting confidence among those who promoted Western imperialism. His text circulated within new worlds, that is, only after the major European powers, which had long been preoccupied with the end stages of the Second Hundred Years' War, were freed from that concern and able to throw resources (including European settlers) overseas. Meanwhile, multiple revolutions in the Americas had created or were creating nations independent of European empires but quite similar to them in their schemes to separate Indian populations from their lands.

Timing was everything. Although Malthus had written his work at a complicated moment in the history of modern European empires, his work received rapid uptake when ambivalence was replaced with a (Western) self-assurance about the justice of resettlement of extra-European territories that would prevail for more than a century. And because of that timing, combined with Malthus's propensity to issue cautions against imperialist exploitation of new world natives only timidly, his moral statements in this regard have been, since 1803, slighted. New world discussions of population quite often warred with Malthus's original principle, or else sided with his growing acceptance of the benefits of emigration and then went back to influence European discussions of population in a constant feedback loop.[1]

This final chapter uses methods from scholarship on the history of the book and other cultures of print to trace the growing presence of Malthus's *Essay* abroad, in its original editions, in translations, and as discussed in other printed matter, principally newspapers, focusing on the time from the publication of the initially expanded *Essay* in 1803 until December 29, 1834, when Malthus died. This analysis establishes that Malthus and his text had notable places within the intellectually engaged public spheres in the new worlds of the early nineteenth century, beyond the more bounded world of governmental activity that characterized his impact (or lack of it) on abolition and colonization. That discovery suggests a global presence for the text that scholars for other parts of the world might profitably explore, building upon the results here, which indicate important engagement with Malthus's text in the Americas, paralleled by some responses in the Pacific. As well, and even though Malthus was trying to place a larger claim on the field of political economy with his 1820 *Principles of Political Economy*, he would always remain primarily identified abroad as the author of "the principle of population." And if anything, the new world template for his population assertions had its clearest implications within new worlds. The first Spanish translation of the *Essay*, for example, produced in 1846, would be of the expanded text, not the original, and even before 1846 discussion of Malthus in Spain and the Iberian colonies would focus on the French translations, also of post-1798 versions of his text; the first Spanish translation of the slimmer 1798 edition was not done until 1966, which guaranteed that Hispanic comprehension of Malthus was overwhelmingly of the expanded version of the *Essay*.[2]

And yet readers in the new worlds did not obediently accept Malthus in his own terms. The tendency in this era, before well-documented indigenous response to any Western texts, was that when free white settlers acquired Malthus's ideas, they bent them to support their appropriation of indigenous lands or desire for dense populations to support manufacturing. But there are some interesting exceptions. They indicate more complex reading and absorption of the principle of population, and they repeat some of the oldest questions about the character of new worlds, above all the implications of those worlds for the linked problems of nature and human nature. The old question that had set Malthus to writing his *Essay*—can humans achieve the highest state of happiness?—and the way he had answered it, negatively, with special reference to the new world sites that had seemed to offer Eden but instead revealed humanity's fallen state, remained (and remain) in play.

* * *

The *Essay on the Principle of Population* went out into the world at a moment when printed material had unprecedented means to do so. Several factors made that possible. The separation of the previously unified roles of printer, publisher, and bookseller meant that production and marketing underwent significant specialization. Industrial methods of printing made the production of reading material faster and cheaper. Even as empires spread over more of the globe, state censorship in the global west was becoming more relaxed, and information spread somewhat more freely. And untroubled by British copyright restriction, US publishers (the best developed in all of the new worlds) were able to reprint authors with impunity, as they did with Malthus.[3]

Malthus's text had its earliest new world uptake in the United States, where concern over population size and growth had been woven into the political fabric. The new republic constituted the clearest legacy of the British Empire's pre-revolutionary emphasis on growing population as an unusual strength of Anglophone colonies. Censuses remained important civic rituals, for example, despite their imperial pedigree; the most important instigator for colonial enumeration had been the British Board of Trade. American patriots of 1776 may have rejected Great Britain but not that nation's fascination with political arithmetic. During the United States' period of Confederation (1781–1789), the states that continued to enumerate their populations were those that had had imperially inspired censuses. Their leaders realized the political significance of population size and disposition, having seen those qualities become important points of argument in the decades before the Revolution. Although they had not originally been linked, the twin Anglo-American ideals of "no taxation without representation" and of a rapidly increasing number of consumer-producer settlers (who demanded their representation in Parliament) eventually merged, until arguments in favor of making political representation directly proportionate to population were the default, as if power lay primarily in numbers. This was a demand that reason-of-state arguments had not supported as such, though the Americans' case followed that old logic in other respects.[4]

The goal of making political representation proportionate to the number of US citizens would require regular and accurate headcounts, which were duly legislated in a national census. Decennial counting of the US population—not estimates of household sizes but what the US Constitution termed "actual enumeration"—was mandated by the constitution ratified in 1789. First carried out in 1790, the US census existed eleven years before England would stage a comparable event (within much smaller territory), though Sweden had led the way, in 1749, with what is considered to be the first accurate modern census on a national scale. Nevertheless, the United States had the first national census to be instituted at regular intervals.

It would be wrong to attribute all of these occurrences of concern—or delight—over expanding US population to Malthus himself, however. Because his principle of population was derivative, resulting from centuries of commentary and analysis on human increase in imperial zones, it cannot be said that any statement on the topic was necessarily due to his particular impact. There was an especially powerful confounding variable within the United States in the lingering influence of Benjamin Franklin, whose exponential catchphrase, that the numbers of North American settlers were "doubling every twenty years" (sometimes every twenty-five years), had taken on a life of its own. Although the idea had precedents in the work of Petty and Wallace, it had never acquired a firm place in public commentary until Franklin gave it renewed and specific life. The phrase had proliferated precisely in the acrimonious run-up to the American Revolution, when it comforted the patriots to think they would simply outbreed the British and it fascinated, if not alarmed, Britons for the same reason.[5]

Without naming him, for example, members of the Continental Congress had discussed Franklin's population estimate during the war. Via a circular letter of 1779, they broadcast his calculation to their constituents, to reassure them that, because their numbers were increasing so quickly, their productive capacity would likewise expand swiftly enough to cover the war debt. Indeed, John Jay, the letter's author, rephrased the matter in purely economic terms: "It is well known that the Inhabitants of this country encreased almost in the ratio of compound interest. By natural population they doubled every twenty years." After the war ended and United States independence was definitively recognized, state histories and compendia continued to celebrate the nation's rapid population growth, often reusing the comparison between rates of increase for Americans and for compound interest, as if proliferating citizens were in effect money in the bank.[6]

The rationale for counting different segments of the US population also followed, unfortunately, the racist configurations of Franklin's (and many others') original observations, as further developed by Malthus, which classified Indians and slaves as less important to the polity, if not entirely unwanted. The US Constitution stipulated that slaves be counted, for the purposes of taxation and representation, as three-fifths of free persons and that untaxed Indians not be counted at all. Both decisions linked property, above all land, to political personhood. Free white men in the early Republic had to own a minimum of property, typically real estate, to claim the franchise. Slaves could not legally own property and were not even property in their own right but instead belonged to others, their owners, who were counted as full persons.

Nor were nonlandholding individual Indians (whatever their claims on the customary community properties of families, tribes, or nations) the equivalent of white male property holders. The "three-fifths clause" would remain in place until 1865, when erased by the post–Civil War Thirteenth Amendment, which abolished slavery; the phrasing about untaxed Indians would be removed only in 1913 with the passage of the Sixteenth Amendment. These adjustments would not mean that free blacks and native Americans would easily gain the franchise, which had been embedded in racialized census requirements since 1789. In any case, Malthus would not live to see a United States that was even beginning to purge itself of the racially configured political arithmetic that had been present at the birth of the first independent new world republic.[7]

The character and results of the US census were in the meantime productive for debate over a distinctively new world rate of growth. US government officials focused on the problem of distributing federal congressmen based on a growing population. Those of a more theoretical bent calculated the absolute rate of growth, which would be statistically possible once the censuses of 1790 and 1800 yielded data for two points in time. Thus Thomas Jefferson estimated a geometric rate of overall population growth in his *Notes on the State of Virginia* (1785), in which he assumed that the black population doubled roughly every twenty-five years, and in 1801 he used census returns to determine, with logarithms, a doubling of the total US population every 22.23 years. But was this rate of growth achieved by natural increase or by immigration? That was a pointed question about new world population taken up by no less than William Godwin, Malthus's original target.[8]

In responding to Malthus's *Essay*, Godwin had taken his time, but, like limping Nemesis, he got there in the end. The two moral philosophers had been exchanging views in private letters and personal encounters. But those conversations had not satisfied Godwin; if anything, they seem to have infuriated him, especially by the time of the *Essay*'s unrepentant fifth edition of 1817. So, in 1820, Godwin published an extensive refutation of Malthus. The text of over six hundred pages is weakened, it must be said, by pique and by repetition. Where he might have scored hits, Godwin instead wandered around and around his target, firing complaints rather than substantial critiques. It would have been interesting had he submitted to reason and firm editorship, because the foundations of his criticism, about Malthus's primordial inspiration, North America, were important. Godwin knew this, which is why he did aim squarely at this old part of the new worlds, stating that his main goal was to refute Malthus's "main principle," the geometrical increase of population based on the North American example. Or, as he said, in parodying Malthus's work: "If America had never been discovered, the geometrical ratio, as applied to the multiplication of mankind, would never have been known." "The entire foundation of his work lies in one simple sentence," Godwin concluded of Malthus. "'In the Northern States of America, the population has been found to double itself for above a century and a half successively, in less than twenty-five years.'" If "Mr. Malthus's discovery is built on 'the American increase,'" then Godwin thought it necessary to get to the bottom of that new world hypothesis. At first he did so by tracing, as Malthus had done, the intellectual genealogy of the phrase "doubling every twenty years" back to its source. He verified that Benjamin Franklin "was the first man that started the idea of the people of America being multiplied by procreation, so as to 'double their numbers every twenty years.'" But the source revealed that the phrase was not a neutral description of a law of nature: "The paper from which these extracts are taken, was expressly written to exalt the importance and glory of his [Franklin's] country."[9]

Godwin sought statistics to challenge or vindicate Malthus's central assumption, and he found them in the US census returns. In that way he interrogated what could have been the strongest evidence for Malthus's claims, which Malthus himself had declined to do, notably (and puzzlingly) when, in his appendix to the 1806 edition of the *Essay*, he refused both to speculate as to the future of US population growth and to consider that data might exist to question his mathematical definitions of increase, population versus food; "at present I see no mode of obtaining such information," he wrote in a footnote to the appendix. Godwin thought that was nonsense, and the several pages of tables based on the US censuses in his text display his contempt for Malthus's timidity. While admitting that the statistics showed a quite staggering rate of population growth, Godwin pointed out the difficulty of determining which of the new Americans had actually been born there, rather than arrived from abroad. Given US encouragement of immigration, some citizens were likely to have been transplants; significantly, US policy revealed little fear of Malthusian population growth. In any case, Malthus himself had not analyzed these figures; his suppositions remained just that. In making this final point, Godwin savaged Malthus in the old terms by which he himself had been criticized, as author of conjectures rather than of laws.[10]

"It has been my purpose to assail his theory at the foundation," Godwin admitted candidly. From the statistical dimensions of the debate, which were focused on the US census returns, he turned back to the question of human happiness and mused over the specific places it might be found. He took his antagonist's point that material circumstances were necessary to felicity, or else their absence was the cause of the opposite condition. But he deplored Malthus's insistence that there was no haven on Earth that offered any promise of present or future relief. Godwin wanted to believe in a new world, some beckoning site of hope for humanity. He was astute enough to register doubt over that possibility, though he expressed it as if a paraphrase of the abbé Raynal's great tragic question: "Has the discovery of America been beneficial or harmful to the human race?" Again, Godwin's version of the query, stated more than once in his book, was that "if America had never been discovered, the geometrical ratio, as applied to the multiplication of mankind, would never have been known," and thus a bleak contribution to moral philosophy, Malthus's principle of population, would never have been made. By connecting the deepest reservation about the human condition to new worlds, Malthus, Godwin complained, was always thus warning "Remember Utopia! Reject every measure, however specious in its appearances, that looks that way!" And that rejection of utopias depended on the insidious comparison of "two worlds!" These were an "Old World" that was "worth living in" and a Malthusian new world, where humans have "fallen into the hands of a remorseless stepmother, Nature."[11]

Godwin was quite obviously motivated, personally and philosophically, to be suspicious of Malthus, though he was not so incapacitated by antipathy that he could not indeed assail the principle of population "at the foundation," meaning in terms of the primordial new world scenario. Compared to other British critics, such as William Hazlitt and Robert Southey, he was far more astute about the American genesis of Malthus's thesis. In sixteen major British reviews of his book, critics were divided on the *Essay*'s merits, but agreed that America lay at the heart of the matter; the US census may have been at no other time so roundly discussed in Britain. Responses variously reproved Godwin for his "rancorous revenge" or praised his most "heartwarming and complete of peaceful victories." But none of the reviews quarreled with Godwin's focus on the North American example: "unimpeachable proof in support of even the highest rate of increase" said one reviewer, though another more skeptically admitted only that "the geometrical and arithmetical ratios" of Malthus's principle "have no other grounds than the supposed doubling of population in America by native births in 25 years." It was "a living and most instructive example." Nor was there doubt that the US census was the right set of statistics to interrogate, whether they agreed with Godwin's conclusions or not. As one reviewer summarized, "No one before Mr. Godwin thought of examining the data on which Mr. Malthus's structure rests." Still, one review noted the terrible irony that Godwin's suspicions about the US example undermined his own faith in utopias: "he seems in some measure so blinded by his passions, that he cannot perceive the support which Mr Malthus's book is calculated to give to some of his own speculations."[12]

Godwin was not alone in being uneasy that, if America offered no haven from disaster, the implication had to be that there was no earthly hope for humanity. There was a more general British peevishness in relation to United States population growth, however empirically established. Although the London- and Edinburgh-published *A New Geographical, Commercial, and Historical Grammar . . .* (1790) had concluded that America's "superior plenty" explained many differences between Europeans and Americans, not least because the latter "doubled every 20 years, exclusive of emigration from Europe," that scenario was not universally accepted as a positive one. The London *New Monthly Magazine*, in an essay reprinted in the *Royal Gazette* of Jamaica in 1821, reproached an invented prototype, the demographically smug white male American: "With Malthus in one hand, and a map of the back settlements in the other, he boldly defies us to a comparison with America, *as she is to be*, and chuckles with precocious exultation over the splendours which the 'geometrical ratio' is to shed upon her story." Actually, the stereotype was not far from the truth.[13]

* * *

Malthus's ideas about population, material constraint, and economic power would find a home within a specific US historical context. As the US census stipulations about "Indians not taxed" made clear, stadial thinking had found favor in British North America and continued to influence American interpretations of population. Settlers in the United States found the theory useful in defining themselves as superior to the precommercial Indians whose lands they had either already taken or were beginning to covet, as white population increased and expanded westward. Franklin may have been careful to remove from his essay his prediction that European settlers would replace American Indians, but his overall point about colonized lands was not lost on a later generation of imperialists. A Philadelphia compendium of travel accounts for young readers explained in 1816 that America's "wandering savages" would inevitably give way to white settlers, whose numbers were "doubled every twenty years."[14]

Because the US reception of Malthus's text was strongly tilted toward his expanded editions, the new world elements of his population principle were present even in the earliest discussions of his book. The Readex compendium of early American newspapers lists no advertisements for the 1798 edition of the *Essay*, nor any reviews of it. Appropriately, however, the Library Company of Philadelphia, the nation's first lending library, founded by Benjamin Franklin among others, had a copy of the *Essay on the Principle of Population* by 1799. The Boston Library and the Library Company of Baltimore each had an *Essay* by 1802, obviously Malthus's 1798 book. These volumes seem to have been exceptional. It is striking that neither the Library of Congress nor the American Academy of Arts and Sciences appears to have held a copy of the first edition. Early comprehension of the book as an intra-European sally against Godwin and Condorcet may have impeded its initial arrival in the new world.[15]

But advertisements for imported copies of the 1803 edition begin to appear in fall of that same year. The earliest notice is in the September 27 issue of the New York *Evening Post*, roughly four months after the book was published. That was speedy for the time. In his study of the acquisitions of the Charleston Library Society from 1748 to 1811, James Raven has found that the fastest rate of American reception for a European book, from sending the order to getting the volume, was 150 days, or five months. This indicates that the American importer of the 1803 edition of Malthus's *Essay* had either anticipated its publication and preordered it or else worked with a bookseller in England who was authorized to select and send volumes on account. In either case, the buyer or seller knew what he was doing, because thereafter advertisements for the 1803 version of the *Essay* proliferate in newspapers published in New York, Philadelphia, Baltimore, and Georgetown. (It is possible that some of the advertisements that do not specify an edition, or number of volumes, are for the 1798 edition, the expanded version having paved the way for the original.) Like so many things in American history, the book then went west. By February 1807 it had been advertised for sale in Lexington, Kentucky. This was most likely still the second edition of 1803, though it is not impossible that the 1806 edition had sped to Kentucky by early 1807. Then, beginning on October 12, 1807, there were advertisements for the third edition, the first appearing in the New York *Daily Advertiser*. Copies that continued to arrive after December 1807 had either been ordered before that date, when President Thomas Jefferson placed an embargo on goods from all warring nations (including Great Britain), or else had somehow arrived in defiance of that ban, which lasted until 1815.[16]

And yet it is Jefferson who supplies the first recorded American reaction to Malthus's text. Jefferson was eager to receive new titles from Europe and was at least beginning to read the 1803 edition of the *Essay* by January 29, 1804, when he praised "the new work of Malthus on population" to another of publisher Joseph Johnson's authors, Joseph Priestley, describing it as "one of the ablest I have ever seen." In that initial reading, from a borrowed copy of the 1803 edition, Jefferson thought that Malthus's "main object is to determine the effects of redundancy of population, and to test the poor laws of England." (He might have gleaned this from secondhand discussions of the first edition.) But Jefferson was further enough into the book three days later to recognize the significance of its argument about America. This did not mean he agreed with Malthus. In a February 1 letter to the French political economist Jean-Baptiste Say, Jefferson stated that while in Europe "the quantity of food is fixed, or increasing in a slow and only arithmetical ratio," in America "the immense extent of uncultivated and fertile lands" not only enabled people to "marry young" but in the confidence that food "may increase geometrically." He underlined his conviction in that hemispheric difference by explaining several questions he posed to Say: "I shall have asked them because I think for America." Jefferson concluded that Malthus was essential reading for Americans, recommending him as part of any standard background in political economy.[17]

Most of the US reception of the *Essay* was similarly favorable. The earliest extended comment occurred in a long article in a Richmond, Virginia, newspaper in August 1804, on the utility of collections of essays as focused thought-experiments in moral philosophy. Malthus makes an appearance in a footnote, where an unnamed author praises his book on population as a counterweight to "the splendid illusions of fanciful speculation respecting the immutable condition of man on earth," a point of value to any "editor, legislator or instructor in Virginia." State-specific that advice may have been, but it was republished, along with the praise of Malthus, in a paper in Norwich, Connecticut. More to Malthus's point, another article in the Richmond *Enquirer*, probably by the same author, extolled Malthus for his warning that humans reproduced "in a geometrical ratio" whereas "the means of subsistence" did so only arithmetically. "Neither any possible state of improved agriculture, nor emigration to new countries, nor, lastly, the perfectibility of man" would offer a solution. Hence the need for moral discipline, if the alternatives were "vice" and "misery." In subsequent references, the *Enquirer* continued to applaud "the celebrated Malthus" and his "celebrated work." In 1809 an editorial in the *American Citizen* of New York City recommended Malthus, not because he described problems in the United States at present, but because he showed how to avoid the evils of human overpopulation and misery in future: "If we avoid the wreck which has befallen other nations, it can only be by shunning the causes which led to their destruction." Malthus proved an unexpected ally during the wartime embargoes. As one essay pointed out, the Englishman had confessed British dependence on the United States and the Baltic for key resources; products of these ghost acres were Great Britain's weak point. Finally, one American admirer concluded that the "unpleasant association connected with his [Malthus's] name" was a "silly prejudice" held by those who could not stomach the truth that "political improvement ... has its limits."[18]

It is impossible to calculate sales for imported copies of Malthus's book, but there is collateral evidence that they must have been decent. By 1807, for example, at least two American printers began to offer to publish, by subscription, an American edition of the *Essay on the Principle of Population*. At first the British edition of greatest interest to them seemed to be the first, rather than any currently being read. That might have been the case because the 1798 edition was in short supply within the United States, because it was missed the first time around. Also, and for the same reason, it would not compete with the imported copies. Finally, the 1798 edition was of course shorter and therefore less expensive (and financially risky) to produce. In the end, however, the printers decided to tackle the expanded edition of 1803, which was in press by late 1808.[19]

That edition, the first to be produced in the new world, appeared in 1809, a two-volume reprint of the third British edition of 1806. It was the product of two printers, Joseph Milligan and Roger Chew Weightman, who joined forces with an imprint based in Georgetown, the District of Columbia. The location indicated belief that interest in Malthus's ideas would be strongest in and around the nation's capital. Indeed, one of the edition's subscribers was President Jefferson, who had a regular account with Milligan and placed his order for the forthcoming work in November 1807, with the two printers and the president all quite aware that the impending US embargo would create significant opportunity for American publishers. (Many British authors would thus be denied profits from American sales—ironic, in Malthus's case, given his support of protective legislation.) That the edition must have been successful is indicated in an 1819 letter Milligan wrote to Jefferson, explaining his interest in publishing Malthus's very latest edition, something he would not have contemplated unless he thought it might sell. But in the end the US edition of 1809 seemed more than enough for American readers, who were accustomed to import British publications from Great Britain in any case, as they would do again after peace in 1815; the next US edition of Malthus would not appear until 1890. Canadian readers remained even more tied to the British publishing industry, with book production in Canada only taking off in the second half of the nineteenth century, though even it was then significantly augmented by imprints from Britain and the United States.[20]

North American responses to Malthus's *Essay* were not entirely uncritical. Some commentators focused on what Malthus had to say about commercial and manufacturing economies, with special reference to workers and the poor, problems still associated with the old world and therefore to be avoided in the new. As early as 1807, an advertisement for his work in a Philadelphia newspaper also offered a "Reply to Malthus on Population," most likely William Hazlitt's *A Reply to the Essay on Population . . .* (1807), which concluded that Malthus's *Essay* constituted a sermon to the poor preached by the rich. That outraged response, available in the United States an impressively short time after its London publication, retained a steady presence in newspaper advertisements. So did an essay on the necessity of manufacturing, even within the putatively land-rich United States. "Malthus has written a book," ran the much-reprinted essay, "which alleges an apparent series of truths, susceptible of mathematical demonstration; it is full of horror, for the people who may live to eat each other in the ninety ninth century." Confidence that the United States could somehow escape a dire Malthusian destiny increased, if anything, toward the end of Malthus's life. In 1834 a writer in Massachusetts complained that Malthus's "notions" were "absurd and monstrous in themselves, and most especially inapplicable to the circumstances of this country."[21]

Canadian public opinion was likewise dismissive, perhaps even more so. It is notable that "Malthus" was an easily recognized name in Canada, never preceded by any introduction other than (sometimes) "Mr.," and always to be dismissed as lacking expertise on new worlds, which by definition, settlers thought, cried out for population. Some of these Canadian critics were, interestingly, oblivious of Malthus's own acceptance of schemes to colonize Upper Canada. Thus the editorialist L. L. M., writing in the Montreal *Free Press* in 1823, declared that "an increase of population as an improvement in the state of every country, notwithstanding the sophistry of Malthus . . . none but system-mongers, or paradox-manufacturers, will deny; and the newer, and the more extensive the country, the greater is the proportionate benefit derived by the birth of every child, and the importation of every emigrant from abroad." In the 1829 *Essay on Marriage* published in Quebec, one commentator accepted that "Mr. Malthus' information may enable us to contrast the wretchedness and misery of European climes with Columbia's enjoyments." The unmiserable Columbia, meaning Canada, needed people. There, early marriages were "the soul and chief prop of empire" and the means by which all souls were brought into existence. The author concluded that "the design of his essay on Population cannot be sufficiently condemned" and approvingly quoted one politician's reaction to Malthus's *Essay*: "*'That is a wicked book.'*"[22]

The most sustained of new world assessments of Malthus appeared in Alexander Hill Everett's *New Ideas on Population: With Remarks on the Theories of Malthus and Godwin*, published in London and Boston in 1823. While serving as US chargé d'affaires to The Hague, Everett visited London, met Malthus at the East India College, and gave a polite description of him in the introduction to his book. That was a disarming lead-in to a bracingly confrontational assessment of both Malthus and Godwin. Everett began by saying that Godwin (and Condorcet) wrote in accord with the political fashions of their time, which made Malthus, as a commentator upon them, also limited by the context. "As the theory which Mr. Malthus undertook to refute was in a great measure the result of the political enthusiasm of the time, so the character of his refutation appears to have been determined or modified by a reaction of this enthusiasm." What dated both Godwin and Malthus, Everett contended, was their overly critical stance toward political institutions. Godwin "considers political institutions as absolutely mischievious," while "Malthus affirms that they are completely indifferent," nature always having the last word. Everett's remarks were very American, reflecting his generation's confidence that the United States had a republican form of government unsullied by the accreted customary powers that plagued Great Britain's—to which Godwin had rightly objected, even as he recommended nothing in their place, and within which Malthus worked without achieving reform. The very existence of the United States proved both of the Englishmen wrong.[23]

Neither was Everett convinced that population increase led to scarcity rather than abundance, and to determine the truth of the matter, he began where Malthus had begun, with North America and its original residents. The "savage" inhabitants had been too preoccupied with subsistence (and warfare) to flourish. But if by some circumstance their numbers did increase, they would surely be better off—"there will now be two hunters where there was before only one"—and a gain in productive capacity would follow. So too would herders and fishermen benefit from increased labor and productivity; so too did agricultural production expand with the assistance of greater numbers of laborers. (Obviously, Everett was ignoring Malthus's point that deer, fish, or grain might not increase as fast as their pursuers or cultivators.) Even where settled nations might seem to have surplus population, this could be sent abroad to colonies, where the trifecta of fresh land, superior agricultural knowledge, and demand for food elsewhere guaranteed economic success. Everett illustrated these suppositions with the contrasting yet interdependent fates of Great Britain and the United States, precisely the exempla Malthus had used, though to reach overtly different (because more optimistic) conclusions about new world population dynamics. Above all, Everett maintained, checks on population resulted from the "moral and physical imperfections of our nature," not the external checks of nonhuman nature beyond. Thus the "pure manners" and purely republican government of the Americans prophesied future glory, rather than the eventual finitude of land guaranteeing their eventual stagnation. Human nature would always triumph over mere nature, and fresh starts for humanity remain possible.[24]

Throughout his critique, Everett accepted that the United States furnished the fastest documented rate of natural population increase, directly contradicting Godwin's suggestion that immigration must account for at least part of it. (Everett analyzed trends in the youngest segments of the population to establish the unlikelihood that immigrants, who tended to be older, made the largest contributions to population growth.) He contrasted this distinctive rate to the less firm, but still striking, supposition that populations elsewhere did not enjoy such growth, instead being either stationary or regressive. The checks he identified as conducive to these trends included barbarism, meaning the lack of agriculture; vicious political systems, which could exist even in agricultural societies; private vice; and natural calamities. From all this he patriotically deduced that the United States of America had unparalleled levels of private and public virtue. This was an "answer to the calumnies on the moral character of the citizens of the United States, in which some European writers are accustomed to indulge." Everett would proceed to give reasons for supporting rather than abolishing the Poor Laws, but it is obvious that his central concern was to describe the US population in terms more favorable than he thought Godwin or Malthus had done. His conclusion was blunt: good morals and social institutions had profited US population, with the natural world as an only incidental factor, as could be seen in the contrasting condition of Indians, who dwelled in the same land yet were "diminishing in number and dying of want."[25]

These varied US responses suggest a fittingly complex response to Malthus, and yet there are some distinguishable patterns that reflected two significant (and divisive) national concerns. The worries were related: how might settler population move westward, and should slavery do so as well? As stated within these two concerns, Malthus became widely cited and discussed in national and regional media, above the local newspapers that had initially welcomed the *Essay*. The Boston-based *North American Review*, which began publication in 1815, was the closest thing that the United States had to a national periodical; it also circulated in other parts of the Americas (it would help disseminate Alexander Hill Everett's ideas, for instance, because it was run by another member of his family and it reviewed his book). The *North American Review* published twenty two articles on Malthus between 1815 and 1860; an additional nine appeared in the *United States Review* between 1837 and 1858. But just as Malthus had been utilized (to his horror) by both sides of the British debate over abolition, so Southern periodicals summoned him in defense of slavery, as in *Debow's Review* (twenty articles, 1846–1860) and in the *Southern Literary Messenger* (ten articles, 1834–1860).[26]

Even as the British argument over Malthus and slavery revolved around the question of population in Africa, focused on the slave trade, and (sometimes) characterized Malthus as proslavery, its American counterpart tended to focus on the possibility of slaves crowding out free white settlers in western regions (even in the absence of an Atlantic slave trade) and used Malthus—contradictorily—as evidence of the evils of either chattel slavery or else wage slavery. As early as 1819, in the pivotal argument over whether Missouri would be admitted to the United States as a free or as a slave state, the *Essay* was used to supply ominous material about the probable rate of increase for black slaves along the US frontier. (Jefferson's earlier calculations had also predicted this.) In a mere twenty years, Daniel Raymond wrote in *The Missouri Question* (1819), 1 million slaves would become 2 million, and as this geometrical increase spun into the future, the land would quickly be lost to free farmers: "If all the product of the earth be consumed by slaves, a white population cannot subsist." Most antislavery observers agreed with Raymond that slaves would curtail a free labor future in the American West. But some proslavery advocates drew on Malthus too when they warned of a dark scenario should population increase among whites lead to wage slavery in factories, once land for farms was no longer readily available anywhere, east or west, north or south.[27]

If slaves were not to be moved west, and if a viable economic function for them in the older regions of the United States might dwindle (itself a point of contention), how then might their particular population be best adapted to the nation? One answer was that they could not, but instead should be removed to Africa in a kind of reverse colonization. Members of the American Colonization Society (founded 1817) planned just such a removal, to prevent the growth of black population in United States. Proslavery writers smelled a rat, seeing the scheme as an oblique attack on slaveholding more generally—which it was, despite its manifest racism in other regards, especially the assumption that free blacks could not be peaceably assimilated to Euro-American culture the United States. One famous defender of slavery, Thomas R. Dew, referenced Malthus to argue that emancipation and removal of slaves to Africa would improve no one's condition. "There is nothing more dangerous than tampering with the elastic and powerful *spring* of population," Dew warned. Africa did not need more population; the slave trade had never diminished the number of its people, as Malthus, citing Franklin, had shown. Finally, Dew echoed Malthus's discouraging comments on new settlements—"the frequent failures of new colonies tend strongly to show the order of precedence between food and population"—hence the likely failure of any African-American colony in Africa.[28]

The fate of freed or enslaved blacks thus intersected with the equally vexed question of where any part of the US population might resettle itself, with western territories a contested destination, contested most obviously by Indians, but also by some white critics of US expansion. The outrageous case in point were the Five Civilized Nations—the Cherokee, Choctaw, Chickasaw, Creek, and Seminole Indians of the US Southeast—who presented themselves as examples of Indian assimilation to settler culture and acceptance of Western definitions of civilization. They assimilated, that is, by adopting definitions of individual property ownership (including land, but also slaves) and education, the latter most clearly announced in the development of a Cherokee syllabary and its use in printed works.

But the Five Nations' prime characteristic, as far as many white Southerners were concerned, was that they occupied land fit for commercial agriculture, and in particular the cultivation of cotton. The indigenous occupation of potentially ripe farmland, according to the longstanding logic of stadial theory, was a contradictory state, in which historically less commercialized peoples were supposed to be less able to develop natural resources and more likely to succumb to natural limitations. Creole population pressure added another reason, at least from the settler perspective, to contemplate the appropriation of native land. As an 1829 editorial in a Georgia newspaper put it, "In ten years our population will perhaps be doubled," even as the "fertility of the Cherokee lands" beckoned migrants into the state. Alone among new world aboriginals, the Cherokee responded to this Malthusian thinking in print, as in their native-language newspaper, the *Cherokee Phoenix*:

> We know very well that tribe after tribe have dwindled away, and that the remnants of some are greatly degraded, and bid far, without judicious measures for their recovery, to trod the foot-steps of their fore fathers. The question, however, comes with great force; will a removal far to the West, remedy the evils which have followed us from the discovery of America? Will a residence west of Missouri, or elsewhere, beyond the limits of any state or territory, prevent the destroying effects of white population, and its concomitants [sic] evils? As regards the Cherokees this question is peculiarly interesting, and ought not to be answered without due consideration. It is now admitted by all, we believe, that we are an improving people; that we are on a constant and gradual march towards a civilized state; and that though we have to encounter many counteracting influences, yet, we are on the increase in numbers; and that the present appearances are favourable to our complete recovery from a savage state.

The statement was interesting both for its acceptance of a correlation between the transition to a commercial state and population growth and for its rejection of any suspicion that Indians could not achieve both. But the majority of Indians could not vote, and none of them had real political power. Even whites who sympathized with the Five Nations (principally from New England) were unable to question entrenched settler assumptions about land, savagery, and population in any effective way.[29]

The Indian Removal Act of 1830 gave Indians in the Five Nations a coercive offer: surrender land within the existing states for its equivalent in western territories. While some Indians resisted, many took the territorial option, embarking on what would be called the Trail of Tears to Oklahoma territory. That US saga, a temporal parallel to the Black Line in Van Diemen's Land, was the latest chapter in the sadly rich history of forced new world removals: the translatlantic slave trade, the flight of Huguenot refugees, all of the earlier native displacements, the trades in indentured servants and convicts, Le Grand Dérangement (the removal of several French-speaking populations of Canada after British victory at Louisbourg during the Seven Years' War), and the exodus of Loyalists from the United States during and after the American Revolution. The persistence of such projects—and the elision of categorical distinctions between free and unfree, white and not—shows how many white

Americans of this later generation were ignoring Malthus's warning about the questionable ethics of driving indigenous populations of the new world into a corner, which is precisely what the Trail of Tears accomplished.[30]

* * *

Circulation of the *Essay* in the parts of the Americas where English was not the dominant language depended on translation of the text, or at the least descriptions of it. To the extent that his book began to circulate more widely, Malthus benefited, as well, from the Atlantic revolutions about which he was critical, whether he enjoyed the paradox or not. Napoleon's invasions of Spain, for example, assisted Spanish discussion of the French translation of Malthus's *Essay*. Across the Atlantic, the Iberian colonists' stock of reading material was significantly expanded in the early nineteenth century, when the waning authority of the metropolitan powers, climaxing in the Spanish American Wars of Independence, lifted censorship. A generally Atlantic discussion of Malthus was apparent in the international character of the polyglot tag-team whose efforts serially translated the *Essay*. The French translation of Malthus's *Principles of Political Economy* was done by a Portuguese man, for example, and read by those whose native language was Spanish. Within the context of these developments, it is notable that Malthus's reputation if not notoriety in political arithmetic always preceded him; even as his writings in political economy were translated into other languages, he was invariably introduced as the author of the *Essay on the Principle of Population*. Still, and as in North America, it was not always the case that the elements of his population thesis that criticized settlers dominated discussion.[31]

The first translation of the *Essay* into French appeared in 1809. It was the Swiss man of science Pierre Prévost, whose main work was in physics, who produced the *Essai sur le principe de population, ou, Exposé des effets passés et présens de l'action de cette cause sur le bonheur du genre humain* (Essay on the principle of population, or exposition of the past and present effects of this cause on the happiness of humanity), which was published simultaneously in Paris and Geneva. (A subsequent edition appeared in Brussels.) Prévost had corresponded with Malthus about the translation; he explained the burden of that exchange to the reader, gave his rationale for choosing certain French words for key Malthusian concepts (*obstacle* for "check"), and related Malthus's general approval of his decisions. The Prévost edition was, therefore, the authorized French prototype through the nineteenth century. As such, its strong emphasis on Malthus's significance for the English poor could not have gone unnoticed. Prévost stated that four English editions of the *Essay* had been published to date (those from 1798 to 1807) and that the last one (the basis for his translation) had been hastened into print a mere year after the preceding edition in order to influence members of Parliament in their discussion of the Poor Laws. Even on this intra-European concern, however, Prévost's translation had omitted four chapters and, strangely, these had immediately followed two on the Poor Laws, encompassing chapters 7 through 10 in Book III: "Of Increasing Wealth as It Affects the Condition of the Poor," "Of the Definitions of Wealth. Agricultural and Commercial Systems," "Different Effects of the Agricultural and Commercial Systems," and "Of Bounties on the Exportation of Corn."[32]

For that reason, when the physiocrat Pierre Samuel Du Pont de Nemours produced an *Examen du livre de M. Malthus sur le principe de population* in 1817, using the 1807 English edition as his reference, he pointed out the gap in Prévost's work and gave translations of the four missing chapters. While his nod to Prévost may have emphasized an ongoing French conversation about Malthus, Du Pont du Nemours in fact published his work in Philadelphia, having fled Napoleonic France for what he expected to be a more enlightened republic. (His son would found the American company DuPont.) Du Pont de Nemours had in private correspondence already praised Malthus, concurring that "the measure of subsistence is that of population." In his translation he referred to the new American edition of Malthus's work, published in Georgetown, the same year as Prévost's translation, and compared the two versions of the text where he thought it helpful to do so, all of which underscores yet again how there was an emerging and multilingual Atlantic conversation about the *Essay*.[33]

But rather than passively relate Malthus's theory, Du Pont de Nemours challenged it. He was in some ways prepared to be sympathetic to his subject's deepest assumptions, including its religious dimensions. Even as physiocracy was a form of political economy, it was also an example of natural theology. It assumed a basic condition of original sin, though it also defined states of justice and a good life to which humans, even in their fallen state, were meant to strive. It is interesting that these definitions of human fulfilment assumed that the body, unlike the soul, could be returned to a state of natural harmony, a position of faith in nature quite different from anything Malthus articulated and that may have been a root problem for physiocrats who were otherwise as a group receptive to his pessimism about human nature.[34]

For example, Du Pont de Nemours celebrated, as Malthus had not, agricultural improvements in Europe, which had raised the standard of living for "even the poorest classes." And he conjectured that these reforms would continue their good work in America, particularly for native Americans—very much against the grain of Malthus's argument. Du Pont de Nemours accepted Malthus's point that "savages" lived most extremely within natural limits, but he added his opinion that preaching population control to them directly would not solve the problem. Agricultural reforms would instead expand Indian subsistence until they understood the principle of population in their own terms: "It is because of this that the excellent Jefferson and his worthy successor Mr. Madison, to give the Cherokees greater ease and make them happier, have not advised them moral restraint, of which they would have understood nothing." The better plan would be to give the Cherokee domesticated livestock, along with agricultural crops and techniques, and to vaccinate them against smallpox—again, not quite what Malthus had outlined, and yet it was wholly of a piece with physiocratic faith that the human body and the rest of nature could be happily aligned. Assistance to the Cherokee would, Du Pont de Nemours predicted, give his adopted nation a large, valuable, and distinctive population: "There will be more Cherokees, and above all happy Cherokees.... The United States will have won, or rather will have created, an ally, which became a formidable military force just for them, useful against enemies they might have, [and] will give more security at their borders, another guarantee of their glorious independence." By referring to Cherokee happiness, Du Pont de Nemours reinstated the original moral philosophy of the Godwin-Malthus interchange while reaffirming Godwin's faith (contra Malthus) that a new world mattered precisely because it offered such glorious opportunities of expanding global felicity. He rejected Malthus's warning about population oscillation, let alone extinction, envisioning only an upward trend.[35]

A final and key Malthusian text in French came from Jean-Baptiste Say, French political economist, who corresponded with Malthus and published four of his letters to him (*Lettres à M. Malthus, sur différens sujets d'économie politique*) in 1820. Say assumed that the *Essay on the Principle of Population* was Malthus's masterwork, with which he had no dispute, in contrast to the *Principles of Political Economy*, which he thought lacked the logical force and moral persuasion of its author's earlier effort. "But this is not an Essay on Population," Say lamented of the newer and, he thought, the lesser work. Because of his admiration for the masterpiece, Say faithfully relayed to French readers Malthus's major point about population: that it must oscillate within

natural limits and did so in every observable instance. Say's antipathy to organized religion made him a somewhat unexpected admirer of Malthus. But
his interest in natural limits inclined him to the principle of population, if
at a slant from its author's assumptions and intent. His engaged and engaging letters to Malthus in French were translated into English the following
year, even before Malthus's *Principles of Political Economy* was translated into
French.[36]

Say's work was significant to the circulation of Malthus's ideas about the
Americas in two ways. First, his scholarship appears to have invited Alexis
de Tocqueville to use Malthus in his *Democracy in America*. Tocqueville drew
upon his 1820s study of Say in the first edition of that work, published in
France in 1835, but was evidently dissatisfied with what he regarded as the
increasingly observational and statistical bent of political economy, which
posited laws of human behavior rather than proposed laws to guide it. He
returned, therefore, to Malthus, as representative of an older generation's fu-
sion of moral philosophy and political economy. Tocqueville's interest in
Jansenism, the primarily French religious movement that emphasized original sin but was nevertheless associated with liberal politics, was probably
significant for his sympathy with Malthus's moral austerity. (And similar to
physiocracy's natural theology too.) Accordingly, Tocqueville endorsed Malthus's warnings against the hopeful perfectibilists who, inspired by the revolution in France, had sought utopias in which individuals would be unbound by
law. That could not happen, Tocqueville believed, as his emphasis on the significance of political institutions within the American republic would make
even clearer in the 1840 edition of his work.[37]

Nonetheless, Tocqueville rejected Malthus's idea of the moral hazard
posed by colonization. His text instead restated all of the prejudices about
savagery that the *Essay* itself had repeated: "It is by agricultural labour that
man appropriates the soil, and the early inhabitants of North America lived
by the produce of the chase" while their "savage virtues, consigned them to
inevitable destruction." More frankly, Toqueville compared North America
to its southern companion continent, where it had been "necessary to extirpate or to subdue a numerous population, until civilization has been made
to blush for their success." In contrast, "North America was only inhabited by
wandering tribes . . . that vast country was still, properly speaking, an empty
continent, a desert land awaiting its inhabitants." He assumed that the process
of inhabitation would be violent, surmising that any movement westward
began with a few thousand soldiers who "drive the wandering races of the
aborigines before them," succeeded by the "pioneers" who "make ready the

triumphal procession of civilization across the waste"; somehow civilization blushed far less, if at all, at this manner of conquest. Tocqueville cited the well-worn statistic about the rapid doubling of settler population and rejoiced in it: "Since the first settlement of the British Colonies, the number of inhabitants has about doubled every twenty-two years [the statistically verified fact]. I perceive no causes which are likely to check this progressive increase . . . for the next hundred years," at which point, he predicted, free Americans would number 100 million and be distributed among forty states that had been cleared of aboriginal people.[38]

Tocqueville was worried about the consequences of an increasingly large and continentally dispersed population, some of which would be clumped into ever larger and denser cities, but its negative impact on Indians left him entirely untroubled. The immediate translation of his book on the United States into English (in England) permitted quick circulation and discussion of his ideas in the United States, with—needless to say, if sadly—no challenge to his representation of Indians as dispensable savages.

Thus had Jean-Baptiste Say led two fellow Frenchmen to entirely different Malthusian conclusions: the American visitor Tocqueville toward optimism over the happiness of settlers; the American transplant Du Pont de Nemours toward optimism over the happiness of the Cherokee. (As on the question of the slave trade, Malthus's principle of population had completely divided implications.) Of equal importance to the history of the circulation of Malthusian ideas through the Americas, Say's letters would be translated from French into Spanish in 1827, and it was in the disintegrating Iberian colonies that Malthus's *Essay* would have some of its most sustained—and thoughtful—discussion.

Iberian America represented the oldest of all new worlds, and yet it was source of some of the newest surprises about American populations, not least for Malthus himself. The Spanish monarchy had released little statistical information about its colonial population, or indeed anything about its colonies. Although it was regular policy for Spanish authorities to gather censuses of different portions of Spain's new world empire, these were not published: hence the at-best partial information of William Robertson (and others) that Malthus had quoted, which failed to convey the powerful presence of native Americans within the Spanish territories. In the 1780s, for example, just a decade before Malthus wrote (and unbeknownst to him, quite obviously), Indians still controlled half the territory within the lands claimed by Spain and they constituted at least one-fifth of the population. And in contrast to the British Empire, or the later United States, Spanish authorities doubted that white settlers would fill up available land, let alone displace the native inhabitants. Instead, they made several attempts to recruit foreign Catholics as buffers against Indian populations and as anchors within territory unattractive to already settled colonial populations.[39]

Again, that these developments were largely invisible to subjects of Spain's rival, Great Britain, was part of a centuries-long imperial strategy. The Black Legend, originally a Spanish self-criticism of cruelty toward Indians, had been repeated so vigorously and frequently that it seemed that natives within New Spain must have been nearly wiped out. Had they? Spanish silence on that matter had fed into the "dispute of the New World," which privileged some information and informants over others, allowing suppositions about the supreme alterity of its American peoples and territories to flourish in the absence of sustained information. *Peninsulares*, persons born in Spain, were regarded as more authoritative than either criollos or mestizos (those of mixed European, Indian, or African parentage), let alone Indians. British conviction that the southern parts of the Americas were naturally and culturally bizarre had in parallel reinforced what turned out to be a blind pride in their own colonies. The prejudices were ingrained and not easily modified, even when reports on Central and South America grew more varied, beginning to hint at the truth—that the Spanish empire contained nearly five times as many people as Anglophone North America. That was because the acknowledged informants changed only slightly. To some extent, political reforms in Bourbon Spain promised a different kind of rule over Spain's colonies, and perhaps access to it by outsiders, which was why it was an outsider, the Prussian naturalist Alexander von Humboldt, who became the foremost authority on Spanish America in its dying days.[40]

Having gained royal permission to enter the new world portions of the Spanish realm in 1799, Humboldt and a companion, Aimé Bonpland, made an extensive American circuit that included, at the end, the United States, with a visit to President Jefferson. Humboldt and Bonpland then returned to Europe in 1804, just in time to experience the wave of Napoleonic warfare that would first convulse Europe and next crack open—then apart—the very places Humboldt and Bonpland had visited.

The peace dictated by the Treaty of Amiens had failed in early 1803; by 1806 Humboldt's Prussia would be at war with France. Bonaparte would invade Spain in 1808 and his forces occupy it until 1814, his own brother, Joseph, serving as monarch. Within the Spanish empire, both criollos and mestizos saw the regime shifts as opportunities to liberate themselves from governments that had favored the peninsulares over themselves, and Spain against any local interests. Colonial liberation from Spain (and, in Brazil, from Portugal) would sustain the trends toward American independence that had begun in 1776 and continued with the revolution in Haiti, which in 1804 became the second independent republic in the hemisphere. So too might revolt bring Spanish- and Portuguese-speaking Americans into line with the modern revolutionary states, primarily the United States but also France, or some version of France. Humboldt's four-volume *Political Essay on the Kingdom of New Spain*, first published (in French) in 1811 and translated into English that same year, therefore used the words "New Spain" to describe a viceroyalty (stretching from southern North America through the Andes, and spanning the Caribbean to the Philippines) in the very last years of that historical entity, which would cease to exist after Mexican rebels declared independence in 1819.[41]

In his *Political Essay*, Humboldt was consistent in stating that the published sources on the population of pre-Columbian New Spain were suspiciously variable and therefore untrustworthy. He conceded that accurate description of populations was difficult, drawing attention, interestingly, to how James Cook had calculated the Tahitians to be 100,000 in number, and yet subsequent estimates of the island's natives had slid inexorably downward. Could new world populations decline so rapidly? Humboldt found it unlikely; his English translator supplied a long footnote disputing him. Nevertheless, Humboldt drew the correct attention to the right problem: at moments of invasion and conquest, both populations and observations of them underwent rapid and contradictory metamorphoses; as symptoms of the ongoing disaster, ignorance and misinformation were as likely to prevail as accuracy. He cited Robertson as an authority who had ignored the contradictions in order to pick a trend that fit his interpretation that native American populations had rarely and barely survived conquest. On the contrary, Humboldt pointed out, Indian populations were in many parts of New Spain healthy and growing, often fulfilling the conjectural prediction that when humans passed from a pastoral to commercial stage, their numbers increased. That observation explained Humboldt's skepticism about Tahiti. While he was wrong that the Spanish-American example might apply elsewhere, he was right about New Spain itself and, therefore, important in observing that different new worlds had different indigenous population dynamics, not a single easily summarized trend—let alone one that indicated a universal pattern of oscillation.[42]

Here is where Humboldt revealed that the Spanish authorities had been enumerating new world populations for some time and in considerable detail. He conceded that hot regions in New Spain had high mortality rates but observed that cooler places had healthier ratios of births to deaths, ranging from 190:100 to 200:100. In relation to the Americas more generally, he remarked on the tendency of populations in thinly settled places with new lands to increase rapidly, pointing out that this occurred in the old world as well as the new, as could be seen in parts of Prussia and Russia: "The newer the cultivation of a country is, so much easier is subsistence on a soil newly torn up." From this Humboldt concluded that the population of New Spain might double in size every nineteen years, aware that the comparable rate for the United States (based on comparisons of the 1790 and 1800 censuses) was about twenty-three, though some subpopulations of the northern republic reproduced even faster, with a "happy cycle" of doubling occurring every thirteen or fourteen years. Throughout all four volumes of the *Political Essay*, moreover, Humboldt provided relentless, up-to-date population statistics. Although he could have used evidence of Indian population vitality to rebuke Malthus in the same way he did Robertson, he instead cited him on the proportion of births to deaths in England and described him as author of "one of the most profound works in political economy which has ever appeared."[43]

Because of its late genesis in relation to the history of New Spain, Humboldt's text might be considered an elegy for Spanish imperialism as well as a prophecy for the future glory of the independent states that were going to emerge out of the former Spanish monarchy. Humboldt knew very well, however, that a burgeoning population would never strengthen any empire, colony, or nation unless it had adequate food. For that reason, he was careful to present harvest statistics for different parts of New Spain, specifically in contrast to both the old world and North America. He referred to the metric he used, grains produced per grain sowed, as a "multiple" that was "one of the first elements of the prosperity of nations." Thus, France, northern Germany, Poland, and Sweden harvested five or six grains per one sowed; Hungary, Croatia, and Saxony eight to ten grains per one; but twelve to seventeen in many parts of New Spain, rising even to twenty-four in equatorial Mexico and thirty-five (admittedly in unusual years) in parts of what would become Colombia. Should plans to expand exportation of this grain to Europe succeed, Humboldt playfully warned any readers in the United States, North American farmers could hardly compete, given that their productivity lagged despite their labor costing more than did its equivalent in New Spain.[44]

Even here Humboldt did not name Malthus as the pundit who had opined the opposite in pretty much every aspect, but Malthus nevertheless took the bait. By the time he did so, the revolutions in Central and South America were nearly over. He published his thoughts on Humboldt in 1824, in the essay for the *Encyclopaedia Britannica* on "population," later printed as a pamphlet, *A Summary View of the Principle of Population*. At that point, the insurgencies of the 1810s and 1820s that were orchestrated or inspired by Simón Bolívar had led to the independence of Venezuela, Colombia, Uruguay, Paraguay, Argentina, Ecuador, Bolivia (named for *El Libertador*), Peru, and Chile; parallel revolutions liberated Mexico and Brazil. Imperial control of the Caribbean and parts of South America would continue, as in Cuba; Russia's North American empire would exist until 1867, when its remaining Alaskan territory would be sold to the United States. But by 1826 Great Britain no longer had a great imperial adversary in Spain (or France for that matter, given Haiti's independence and Napoleon's sale of the Louisiana territory). Instead, Britons were becoming accustomed to thinking of themselves not only as having the most powerful empire on Earth but having one that, despite the disruptions of the Seven Years' War (principally in the form of the American Revolution), had a long historical presence, starting in the new world.

However respectful he might have been of the newfound independence of the peoples of the former New Spain, Malthus seasoned Humboldt's statistics about the varying produce of "a single grain of wheat" with several grains of salt. Happy news the harvests of Mexico may have been, but Malthus noted, accurately, that they were static measures, not predictions of a food supply that was increasing, let alone geometrically increasing. Population would still be "checked" at a future point. It is particularly notable that at this time, as colonization was accelerating, Malthus restated his warning about "the great natural barrenness of a very large part of the surface of the earth." Only then, after rebuking Humboldt's Godwinian optimism about the Americas, did Malthus use the rest of his essay to restate the principle of population he had formulated in his longer works, beginning in 1798. Thus he tackled what might have constituted the biggest objection to his principle, based on the new world, from Humboldt's well-read work, and crisply identified its mathematical limitations and therefore its utility for future planning. Having vanquished the vegetable imaginary yet again, Malthus used an interior portion of the essay to warn about the busy sexual dyads in "those territories of the New World which lately belonged to Spain," whose rates of increase dangerously resembled those of the United States. Indeed, Malthus was incredulous that the rate, the average of which indicated a doubling of the population within 27½ years (approximating that of the United States), might not be sustainable. Here he was as much questioning the healthfulness of "a tropical climate" (Humboldt having supplied the first serious population statistics for such environments) as the potential for the new nations of the new world to maintain good political institutions and pure manners among their citizens.[45]

The residents of the places Humboldt and Malthus had discussed were, no less than their counterparts in the United States, eager to debate population matters themselves. Peninsular publications in Spanish may have been the first printed materials to introduce Malthus to the Hispanic colonies. At two different points in the early 1800s, the *Gazeta de Madrid* produced short-run sequences on Malthus. The first began in June 1808 with seventeen installments, over roughly six weeks, synopsizing the 1803 edition of the *Essay*. The second occurred in 1811, with three extracts from the French translation of the work. At both points, the French influence was essential, given that Spain was from 1808 to 1813 occupied by French forces, with an influence via journalism that would stretch across the Atlantic. Foreign journals were also likely to have sent Malthus's name into Spanish and Portuguese territories; the most influential there were the *Revue des deux mondes* (Paris), *The Economist* (London), and to a lesser extent the *North American Review* (Boston). By the late 1820s and early 1830s, Malthus's *Essay* itself was being exported to the Iberian colonies. Editions (title and language unspecified) were offered in Rio de Janeiro's *Jornal do Commercio* (1827 and 1830; the newspaper was founded by an emigré Frenchman) and in *El Mercurio de Valparaiso* (1834).[46]

If Franklin was a confounding factor for reception and discussion of Malthus in the United States, Humboldt played the same role in relation to the Hispanic world. Because of the context of political liberation in the first quarter of the nineteenth century, Spanish creole patriots were quick to crow over Humboldt's predictions of their material success. In his 1832 *México considerado como nacion independiente y libre* ("Mexico considered as an independent and free nation"), Tadeo Ortiz dwelled on Humboldt's point that, except in extraordinary times, the Mexican population "should double every 19 years." Ortiz drew attention to how this swift growth exceeded that in the United States, though he accepted the general point (which he supported with statistics on different parts of Europe and the Americas) that new-settled countries in general had faster rates of population growth. And he remarked that good laws were needed to properly foster population growth, so that its advances in times of peace would not somehow result in conflict; he spared a thought, here, for what he considered to have been the contrastingly lamentable state of Indians under the original Spanish conquistadores.[47]

For Brazil, a main promulgator of Malthus's ideas was the political econo-mist José da Silva Lisboa, visconde de Cairu, whose 1819 *Estudos do bem-commum e economia politica* ("Studies on the common good and political econ-omy") was the earliest serious engagement with Malthus in Portuguese. In the year of that book's publication, Brazil was still part of the Portuguese empire and Silva Lisboa was loyal to the monarchy, which authorized the printing of his text. (He would change direction as demands for independence began to indicate the likelihood of that outcome, which arrived in 1822.) Silva Lisboa gave an accurate précis of Malthus's principle of population (citing the fifth edition of 1817), as well as praise for the field of political economy generally, as the branch of learning that, alongside natural science, would overcome the malice of humanity, and on those grounds declaring Malthus "the Newton of Political Economy." Here, however, the admiration dwelled on what Malthus had said about the Poor Laws, which Silva Lisboa characterized as "a costly compulsory charity tax" that produced "only inertia, ingratitude, and immo-rality." And in his statements that the level of economic development within a society determined its state of happiness, with a large population often a positive indicator of this status, Silva Lisboa was not quite on the same page as his admired source, aligning himself instead with Portuguese and Brazilian advocates of economic development, which might require ample labor.[48]

Where Silva Lisboa addressed Malthus's American material, he was more critical. He accepted Malthus's point that slow agrarian growth provided more lasting power for colonial regions: "luckily" for Anglo-America, "no silver or gold mines were discovered" there to deter settlers from agricultural activities. And he approved the point he thought both Humboldt and Malthus had made, that in the Spanish colonies, where much land was held in few hands, there was low government investment in roads and little manufacturing. But he protested Malthus's statement that idleness was, in New Spain, as endemic as it was in Ireland or India, where food was more plentiful than capital or manufactures. Here again Franklin was a confounding factor. Silva Lisboa de-voted a chapter to the American philosopher, principally a list Franklin made, unpublished during his lifetime, of "positions to be examined" (1769), which restated his belief that humans had to live within the bounds of the cultivable land available to them, as if sustained analysis of this phenomenon were not more aptly attributed, by this point in time, to Malthus.[49]

As well, direct Iberian-American engagement with Malthus's critical thoughts on settler societies was inconsistent, with readers south of the United States just as unlikely as their US counterparts to dwell on Malthus's full warning about new worlds. A short essay of 1827 in the *Noticioso Mercantil* of

Havana presented Alexander Hill Everett's North American case against Malthus entirely in terms of the question of the swiftness of American population increase, arguing that new world settler societies benefited economically from such growth. In his 1833 *Origen, progresos y límites de la población*, Agustín de Blas related Malthus's thoughts on ancient Rome but not on modern new world colonies, even as he recited the quick population growth of the United States as central to any population's dependence on an ample supply of land. In the same year, a long editorial in the *Mercurio Peruano* of Lima ran through the basic elements of Malthus's principle of population accurately—and while praising what he had done for the laws of moral order, comparable to what Newton had done for the laws of nature—only to conclude that they remained matters of dispute. The editorial cited Everett's objections, showing that this North American critique had circulation within the Americas that rivaled Malthus's. And the article's recommendation of Peruvian reforms to restore public happiness only partly resembled what Malthus might have supported. The United States was the editorialist's model of economic success, both for agriculture and commerce, which implied approval of immigration; the article duly offered a plan to attract "laboring families from the Canary Islands and Ireland." But Malthus might have smiled upon another suggestion: to "abstain from harassing in any way the independent tribes who inhabit those fertile lands" outside the areas of settlement, and even "distributing to the Indians who are without property, the remaining lands of the Republic."[50]

The same pattern of yes-but-no followed in the greater anglophone Caribbean. Newspaper advertisements in the *Bermudian* show that Malthus's *Essay*, along with the foundational texts of Smith and Ricardo, was sold in the islands as early as November 1820. But the burden of discussion of Malthus tended, when it did not focus on slavery, to take up Malthus's contentions in relation to the Poor Laws, and thus to a state of economic development more closely associated with the old world than the new. An essayist in Grenada praised the United States, with its burgeoning population and independent economy, over and above Britain and its dependencies, where the rich benefited from trade restrictions while the poor starved, just as Malthus had warned. An article in a paper on St. Christopher went further in defying Malthus's conclusions, pleading instead that any excess British population might be used to fill up "colonies in both hemispheres as yet more than half unpeopled." A piece in the *Port of Spain Gazette* pointed to recent statistics indicating growth in the slave population and, citing Malthus, predicted that the island would, in future, be unable to employ and feed all the slaves, some of whom would need to be exported to the cotton-growing states of the US

South. Appearing in 1833, on the eve of British abolition of slavery, this last piece contemplated the chronological and geographical extension of new world slavery, using Malthusian logic in a direction Malthus himself would have deplored.[51]

* * *

Because of the more recent settlement of Australia, and its resulting delay in developing a print culture, Malthus's *Essay* arrived there about two decades after its first publication, representing a later cultural presence for him there than in the Americas, though still occurring within his lifetime. Newspapers were the main expression of antipodean print culture; Australia would continue to import books, principally from Great Britain, until its own book publishing industry took off after the 1850s. The first evidence of a (necessarily imported) copy of the *Essay on the Principle of Population* occurs in 1821, in a newspaper advertisement for an auction of some books in Sydney: "Malthus on Population, 2 vols . . . of a late Edition." The original owner is unspecified, therefore it is impossible to pinpoint how long the book might have been in the colony. The two-volume format of this "late Edition" indicates that the books were either the third or fourth British edition (1806 or 1807) or else the American edition of 1809; the 1817 British edition was published in three volumes, and news of its printing might not, in any case, have been well known in New South Wales by 1821. Copies of the *Essay* presumably continued to accumulate, though in small numbers, even past Malthus's death. The first order of books for the Melbourne Public Library, in 1853, would include, under the category of "Political Economy," titles by both Malthus and his English popularizer Harriet Martineau (plus Smith and Ricardo).[52]

In the Australian colonies, as probably everywhere, not having read the actual *Essay on the Principle of Population* was no impediment to discussing it or its author. And overwhelmingly the sense was that Malthus should be read in support of colonization and the greater peopling of Pacific new worlds, his measured criticisms of just those goals notwithstanding. From 1822 to 1834, newspaper articles and editorials in the Australian press raised his name in this regard almost indiscriminately: to advocate the export of brides for men in New South Wales, to promote British settlement in Borneo, to ponder the depopulation of Ireland that would surely result from outmigration to the antipodes, to propose the "Exportation of Ladies" to Van Diemen's Land, and to recommend the use of free migrants rather than convicts. On the Borneo question, the author of an 1822 piece in the *Sydney Gazette* quoted Malthus,

"in a work we have not yet seen," as a critic of emigration yet with the qualification that "with a view to the more general cultivation of the earth and the
wider extension of civilization, it [emigration] seems to be both useful and
proper," an interesting example of an idea arriving before its surrounding text
did. If anything, once the book was more widely present, disagreement became more manifest. In an editorial fracas that occurred slightly later in the
Sydney Gazette, one pro-emigration correspondent said of "Mr. Malthus" that
his "doctrines I consider worse than sophistical." An editorialist in Hobart
went further in denouncing the "sect of Philosophers, Mr. Malthus at their
head," whose "detestable doctrines" defied the divine mandate to "encrease
and multiply." Had the settlers of British America followed that advice, "the
great and powerful [United] States of America would still have continued in
the solitary desolation of its native wildernesses."[53]

And yet there was debate over the likelihood of this outcome. One Tasmanian colonist speculated on the significance of the postdiluvian reproducing dyad in 1831. "The increase of population in all new countries is
subject matter of the deepest interest to their prosperity," he claimed. But
the power to double four times in a century—the claim made by "all the
polished economists"—was surely spurious. If nothing were to prevent this
power of increase "the descendants of Noah and his family would have now
increased to the following number: 1,496,577,676,626,844,588,249,573,268,
701,473,812,126,674,924,007,424." For this editorialist, the obvious significance of Malthus's "checks" trumped settler colonialist claims. And yet the
Tasmanian in April 1831 featured just the check that most troubled Malthus:
war and extermination in the settler colonies of Australia. In graphic detail,
readers learned of the latest Aboriginal wars.[54]

Australia would be the only Pacific site that had significant discussion
of Malthus's principle of population during his lifetime. None of the other
European-settled islands had newspapers or libraries at comparably early
points in time. The exceptions, two Sandwich Islands (Hawai'i) newpapers,
Ke Kumu Hawaii and *Ka Lama Hawaii*, which began in 1834, did not include
any Malthus-related material for that year, the final one in his life. American
missionaries established a circulating library in what would later be called
Hawai'i as early as 1832, but its catalog for 1837 does not include any of
Malthus's works. Meanwhile, the *New-Zealand Gazette* would not begin
publication until 1839, and not within New Zealand itself until a year later;
French-Polynesian newspapers have even later founding dates. The reception
history of the *Essay on the Principle of Population* in these places, therefore, took
place after its author's death. If scattered individuals (missionaries, whaling

captains, and so on) owned or had read the book, their possession of this knowledge did not enter into public life before 1834.[55]

And yet the specifically new world discussions of the *Essay* that did occur had at least one extraordinary legacy. When Charles Darwin made his celebrated voyage on HMS *Beagle*, he traveled as an acolyte of Humboldt, envious and emulous of that earlier scientific traveler's journey to America. Even so, Darwin ended up taking Malthus's side against Humboldt's happier reading of new world places. Reflecting on his journey down and through South America, continuing on to Australia and around the world, Darwin cited the 1826 edition of the *Essay on the Principle of Population*. From it, he concluded that however many new world natives had survived conquest, whatever new world grain might be grown to feed them and other eaters, "Wherever the European had trod, death seemed to pursue the aboriginal." And from that new world observation, supported by Malthus's restatement of Franklin on fennel running riot over land that had been "cleared" of competitors, Darwin derived his theory of evolution based on natural selection, complete with the bleak prospect of extinction. Daniel Malthus's desire that his younger son produce scientific knowledge had paid off, though neither of them were ever to know it.[56]

*   *   *

But where are the imaginary new worlds, the alternatives, utopian or dystopian, that had inspired Malthus's objections to Godwin and Condorcet in the first place? No concept is fully present in public consciousness unless it has been represented in fiction or other art, which are ways of imagining the world, certainly as it seems to be, perhaps as it ought to be, and this truism may be especially true for political and economic ideas that otherwise inhabit only the mental worlds of government and academic specialists, as Malthus himself had been.

In Malthus studies, for example, Charles Dickens has held pride of place as the political arithmetrician's artistic nemesis. Dickens was a consistent critic, that is, of Malthus's warnings that the procreating poor would be the doom of England. (Because this occurred during Dickens's Victorian heyday, after Malthus's death, it has contributed to the widespread if wrong-headed notion that Malthus was a Victorian author.) "Boz" satirized the principle of population multiple times. He did so offhandedly, as in his parodistic remark that London's cats who, "made selfishly ferocious by ruminating on the surplus population around them, and on the densely crowded state of all the avenues to cat's meat," increased their families in savage disregard of Malthus's warnings. In *A Christmas Carol* (1843), Ebenezer Scrooge, byword for moral indifference, is Dickens's more direct hit. Told that the poor dread the cold charity of the establishments to which he makes calculated contributions, that they prefer death to that soul-stealing experience, Mr. Bah Humbug gives his famous Malthusian reply: "If they would rather die," said Scrooge, "they had better do it, and decrease the surplus population." Dickens's first attack on Malthus was, however, more elliptical yet most pointed. In *Oliver Twist; or, the Parish Boy's Progress*, published serially from 1837 to 1839, Dickens addressed the humiliating, invasive nature of the 1834 Poor Laws, written precisely to discourage the poor from marrying and having children. It became policy that anyone seeking public assistance would be separated from other family members—spouses from each other, parent from child. By creating the orphaned character Oliver Twist, deprived of his dying mother's family and (for most of the story) denied any knowledge of her or of them, and by emphasizing Twist's morally superior nature, Dickens argued that the "poor" were not an insidious mass but instead individual human beings of merit. Twist the "parish boy" is not worthless, but worth more than most of the other characters combined, a twisty paradox that his surname had implied all along.[57]

But what is the anti-Malthusian novel of *new worlds*, the fiction that addresses how those places constituted the principle of population in the first place? *Oliver Twist* is the great anti-Malthusian novel only if Malthusianism is conceived in its standard definition as an argument, inherited from the age of revolutions, over European nations' ability to foster the continuing happiness of even their poorest citizens. All this has been long understood, ever since Dickens took on Malthus. But if the new worlds of Thomas Robert Malthus were important to the history of population theories, however overlooked they have been, then some fiction must exist by an author who expressed contemporary understanding that this was so. There are two contenders for this honor, one English, one American. Even better, and unlike Dickens's works, they were published within Malthus's lifetime.

The first contender is Mary Wollstonecraft Godwin Shelley, daughter of Malthus's great anarchist antagonist. If William Godwin had tried to refute Malthus, his daughter refuted them both. While Godwin's anti-Malthus book is now largely forgotten, not so the near-contemporaneous work of Shelley, who had published *Frankenstein; or, The Modern Prometheus* two years earlier in 1818. The plot of that novel would seem somewhat to the side of Malthusian concerns, focused as it is on the prospect of giving life by means other than sexual reproduction. But when Victor Frankenstein's monster pleads for a female companion, like him made from reanimated human flesh, the request frightens even Dr. Frankenstein. Initially he complies, especially once his creature assures him that he will take his bride to America, there to live at a safe distance from other people and to subsist by hunting animals. But so confident is the doctor that he can create humans with every capacity equal to those bred the normal way, that he worries his uncanny Adam and Eve, the un-*heimlich* dyad, might breed a new race:

> Even if they were to leave Europe, and inhabit the deserts of the new world, yet one of the first results of those sympathies for which the daemon thirsted would be children, and a race of devils would be propagated upon the earth, who might make the very existence of the species of man a condition precarious and full of terror.

It was the Malthusian nightmare reimagined very imaginatively, with the central elements of the principle of population put into play in order to conjure new horrors for the typological new world scenario Malthus had proposed—and in fact that Franklin had proposed. The American philosopher had been "the modern Prometheus" of Immanuel Kant's designation, alluded to in Shelley's title, then within her text (as is commonly noted) in reference not only to the electrical power thought at the time capable of imparting life but also (not commonly noted) in relation to his status as commentator on life, death, and human populations, particularly in America. Above all, it is striking that Shelley disagreed with her father: she thought Malthus had a point.[58]

Shelley reimagined the new worlds of Thomas Robert Malthus even more thoroughly in her later novel, *The Last Man* (1826), published the same year as the final edition of Malthus's *Essay*. If *Frankenstein* is the progenitor of mad-scientist science fiction, *The Last Man* is its counterpart for apocalyptic biological scenarios that predict the end of the human race. "Last man" plots were common in the early 1800s; Shelley's contribution was to give specific dates and a mechanism for the disaster, details that still prevail in the genre. Only one scholar, however, has noted Shelley's Malthusian influences, and none so far have explicated the significance of new world places within it. Shelley had read both Malthus and her father's response by 1821, and she absorbed both authors' arguments in order to assess them. Indeed, she seems to have taken up one of her father's throwaway lines in his *Of Population*: Might the human races not simply "wear out?" That was the possibility Shelley pursued. The central plot mechanism of her novel reverses an important part of Malthus's principle of population: the novel's Earth is boundless, teeming in life-giving life, but the human species somehow cannot keep up with it. The novel begins at the end of the twenty-first century, with a new and utopian government poised "to render England one scene of fertility and magnificence; the state of poverty was to be abolished . . . disease was to be banished . . . food sprung up, so to say, spontaneously." Behold the Godwinian vision. But Malthusian doom lurks in the form of warfare abroad, and disaster strikes when "plague" arrives in England, possibly from a North American sailor, whose blackened corpse disastrously connects the old world with the new.[59]

Refugees arrive before the full-blown epidemic does, even as imports are cut off. There is such consequent pressure on English resources that livestock and wild animal populations significantly diminish; private parks are put to the plow; every inch of land is gardened, just as Malthus had conjectured it might be. Shelley emphasizes that the short-term population pressure reverses the historical outward flow from England. To outrun death, citizens of the United States strike out first for Ireland and then, gathering up Irish refugees, sail for England, where they are joined by the English poor. Together, these disparately historical antagonists of England, Britain, and the British Empire "talked of taking London, conquering England—calling to mind the long detail of injuries which had for many years been forgotten." The full disaster unfolds as, eventually, every sector of England's population suffers death and the island is emptied of humans: "An uninhabited rock in the wide Pacific, which had remained since the creation uninhabited, unnamed, unmarked, would be of as much account in the world's future history, as desert England."[60]

Just as the American refugees had retraced their ancestors' passage across the Atlantic, so Shelley's small band of English survivors retrace their progenitors' putative migration from the ancient Mediterranean back toward Eden and the globe's primordial parents. The eventual last man, Lionel Verney, describes himself as being one only of "fifty, the only human beings that survived of the food-teeming earth," another of Shelley's digs at Malthus, via the vegetable imaginary. Verney goes to Italy, then to Greece, as he loses all family and companions and even strangers, who might at least remind him of the human world of language and custom. "I lived upon an earth," he reports, "whose diminished population a child's arithmetic might number." Alone, he plans to sail for Africa and lives in hope that an anonymous Adam and Eve had somewhere, somehow, survived to begin human history all over

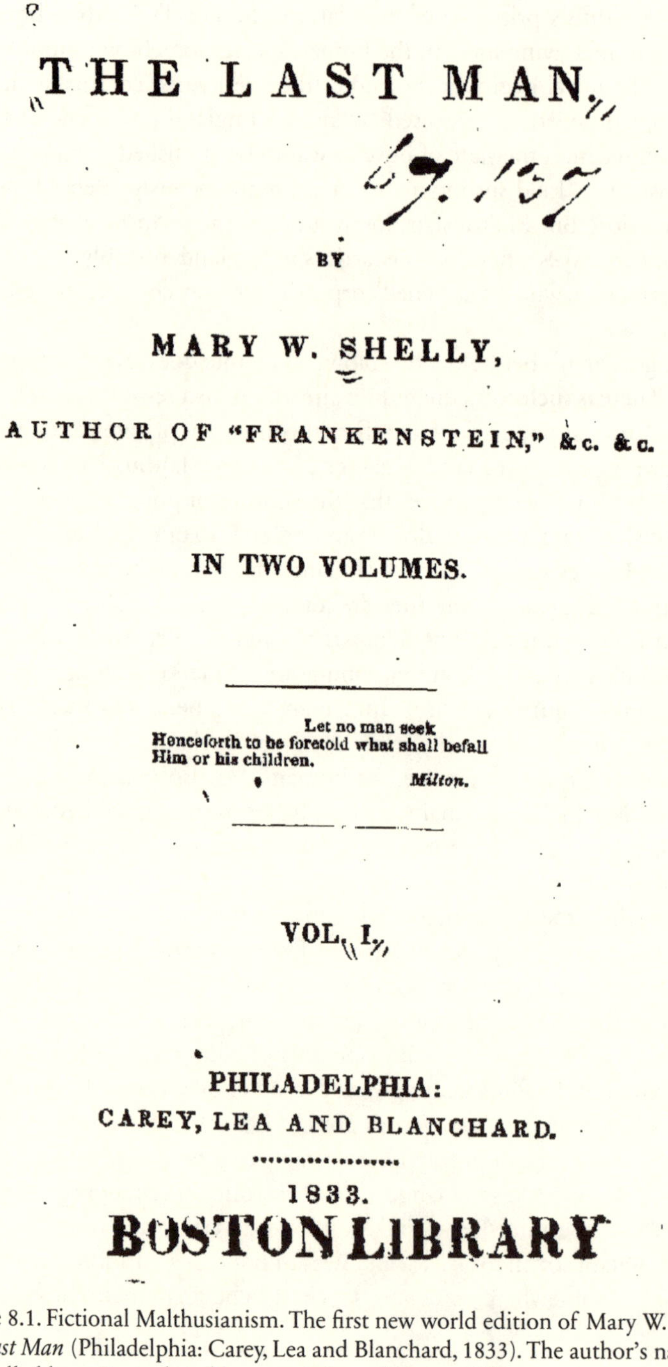

THE LAST MAN,

BY

MARY W. SHELLY,

AUTHOR OF "FRANKENSTEIN," &c. &c.

IN TWO VOLUMES.

Let no man seek
Henceforth to be foretold what shall befall
Him or his children.
Milton.

VOL. I.

PHILADELPHIA:
CAREY, LEA AND BLANCHARD.

••••••••••••••••••

1833.

BOSTON LIBRARY

Figure 8.1. Fictional Malthusianism. The first new world edition of Mary W. Shelley, *The Last Man* (Philadelphia: Carey, Lea and Blanchard, 1833). The author's name is misspelled here. Reproduced by permission of Harvard Library.

again: "'Yet, will not this world be re-peopled, and the children of a saved pair of lovers, in some to me unknown and unattainable seclusion, wandering to these prodigious relics of the ante-pestilential race, seek to learn how beings so wondrous in their achievements, with imaginations infinite, and powers godlike, had departed from their home to an unknown country?'" Not only were humans fallen, never to recover paradise despite their seemingly godlike powers, but fallen even unto extinction. Astonishingly modern in its pessimism, Shelley's apocalypse rejected both her father's utopianism and his antagonist's insistence that humans could, should, struggle against nature's laws. She put her faith neither in nature nor in human nature.[61]

The other and American contender for Malthusian novelist of new worlds is James Fenimore Cooper, long noted for his role in inscribing belief in an inevitable native population recession and white settler increase within new world national mythology. Cooper's five Leatherstocking Tales, published from 1823 to 1841, feature that central collision between Indians and settlers, with the main character Nathaniel Bumppo representing a small possibility of peaceful amalgamation between the two populations. Readers understood the frontier setting as central to the drama, even as some of them smirked at the studied archaicisms, such as the backwoods patois that one British reviewer mocked as "transatlantic Doric." But Cooper needed that period detail to contextualize the adventures of "Natty" Bumppo, alias the Deerslayer (also La Longue Carabine, Hawkeye, and Leatherstocking), within the phases of the Second Hundred Years' War that had brought imperial ambitions into violent conflict. Beginning in *The Pioneers* (1823), Cooper traces settler migration westward, relentless despite the pauses that recurring warfare poses. Indian's noble savagery yet inevitable extinction, paired with settlers' unceasing migration westward, are the twin themes of the books. To that extent, they might be interpreted as showing the demographic inheritance of Franklin, without any Malthusian complexity—or warning.[62]

Indeed, Cooper's nonfiction *Notions of the Americans* (1832), designed to correct European ignorance, stated that the US population "has doubled in about twenty-three years," remarking that while "to an Englishman, who knows that excess population is the greatest burden on his country," US population surplus was on the contrary a good thing. But Cooper had ample opportunity to absorb the ongoing discussions of Malthus. One of the American journals to which he made regular contributions, the *Literary and Scientific Repository*, had mentioned Malthus's work on population several times in the 1820s. Later, when he lived in London, Cooper met Godwin and Coleridge. He opened his first Leatherstocking novel, *The Pioneers*, with the entirely

Malthusian admonition that, the population of western New York state having blossomed inordinately, it could "look forward to ages before the evil day must arrive, when their possessions shall become unequal to their wants." Slightly later still, in his *Gleanings in Europe: England* (1837), Cooper would cite the *Essay on the Principle of Population*. Obviously, like most of the reading public, he knew his Malthus.[63]

And in *The Last of the Mohicans* (1826), Cooper questioned settler optimism about displacing Indian populations in Malthusian terms. Set in 1757, the novel expresses nostalgia for the Seven Years' War, as a moment when empires and colonies might have developed in more harmonious directions. In contrast to Shelley's fictional pathos of the last man on Earth, Cooper examines the historical tragedy of those native individuals who found themselves to be the last of their nation or tribe, precisely as a consequence of colonial expansion. Indians "disappear before the . . . inroads of civilisation, as the verdure of their native forests falls before the nipping frost." A white settler is a person who wants everything in nature, one native man complains: "His gluttony makes him sick." Cooper had already introduced the novel with the warning that, in New York State, Indians "have disappeared, either from the regions in which their fathers dwelt, or altogether from the earth." Indeed, the novel's conventional marriage plot, which annoys many present-day readers, is not sentimental garnish but intrinsic to the Malthusian outcome. The fates of five marriageable characters—a pair of white lovers, plus two Indian men who are vying for a woman of mixed black-white parentage—dominate the story. But only the white dyad, Alice Munro and Duncan Heyward, survive to marry and, presumably, to fill territory that has been orphaned of its indigenous population. The Mohican character Uncas dies, along with his Huron rival, Magua, and their mutually sought prize, Cora. Uncas's father, Chingachgook, now a childless parent and the last surviving Mohican, laments: "I am alone." A Delaware elder agrees that he has "seen the last warrior of the wise race of the Mohicans!" "The pale-faces are masters of the earth," he says, "and the time of the red-men has not yet come again."[64]

Not yet come again. It is a hopeful if ambivalent thought and a surprise, given that it does not match the title of the book, or indeed the whole, tragic "last man" genre. The four words express a sentiment not unlike that contained in Malthus's warning against "exterminating, or driving into a corner" the new worlds' indigenes, which, given Malthus's emphasis on having enough resources to thrive, amounted to the same thing—as Cooper's novel had also indicated. The two warnings, English and American, would, slightly later, both be printed by the same London publisher, John Murray, who had taken up

Malthus's *Essay on the Principle of Population* after Joseph Johnson's death and who would produce the English editions of Cooper's novels. However much in fragments and contested, the principle of population's warning about the moral hazard of new worlds had survived several sea crossings, taken root in new worlds, and was transplanted back to its native land.[65]

Coda

IT TOOK A MERE MONTH FOR WORD OF MALTHUS'S DEATH to begin to circulate in new worlds. He died in Bath, age sixty-eight, on December 29, 1834, leaving a widow and two children, having outlived his older brother Sydenham and one of his own children, a daughter. In the earliest known report of his demise on the opposite side of the Atlantic, on January 1, 1835, the *Commercial Advertiser* of New York City (in a section of news titled "Very Late from England") announced that "the Rev. Mr. Malthus, author of the Malthusian system, as it is called, and celebrated for his works on political economy, died in the latter part of December." The news moved west and south, reaching Albany, New York, and Charleston, South Carolina, by February 7. Some of the death notices were also miniature editorials on the Malthusian system. One coolly critical version that made the rounds described Malthus as "the celebrated writer on political economy . . . whose notions on *population* were rather singular." This was the wording that William Lloyd Garrison chose for his Boston antislavery newspaper, the *Liberator*, to run on Valentine's Day 1835, which happened to be Malthus's birthday, the first instance of that vital statistic he would not be alive to celebrate.[1]

In the Australian colonies, where opinion on Malthus was even more negative than it was in the Americas, news of his death did nonetheless briefly slow the stream of vituperation. On May 21, 1835, a correspondent to the *Sydney Morning Herald* was busy asserting, though not it must be said with full truth, that "Mr. Malthus had ten children, and consequently as many reasons for impressing on the Home Government the necessity of stopping in embryo such a torrent of destruction. Mr. Godwin very kindly, in answer to Mr. Malthus, proved that the torrent, which was the incubus of the dreams of Mr. Malthus, need neither be stopped nor diverted." Three weeks later, on June 11, the *Launceston Advertiser* in Van Diemen's Land respectfully broke the news of Malthus's death "on the 29th ulto. [last year], at Bath." It did not take long, however, for the jabs at Malthus to start up again. On July 2 another Sydney newspaper announced the new construction and availability of a hearse. "We must say that it is a dashing affair of the kind," the paper said, praising the hearse's constructor and owner, a Mr. Gannon. "Now as the colony must advance in population so it must advance in deaths; and Mr. Gannon being as good a politician and idolater of Mr. Malthus . . . he, statesman-like, gets ready to bury all who choose to die." The settler facetiousness about Malthusian oscillation between life and death reasserted itself just over a half year after Malthus's death. And of course the name "Malthus" and a system that might be described as "Malthusian" survive.[2]

* * *

"Mr. Malthus's gospel is preached only to the poor!" Thus William Hazlitt in 1819 gave an indelible and lasting if not infamous character to the author of the *Essay on the Principle of Population*. The stereotype of Malthus as cruel browbeater of the English poor begs a question: if the place of new worlds within Malthus's moral philosophy and political economy is to be taken seriously, does it (should it) alter the persistent characterization of Malthusianism as heartlessness to the have-nots? If the name "Malthus" and the neologisms based on it are going to continue signifying something well into the twenty-first century, if not beyond, what should their meanings be?

Malthus defined two moral hazards that he considered to be central to his principle of population, but he did not reconcile them. Famous, as in Hazlitt's portrayal, for his warning against expecting a perfected human society within Europe, he notoriously identified material constraint as the element that guaranteed human misery unless vice were resorted to, which he did not recommend. It was not for him a matter of whether doom would arrive but to whom and, importantly, to what extent. Given that the poor were already unfortunate, living as they did at the margins, they were likeliest to suffer worst and first. And yet the least recognized ambition of Malthus's thesis, as well as of his personal concern and inclination, was the attempt to work out how such suffering might be minimized in the long run and overall. The poor might and probably would suffer, according to Malthus, but there were any number of interventions—economic, educational, and political—that could and should ameliorate that want. Hence the moral imperative within Europe of preventing the worst rather than hoping for the best. The same constraints, but also possibilities, held true for those people who lived most marginally outside Europe, meaning the noncommercial peoples of new worlds, in both the Atlantic and the Pacific. They represented the second moral hazard that Malthus identified and for which he proposed some elements of a solution. Like the poor (or so Malthus reasoned), the hunting "savages" and semipastoral "barbarians" of new worlds were likeliest in times of want to resort to war, infanticide, cannibalism, violence toward childbearing women, abortion, and other desperate measures, unless starvation thinned their ranks involuntarily. Or unless other more "civilized" measures were introduced.

Could both problems be solved—at all, let alone at the same time? It says a great deal about the thoroughness of Malthus's moral reasoning that he tried to do so when a great many of his contemporaries saw, at best, only one of the two hazards he had spotted (and not in the fine level of detail he did). Although it had been thought for centuries that to colonize new lands would offer employment for those who needed work, plus ghost acres to feed those who stayed behind, Malthus queried that solution. His insistence that human population growth was always—necessarily—limited by availability of food was based on a belief that humans could not endlessly develop and improve nature; neither human nature nor the nature that lay beyond humanity could, he thought, bear such optimistic expectations. There would always be diminishing returns. In that case, European settlement in new worlds was not unjust merely because it took land from its prior occupants but also because it held out false hope: it exacerbated rather than solved the paired problems. For that reason, Malthus's insistence that population within Europe (including perhaps especially England) needed to be controlled, lest it double as quickly as on the North American frontier, represented an idea of reform at home but also abroad. His principle signaled that "civilization" demanded different kinds of check—not starvation, infanticide, or violence, but delayed marriage and abstinence before it. This prudence and an expectation of "improvement" could result from better forms of education and government, mitigating the numbers and conditions of the poor, he thought, though never fully ameliorating this fate for at least some.

At its base, his point was that rapid increase of population was for civilized, Christian people never an excuse for bad behavior, exactly the observation he would make in response to those who defended the slave trade on the grounds that it did not deplete a constantly replenishing West African population. He considered that hardly a fit justification. Emigration policies that sought to raise the standard of living for the poor at home were for that reason, he thought, threats to the happiness if not actual lives of new world peoples.

And yet he backed down. It is perhaps not entirely surprising, given the optimistic clamor supporting settlement schemes after 1815, when British energies could turn from war to colonization, that even Malthus would modify his warnings against the quick fix (as he had seen it) of shifting the able-bodied poor abroad. And given that he had stated his reservations against settlers driving any new world natives into a corner only fleetingly, his eventual capitulation had its own logic. It is in contrast, however, to the quiet way he had criticized the slave trade and yet stood against it when it mattered that he do so. Small wonder that his second moral hazard has seemed much less important than the first; the poor we have always with us, but the "vanishing races" have been much less of a public concern, except of course to themselves.

Their continuing plight, and the way in which the ethical considerations of modern economic development have rarely included attention to it, should nevertheless prompt a broader definition of what we talk about when we talk about "Malthusianism." Given the prejudices of his contemporaries in Europe, it is not surprising Malthus questioned the justice of displacing new world peoples only hesitantly. But his caution does not erase the fact that he did articulate and publish those reservations. Had his principle of population in relation to new worlds undergone careful and thorough discussion since 1803, today's world might look different, though doubtless still with the unfinished work of undoing the legacies of imperialism. Put another way, which population problems could be adequately discussed in the terms laid out in the 1798 edition of the *Essay on the Principle of Population*, and which would necessitate some understanding of the editions from 1803 and after? This is not an absolute distinction, of course. But the "1798 thesis" could represent how the first edition of the *Essay* has been seen to emphasize Malthus's first moral hazard, while the "1803 thesis" represents a significant shift toward the second, not a full break, but an elaboration.

Today the name "Malthus" typically evokes the main points of the 1798 thesis, as they are commonly understood, in relation to parts of the world where population is growing most swiftly, usually meaning Asia and Africa, and yet which seem also to suffer disproportionately from material want. To a large extent, these populations in the developing world stand to those in the developed global west as the poor did to Malthus, and they are often discussed with the same sense of pitying, unhelpful inevitability: "a strong and constantly operating check on population from the difficulty of subsistence" is a "difficulty that must fall somewhere; and must necessarily be felt severely by a large portion of mankind." The difficulties are true enough, though the necessity of them falling on only some of humanity is less so. For this line of argument, the Hazlitt criticism is apt: why do people in the developed world, who consume resources disproportionately, have the right to browbeat people in South Asia and West Africa for their choice of family size?

Less rarely is the continuing struggle or decline of new world peoples considered to be as serious a problem. It must first be said that their central position within Malthusian population analysis was based on a falsehood, at least with regard to the Americas, the first of new worlds. Malthus had repeated, without criticism, the most extreme scenarios of native American population collapse and (beyond South and Central America) of Indians' small population size in the first place. He then transferred these assumptions to the new worlds of the Pacific, even as others, including Alexander von Humboldt, presented contrary evidence for precisely the parts of the Americas first known to Europeans. Historians and archeologists have since validated Humboldt's suspicions: pre-Columbian indigenous populations were larger than the stereotypes had allowed; native decline was in many places exaggerated. Malthus's "principle of population" was wrong in its insistence that new world peoples were by nature inclined toward extinction. But it was correct in its proposal that settler behavior toward the indigenes was an important factor in population dynamics, and therefore the ultimate disposition of land. In Australia and much of the Pacific, the decline in numbers was rapid, but all along this constituted a principle of colonization, not a principle of population. To some extent Malthus understood that, but he persisted in seeing the former as somehow part of the latter, following the primordial American stereotype that itself was turning out to be wrong.[3]

And yet, in purest terms, new world communities are absolutely examples of Malthusian population dynamics because of the rapid settler proliferation that drove indigenous people into various corners. This plight indeed continues under conditions uncomfortably similar to those Malthus laid out at the start of the nineteenth century: shrinking resources, oscillating population, and limited public intervention on their behalf—driven into "a corner" indeed. Even when indigenous populations do better (as could be argued for New Zealand and parts of Canada), they rarely enjoy material benefits comparable to the descendants of the settlers who originally edged them away from ancestral homelands. If there is a Malthusian thesis to be evoked here, it is quite definitely that of 1803, which identifies problems of the late eighteenth and early nineteenth century as unresolved.[4]

It is perhaps still more critical to inform public debate over resources and population with the terms of the 1803 thesis because the indigenous populations of new worlds will struggle all the more as natural resources diminish and global climates change. The fragile communities of the South American tropics and of the far Canadian Arctic, as well as island populations in the Pacific, could represent some of the worst of the worse-case new world scenarios, as rainforest is logged, ice melts, and seas rise. Again, and sadly, the terms in which Malthus originally made that case for such people need remarkably little in the way of update. Even worse, many new world language groups have already been "exterminated" in the second sense in which Malthus used the word in the English language, and just as he predicted. As he had said, "to exterminate the inhabitants of the greatest part of Asia and Africa, is a thought that could not be admitted for a moment," even as there is passive public acceptance that new world populations still "inevitably" shrink. Any comprehension of those tragedies is absolutely dependent on Malthus's principle of population. Charles Darwin, informed by the long edition of the *Essay*, and therefore the 1803 thesis, could see and apply the principle of population, not only to the natives of South America and Australia whom he observed as dwindling before the tread of the white man, but also to the overall scientific definition of extinction as part of natural selection and of evolution, in which the preventive checks that Malthus thought human action and natural limits exerted on population could be used to explain all other living beings.[5]

It is crucial to remember that Malthusian new worlds may still exist, and to think critically about those that might come into being. Are there any? New frontiers of material plenty might be available, certainly there is perennial discussion of them, which Malthus would have recognized as aspects of the old fantasy that fresh starts for humanity must exist somewhere. Perhaps asteroids could be mined for something or other. Maybe the Moon or Mars have untold economic opportunities. Obviously, Earth's seabed offers new sites for petroleum extraction. And yet these places are not new worlds in the same sense that the Americas or the South Seas were, because they lack human inhabitants. There are no competitor beings with whom rights would need to be brokered—or ignored. The asteroids and Mars in particular, far from Earth, represent pure cases of optimism that the nonhuman parts of material nature always contain something for human use, that our ingenuity will perpetually invent novel opportunities even as new resources will be identified. This was one half of the problem, as Malthus saw it: misplaced faith that the Creation (as he would have called it) was inexhaustible, even to the point of relinquishing the obligation to face the deficiencies of nature and human nature: "Necessity, that imperious all pervading law of nature, restrains them within the prescribed bounds." Here is where his 1798 warning that humans tend to use resources faster than they could be replenished could, in secular terms, still be debated. If so, the argument is likely to be over whether there are economic and ethical models that might represent a break from the many historical examples of human behavior that he (and others) have used to express skepticism over human nature rather than optimism about it.[6]

But new worlds in the classic sense would have to represent the moral hazard represented in the 1803 thesis: competition with the human beings who have prior rights to a place, which would make them worlds of the kind

Bennelong had inhabited. If they exist, they lie far away, possibly as inhabited "Goldilocks" planets capable of sustaining human life. Should Earthlings ever venture to such a place, Malthus's principle of population would yet again be put to the test. And so in that far-off possible new world, the useful edition of the *Essay on the Principle of Population* to peruse could not be that of 1798. It would have to be any of the editions from 1803 onward, those that identify the fully problematic interplay between human needs and material limits in inhabited new worlds as a yet-unsolved ethical dilemma. However bound to Malthus's historical context and whatever the weaknesses or flaws in its moral logic, the 1803 thesis is still the only definition of Malthusian analysis that would be of universal value, meaning over the Earth and even beyond, in whatever new worlds might exist, and therefore that thesis begs the question of how settlers might be able to enter new places without exterminating any others who also deserve to live if not also to be happy there.

*   *   *

Over time, it was the old world Malthuses who bordered on extinction, perhaps by too much preventive checking of one kind or another. Malthus himself married very late, and as a result—axiomatic to his own social and economic plan—had only three children, contrary to the rumors that so early spread as far as the southwestern Pacific, that he was father of ten. For various reasons, Henry, Emily, and Lucy Malthus did not reproduce (though his son did go on to be a more diligent vicar than the father ever was). However, their uncle Sydenham and his sugar-enriched cousin and wife, Marianna Georgina, spawned two more generations of Sydenham Malthuses, a direct line that also self-extinguished in the United Kingdom. But Sydenham Malthus IV had two brothers, Charles Edward Daniel Malthus and Henry Percival Malthus, who emigrated to New Zealand in the 1860s, after the Wakefield-inspired New Zealand Company had cleared land for new settlers and as the New Zealand wars were still being fought between Māori and British. The Malthus tribe removed to a distant corner of the British Empire, where they were beneficiaries of the linked population policy and land policy that had been at the heart of new world settlements, whatever Malthus's and others' criticisms of them.[7]

Meanwhile, and in notable contrast, William Godwin's line has continued within England, albeit not under his name. Despite losing most of her children while they were still quite young, Mary Wollstonecraft Godwin Shelley, daughter of Godwin, mother of *Frankenstein*, wife of the poet Percy Bysshe Shelley, was female parent of the heir to the Shelley estate at Penshurst and to the title of baronet. The family title has since then been changed twice, but as this book is published it survives in the person of the second Viscount De L'Isle, lineal descendent of Malthus's foe. Condorcet was not so fortunate. His one child, Eliza, married one of the early members of the radical Society of United Irishmen, which sought an independent and republican future for Ireland, along the lines of the United States and inspired, as well, by at least some of the principles of the French Revolution. In honor of his guillotined father-in-law, Daniel O'Conner added the name of Condorcet to his own, and therefore to his and Eliza's four children. But the line failed in the fourth generation; there are no surviving Condorcet–O'Conners.

Ironies abound. Godwin the philosophical anarchist has an aristocratic descendant within England, his line protected from material want by inherited wealth that no revolution ever did away with, to which no lasting utopia has defined an alternative of the radical type Godwin would have preferred and whose very continuance proves Malthus's point that the passion between the sexes has not so far been extinguished. Meanwhile, Condorcet the aristocrat though also social reformer had a daughter who survived the French Revolution and married an Irishman who eventually supported Bonaparte, an interesting and revolutionary amalgam indeed, the history of which failed to survive within that family line. Finally, Malthus, the cautious liberal who put his faith in law and custom, who so often wrote against emigration, and who was anxious about new world people, had a family line that without the property of a titled family or the inclinations toward diasporic political dissent was eventually driven to the empire in the Pacific. Only the 1803 thesis could possibly make sense of the material and moral dimensions of this story. And thus it is only in the new world, on (so far) alienated Māori land, that the Malthus family name has endured, even as the Malthusian dilemmas of the 1803 thesis persist.

ACKNOWLEDGMENTS

For comment and reflection on our project we are grateful to many friends and colleagues, including in particular John Pullen, Donald Winch, Alan Atkinson, Michael McDonnell, Kirsten McKenzie, Ann Curthoys, John Gascoigne, Stephen Heath, Linford Fisher, Paul Warde, Robert Mayhew, Dore A. Minatodani, Hi'ilei Julia Hobart, John Womack, Gabe Paquette, Carlos Marichal Salinas, Jose Enrique Covarrubias, Francisco J. Vanaclocha Bellver, Kathryn Sampeck, Leah Price, Fredrik Albritton Jonsson, Deborah Cohen, Alexander F. More, Nicholas Crawford, Rebecca Goetz, E. G. Gallwey, and Caitlin Fitz. John Pullen generously shared his comprehensive list of Malthus's surviving letters. We are grateful for the research assistance of João Rangel del Almeida, Chris Holdridge, Matthew Kennedy, Ewan Lusty, Louise Moschetta, and Sonia Tycko, partly funded by the Australian Research Council, the Harvard University Dean's Startup Fund, and the Neubauer Family (through the Neubauer Collegium at the University of Chicago). Our thanks to the Master and Fellows of Jesus College, Cambridge, for access to the Malthus Collection in the Old Library and to the James Papers.

ABBREVIATIONS

CO	Colonial Office records, the National Archives, Kew
DM	Daniel Malthus
DRO	Derbyshire Record Office, Matlock
KJV	King James Version
JC	Jesus College, Old Library, Cambridge
MP	Member of Parliament
MUP	*T. R. Malthus: The Unpublished Papers*
NLA	National Library of Australia (Canberra)
OED	*Oxford English Dictionary*
PBF	*Papers of Benjamin Franklin*
TNA	The National Archives, Kew, England
TRM	Thomas Robert Malthus

Unless otherwise noted, all translations done by Joyce E. Chaplin.

NOTES

NOTES TO INTRODUCTION

1. *OED*, s.v., "Malthusian" and "Malthusianism."
2. The Library of Congress lists 79 books with "Malthus" as the key subject, but more than twice that number, 183, under "Malthusianism." On Malthusianism in the developing world (both for scholars who broadly agree with his proposition and those who do not): Sachs, "Are Malthus's Predicted 1798 Food Shortages Coming True?"; Rao, *From Population Control to Reproductive Health*; Rao and Sexton, *Markets and Malthus*. On the "conversation with a friend": [Malthus], *An Essay on the Principle of Population*; Pullen, "Correspondence between Malthus and his Parents." On the centrality of the English poor: Huzel, "Malthus, the Poor Law and Population"; Petersen, *Malthus*; James, *Population Malthus*; Winch, *Riches and Poverty*; Hilton, *Age of Atonement*; Hollander, *Economics of Thomas Robert Malthus*; Jones, *An End to Poverty*. In a different tradition, see Dean, *Constitution of Poverty*; Dean, "The Malthus Effect." And on Malthus as a political economist, Pullen, "Last Sixty-five Years of Malthus Scholarship."
3. Wrigley, "Standing Between Two Worlds." As coeditor of Malthus's complete works, Wrigley is naturally aware of the geographic range of the *Essay*. See Wrigley and Souden, *Works of Thomas Robert Malthus*.
4. Kupperman, "Changing Definition of America"; Miller, *Errand into the Wilderness*; Nash, *Wilderness and the American Mind*; Banner, *Possessing the Pacific*; Fitzmaurice, *Sovereignty, Property, and Empire*.
5. On the frontier: Turner, "Significance of the Frontier"; Slotkin, *Regeneration through Violence*. Comparison among frontiers was of interest in roughly the middle of the twentieth century; see, for instance, Wyman, *Frontier in Perspective*, though focused comparisons among two or a few specific places are now more common, as for example with Hogg, *Men and Manliness on the Frontier*. For critiques of the frontier thesis: White, *Middle Ground*; White and Limerick, *Frontier in American Culture*. On borderlands: Bolton, *Spanish Borderlands*; Adelman and Aron, "From Borderlands to Borders"; Readman, Radding, and Bryant, *Borderlands in World History*. On creoles and nationhood: Brading, *First America*; Anderson, *Imagined Communities*, 49–68. On settler colonialism/settler society: Wolfe, "Land, Labor, and Difference"; Belich, *Replenishing the Earth*; Bateman and Pilkington, *Studies in Settler Colonialism*. For Malthus, Malthusianism, and frontiers within imperial and global contexts, see Richards, "Malthus and the Uses of British Emigration"; Bashford, *Global Population*, 31–36.
6. For brief versions of the Franklin-Malthus connection, see Aldridge, "Franklin as Demographer"; Zirkle, "Benjamin Franklin,"; James, *Population Malthus*, 106–7; Appleman, "Introduction," xvi; Hodgson, "Benjamin Franklin on Population." For a fuller account, see Chaplin, *Benjamin Franklin's Political Arithmetic*.

7. Malthus as ethnographer: Godelier, "Malthus and Ethnography"; Hamilton, "Malthus, Yesterday and Today—and Tomorrow?"; Brantlinger, *Dark Vanishings*, 33–36; Blainey, *Triumph of the Nomads*, 93–95, 99; Mulvaney, "Australian Aborigines, 1606–1929," 141; Frost, "Pacific Ocean"; Strong, "Fathoming the Primitive"; Konishi, "The Tantalising Cannibal,"; Konishi, " 'Wanton with plenty.' " Cf. the invisibility of Malthus's chapter on New South Wales in "Malthus and his Legacy," though this does not include all papers delivered. For glancing appreciations of Malthus's attention to extra-European worlds: Caldwell, "Malthus and the Less Developed World"; Winch, *Classical Political Economy and Colonies*; Richards, "Malthus and the Uses of British Emigration"; Ghosh, "Malthus on Emigration and Colonization"; Toye, "Keynes on Population and Economic Growth," 8. See Bashford, "Malthus and Colonial History."

8. Jonsson, *Enlightenment's Frontier*, 193–95, 251–52; Richards, "Malthus and the Uses of British Emigration," 42–43.

9. Borgstrom, *Hungry Planet*, 70–85.

10. Pomeranz, *Great Divergence*, 276, 313–14; Wrigley, *Energy and the English Industrial Revolution*, 99, 174, 208; Belich, *Replenishing the Earth*, 443–46; Bashford, *Global Population*, 362; Mayhew, *Malthus*, 3, 103–27; Albion, *Forests and Sea Power*; Grove, *Green Imperialism*, 57–67; Williams, *Deforesting the Earth*, 193–209; Appuhn, *Forest on the Sea*; Warde, "Invention of Sustainability"; Wing, "Keeping Spain Afloat."

11. British economic historians certainly frame Malthus in terms of land and organic economies, but rarely in terms of the politics of colonial land. However, for organic economies and extra-European land figured as "areas of recent settlement," see Wrigley, *Poverty, Progress, and Population*, 4–5, 12, 219; quotation from Malthus, *An Essay* (1803), 6.

12. Malthus, *An Essay* (1803), 6; Bayly, *Birth of the Modern World*, ch. 12 "The Destruction of Native Peoples and Ecological Depredation" and "Conclusion: The Great Acceleration."

13. "Chapters iii to xiv omitted from this edition": Malthus, *An Essay*, ed. Donald Winch, 29; James, *Population Malthus*, 93–94.

14. Malthus, *An Essay* (1826), vol. 1, 67.

15. *MUP*; [Graves], "A domestic scene in rural life." Graves noted, "This is a real though imperfect sketch of a worthy family, who have happily united in their domestic economy, the elegant simplicity of the pastoral ages with the refinement of modern life" (40).

16. We engage with historians of stadial theory, including Hont and Ignatieff, *Wealth and Virtue*; Chaplin, *An Anxious Pursuit*, 23–65; O'Brien, "Between Enlightenment and Stadial History"; Pocock, *Barbarians, Savages and Empires*; Wolloch, "Civilizing Process, Nature, and Stadial Theory"; Sebastiani, *Scottish Enlightenment*. We are also in dialogue with scholars of theories of human nature more generally, as with Meek, *Social Science and the Ignoble Savage*; Pagden, *Fall of Natural Man*; Jones, *Science of Man in the Scottish Enlightenment*; Garrett, "Anthropology: The 'Original' of Human Nature"; Wolff and Cipolloni, *Anthropology of the Enlightenment*.

17. Hodgson, "Malthus' Essay on Population."

Chapter 1: Population, Empire, and America

1. KJV Genesis 1:28, 3:16–19, 9:1; Cohen, *Be Fertile and Increase*.
2. Braude, "Sons of Noah.".
3. KJV Acts 17:26; Grafton, *New Worlds, Ancient Texts*, 11–58, 95–158; Almond, *Adam and Eve*; Gliozzi, *Adam et le Nouveau Monde*.
4. Delumeau, *History of Paradise*, 109–15; Householder, "Eden's Translations."
5. De Bry, Grands Voyages, pt. 1, pt. 7.
6. Laiou, "Economic Thought and Ideology," 1142–44; Jordan, *Great Famine*; Bartlett, *Making of Europe*, esp. pp. 106–66.
7. KJV 1 Chron. 21:1; Cohen, *Be Fertile and Increase*; Cohen, *A Calculating People*, 56–65.
8. Machiavelli, *Machivael's Discourses*, 221–22.
9. Bodin, *Six Bookes*, 387, 637–41.
10. Botero, *Reason of State*, 227, 276, 278.
11. Glacken, *Traces on the Rhodian Shore*, 369–74.
12. Botero, *Reason of State*, 278; Thomas Hariot Mathematical Papers, British Library; Chaplin, *Subject Matter*, 124–25; Smith, "Reception of Malthus' Essay," 550.
13. Bodin, *Six Bookes*, 621; Botero, *Reason of State*, 156–57; Chaplin, *Subject Matter*, 126–27.
14. Glacken, *Traces on the Rhodian Shore*, 625; Chaplin, *Subject Matter*, 126–27; Richards, *Unending Frontier*.
15. Chaplin, *Subject Matter*, 151–52.
16. Pagden, *Fall of Natural Man*; Pagden, *Lords of All the World*, 87, 116.
17. Cassedy, *Demography in Early America*; Wells, *Population of the British Colonies*, 5, 8–11, 13–23; Cohen, *A Calculating People*, 56–65, 78.
18. [Vincent], *A True Relation of the Late Battell*, [1], 21; Chaplin, "Natural Philosophy"; Jones, *Rationalizing Epidemics*, 21–67.
19. Chaplin, *Subject Matter*, 243–79; Morgan, "'Some Could Suckle over Their Shoulder.'"
20. Sokol, "Thomas Harriot," 212; [Winslow], *Mourt's Relation*, 84.
21. [John Locke], *Two Treatises of Government*, book II, ch. 5, § 49.
22. Buck, "People Who Counted," 28–29.
23. Glacken, *Traces on the Rhodian Shore*, 398–99.
24. Glacken, *Traces on the Rhodian Shore*, 398–99; Riley, *Population Thought*, 7–15; Rusnock, "Biopolitics," 56–57; Daston, *Classical Probability in the Enlightenment*, 127–29. On the doubling idea beyond Malthus, see Bashford, *Global Population*, 37, 38, 47, 49, 92, 110–11, 202, 276, 348.
25. Daston, *Classical Probability*, 129–38.
26. Marquis of Lansdowne, *Petty-Southwell Correspondence*, 154.
27. Chaplin, *Subject Matter*, 318–20; McCormick, *William Petty*.
28. Petty, *Political Arithmetick*, 94, 97–98.
29. Webb, *Governors-General*.
30. Boyle, "General Heads for a Natural History," 188; Chaplin, "Creoles in British America," 46–65.

31. Rothschild, *Economic Sentiments*, 2; Marouby, "Adam Smith and the Anthropology of the Enlightenment," 85–102; Cañizares-Esguerra, *How to Write the History of the New World*, 44–51.

32. Pagden, *Fall of Natural Man*.

33. Pagden, *Fall of Natural Man*, 198–209.

34. Montesquieu, *The Persian Letters*, 390–411; Montesquieu, *Spirit of Laws*, 302–18.

35. Hume, "Of the Populousness of Ancient Nations" (1752), in Hume, *Essays Moral, Political, and Literary*, 371–464; Riley, *Population Thought*, 47–57.

36. Wallace, *A Dissertation*, 1–8, 8n., 12–13.

37. Wallace, *A Dissertation*, 15–20, 91, 107–8, 147, 168–208, 268–69, and passim for moralizing analysis of the ancient world.

38. Wallace, *A Dissertation*, 95–96, 160, 270–71.

39. Wallace, *A Dissertation*, 149; Glacken, *Traces on the Rhodian Shore*, 630–31, 632–34.

40. Meek, *Social Science and the Ignoble Savage*, esp. 37–67; Pocock, "Gibbon and the Shepherds," 193–202; Marouby, "Adam Smith and the Anthropology of the Enlightenment," 85–102; Montesquieu, *Persian Letters*, 406; Montesquieu, *Spirit of Laws*, 304, 314.

41. Palmeri, "Conjectural History and Satire."

42. Meek, *Social Science and the Ignoble Savage*, 131–76; Marshall and Williams, *Great Map of Mankind*; Schiebinger, *Nature's Body*, 48–74; Sebastiani, *Scottish Enlightenment*, 80–90.

43. Dent, *Rousseau*, esp. 37–112; Wokler, *Rousseau*, 1–28.

44. Appleby, "Ideology and Theory"; Winch, *Riches and Poverty*, 57–89; Montes, *Adam Smith in Context*; Waterman, *Political Economy and Christian Theology*), 1–15, 107–113; Buck, "People Who Counted," 28–29.

45. Rothschild, *Economic Sentiments*; Sebastiani, *Scottish Enlightenment*, 133–62.

46. Oldmixon, *British Empire in America*, vol. 1, xvi, xxi–xxv, xxix, 161.

47. Swift referred to the new world on pp. 3 and 6 of *A Modest Proposal* (q.v.).

48. Franklin, "The Speech of Miss Polly Baker" (1747), *PBF*, vol. 3, 123, 124, 125.

49. Benjamin Franklin, 'Observations Concerning the Increase of Mankind' (1751), *PBF*, vol. 4, 225–31.

50. Franklin, "Observations," 228, 230–31, 234.

51. Franklin, "Observations," 228, 234.

52. Franklin, "Observations," 233; Chaplin, *Benjamin Franklin's Political Arithmetic*.

53. Franklin, "Observations," 231.

54. Ezra Stiles, *A Discourse on the Christian Union*, 108–9; Price, *Observations on Reversionary Payments*, 197–98, 203–5; Mayhew, *Malthus*, 30–35.

55. Chaplin, "Pacific before Empire," 53, 74.

56. Cook, *Journals*, vol. 1, cclxxxiii.

57. Marshall and Williams, *Great Map of Mankind*, ch. 9; Gascoigne, *Encountering the Pacific*.

58. Cheek, *Sexual Antipodes*.

59. Marshall and Williams, *Great Map of Mankind*, 258–98; Banks, *Endeavour Journal*, vol. 1, 400–3, 268–71, vol. 2, 122–30, 142.

60. Pitts, *A Turn to Empire*, 1–21.

61. Gibbon, *Decline and Fall*, vol. 1, 227; Pocock, "Gibbon and the Shepherds."

62. Smith, *Wealth of Nations* (1776), book 4, ch. 7, para. 29, book 5, ch. 3, para. 76. See also Winch, *Classical Political Economy and Colonies*, 6–24; Pitts, *A Turn to Empire*, 25–58.

63. Smith, *Wealth of Nations* (1776), book 4, ch. 7, para. 23–25, 37–43.

64. Smith, *Wealth of Nations* (1776), book 1, ch. 8, para. 23, 23n., book 4, ch. 8, para. 49.

65. *Annual Register*, 191–92; Burgh, *Political Disquisitions*, vol. 2, 287; *Politician's Dictionary*, vol. 1, 147.

66. Braithwaite, *Romanticism, Publishing, and Dissent*, chs. 1, 2; [Joseph] Johnson to BF, November 4, 1766, *PBF*, vol. 12, 484.

67. Franklin, *Political, Miscellaneous, and Philosophical Pieces*, 1–23.

Chapter 2: Writing the *Essay*

1. [Malthus], "An Essay on the Advantages of Colonies," 275.

2. Jean-Jacques Rousseau to François Henri d'Ivernois, May 13, 1764 (*Il me paroit homme de mérite et fort instruit*), in Rousseau, *Correspondance complète*, vol. 20, 53; DM to Rousseau, January 16, 1766, January 20, 1766, and January 24, 1766; Rousseau, *Correspondance complète*, vol. 28, 194–95, 209, 221–22; DM to Rousseau, [December 1, 1766], Rousseau, *Correspondance complète*, vol. 31, 235–37; Rousseau to DM, [March 3, 1766], DM to Rousseau, April 1, 1766 (Je m'étois flatté de vous avoir fait passer e quelques jours au moinse, vous & Mademoiselle Le Vasseur, dans ma famille), and Rousseau to DM, [April 15?, 1766] (vous avez trop de sens), Rousseau, *Correspondance complète*, vol. 29, 9, 84–85, 117–18; Cranston, *Solitary Self*, 163–73; David Hume to Rousseau [February or March 1766] and Hume to Rousseau, March 27, 1766, in Hume, *Letters of David Hume*, vol. 2, 23–24, 32–33.

3. Malthus Family, Newsclipping Album, MA 7.5, JC. On the *St. James's Chronicle*, see Rea, *English Press in Politics*, 98–99, 147, 152, 156–57, 165, 177, 204; Barker, *Newspapers, Politics, and English Society*, 163, 189; DM to Rousseau, July 18, 1766, in Rousseau, *Correspondance complète*, vol. 30, 112–14; DM to Rousseau, [December 1, 1766] (Vivant a la campagne, ou je ne lis que rarement les papiers publics), Rousseau, *Correspondance complète*, vol. 31, 235–36.

4. [Graves], "A domestic scene in rural life."; DM to Rousseau, July 18, 1766, *Correspondance complète*, vol. 30, 113; Cook, "Bernardin de Saint-Pierre's English Correspondents," 18–21; letters from Jane Dalton to Jacques Henri Bernardin de Saint-Pierre, Electronic Enlightenment (www.e-enlightenment.com).

5. On p. 39, the "n" in "Dunny's" is more rounded than in TRM's hand; on p. 87, the "P" in "Petition" carries a tail, which TRM's handwriting does not have; apostrophic contractions occur on p. 116, "appear'd," and p. 127, "walk'd." Compare to this the contrasting forms in the father-son correspondence: on June 16, [1787], DM wrote "lock'd," "receiv'd," "resolv'd," "enjoy'd," and "wish'd"; on April 17, 1788, in a letter of roughly the same length, TRM used "call'd" but otherwise spelled out "received," "obliged," "finished," "polished," and "overwhelmed," in *MUP*, vol. 1, 50–51, 53–54.

6. McLachlan, *Warrington Academy*, 32; Wykes, "Contribution of the Dissenting Academy," 132–36; Safford and Safford, *A History of Childhood and Disability*, 13–14, 27–28, 50–54; Woodley, " 'Oh Miserable and Most Ruinous Measure' "; Cohen, " 'Familiar Conversation,' " 109. 113–15; Gill, *Education Philosophy in the French Enlightenment*, esp. 181–270.

7. Malthus, "An Essay on the Advantages of Colonies," 275–77.

8. DM to TRM (April 7, [1784]), *MUP*, vol. 1, 21; TRM to DM (November 14, 1784), *MUP*, vol. 1, 29; DM to TRM (January 13, 1786), *MUP*, vol. 1, 36; DM to TRM (January 31, 1786), *MUP*, vol. 1, 41; TRM to DM (February 11, 1786), *MUP*, vol. 1, 41, 42.

9. James, *Population Malthus*, 30, 33; TRM to DM (April 17, 1788), *MUP*, vol. 1, 53.

10. James, *Population Malthus*, 40, 43–44; TRM to DM, April 19, 1786, *MUP*, vol. 1, 47; editorial note in *MUP*, vol. 2, 53.

11. Winch, *Riches and Poverty*, 127–36; Mayhew, *Malthus*, 35–46.

12. James, *Population Malthus*, 50–54; DM to TRM (April 14, [1796], *MUP*, vol. 1, 62.

13. Emsley, "Repression, 'Terror' and the Rule of Law"; Dickinson, *British Radicalism and the French Revolution*; Barrell, *Spirit of Despotism*.

14. Braithwaite, *Romanticism, Publishing, and Dissent*, 162–69.

15. Zall, "Cool World of Samuel Taylor Coleridge"; Tyson, "Joseph Johnson"; Braithwaite, *Joseph Johnson*.

16. Tyson, "Joseph Johnson," 11–14.

17. Tyson, "Joseph Johnson," 14; Braithwaite, *Joseph Johnson*, 155–69; Joseph Johnson to Ralph Mather, July 15, 799, Joseph Johnson Business Correspondence, RP 5898, BL.

18. Joseph Johnson to Joseph Priestley, March 15, 1805, Joseph Johnson Business Correspondence; see Jane Dalton to Bernardin de Saint-Pierre, September 1, 1789, in which she gives her address for correspondence at a London bookseller and passes respects from "M. Malthus," probably Daniel Malthus.

19. [Malthus], *An Essay* (1798), 2, 7.

20. [Malthus], *An Essay* (1798), 10, 11, 13, 14, 17.

21. Malthus's slant toward Godwin, compared to Condorcet, may also have resulted from his book's origins in an argument with his father about one of Godwin's essays. See [Malthus], *An Essay* (1798), v.

22. On famine: Minchinton, "Agricultural Returns and the Government"; Sheridan, "Crisis of Slave Subsistence"; Arnold, "Hunger in the Garden of Plenty"; Taylor, " 'The Hungry Year,' ", chs. 4 and 6; Johnson, "El Niño, Environmental Crisis, and the Emergence of Alternative Markets." On agricultural reform and empire: Gascoigne, *Science in the Service of Empire*; Drayton, *Nature's Government*; Jonsson, *Enlightenment's Frontier*. On the poor and reform within Europe: Winch, *Riches and Poverty*, 198–287.

23. Godwin, *An Enquiry*, vol. 1, vi, 203, 204, vol 2, 813.

24. [Malthus], *An Essay* (1798), 361, 393; see also LeMahieu, "Malthus and the Theology of Scarcity"; Santurri, "Theodicy and Social Policy "; Pullen, "Malthus' Theological Ideas," 39–54.

25. [Malthus], *An Essay* (1798), 20–21.

26. [Malthus], *An Essay* (1798), 21–23, 25–26; Bashford, *Global Population*, 25–30.

27. [Malthus], *An Essay* (1798), 27, 37.
28. [Malthus], *An Essay* (1798), 38–44.
29. [Malthus], *An Essay* (1798), 20, 108.
30. [Malthus], *An Essay* (1798), 101–6.
31. [Malthus], *An Essay* (1798), 104–5, 185; Stiles, *A Discourse on the Christian Union*, 108–9; Price, *Observations on Reversionary Payments*, 203, 204, 206; *Malthus Library Catalogue*, 138, 165; Chaplin, *Benjamin Franklin's Political Arithmetic*, 41. See Malthus Family, Newsclipping Album, JC, 30–31.
32. Franklin, "Observations," 233; [Malthus], *An Essay* (1798), 127–28; Godwin, *Political Justice*, vol. 2, 862; Chaplin, *First Scientific American*, 335, 337–38.
33. [Malthus], *An Essay* (1798), 341–42; Price, *Reversionary Payments*, 203–5.
34. Godwin, *Political Justice*, vol. 2, 860, 870–72; [Malthus], *An Essay* (1798), 210–18.
35. "Political Economy," *Monthly Magazine and British Register* 6 (July 1798): 496–97; *New Annual Register*, 229.
36. "S. A.," review of *Essay on the Principle of Populations* (which is corrected as "Population" in the running heading for the review), *The Analytical Review: Or, History of Literature* 28, no. 2 (August 1798): 119–25.
37. Unsigned review, *Analytical Review*, 125–33.
38. Bayly, *Imperial Meridian*, 100–32, 217–47; Nick Cullather, *The Hungry World*, 12; Bashford, *Global Population*, chs. 7, 10.
39. Malthus, *An Essay* (1803), iii; James, *Population Malthus*, 69; James, *Travel Diaries of Thomas Robert Malthus*, 59, 81, 117, 137–38, 140, 152, 156–57.
40. James, *Population Malthus*, 92.
41. Brewer, *Sinews of Power*, esp. 167–217; Colley, *Britons*, 283–319; Bell, *First Total War*, 148–49, 162–62, 210, 234, 245.
42. Bayly, *Imperial Meridian*, 89–95, 164–92; DuBois, *Avengers of the New World*.
43. [Malthus], *Causes of the Present High Price of Provisions*, 4, 8, 9, 16, 26, 27–28; James, *Population Malthus*, 86–92.
44. Barnes, *A History of the English Corn Laws*, 69, 72; Hunter, "Wheat, War, and the American Economy," 505–26 (Jefferson cited on p. 505); Fichter, *So Great a Proffit*, 56–81.
45. [Malthus], *Causes of the Present High Price of Provisions*, 27–28.
46. Malthus, *An Essay* (1803), iii–vi.
47. Malthus, *An Essay* (1803), vii, ix–xi; notes for four sermons, *MUP*, vol. 2, 1–24.
48. Malthus, *An Essay* (1803), vii.
49. TRM to DM (February 4, 1799), in *MUP*, vol. 1, 64–65; McLachlan, *Warrington Academy*, 42, though Malthus and Aikin were not at Warrington at the same time.
50. Malthus, *An Essay* (1803), 2, 3, 4, 5.
51. Chaplin, *Franklin's Political Arithmetic*, 7–8, 12–19, 25–35; Schofield, *Enlightened Joseph Priestley*, 59–76, 263–89; Pullen, "Malthus' Theological Ideas," 203–16; Winch, *Riches and Poverty*, 236–37; Waterman, *Political Economy and Christian Theology*, 116–18.
52. Malthus, *An Essay* (1803), 7–12.
53. Malthus, *An Essay* (1803), 2–4.
54. Malthus, *An Essay* (1803), 5–8.
55. Malthus, *An Essay* (1803), 6.

56. Malthus, *An Essay* (1803), 6, 15.
57. Malthus, *An Essay* (1803), 354–61, 364, 366–86.

CHAPTER 3: NEW HOLLAND

1. Malthus, *An Essay* (1803), 18. Cited as a quotation from *"Cook's First Voyage,"* vol. 3, p. 240 [23 August 1770]. This was [Hawkesworth], *Account*, vol. 3, 644.
2. Malthus, *An Essay* (1803), 47.
3. TRM to the Reverend George Turner, November 28, 1800, AL82i, Senate House Library, University of London.
4. For eighteenth-century voyaging and Enlightenment thought, see Frost, "Pacific Ocean"; Gascoigne, *Encountering the Pacific*.
5. [Hawkesworth], *Account*, vol. 2, 57–59; Malthus, *An Essay* (1803), 17. Malthus also read the accounts of Tierra del Fuego in the second voyage, *A voyage towards the South Pole*, vol. 2, 187. For early voyagers, see Chaplin, *Round about the Earth*, 25.
6. [Hawkesworth], *Account*, vol. 2, 59; Malthus, *An Essay* (1803), 17; Smith, *European Vision*, 39–41.
7. Cook, *Journals*, vol. 1, ccliii; Benjamin Franklin to Jan Ingenhousz, September 30, 1773, *PBF*, vol. 20, 434–45. For Hawkesworth and Cook's voyage accounts, see Abbott, *John Hawkesworth*, 137–86; Beaglehole, *Life of Captain James Cook*, 290–1, 439–40, 457–9; Lamb, *Preserving the Self*.
8. Vancouver, *A Voyage of Discovery*. See Symes, *An Account of an Embassy*, vol. 1, 300–3. Malthus cited chapter 1, p. 129, but the equivalent material is bound as one volume with continuous pagination in Jesus College Old Library. See also Vaidik, "Wild Andamans," 19–42.
9. Register of Borrowers, 1791–1805 (November 17, 1801), B.15.14, p. 70, JC.
10. Colebrooke, "On the Andaman Islands," 401–411; Malthus, *An Essay* (1803), 17–18.
11. Smith, *Lectures on Jurisprudence*, 14; Gibbon, *Decline and Fall* vol. 6, 411; Home, *Sketches*, vol. 1, 54.
12. Malthus, *An Essay* (1803), 18, 47; Malthus, *A Summary View*, 44.
13. Banks continued, "They were indeed generaly furnishd with plenty of weapons whose points of the stings of Sting-Rays seemd intended against nothing but their own species, from whence such an inference might easily be drawn." In Banks, *Endeavour Journal*, vol. 2, 123 [August 1770]. There does not appear to be extant correspondence between Malthus and Banks, but we know they met once at the very least, when Malthus was elected fellow of the Royal Society in 1818.
14. Secret Instructions for Lieutenant James Cook Appointed to Command His Majesty's Bark the Endeavour, July 30, 1768, in Cook, *Journals*, vol. 1, cclxxix–cclxxxiv.
15. Description of New Holland, August 22, 1770, in Cook, *Journals*, vol. 1.
16. Banks, *Endeavour Journal*, vol. 1, 122–23 [August 1770].
17. Bunbury Committee on Transportation, *Journal of the House of Commons*. 37 (1779): 311.

18. Christopher and Maxwell-Stewart, "Convict Transportation," 68–69; *St. James's Chronicle*, December 5, 1786. For *St. James's Chronicles* clippings see Malthus Family, Newsclipping Album, MA 7.5, JC.

19. Governor Phillip to Under Secretary Nepean (June 29, 1789), Watson, ed. *Historical Records of Australia*, ser. 1 vol. 1, 56; Banks, *Endeavour Journal*, vol. 1, 122 [August 1770].

20. David Collins, *An Account*. All of Malthus's examples and information were derived from the appendices of this volume. David Collins produced a second volume published in 1802. Collins's *Account* was reviewed in the British press, sometimes with long extracts including mention of Ben-nil-long and Colebe, for example, in *Monthly Review*, November 1798, 242–57; *Annual Review* 1 (January 1802): 31–35. See Smith, "Bennelong among his People."

21. Tench, *Complete Account*; Phillip, *Voyage of Governor Phillip*; Barrington, *A Voyage to New South Wales* (for smallpox, see pp. 72 ff). Barrington also detailed Bennelong, or Banalong, extensively. Chapbooks also detailed the "Customs and Manners" of the natives, for example, in *An Authentic and Interesting Narrative*.

22. "His account is as detailed as a film's shooting-script." Clendinnen, *Dancing with Strangers*, 254.

23. Malthus, *An Essay* (1803), 19. Archaeologists' understanding now is that Aboriginal people engaged more in resource management than cultivation in this period. There is evidence of water and eel management, as well as fire management of land. There were fish traps in various places, involving tidal and flood harvesting, and there were the bunya nut festivals in northern New South Wales, along with processing of the poisonous macrozamia. However, there is no consensus as to whether these were managed or serendipitous harvests, during bumper seasons. In the north tuber tops (yams) may have been replanted to regrow, and there is an argument that patches of fruit trees on the far northeastern coast may have been managed by fire to increase production. Cultivation, per se, then, is not proven. Interview, Alison Bashford with Dr. Anne Clarke, May 19, 2014. For the persistence of the idea of the Australian "hunter-gatherer," see White, "Revisiting the 'Neolithic Problem.'"

24. Malthus, *An Essay* (1803), 20–21.

25. Collins, *An Account*, quoted in Malthus, *An Essay* (1803), 20–22; Collins, *An Account*, app. XI, 608. For masculine honor in this context, see Atkinson, *Europeans in Australia*, 160; Malthus, *An Essay* (1803), 23.

26. Malthus, *An Essay* (1803), 22–23. In February 1790 Governor Phillip reported that one Aboriginal man who lived with him thought "one-half of those who inhabit this part of the country died." Governor Phillip to Lord Sydney, February 13, 1790, Watson, ed. *Historical Records of Australia*, ser. 1, vol. 1, 159.

27. Phillip noted that "it never appeared on board any of the ships in our passage . . . nor has it ever appeared in the settlement except on that man [from the *Supply*] and the native who caught the disorder from the children." Governor Phillip to Lord Sydney, February 12, 1790, Watson, ed. *Historical Records of Australia*, ser. 1, vol. 1, 145. Malthus, *An Essay* (1803), 22. In the appendix, Collins did attribute venereal disease to the English : "The venereal disease also had got among them;

but I fear our people have to answer for that." For smallpox in eighteenth-century Australia, see Campbell, *Invisible Invaders*; Bennett, "Smallpox and Cowpox.".

28. Fenn, *Pox Americana*; Collins, *An Account*, app. VIII, 597–98.

29. Moorehead, *Fatal Impact*.

30. Malthus, *An Essay* (1803), 19; Collins, *An Account*, apps. V and VI, 560–65. For Malthus and anthropology see Godelier, "Malthus and Ethnography."

31. Fullagar, *Savage Visit*. "New Holland," *London Packet (New Lloyd's Evening Post)*, May 29–31, 1793, 1d.

32. Collins, *An Account*, 543; Coleman, *Romantic Colonization*, 170; Letter from George Cherry, Victualling Commissioner, June 1797, HO 42/41/92, TNA; Fullagar, "Bennelong in Britain"; Altick, *Shows of London*, 31–2; Smith, *Bennelong*.

33. Banks, *Endeavour Journal*, vol. 2, 145 [September 3, 1770]; Collins, *An Account*, 251; Chaplin, "Earthsickness."

34. "The Crisis," quoted in Empson, "Life, Writing, and Character," 479; Bennelong to Mr Phillips, 29 August 1796, in Jose, *Macquarie Penn Anthology*, 60.

35. "Here, if the reader pauses for a moment to consider the difference between the general conduct of our baptismal sponsors (to whose duties this custom bears much resemblance) and the humane practice of these uncivilised people, will not the comparison suffuse his cheek with something like shame, at seeing the enlightened Christian so distanced in the race of humanity by the untutored savage, who has hitherto been the object of his pity and contempt?" Collins, *An Account*, app. I, 545; Rev. W. Pascoe Crook to Hardcastle, Parramatta, May 5, 1805, Bonwick Transcripts, Box 49, 141, Mitchell Library (Sydney): *New South Wales Pocket Almanac, 1818*, 60; *Sydney Gazette*, January 9, 1813: 2a.

36. Bennelong's departure was announced in the *St. James's Chronicle*, July 17–19, 1794; Bennelong saw *The Suspicious Husband: A Comedy*, by Benjamin Hoadly, at Covent Garden on December 23, 1793; *The Tender Husband*, by Richard Steele, on February 24, 1794; and *The Glorious First of June*, by Richard Sheridan, on July 3, 1794. The Malthus family had copies of each of these plays in their library. For an exchange on London theater, see TRM to DM (November 20, 1783), DM to TRM, (January 5, 1784) TRM to DM, (January 14, 1784), in *MUP*, vol. 1, 12, 17, 18. See also multiple newsclippings on London theatre in Malthus Family, Newsclipping Album, MA 7.5.

37. Collins, *An Account*, 354.

38. Pocock, *Barbarians, Savages and Empires*, 157–56; Fabian, *Time and the Other*; Wilson, "Thinking Back."

39. TRM to David Ricardo, October 9, 1814, AL83, Senate House Library, University of London.

40. David Collins to Philip Gidley King, November 5, 1803, Philip Gidley King Letter Book, 1797–1806, A2015, p. 329, Mitchell Library (Sydney).

41. David Collins to Joseph Banks, August 19, 1804, Ab 67/14b 23, Mitchell Library (Sydney); Robson, *A History of Tasmania*, 32–44.

42. *Colonial Times and Tasmanian Advertiser*, December 1, 1826, 2.

43. Malthus, *An Essay* (1803), 6.

44. Malthus, *An Essay* (1826), vol. 2, 451.

45. Malthus, *A Summary View*, 29.

CHAPTER 4: THE AMERICAS

1. Malthus, *An Essay* (1803), 6.
2. In her variorum edition of Malthus's *Essay*, Patricia James did give bibliographic information about his citations, but without assessing the pattern of citation and their larger history in relation to reporting on the Americas. See Malthus, *An Essay on the Principle of Population . . .* , ed. James, vol. 2, 253–357.
3. Malthus, *An Essay* (1803), 25n; Armitage, "New World and British Historical Thought," 66–67; Grafton, *The Footnote*.
4. Robertson, *History of America*, vol. 1, xi (quotation), xxix–li (bibliography); Brown, *William Robertson*; Paquette, "Image of Imperial Spain," 189–94, 202–4.
5. Burke, "America and the Rewriting of World History," 46; Armitage, "New World and British Historical Thought," 66–67; Sebastiani, *Scottish Enlightenment*, esp. 90–101; Festa, *Sentimental Figures of Empire*, 205–32.
6. Hodgen, *Early Anthropology*; MacCormack, "Limits of Understanding"; Wolff and Cipolloni, *Anthropology of the Enlightenment*; Robertson, *History of America* (1780), vol. 1, v–vi.
7. Malthus, An *Essay*, ed. James, vol. 2, 349.
8. Hargraves, "Beyond the Savage Character"; Malthus, *An Essay*, ed. Winch, 128; for citations of "America" and "United States," keyword searches for the 1798 and 1803 editions of Malthus, *An Essay*, Eighteenth Century Collections Online, Making of the Modern World.
9. Malthus, *An Essay* (1803), 24, 38, 41–42, 44, italics added.
10. Malthus, *An Essay* (1803), 388.
11. Malthus, *An Essay* (1803), 24–25.
12. Malthus, *An Essay* (1803), 25–30.
13. Malthus, *An Essay* (1803), 29; cf. Robertson, *History of America*, vol. 1, 95, 125, 129, 329, 331, 354, 397, 471, vol. 2, 40, 96, 325, 375, 454, and there are still further references to Indian agriculture that do not mention maize per se.
14. Malthus, *An Essay* (1803), 33–34.
15. Malthus, *An Essay* (1803), 34–36; Simpson, *Cannibalism and the Common Law*.
16. Malthus, *An Essay* (1803), 34–37; Robertson, *History of America* (1777), vol. 1, 351; Bell, *First Total War*; Paine, *Common Sense*, 84.
17. Malthus, *An Essay* (1803), 40.
18. Malthus, *An Essay* (1803), 37–38.
19. Malthus, *An Essay* (1803), 39–40.
20. Malthus, *An Essay* (1803), 41–43.
21. Rountree, *Pocahontas, Powhatan, Opechancanough*, 176–86; Hinderaker, "The 'Four Indian Kings' "; Oliphant, "Cherokee Embassy to London, 1762"; Thompson Kelsay, *Joseph Brant*; Miller, "Petitioning the Great White Mother," 301–5; Hackforth-Jones, et al., *Between Worlds*.
22. Malthus, *An Essay* (1803), 43–44.
23. Malthus, *An Essay* (1803), 30, 31–33; Chaplin, "Natural Philosophy"; Jones, *Rationalizing Epidemics*.
24. Malthus, *An Essay* (1803), 44; Mancall, *Deadly Medicine*.
25. Malthus, *An Essay* (1803), 44–45, 45n.

26. Malthus, *An Essay* (1803), 31, 44, 45, and see also 40, 532 for other quarrels with Raynal; Franklin, "Remarks Concerning the Savages of North America," *PBF*, vol. 41, 412.

27. Robertson had cited Colden in the first volumes published in his study, *History of America* (1777), vol. 1, 351, 360, 412, 476; these citations were also present in the 1780 edition Malthus consulted.

28. "M. T.," writing in *The Analytical Review: or, History of Literature* 14 (November 1792): 241–54; Lowes, *Road to Xanadu*, 277–80; Wu, *Wordsworth's Reading, 1770–1790*, 9; Wu, *Wordsworth's Reading, 1800–1815*, 14, 167–68; Watson, "Continuity in Commerce," 551–52.

29. Pratt, *American Indians in British Art*, 45–48.

30. Dowd, *A Spirited Resistance*.

31. Home, *Sketches*, vol.1, 98–99n., 99–100.

32. Malthus, An *Essay* (1803), 37–38, 41–43.

33. Malthus, *An Essay* (1817), vol. 1, 11.

34. *Malthus Library Catalogue*, 85; Thomas Jefferson, account with Joseph Milligan, November 7, 1807, Jefferson, *Papers of Thomas Jefferson: Retirement Series*, vol. 1, 35; Thomas Jefferson to Meriwether Lewis, June 20, 1803, Jackson, *Letters of the Lewis and Clark Expedition*, 63.

35. Malthus, *An Essay* (1803), 387–89.

36. Malthus, *An Essay* (1803), 389, 391, 395.

37. McCallum, *Unequal Beginnings*, 11–22; McCalla, *Planting the Province*, 24–25.

38. Barnes, *A History of the English Corn Laws*, 460, 464.

39. Malthus, *An Essay* (1817), vol. 2, 475.

40. Malthus, *An Essay* (1817), vol. 2, 274, 405–6, 458; vol. 3, 16n.

41. Mintz, *Sweetness and Power*.

42. *MUP*, vol. 1, 69–70, incl. 69n.

43. Innis, *Fur Trade in Canada*, 335–37; Rich, *Hudson's Bay Company*, 112–13, 164–67.

44. Frank Palmeri, "Conjectural History and Satire," 79–81.

Chapter 5: The South Sea

1. Fullagar, *Savage Visit*, 126–50. See also Smith, "Banks, Tupaia, and Mai"; Guest, "Ornament and Use."

2. Guest, *Empire, Barbarism, and Civilisation*, 12.

3. The account of the second voyage was in the Malthus library, *A voyage towards the South Pole, and round the World*. Malthus refers to volumes 1 and 2 of the third voyage account, *A Voyage to the Pacific Ocean*. Smith, *Imagining the Pacific*, 208.

4. Secret Instructions for Lieutenant James Cook Appointed to Command His Majesty's Bark the Endeavour, July 30, 1768, in Cook, *Journals*, vol. 1, cclxxix–cclxxxiv; Malthus, *An Essay* (1803), 52, 47.

5. More, *Utopia*; Bacon, *New Atlantis*; Defoe, *Life and Strange Surprizing Adventures*; Smith, *Lectures on Jurisprudence*, 14. On islands, see Grove, *Green Imperialism*; Edmond and Smith, *Islands in History and Representation*; Lamb, *Preserving the Self*.

6. Brosses, *Histoire des navigations*; Diderot, *Supplément au voyage de Bougainville*.

7. Home, *Sketches*, vol. 1, 15. "Food and population" was the author's second "sketch," 44–60. See also Ross, *Lord Kames*, 333–35; Gascoigne, *Encountering the Pacific*. "Dangerous Liaisons in the Pacific," special issue, *Eighteenth-Century Studies* 41 (2008).

8. *Gentleman's Magazine* 70 (March 1800): 281. One of two copies of *Paul and Mary* in the British Library has a penciled attribution: "trans by Daniel Malthus," now corrected in the online catalog. The copy in the Malthus Collection, Jesus College, also contains a cataloguers' attribution to Daniel Malthus (ME.5.79). Saint-Pierre, *Paul and Mary*, vol. 1, 2, vi. Letters from Jane Dalton to Jacques Henri Bernardin de Saint-Pierre, Electronic Enlightenment (www.e-enlightenment .com). See also Cook, "Bernardin de Saint-Pierre's English Correspondents." Daniel Malthus Will, Prob, II/1335/317, TNA.

9. Wilson, *Island Race*; Godwin to TRM, August 15, 1798, *Letters of William Godwin*, vol. 2, 328; Bashford, *Global Population*, 56–7.

10. Malthus used the 1795 French edition of Raynal; Malthus, *An Essay* (1803), 46–47. For Malthus on the globe and on islands, see Bashford, *Global Population*, 29.

11. Malthus, *An Essay* (1803), 57. For Tahiti and populousness, see Smith, "Crowd Scenes."

12. Malthus, *An Essay* (1826), vol. 2, 447; Cook, *Journals*, vol. 1, 120 (13 July 1769). This paragraph was added in the Admiralty copy. Forster, *Observations Made*, 145–46, 195.

13. *A Missionary Voyage*, 191–92, 385. See also Sivasundaram, *Nature and the Godly Empire*. For the missionaries and Peter the Swede, see Thomas, *Islanders*, 33, 36.

14. Malthus, *An Essay* (1803), 50, 51.

15. Malthus, *An Essay* (1803), 53, 51.

16. Malthus, *An Essay* (1803), 51–56. For Arreoy, see Russell, "An 'Entertainment of Oddities'"; Oliver, *Ancient Tahitian Society*.

17. Malthus referred to David Hume, "On the Populousness of Ancient Nations," in *Essays and Treatises on Several Subjects*, 2 vols. (London: Millar, 1764), vol. 1, 415–16. Hume's essay had first appeared in 1752; Malthus's cited edition was from 1764.

18. Smith, *Theory of Moral Sentiments*, 210; See Kipp, "Naturally Bad or Dangerously Good," 241; Malthus, *An Essay* (1803), 57.

19. Malthus, *An Essay* (1803), 54; *A Missionary Voyage*, p. a3, a4.

20. *A Missionary Voyage*, 192.

21. Malthus, *An Essay* (1803), 56.

22. [Hawkesworth], *Account*, vol. 2, 285 [8–9 October 1769].

23. Collins in fact recounted far more recent information on New Zealand in the conclusion of part 1 of *An Account of the English Colony in New South Wales*, vol. 1, "Particulars of the *BRITANNIA'S* VOYAGE to ENGLAND; with Remarks on the STATE of NORFOLK ISLAND, and some Account of NEW ZEALAND."

24. [Hawkesworth], *Account*, vol. 2, 284 (7–8 October 1769); Malthus, *An Essay* (1803), 50; Banks, *Endeavour Journal*, vol. 1, 471 [4 March 1770].

25. "Cook's Third Voyage" [Cook, *A Voyage to the Pacific Ocean*], quoted in Malthus, *An Essay* (1803), 48; Collins, *An Account*, 549. In reading for his earlier chapter, Malthus had read of the Andaman Islanders eating human flesh, but Symes, his source, also commented that "it probably arose more from the impulse of

excessive hunger, than from voluntary choice; a conclusion, that well authenti-cated instances of the distress they at times endure, appear to authorize." Symes, *An Account of an Embassy*, 296–97. See also Konishi, *Aboriginal Male*.

26. Malthus, *An Essay* (1803), 60–61.

27. Malthus, *An Essay* (1803), 58–9. For Hawkesworth's rendition of Tahiti and feu-dal Europe, see Williams, "Seamen and Philosophers," 11. Williams calls this an "absurdity," but in the context of stadial theories, and at a time when the natives of the world were actively being fitted to European historical time, this is perhaps more normative than absurd for the intellectual milieu. Alternatively, we might think the whole project of such universal history absurd.

28. Malthus, *An Essay* (1803), 63.

29. [Malthus], *An Essay* (1798), 51.

30. Malthus, *An Essay* (1803), 62–3.

31. [Malthus], *An Essay* (1798), 32; Malthus, *An Essay* (1803), 68. Malthus was com-menting on Abū al-Ghāzī Bahādur, *A General History*.

32. [Malthus], *An Essay* (1798), ch. 3.

33. "I have laid aside my chemistry for a while, & am at present endeavouring to get some little knowledge of general history & geography. I have been lately reading Gibbon's decline of the Roman Empire. He gives on some useful information concerning the origin & progress of those nations of barbarians which now form the polished states of Europe; & throws some light upon the beginning of that dark period which so long overwhelmed the world, & which cannot I think but excite one's curiousity. He is a very entertaining writer, in my opinion; his style is sometimes really sublime, ever where interesting & agreeable, tho perhaps it may in general be call'd rather too florid for history. I shall like much to see his next volumes." TRM to DM, April 17, 1788, in *MUP*, vol. 1, 53.

34. Guest, *Empire, Barbarism, and Civilisation*, 12.

35. See Fabian, *Time and the Other*; Stern, *Varieties of History*; Bender and Wellerby, *Chronotypes*.

36. Malthus, *An Essay* (1803), 47; "it is extraordinary that the same Nation should have spread themselves over all the isles in this Vast Ocean from New Zealand to this Island which is almost a fourth part of the circumference of the Globe," Cook, *Journals*, vol. 2, 354; Guest, *Empire, Barbarism, and Civilisation*, 5.

37. Malthus, *An Essay* (1803), 63–4; Sebastiani, *Scottish Enlightenment*, 40; Pocock, "Cam-bridge Paradigms and Scotch Philosophers," 242–43.

38. Malthus, *An Essay* (1803), 65–66; Home, *Sketches*, vol. I, 41–42.

39. The translation used was Abū al-Ghāzī Bahādur, *A General History*.

CHAPTER 6: SLAVERY AND ABOLITION

1. Malthus, *An Essay*, (1806) vol. 2, 559. For Wilberforce, see *The Times*, February 24, 1807, 2; TRM to Clarke, February 27, 1807, PP/87/40/1, Keynes Papers, Archive Centre, King's College, Cambridge; Malthus, *An Essay*, ed. Winch, 364.

2. Drescher, *Mighty Experiment*, 42. Sergio Cremaschi explores Malthus as an "oppo-nent of the slave trade," placing too much emphasis on the single 1806 footnote. Cremaschi, *Utilitarianism and Malthus's Virtue Ethics*.

3. Drescher, *Abolition*, 206; Higman, *Slave Population and Economy*; Wakefield, *Memoirs*, vol. 1, 300–8. Wakefield and Wilberforce were Cambridge contemporaries, see Wakefield, *A Letter to William Wilberforce*.

4. On political economy's appeal to slaveholders, see Chaplin, *An Anxious Pursuit*, esp. pp. 36–37. On Malthus's appeal specifically; Paugh, "Rationalizing Reproduction"; Paugh, "Politics of Childbearing"; Drescher, *Mighty Experiment*. On reforms of West Indian slavery intended to maintain the institution, see Luster, *Amelioration of the Slaves*; Lambert, *White Creole Culture*, 41–72; Petley, *Slaveholders in Jamaica*, 7, 48–50, 83, 87, 115, 40; Fergus, *Revolutionary Emancipation*, 36–51,142–60.

5. Solow and Engerman, *British Capitalism and Caribbean Slavery*; Brown, *Moral Capital*, 1–30.

6. Roach, *Cities of the Dead*; Brown, *Reaper's Garden*; Armstrong, "Slavery, Insurance, and Sacrifice"; Walvin, *Zong*.

7. Davis, *Problem of Slavery*; Brown, *Moral Capital*, esp. 209–58; Sheridan, "Crisis of Slave Subsistence."

8. Brown, *Moral Capital*, 192–99, 352–64; Glasson, *Mastering Christianity*.

9. [Malthus], *An Essay* (1798), 41; Malthus, *An Essay* (1803), 389.

10. Park, *Travels in the Interior*. The *Malthus Library Catalogue* indicates his access to Volney, *Voyage en Syrie et en Egypte*. However, Volney's exposition on Egyptian peasants is in Volney, *Les Ruines*, 173. For Malthus and Volney, see Cook, "Philosophy of Constantin Volney," 206–36. Bruce, *Travels*. For Sierra Leone see Carretta, *Equiano the African*, 202–35; Everill, *Abolition and Empire*. On geographic knowledge of Africa and its connections to slavery, see Lambert, *Mastering the Niger*.

11. Malthus, *An Essay* (1803), 102, 110–11.

12. Malthus, *An Essay* (1803), 103–5.

13. Malthus, *An Essay* (1803), 105, citing Park, *Travels in the Interior*, 295. Malthus, *An Essay* (1803), 110, citing Bruce, *Travels*, vol. 3, 88; Malthus, *An Essay* (1803), 112.

14. Malthus, *An Essay* (1803), 104; Wallace, *A Dissertation*; Home, *Sketches*, vol. 1, 55.

15. For eighteenth-century debate on slave labor and free labor, see Sebastiani, *Scottish Enlightenment*, 38–43; Drescher, *Mighty Experiment*, 55.

16. Malthus, *An Essay* (1803), 172, 173.

17. Henry Thornton, House of Commons, March 16, 1807, *Hansard*, ser. 1. vol. 9. For further comparisons of West Indian slavery to other forms, "ancient and modern," as deployed by both sides in abolition debates, see Stephen, *Slavery of the West India Colonies*; McDonnell, *Considerations on Negro Slavery*.

18. Malthus, *An Essay* (1803), 176–77; Malthus, *An Essay* (1806), vol. 2, appendix.

19. Malthus Family, Newsclipping Album, MA 7.5, JC. Muncaster, *Historical Sketches of the Slave Trade*; Francklyn, *Observations*; More, *Slavery*; Equiano, *Interesting Narrative*; A Friend to Commerce and Humanity, *Thoughts on Civilization*; Lowe, *An Inquiry*. Many books in Jesus College Old Library display Jane Dalton's bookplate, however neither Malthus nor his father had bookplates.

20. Drescher, *Mighty Experiment*, 35–36; Higman, "Slavery and the Development of Demographic Theory," 164–94; Higman, *Slave Populations*; Manning and Griffiths, "Divining the Unprovable"; Caldwell, "Social Repercussions of Colonial Rule," 458–61.

21. For Cooper, see Drescher, *Mighty Experiment*, 39–41; review of *A Concise Statement of the Question Regarding the Abolition of the Slave Trade* (1804), *Edinburgh Review* 8 (1804): 477; Wilberforce, House of Commons speech in *Heads of the Speeches*, 57, 58; Drescher, *Mighty Experiment*, 45; Higman, *Slave Populations*, 72, 307; Dunn, "Sugar Production and Slave Women," 51; Brown, *Reaper's Garden*.

22. Eckersall Diary, 1740, notes from "Eckersall Diaries owned by N. H. Vicars-Harris," Patricia James Papers, Box 3, 2006–2007; James, *Population Malthus*, 7; Pettigrew, *Freedom's Debt*, 237. For Sydenham Malthus, see *The London Magazine, Or, Gentleman's Monthly Intelligencer* 20 (1751): 90, 141.

23. Landholders in the island of Jamaica, Quit Rent Books, 1754, and *Gentleman's Magazine* 67 (April 1797): 350, both copied in Clinton V. Black, Jamaican Government Archivist to Patricia James, September 25, 1985, Patricia James Papers, Box 3, 2471.

24. Returns of Givings-in for the March Quarter, 1819, County of Middlesex, St. Mary, Jamaica Almanac, 1820, and Crop Accounts for Oxford Plantation, vol. 24, f. 3; vol. 53, f. 83, Jamaica Archives, Spanish Town, both copied in Black to James, September 25, 1985, Patricia James Papers, Box 3, 2471.

25. See *Symes v Swann*, November 19, 1807, C13/3008/31, TNA. On absenteeism and plantation management, see Smith, *Slavery, Family, and Gentry Capitalism*, 226–59.

26. *Hibbert v Malthus*, January 15, 1805, C13/610/7, TNA; *Malthus v Swann*, May 19, 1806, C13/2751/40, TNA.

27. Will of Robert Symes (senior), May 13, 1783, PROB 11/1109/161, TNA; *Symes v Swann*, November 19, 1807, C13/3008/31, TNA.

28. *Cannell v Malthus*, answer of Robert Symes, October 20, 1825, C13/2588/7, TNA.

29. Legacies of British Slave-ownership, https://www.ucl.ac.uk/lbs/claim/view/18607.

30. William Bray, solicitor, letters to Thomas Robert Malthus, June 7, 1815, in Warrens (solicitors), letter books and correspondence, London Metropolitan Archives, LMA/4031/01/11–17, see also August 18, 1814, p. 431, May 4, 1815, p. 1008, January 10, 1817, p. 61; Bray to Mariana Georgina Malthus, November 29, 1822, Warrens letter books, March 1821–December 1822, p. 1053, copy in Patricia James Papers, Box 3, 2245; William Bray to Mariana Georgina Malthus, July 23, 1822, Patricia James Papers, Box 3, 2243; Marianna Malthus to TRM (January 9, 1822), in *MUP*, vol. 1, 69–70.

31. William Bray to TRM, January 10, 1817, Warrens letter books, notes in Patricia James Papers, Box 3, p. 2220. See also letters for March 5, 1817 and April 10, 1817; William Bray to TRM, April 23, 1818. Patricia James Papers, Box 3, 2235–36; Bray to TRM, April 30, 1819, Patricia James Papers, Box 3, 2239. "I think it right to make known to you my determination not to pay one shilling of his [Symes'] Fortune to Mr Malthus until I hear from Lieut. Symes on the subject." Warrens letter books, June 29, 1818, Patricia James papers, Box 3, 2237.

32. Said, *Culture and Imperialism*, 80–97; Hall, et al., *Legacies of British Slave-Ownership*, and the ongoing "Legacies of British Slave-ownership" project, https://www.ucl.ac.uk/lbs/.

33. TRM to Clarke, February 27, 1807, PP/87/40/1, Keynes Papers, Archive Centre, King's College, Cambridge.

34. Cobbett, "Jamaica Complaints"; Cobbett, "Slave Trade"; Cobbett to George Hibbert, December 29, 1805, Melville, *Life and Letters of William Cobbett*, vol. 1, 292–93.

35. "Senex," "An Address."

36. Malthus, *An Essay* (1806), vol. 2, app., 556.

37. "Consequently, if by the abolition of the trade to Africa, the slaves in the West Indies were placed only in a *tolerable* situation, if their civil condition and moral habits were only made to *approach* to those which prevail among the mass of the human race in the worst-governed countries of the world, it is contrary to the general laws of nature to suppose, that they would not be able by procreation fully to supply the effective demand for labour; and it is difficult to conceive that a population so raised would not be in every point of view preferable to that which exists at present. It is perfectly clear, therefore, that a consideration of the laws which govern the increase and decrease of the human species, tends to strengthen, in the most powerful manner, all the arguments in favour of the abolition." Malthus, *An Essay* (1806), vol. 2, app., 558.

38. Malthus, *An Essay* (1806), vol. 2, app., 558.

39. Drescher, *Mighty Experiment*, 41, 47.

40. Malthus, *A Letter to the Rt. Hon. Lord Grenville*; Malthus, *Statements Respecting the East-India College*. Grenville's personal and heavily annotated copy of Malthus's *Principles of Political Economy* (1820) has been analyzed in Pullen, "Lord Grenville's Manuscript Notes," 217–37. It demonstrates Grenville's strong critique of Malthus's theories on value, labor, rent, and the definition of wealth.

41. Lord Grenville, Slave Trade Abolition Bill, House of Lords, February 5, 1807, *Hansard*, ser. 1, vol. 8; The Earl of Selkirk, House of Lords, February 5, 1807, *Hansard*, ser. 1. vol. 8. Selkirk and Malthus had crossed paths in Bath in December 1804, likely dining together at the home of Dr Currie. See James, *Population Malthus*, 167.

42. Lord Howick, House of Commons, February 23, 1807, *Hansard*, ser. 1, vol. 8.

43. Lord Mahon, House of Commons, February 23, 1807, *Hansard*, ser. 1, vol. 8.

44. Furness, "George Hibbert and the Defence of Slavery." Robert Hibbert (1769–1849) befriended William Frend at Cambridge.

45. George Hibbert, House of Commons, February 23, 1807, *Hansard*, ser. 1, vol. 8; *A Catalogue of the Library of George Hibbert*, 273; Cobbett to George Hibbert, December 29, 1805, Melville, *Life and Letters of William Cobbett*, vol. 1, 292–93.

46. *The Times*, February 24, 1807, 2. In Hansard this passage was reported thus: "It had been contended that Mr Malthus, in his Essay on Population, had favoured the slave trade; the fact, however, was not so. Indeed Mr Malthus had called upon him that day, and expressed his surprise to have learned, that in some publications of the day he was regarded as a favourer of the slave trade; and stated that he had written an appendix to his work, to remove that impression." William Wilberforce, House of Commons, February 23, 1807, *Hansard*, ser. 1, vol. 8.

47. George Hibbert, House of Commons, March 16, 1807, *Hansard*, vol. 9.

48. Hibbert, *Substance of Three Speeches*, 133.

49. "Summary of Politics—Proceedings in Parliament," *Cobbett's Weekly Political Register*, March 7, 1807, 361.
50. Mayhew, *Malthus*.
51. For Malthus and Whig circles, see James, *Population Malthus*, 50–51, 81–86. He was on friendly and casual terms with Scottish lawyer Henry Brougham, co-founder of the *Edinburgh Review*, liberal abolitionist, and lord chancellor toward the end of the Malthus's life (1830–34).
52. Marshall, *Bengal*, 137–79; Bayly, *Imperial Meridian*, 100–32, 217–47.
53. Mr. Roscoe, February 23, 1807, House of Commons, *Hansard*, ser. 1, vol. 9.
54. East India Sugar; Clarkson, *Thoughts*, 47–48. Macaulay *East and West India Sugar*. On the connections between abolition, humanitarianism, and India, see Laidlaw, "'Justice to India'"; Naidis, "Abolitionists and Indian Slavery"; Major, "'Slavery of East and West.'"
55. Malthus acceptance of Professorship of General History, July 10, 1805, J/1/19/ 468–69, India Office Records, BL; Embree, *Charles Grant and British Rule*; James, *Population Malthus*, 223–24.
56. George Frederick Symes's certificates from the Forces of the United Company of Merchants trading to the East Indies (1813, 1818, 1825) were kept with other Malthus family documents, original in Kanto Gakuen University Malthus Collection, copies in BL RP 3269.
57. "A Preliminary View of the Establishment of the Honourable East India Company in Hertfordshire for the Education of Young Persons appointed to the Civil Service in India" (1806), J/2/1 ff. 75–87, India Office Records, BL; Examination Papers of the Principal and Professors of the East India College, 1808, Bodleian Library; Smith, *Wealth of Nations* (1786), vol. 2, 394.
58. Malthus, *Principles of Political Economy*; Malthus, *An Essay* (1826), vol. 1, 150.
59. Select Committee, House of Lords, 1832, quoted in Higman, *Slave Populations*, 99. Macaulay, Ministerial Plan for the Abolition of Slavery, House of Commons, July 24, 1833, *Hansard*, ser. 3. vol. 19; *Political Economy Club*, 22. For the later use of Malthus's arguments see Drescher, *Mighty Experiment*, 49.
60. *Courier*, December 31, 1834.
61. On the East India Company and abolition, see Drescher, *Abolition*, 205–41.

CHAPTER 7: COLONIZATION AND EMIGRATION

1. Malthus, *An Essay* (1803), 393.
2. Malthus, *An Essay* (1803), 464, 468.
3. *A Statement of the Principles*, 67.
4. "When British settlers made a property of land in Australia and New Zealand, Malthus and Darwin had parts to play in the theorization and representation of their efforts." Lamb, *Preserving the Self*, 8.
5. TRM to William Whewell, February 28, 1831, quoted in Marchi and Sturges, "Malthus and Ricardo's Inductivist Critics," 389; Malthus, *A Summary View*, 29.
6. Malthus *An Essay* (1803), 387.
7. Malthus, *An Essay* (1803), 388–89.

8. Malthus, *An Essay* (1803), 389–90.

9. Malthus, *An Essay* (1803), 390.

10. Malthus, *An Essay* (1803), 391.

11. Malthus, *An Essay* (1803), 392.

12. Smith to Sir John Sinclair, October 14, 1782, quoted in Winch, *Classical Political Economy and Colonies*, 20; Examination Papers of the Principal and Professors of the East India College, 1808, Bodleian Library.

13. Winch, *Classical Political Economy and Colonies*, 35. For *Panopticon versus New South Wales*, see Gascoigne, *Enlightenment*, 123–31; Schofield, *Utility and Democracy*, 216, n. 60.

14. Malthus, *An Essay* (1803), 394–5.

15. Malthus, *An Essay* (1803), 392.

16. Malthus, *An Essay* (1803), 392–5. A very similar passage appears near the beginning of *Statement of the Principles*, 4–5. Richards, "Malthus and the Uses of British Emigration," 46–47.

17. Malthus, *An Essay* (1803), 395.

18. Malthus, *An Essay* (1826), vol. 2, 61–2.

19. Wilmot Horton to TRM, September 3, 1830, D3155/WH/2843, ff. 80–81, WHP, DRO, original emphasis. In this letter, Wilmot Horton extracted and quoted the 1819 parliamentary debate with Cobbett. Note that WH/2843 are clerks copies of originals in WH/2842, WHP, DRO.

20. Wilmot Horton to TRM, [n.d.], 1828, D3155/WH/2843, ff. 2–3, WHP, DRO.

21. See Wilmot Horton's dispatches in Watson, ed. *Historical Records of Australia*, ser. 1, vol. 7.

22. Wilmot Horton to TRM, [n.d.], 1828, D3155/WH/2843, f. 3, WHP, DRO. Wilmot Horton sought to gather and publish this correspondence after Malthus's death, a means by which his own position—by then overtaken and overturned by Edward Gibbon Wakefield—might be vindicated. A preliminary note on the transcribed correspondence between Wilmot Horton and Malthus reads: "I publish these letters without note or comment." But he also noted that Malthus's "*fame* will be of a future day." D3155/WH/2843, WHP, DRO.

23. Wilmot Horton to TRM, July 24, 1830, D3155/WH/2843, f. 52, WHP, DRO.

24. Wilmot Horton to TRM, [n.d.] 1828, D3155/WH/2843, f. 13, WHP, DRO.

25. For example, TRM to Nassau William Senior, May 24, 1829, working together through a set of Wilmot Horton's questions, D3155/WH/2843, ff. 22–23, WHP, DRO; TRM to Wilmot Horton, February 22, 1830, D 3155/WH/2843, ff. 28–29, WHP, DRO. For comments of Chalmers, Thomas, Tooke, and Torrens, see D3155/WH/2291, WHP, DRO. See also Ghosh, "Colonization Controversy." Malthus was one of twenty original members of the Political Economy Club, including Ricardo, James Mill, and Robert Torrens. Later members included Wilmot Horton, McCulloch, Nassau Senior. See Pullen "Introduction," liv. Political Economy Club, 358.

26. Wilmot Horton, *Outline of a Plan of Emigration*; TRM to Wilmot Horton, February 21, 1823, D3155/WH/2841, WHP, DRO. See James, *Population Malthus*, 390.

27. Gourlay, *General Introduction*, cii, cccxxxvii. Gourlay was also cited at length in *Statement of the Principles*, 25.

28. TRM to Wilmot Horton, February 21, 1823.
29. TRM to Wilmot Horton, April 8, 1827 and April 22, 1827, D3155/WH/2841, WHP, DRO; Minutes of Evidence and Petition of Glasgow Tradesmen, *Second Report, Select Committee on Emigration from the United Kingdom*, February 20, 1827, 9–10; *Third Report*, 1827, app., 507.
30. Wilmot Horton, "Remarks on the Province of Upper Canada, by the Founder of the 'Talbot Settlement', " app. B, *Outline of a Plan of Emigration*, xi–xv; Outline of a Plan for the Conveyance and Settlement of Paupers at New South Wales, *First Report, Select Committee on Emigration*, April 27, 1826, 238.
31. Andrew Angus to his parents [January 12, 1822, June 2, 1824], in Minutes of Evidence, *Second Report, Select Committee on Emigration*, March 20, 1827, 128–29.
32. Wilmot Horton, "Remarks on the Province of Upper Canada, by the Founder of the 'Talbot Settlement'," app. B, *Outline of a Plan of Emigration*, xiv–xv.
33. Quoted in Bumsted, *Collected Writings of Lord Selkirk*, vol. 1, 53.
34. Editor, *The Sydney Gazette and New South Wales Advertiser*, December 20, 1822, 3.
35. "Outline of a Plan for the Conveyance and Settlement of Paupers at New South Wales," *First Report, Select Committee on Emigration*, 1826, app., 237–38
36. Minutes of Evidence, *Third Report, Select Committee on Emigration*, May 5, 1827, 311; Malthus, *An Essay* (1826), vol. 1, 470; Winch, *Classical Political Economy and Colonies*, 52–53. See also Mills, *Colonization of Australia*.
37. Wilmot Horton to TRM, July 24, 1830, D3155/WH/2843, f. 58, WHP, DRO.
38. Malthus, *An Essay* (1826), vol. 1, 470. For Irish population, see Connell, "Population of Ireland"; Mokyr, "Malthusian Models and Irish History." 6.
39. Malthus was citing Daniel Augustus Beaufort, *Memoir of a Map of Ireland* (1792); Abstract *of the Answers and Returns Made Pursuant to . . . An Act to Provide for Taking Account of the Population of Ireland* (House of Commons, London, 1823), 378.
40. Minutes of Evidence, *Third Report, Select Committee on Emigration*, May 5, 1827, 327; Minutes of Evidence, *Second Report, Select Committee on Emigration*, March 27, 1827, 166–67.
41. TRM to Wilmot Horton, June 9, 1830, D3155/WH/2843, f. 47, WHP, DRO.
42. Minutes of Evidence, *Third Report, Select Committee on Emigration*, May 5, 1827, 319–21.
43. Nally, *Human Encumbrances*, 31–33.
44. [Parnell], *An Inquiry into the Causes of Popular Discontents in Ireland*, 6. The Malthus library copy of this pamphlet was bound as "Tracts of Ireland and the West Indies," with Lowe, *An Inquiry*. [Malthus], "Newenham and others," 351.
45. Minutes of Evidence, *Third Report, Select Committee on Emigration*, May 5, 1827, 320.
46. TRM to Wilmot Horton, March 8, 1827, D3155/WH/2841, WHP, DRO. See also Minutes of Evidence, *Third Report, Select Committee on Emigration*, May 5, 1827, 325.
47. Minutes of Evidence, *Third Report, Select Committee on Emigration*, May 5, 1827, 312.
48. TRM to Wilmot Horton, March 8, 1827, D3155/WH/2841, WHP, DRO.

49. Minutes of Evidence, *Third Report, Select Committee on Emigration*, May 5, 1827, 312; *Report*, 41.

50. TRM to Wilmot Horton, March 8, 1827, D3155/WH/2841, WHP, DRO.

51. Minutes of Evidence, *Second Report, Select Committee on Emigration*, March 27, 1827, 167.

52. Minutes of Evidence, *Third Report, Select Committee on Emigration*, May 5, 1827, 319, 315.

53. [Malthus] "Newenham and Others," 336–55; [Malthus], "Newenham on the State of Ireland," 151–70. The review was of recently published work on Ireland: Newenham, *A Statistical and Historical Inquiry into the Progress and Magnitude of the Population of Ireland* (1805); Dudley, *A Short Address* (1808); Croker, *A Sketch of the State of Ireland, Past and Present* (1808). Malthus's reviews are inappropriately diminished in Irish historiography, perhaps because of the political difficulty in reconciling Malthus with support of the Catholic cause. See for example, Ó Gráda, *Ireland before and after the Famine*, 1. Francis Horner to Richard Sharp, 29 March 1806, Francis Jeffrey to Francis Horner, 5 August 1804, in Bourne and Taylor, *Horner Papers*, 410, 341.

54. [Malthus], "Newenham and Others," 339; Pullen, "Introduction," xx.

55. [Malthus], "Newenham and Others," 342, 336, 351.

56. [Malthus], "Newenham and Others," 349–350, 353.

57. Brantlinger, *Dark Vanishings*, 106. Nally, *Human Encumbrances*, 88; [Malthus], "Newenham and Others," 353–54.

58. [Malthus], "Newenham and Others," 342. These were Newenham's figures.

59. Minutes of Evidence, *Third Report, Select Committee on Emigration*, May 5, 1827, 326, 319.

60. James, *Population Malthus*, 154; [Malthus], "The Crisis" quoted in Empson, "Life, Writing, and Character", 479–83.

61. Petty, *Political Anatomy of Ireland*, 29. For Petty and the transmutation of the Irish, see McCormick, *William Petty*, 168–208, 193, 194, 207. For the economy of the family as an assimilationist project in Petty's manuscript, "About Exchanging of Women," (1674), see McCormick, *William Petty*, 201–202.

62. "He was of opinion that the general wealth of the empire would be increased by an accession of population in the Colonies, independently of the advantageous consequences resulting to this country form the abstraction of that population which is here in redundance; and that the introduction of English population into those colonies would tend to furnish a very valuable market for the labourers of this country, even if they were not to continue to belong to the British Empire." *Third Report, Select Committee on Emigration*, June 29, 1827, 9, 38–9.

63. Torrens to Wilmot Horton, May 22, 1827, D3155/WH/2991, and Thomas Chalmers "On Emigration," June 12, 1827, D3155/WH/2991, WHP, DRO; Wilmot Horton, House of Commons, 4 March 1828, *Hansard*, ser. 2, vol. 18.

64. *Third Report, Select Committee on Emigration*, June 29, 1827, 39.

65. TRM to Wilmot Horton, February 22, 1830, D3155/WH/2843, f. 29; [Wakefield], *Sketch of a Proposal*; Gouger, ed. *Letter from Sydney*. For the *Letter from Sydney*, see Ballantyne, "Remaking the Empire."

66. For Wilmot Horton and Malthus's inspiration of Wakefield, see Ghosh, "Colonization Controversy," 390.
67. "On the State and Prospects of the Country". Malthus's indecision about emigration was noted, but also that ultimately "he expresses himself strongly as to the occasional expediency of emigration," (388). Gouger, ed. *Letter from Sydney*, v–x.
68. Gouger, ed., *Letter from Sydney*, 180–81, 201, 6, 40.
69. TRM to Wilmot Horton, August 17, 1830, D3155/WH/2843, f. 63, WHP, DRO; *Statement of the Principles*.
70. *Statement of the Principles*, 66.
71. *Statement of the Principles*, 66, 1, 4; Gouger, ed., *Letter from Sydney*, app., "Outline of a System of Colonization," i–xxiv.
72. *Statement of the Principles*, 26–29; For Robert Torrens and the Colonial Office, see Attwood, "Returning to the Past," 54–55. The Swan Hill Colony (1829) saw the dispersal of the colonists, with large grants of land. Huge grants were allocated: by 1832 one million acres was granted, much of its unsurveyed. But the colony was almost stagnant, the population as late as 1849 still below 4,500. See Hartwell, "Pastoral Ascendancy," 46–97.
73. Wilmot Horton to TRM, n.d. [1828], D3155/WH/2843, f. 4, WHP, DRO.
74. TRM to Wilmot Horton, n.d. [1828], D3155/WH/2843, f. 21, WHP, DRO.
75. Evidence, *Third Report, Select Committee on Emigration*, May 5, 1827, 318.
76. [Wakefield], *England and America*.
77. *Statement of the Principles*, 37.
78. TRM to Wilmot Horton, August 17, 1830, D3155/WH/2843, f. 63, WHP, DRO.
79. TRM to Wilmot Horton, August 25, 1830, D3155/WH/2843, ff. 74–79, WHP, DRO.
80. TRM to Wilmot Horton, June 9, 1830, D3155/WH/2843, ff. 41–48, WHP, DRO.
81. TRM to Wilmot Horton, May 31, 1830, D3155/WH/2843, f. 31, WHP, DRO.
82. TRM to Wilmot Horton, June 9, 1830, D3155/WH/2843, ff. 41–46, WHP, DRO.
83. TRM to Wilmot Horton, August 23, 1830, D3155/WH/2843, ff. 68–69, WHP, DRO.
84. Sadler, *Ireland*, vol. 1, ix–xv, vol. 2, 621; TRM to Macvey Napier, January 18, 1830, BL; Malthus, *A Summary View*, 28.
85. Malthus, *A Summary View*, 44.
86. Malthus, *A Summary View*, 29, 31.
87. Plomley, *Aboriginal-Settler Clash*, 6. "An Emigrant" to the Editor, *The Tasmanian*, April 8, 1931, 6.
88. On 10 February 1828 about thirty Aborigines were killed in reprisal, and an Aboriginal woman was murdered at Emu Bay on August 21, 1829. "The sad story of Company race relations saw at least two white men and possibly 36 Aborigines killed." Lennox, "Van Diemen's Land Company."
89. Bathurst to Edward Curr, April 15, 1825, *Minutes of the Intended Arrangements*, 7; "J. E.,". *Launceston Advertiser*, September 26, 1831, quoted in Reynolds, *History of Tasmania*, 64–65; Earl Bathurst to Governor Darling, July 14, 1825, Watson, *Historical Records of Australia*, ser. 1, vol. 12, 21; *Military Operations Against the Aboriginal Inhabitants*, 5–7. Henry Reynolds persuasively argues that at the end of the Black War the Van Diemen's Land Aborigines came to the governor, and

were permitted to do so, both armed and unshackled, that is, surrendering as prisoners or war, not as rebels or criminals. Reynolds, *History of Tasmania*, 63–64. For treaties, see Attwood, *Possession*. For sovereignty in the 1820s and 30s, see Ford, *Settler Sovereignty*.

90. Grey to Torrens, December 15, 1835, CO13/3, TNA. See Attwood, "Returning to the Past," 64; Reynolds, *Law of the Land*, 105–6.

91. "Public Meeting," *Colonial Times* (Hobart), September 24, 1830, 3. For the diplomatic mission and Flinders Island (Wybalenna) Reserve, see Johnston and Rolls, *Reading Robinson*; Ryan, *Aboriginal Tasmanians*; Lawson, *Last Man*.

92. Macbean, "Late Riots in Ross-Shire." In that context, *extermination* was also linked to *extirpation*, "to pull up by the roots," "to abolish and totally destroy," "to eliminate." Thus the method of Highland clearances was described in *The Times*: "[T]he proprietor has hit upon a novel expedient of carrying out 'the principle' of extermination . . . to *turn away two families every year, until the complement of cotters is extirpated.*" *The Times*, October 22, 1846, quoted in Richards, *Highland Clearances* (Edinburgh: Birlinn, 2008), 28. In Scotland, the term "clearance" became common late in the Highland process. The contemporary term, as Eric Richards shows, tended to be "removal." Richards, *Highland Clearances*, 6. For Malthus, extermination and smallpox, see Malthus, *An Essay* (1826), vol. 2, 306–7: "Dr. Haygarth, in the Sketch of his benevolent plan for the extermination of the casual small-pox, draws a frightful picture of the mortality which has been occasioned by this distemper, attributes to it the slow progress of population, and makes some curious calculations on the favourable effects which would be produced in this respect by its extermination."

93. West, *History of Tasmania* (1852), quoted in Reynolds, *History of Tasmania*, 47. For demographic decline, see Reynolds, *History of Tasmania*, 57. Darwin, *Narrative of the Surveying Voyages*, vol. 3, 533–34. Browne, *Charles Darwin*, 386–68. For Malthus and Darwin, see also McCalman, *Darwin's Armada*, 72–73. For Darwin's further reference to Van Diemen's Land, see Darwin, *Descent of Man*.

94. Lyndall Ryan put the Black Line in the context of Scottish clearances in "Black Line in Tasmania." See also Connor, "British Warfare Logistics and the 'Black Line,' Van Diemen's Land (Tasmania), 1830," 43–158. For "age of emigration," see TRM to William Whewell, February 28, 1831, Marchi and Sturges, "Malthus and Ricardo's Inductivist Critics," 389.

CHAPTER 8: THE *ESSAY* IN NEW WORLDS

1. Brantlinger, *Dark Vanishings*, 30–36.
2. Amory and Hall, *Colonial Book*; Howsam and Raven, "Introduction"; McCoy, *Elusive Republic*, 191–92; Gibson, *Americans versus Malthus*); Smith, "Reception of Malthus' Essay," 551. The reception history of the *Essay* within Malthus's lifetime has been overwhelmingly focused on Great Britain; see Huzel, *Popularization of Malthus*; Mayhew, *Malthus*. Exceptions to this Eurocentric pattern appear in notes below.
3. Finkelstein, "Globalization of the Book, 329, 331–34.

4. Bureau of the Census, *A Century of Population Growth*, 3; Wells, *Population of the British Colonies*, 7.

5. Chaplin, *Benjamin Franklin's Political Arithmetic*, 34–41.

6. [Jay], *A Circular Letter*, 6–7; "A Citizen," *Observations on the Peculiar Case of the Whig Merchant*, 8; Ramsay, *History of the Revolution of South-Carolina*, vol. 2, 419; *Collections of the Massachusetts Historical Society*, vol. 3, 174; Pemberton, *An Historical Journal*, 126; *Journals of Congress*, vol. 5, 262; Zirkle, "Benjamin Franklin," 59–60, 60n.

7. Finkelman; *Slavery and the Founders*, 3–36.

8. Cohen, *Science and the Founding Fathers*, 89–97; Thomas Jefferson, calculation of population increase [October 1801], *Papers of Thomas Jefferson*, vol. 35, 531–32.

9. Godwin, *Of Population*, vii, ix, 25, 126–27, 141.

10. Godwin, *Of Population*, 49; Malthus, *Reply to the Chief Objections*, 12n., 279–80, 289–94 (tables), 375–76.

11. Godwin, *Of Population*, ix, 139–40, 539, 589, 619.

12. Graham, *William Godwin Reviewed*, 379, 382, 384, 389, 393, 395, 397, 399, 40, 403, 406, 410, 412, 416, 418 (quotations on pp. 377, 379, 382, 389, 397, 417).

13. *Annual Register*, 191–92; Burgh, *Political Disquisitions*, vol. 2, 287; *Politician's Dictionary*, vol. 1, 147; Guthrie, *A New Geographical, Commercial, and Historical Grammar*, vol. 2, 490–91; *Royal Gazette*, Jamaica, May 26, 1821.

14. Chaplin, *An Anxious Pursuit*, 33–34, 37, 48–50, 53–54, 60–63; Richter, "'Believing That Many of the Red People Suffer Much,'" 601–28; Charles Lloyd, *Travels at Home*, vol. 2, 293.

15. *Fifth Supplement to the Catalogue of Books*, 21; *Catalogue of Books in the Boston Library*, 38. And see lack of Malthus in *Catalogue of Books, Maps, and Charts Belonging to . . . Congress* and *Catalogue of Books, in the Library of the American Academy of Arts and Sciences*.

16. New York *Evening Post*, September 27, 1803 (and other search results from Readex, *Early American Newspapers*, s. v., "essay" and "population"); Raven, *London Booksellers and American Customers*, 140.

17. Thomas Jefferson to Joseph Priestley, January 29, 1804, in Jefferson, *Writings of Thomas Jefferson*, vol. 8, 295–96; Jefferson to Jean-Baptiste Say, February 1, 1804, Jefferson, *Works of Thomas Jefferson*, vol. 4, 526–27; Jefferson, *Papers of Thomas Jefferson: Retirement Series*, vol. 7, 628.

18. *Enquirer*, August 11, 1804; *True Republican*, September 26, 1804; *Enquirer*, November 17, 1804, May 3, 1805, November 5, 1805; *American Citizen*, May 17, 1809; *Suffolk Gazette*, July 1, 1809; Thomas Cooper to Thomas Jefferson, August 17, 1814, *Papers of Jefferson: Retirement Series*, vol. 557, 560.

19. *United States Gazette* (November 30, 1807); *Petersburg Intelligencer*, September 27, 1808.

20. Thomas Jefferson, account with Joseph Milligan, November 7, 1807, *Papers of Jefferson: Retirement Series*, vol. 1, 35; Joseph Milligan to Thomas Jefferson, January 18, 1819, forthcoming in *Papers of Thomas Jefferson: Retirement Series*, vol. 13; Finkelstein, "Globalization of the Book," 335–36.

21. *Poulson's American Daily Advertiser*, December 10, 1807; *Democratic Press*, December 11, 1807; *Daily Advertiser*, December 15. 1807; "Home Manufactures," *Wash-*

ington Reporter, December 19, 1808, originally in the *Aurora*; *Newburyport Herald*, April 8, 1834.

22. *Free Press* (Montreal), February 20, 1823, 141; *Essay on Marriage* (n.p.).

23. Everett, *New Ideas on Population*, viii–ix, 15, 19. See also overview in Spengler, "Alexander Hill Everett."

24. Everett, *New Ideas on Population*, 31–33, 39–42, 61.

25. Everett, *New Ideas on Population*, 70–71, 75–80, 83–85, 88, 92, 123.

26. Hodgson, "Malthus' Essay on Population," 747.

27. Hodgson, "Malthus' Essay on Population," quotations from 745–46.

28. Hodgson, "Malthus' Essay on Population," 756–58; Dew, *Review of the Debate*, 40, 53, 74.

29. *Daily Georgian*, May 28, 1829; *Cherokee Phoenix*, April 24, 1828, English transcription from http://www.wcu.edu/library/DigitalCollections/CherokeePhoenix; Lepore, *Name of War*, 191–226.

30. Rawley, *Transatlantic Slave Trade*; Treasure, *Huguenots*; Ekirch, *Bound for America*; Faragher, *A Great and Noble Scheme*; Jasanoff, *Liberty's Exiles*; Perdue and Green, *Cherokee Nation*.

31. Vasconcelos, "From the French or Not," esp. 212–17; Vera, " 'Learning from Abroad?'," 233–56; Smith, "Reception of Malthus' Essay," 551.

32. Malthus, *Essai sur le principe de population*, vii–xiv, xxiii.

33. Du Pont de Nemours to Thomas Jefferson, January. 25, 1812, Jefferson, *Papers of Thomas Jefferson: Retirement Series*, vol. 4, 440; Du Pont de Nemours, *Examen du livre de M. Malthus*, 39, 40.

34. Sonenscher, "Review Article," 326–39.

35. Du Pont de Nemours, *Examen du livre de M. Malthus*, 11–12.

36. Say, *Lettres à M. Malthus*; Whatmore, "Democrats and Republicans in Restoration France," esp. 45–48.

37. Drolet, "Democracy and Political Economy."

38. Tocqueville, *Democracy in America*, vol. 1, 14, vol. 2, 207, 208, 390–91.

39. Paquette, *Enlightenment, Governance, and Reform*, 87–89, 97–99.

40. Belich, *Replenishing the Earth*, 3–4; Cañizares-Esguerra, *How to Write the History of the New World*.

41. Brading, *First America*; Anderson, *Imagined Communities*, 47–65.

42. Humboldt, *Political Essay*, vol. 1, 89–95.

43. Humboldt, *Political Essay*, vol. 1, 96–110.

44. Humboldt, *Political Essay*, vol. 2, 475–80.

45. Malthus, *A Summary View*, 2–3, 5, 18–21.

46. Smith, "Reception of Malthus' Essay," 550–51; Vanaclocha, "La recepción de Malthus en la España de 1834; *Jornal do Commercio*, November 26, 1827, May 1, 1830; *El Mercurio de Valparaiso*, October 28, 1834. On the *Jornal do Commercio*, see Vasconcelos, "From the French or Not," 215.

47. Ortiz. *México considerado como nacion independiente y libre*, 465 ("la población de México debería duplicar cada 19 años"), 466, 472–76.

48. Paquette, "José da Silva Lisboa"; Cairu, *Estudos do bem-commum e economia politica*, vol. 1, t.p., 72–74, 111, 171, 192–202, 225.

49. Cairu, *Estudos do bem-commum*, vol. 1, 192–202, vol. 2, 92–93, 94; *PBF*, vol. 16, 107–8, also 126. With thanks to João Rangel de Almeida for his help translating these sections of the Portuguese text.

50. Blas, *Origen, progresos y límites*, 87–88, 110–14; *Noticioso Mercantil* (Havana), September 11, 1827; *Mercurio Peruano* (Lima), September 3, 1827.

51. *Bermudian*, November 29, 1820; *Jamaica Journal and Kingston Chronicle*, September 18, 1824; *St. George's Chronicle and Grenada Gazette*, June 3, 1806; *St. Christopher Gazette; and Charibbean Courier*, Basse Terre, St. Christopher, December 14, 1827; *Port of Spain Gazette*, April 19, 1833.

52. Finkelstein, "Globalization of the Book," 335; *Sydney Gazette and New South Wales Advertiser*, June 16, 1821; Overell, *Early Book Purchases*.

53. *Sydney Gazette and New South Wales Advertiser*, December 20, 1822, and July 24, 1823; *Hobart Town Gazette*, March 26, 1824; *Colonial Times and Tasmanian Advertiser*, August 4, 1826; see similar pro-colonialist sentiments in the *Australian*, February 24, 1832; *Perth Gazette and Western Australia Journal*, March 23, 1833.

54. *Tasmanian*, April 8, 1831.

55. Mookini, *Hawaiian Newspapers*, 42; Chapin, *Shaping History*, 15–18; "Helen Chapin's Guide to Newspapers of Hawai'i, 1834–2000," Hawaiian Historical Society, http://www.hawaiianhistoricalsociety.org/ref/chapinpdfs.html; keyword searches for "Malthus," "kanaka," and "heluna kanaka" in the Hawaii newspaper database (http://gdc.gale.com/products/19th-century-u.s.-newspapers) and Papakilo database (http://papakilodatabase.com/pdnupepa/cgi-bin/pdnupepa?a=d&cl=CL2); Tachihata, "The History and Development of Hawaii Public Libraries," *Catalog of Books in the Libraries of the A.B.C.F.M.*; Finkelstein, "Globalization of the Book," 334.

56. Darwin, *Narrative of the Surveying Voyages*, 520; Chaplin, *Benjamin Franklin's Political Arithmetic*, 44–47; Bashford, *Global Population*, 11–12, 36–43.

57. Dickens, *The Uncommercial Traveller* (1861), in Dickens, *Works of Charles Dickens*, vol. 27, 116–17; Dickens, *Oliver Twist*; Dickens, *A Christmas Carol* (1843), in Dickens, *Works of Charles Dickens*, vol. 22, 9–10.

58. Shelley, Frankenstein, 138.

59. Godwin, *Of Population*, 365; Shelley, *Last Man*, 76. On last-man narratives, see Stafford, *Last of the Race*, which does not discuss Malthus in relation to Shelley; on population in literature (including Shelley's works), see McLane, *Romanticism and the Human Sciences*, which does not discuss Malthus; on Shelley and Malthus, see Cameron, "Mary Shelley's Malthusian Objections," 177–203.

60. Shelley, *Last Man*, 213, 215, 272, 276.

61. Shelley, *Last Man*, 285, 303, 339.

62. Slotkin, *Regeneration through Violence*, 466–516; Stafford, *Last of the Race*, 232–60; Brantlinger, *Dark Vanishings*, 60–67; "American Novels," *The British Critic*, July 1826, 422.

63. Franklin, *James Fenimore Cooper*, 288–301; *Literary and Scientific Repository* 1 (1820): 229, and 2 (1821): 150–57 (a long review of Wallace and Malthus); Cooper, *Letters and Journals*, vol. 1, 253–54, 261; Cooper, *Notions of the Americans*, vol. 1, 230, vol. 2, 270, 322; Cooper, *Leatherstocking Tales*, vol. 1: *The Pioneers*, 14; Cooper, *Gleanings in Europe: England*, vol. 2, 166.

64. Cooper, *Leatherstocking Tales*, vol. 1: *The Last of the Mohicans*, 475, 476, 820, 877, 878.
65. Murray also published at least one attack on Malthus. Carpenter, *Seven Lives of John Murray*, 161.

Coda

1. *Commercial Advertiser* (New York), January 1, 1835; *Albany Argus*, February 7, 1835; *Charleston Courier*, February 7, 1835; *Liberator*, February 14, 1835.
2. *Sydney Morning Herald*, May 23, 1835; *Launceston Advertiser*, June 11, 1835; *Sydney Gazette and New South Wales Advertiser*, July 2, 1835.
3. For the Americas, see Denevan, "Pristine Myth"; Stannard, *American Holocaust*; Wylie, "Invented Lands/Discovered Pasts; Dent, "False Frontiers"; Madley, "Reexamining the American Genocide Debate." For Australia, see Butlin, *Our Original Aggression*; Lourandos, *Continent of Hunter-Gatherers*; Briscoe and Smith, *Aboriginal Population Revisited*; McCalman and Kippen, "Population and Health."
4. [Malthus], *An Essay* (1798), 14; Malthus, *An Essay* (1803), 6.
5. Malthus, *An Essay* (1803), 6.
6. [Malthus], *An Essay* (1798), 15.
7. For Henry Malthus's diligence, see notebook, 24 March, 1822, MG.6.17, JC.

BIBLIOGRAPHY

ARCHIVAL SOURCES

Archives Centre, King's College, Cambridge

T. R. Malthus to E. D. Clarke, February 27, 1807, Keynes Papers

Bodleian Library, Oxford

Examination Papers of the Principal and Professors of the East India College, 1808

British Library

India Office Records and Private Papers
Thomas Harriot Mathematical Papers
Joseph Johnson Business Correspondence
T. R. Malthus, acceptance of Professorship of General History, July 10, 1805, India
    Office Records and Private Papers
T. R. Malthus, Collection of manuscripts by, or relating to, Malthus and his family
Macvey Napier, Correspondence with T. R. Malthus
Arthur Young, Correspondence with T. R. Malthus

Derbyshire Record Office, Matlock

Sir Robert Wilmot Horton Papers

London Metropolitan Archives

Warrens (solicitors), letter books and correspondence

Mitchell Library, Sydney

Bonwick Transcripts, May 1805
Philip Gidley King Letter Book, David Collins correspondence with Sir Joseph Banks,
    1797–1806

Old Library, Jesus College, Cambridge

Patricia James Papers
Malthus Family, Newsclipping Album
Henry Malthus Notebook
Register of Borrowers, 1791–1805

Senate House Library, University of London

T. R. Malthus to George Turner, November 28, 1800
T. R. Malthus to David Ricardo, October 9, 1814

The National Archives, Kew

Court of Chancery Records
Malthus v Swann, 1799
Hibbert v Malthus, 1804–1805
Malthus v Swann, 1806
Symes v Swann, 1807
Cannell v Malthus, 1825

Home Office Records

George Cherry, Victualling Commissioner, August 24, 1797
Daniel Malthus Will, January 29, 1800
Mariana Georgina Malthus Will, March 18, 1831
Thomas Robert Malthus Will, February 12, 1835

Periodicals and Newspapers

Albany Argus (Albany, NY)
American Citizen (New York, NY)
Analytical Review, or History of Literature (London)
Annual Review (London)
Asiatic Researches (London)
Australian (Sydney, New South Wales)
Bermudian, a Commercial, Political, and Literary Journal (St. George's, Bermuda)
British Critic (London)
Charleston Courier (Charleston, SC)
Cherokee Phoenix (New Town, GA)
Cobbett's Weekly Political Register (London)

Colonial Times (Hobart, Tasmania)
Colonial Times and Tasmanian Advertiser (Hobart, Tasmania)
Commercial Advertiser (Kingston, Jamaica)
Daily Advertiser (New York, NY)
Daily Georgian (Savannah, GA)
Democratic Press (Philadelphia, PA)
Edinburgh Review (Edinburgh)
Enquirer (Richmond, VA)
Evening Post (New York, NY)
Free Press (Lancaster, PA)
Free Press (Montreal)
Gentleman's Magazine (London)
Hobart Town Gazette (Hobart, Tasmania)
Jamaica Journal and Kingston Chronicle (Kingston, Jamaica)
Jornal do Commercio (Rio de Janeiro)
Launceston Advertiser (Launceston, Tasmania)
Liberator (Boston, MA)
Literary and Scientific Repository (New York, NY)
London Magazine, Or, Gentleman's Monthly Intelligence (London)
London Packet (New Lloyd's Evening Post) (London)
Mercurio Peruano (Lima, Peru)
Mercurio de Valparaiso (Valparaiso, Chile)
Monthly Magazine and British Register (London)
Monthly Review (London)
New Annual Register (London)
Newburyport Herald (Newburyport, MA)
New South Wales Pocket Almanac (Sydney, New South Wales)
Noticioso Mercantil (Havana)
Perth Gazette and Western Australian Journal (Western Australia)
Petersburg Intelligencer (Petersburg, VA)
Port of Spain Gazette (Port of Spain, Trinidad)
Poulson's American Daily Advertiser (Philadelphia, PA)
Quarterly Review (London)
Royal Gazette (Kingston, Jamaica)
Scotsman (Edinburgh)
St. Christopher Gazette, and Charibbean Courier (Basseterre, St. Kitts)
St. George's Chronicle and Grenada Gazette (St. George's, Grenada)
St. James's Chronicle (London)
Suffolk Gazette (Sag Harbor, NY)
Sydney Gazette and New South Wales Advertiser (Sydney, New South Wales)
Sydney Morning Herald (Sydney, New South Wales)
Tasmanian (Hobart, Tasmania)
Times (London)

True Republican (Norwich, CT)
United States Gazette (Philadelphia, PA)
Washington Reporter (Washington, PA)

OTHER WORKS CITED (PRIMARY SOURCES)

Abstract of the Answers and Returns Made Pursuant to . . . An Act to Provide for Taking Account of the Population of Ireland. London: House of Commons, 1823.

Abū al-Ghāzī Bahādur, *A General History of the Turks, Moguls, and Tatars*, 2 vols. (London, 1729/30).

A Catalogue of the Books, &c. Belonging to the Library Company of Baltimore. Baltimore: Prentiss and Cole, 1802.

A Catalogue of the Library of George Hibbert, Esq., of Portland Place. London: W. Nicol, 1829.

"A Citizen" [Hazard, Nathaniel]. *Observations on the Peculiar Case of the Whig Merchants, Indebted to Great Britain at the Commencement of the Late War.* New York, 1785.

A Friend to Commerce and Humanity. *Thoughts on Civilization and the Gradual Abolition of Slavery in Africa and the West Indies.* London: J. Johnson, [1790?].

The Annual Register, or a View of the History, Politicks, and Literature, of the Year 1760. London: R. and J. Dodsley, 1761.

An Authentic and Interesting Narrative of the Late Expedition to Botany Bay. Aberdeen: Alexander Keith, 1789.

A Statement of the Principles and Objects of a Proposed National Society for the Cure and Prevention of Pauperism, by Means of Systematic Colonization. London: J. Ridgway, 1830.

Bacon, Francis. *New Atlantis: A Worke Unfinished.* London, 1627.

Banks, Joseph. *The Endeavour Journal of Joseph Banks, 1768–1771.* Edited by J. C. Beaglehole. 2 vols. Sydney: Angus and Robertson, 1962.

Barrington, George. *A Voyage to New South Wales, with a Description of the Country; the Manners of the Natives, in the Vicinity of Botany Bay.* London: Sadler, 1795.

Beaufort, Daniel Augustus. *Memoir of a Map of Ireland; Illustrating the Topography of that Kingdom, a Short Account of its Present State, Civil and Ecclesiastical.* London: Faden &c, 1792.

Blas, Agustín de. *Origen, progresos y límites de la población . . .* Madrid: E. Aguado, 1833.

Bodin, Jean. *The Six Bookes of a Commonweale.* Edited by Kenneth Douglas McRae. Cambridge, MA: Harvard University Press, 1962.

Botero, Giovanni. *The Reason of State* (translated by P. J. and D. P. Waley) and *The Greatness of Cities* (translated by Robert Peterson). New Haven, CT: Yale University Press, 1956.

Bourne, Kenneth, and William Banks Taylor. *The Horner Papers: Selections from the Letters and Miscellaneous Writings of Francis Horner, 1795–1817.* Edinburgh: Edinburgh University Press, 1994.

Boyle, Robert. "General Heads for a Natural History of a Country, Great or Small." *Philosophical Transactions* 1 (1665): 186–89.

Brosses, Charles de. *Histoire des navigations aux Terres Australes.* 2 vols. Paris: Durand, 1756.

Bruce, James. *Travels to Discover the Source of the Nile.* 5 vols. London: J. Ruthven, 1790.

Bry, Theodor de. *Grands Voyages: Americae.* Frankfurt, 1590-1634.

Bumstead, J. M., ed. *The Collected Writings of Lord Selkirk, 1799–1809.* Winnipeg: Manitoba Record Society, 1984.

Bureau of the Census. *A Century of Population Growth from the First Census of the United States to the Twelfth, 1790–1900.* Washington, DC: Government Printing Office, 1909.

Burgh, James. *Political Disquisitions....* 3 vols. London: E. and C. Dilly, 1774–1775.

Cairu, visconde de (José da Silva Lisboa). *Estudos do bemcommun e economia politica.* 2 vols. Rio de Janeiro: Impressão Regia, 1819–1820.

Catalog of Books in the Libraries of the A.B.C.F.M.[American Board of Commissioners for Foreign Missions] and the Maternal Association, at the Sandwich Islands. Honolulu: A.B.C.F.M., 1837.

Catalogue of Books in the Boston Library, May 1, 1802. Boston, 1802.

Catalogue of Books, in the Library of the American Academy of Arts and Sciences. Boston, 1802.

Catalogue of Books, Maps, and Charts, Belonging to the Library of the Two Houses of Congress. April, 1802. Washington City [DC]: William Duane, [1802].

Clarkson, T. *Thoughts on the Necessity of Improving the Condition of the Slaves in the British Colonies with a View to Their Ultimate Emancipation.* London: Richard Taylor, 1823.

Cobbett, William. "Jamaica Complaints." *Cobbett's Weekly Political Register,* February 16, 1805: 230–231.

———. "Slave Trade." *Cobbett's Weekly Political Register,* January 1806: 65.

Colebrooke, R. H. "On the Andaman Islands." *Asiatic Researches* 4 (1799): 401–411.

Collections of the Massachusetts Historical Society, for the Year 1793. Vol. 2. Boston: Apollo Press, Belknap and Hall, 1793.

Collins, David. *An Account of the English Colony in New South Wales, with Remarks on the Dispositions, Customs, Manners, &c of the Native Inhabitants of that Country.* London: T. Cadell and W. Davies, 1798.

Cook, James. *The Journals of Captain James Cook on his Voyages of Discovery.* Edited by J. C. Beaglehole. 4 vols. Cambridge: Hakluyt Society, 1955.

———. *A Voyage towards the South Pole, and round the World: Performed in His Majesty's Ships the Resolution and Adventure in the Years 1772, 1773, 1774, and 1775.* 2 vols. London: W. Strahan and T. Cadell, 1777.

———. *A Voyage to the Pacific Ocean: Undertaken by the Command of His Majesty, for Making Discoveries in the Northern Hemisphere.* 3 vols. London: W. and A. Strahan, 1785.

[Cook, James]. *A Voyage to the Pacific Ocean: Undertaken, by the Command of His Majesty, for Making Discoveries in the Northern Hemisphere.* 3 vols. London: W. and A. Strahan, 1785.

Cooper, James Fenimore. *Gleanings in Europe: England.* 2 vols. Philadelphia: Carey, Lea, and Blanchard, 1837.

———. *The Leatherstocking Tales.* 2 vols. New York: Library of America, 1985.

————. *Letters and Journals*. Edited by James Franklin Beard. 6 vols. Cambridge, MA: Harvard University Press, 1960–1968.

————. *Notions of the Americans: Picked Up by a Travelling Bachelor.* 2 vols. Philadelphia: Carey, Lea & Carey, 1828.

Croker, John Wilson. *A Sketch of the State of Ireland, Past and Present.* Dublin: M. Mahon, 1808.

Darwin, Charles. *The Descent of Man and Selection in Relation to Sex.* 2nd ed. London: John Murray. 1913.

————. *Narrative of the Surveying Voyages of His Majesty's Ships Adventure and Beagle Between the Years 1826 and 1836.* 3 vols. London: Henry Colburn, 1839.

Defoe, Daniel. *The Life and Strange Surprizing Adventures of Robinson Crusoe.* London: W. Mears and T. Woodward, 1726.

Dew, Thomas R. *Review of the Debate in the Virginia Legislature of 1831 and 1832.* Richmond: T. W. White, 1832.

Dickens, Charles. *Oliver Twist; or, the Parish Boy's Progress.* London: Richard Bentley, 1838.

————. *The Works of Charles Dickens.* 40 vols. London: Chapman and Hall, 1906.

Diderot, Denis. *Supplément au voyage de Bougainville.* Paris: Vauxcelles, 1796.

Dudley, H. *A Short Address Recommendatory of Rome Commutation or Modification of the Tithes of that Country.* London, 1808.

Du Pont de Nemours, Pierre Samuel. *Examen du livre de M. Malthus sur le principe de population: Auquel on a joint la traduction de quatre chapitres de ce livre supprimés dans l'édition française et une lettre à M. Say sur son Traité d'économie politique* Philadelphia: P. M. Lafourcade, 1817.

Early American Newspapers, 1690-1922, Readex. http://www.readex.com/content /early-american-newspapers-1690-1922.

East India Sugar. Pamphlet printed by J. Blackwell, Sheffield. Copy in the Religious Society of Friends Library, London, 1825.

Empson, William. "Life, Writing, and Character of Mr Malthus." *Edinburgh Review* 64 (1837): 469–506.

Equiano, Olaudah. *The Interesting Narrative of the Life of Olaudah Equiano.* London: Printed for the author, 1789.

Essay on Marriage. Québec: P. and W. Ruthven, 1829.

Everett, Alexander Hill. *New Ideas on Population: With Remarks on the Theories of Malthus and Godwin.* Boston: O. Everett, 1823.

Fifth Supplement to the Catalogue of Books, Belonging to the Library Company of Philadelphia. Philadelphia: Zachariah Poulson, Jr., 1799.

Forster, Johann Reinhold. *Observations Made during a Voyage round the World.* Edited by Nicholas Thomas, Harriet Guest, and Michael Dettelbach. Honolulu: University of Hawai'i Press, 1996.

Francklyn, Gilbert. *Observations: Occasioned by the Attempts Made in England to Affect the Abolition of the Slave Trade.* London: Logographic Press, 1789.

Franklin, Benjamin. *The Papers of Benjamin Franklin.* Edited by Leonard W. Labaree, et al. 42 vols. to date. New Haven, CT: Yale University Press, 1959-.

————. *Political, Miscellaneous, and Philosophical Pieces.* London: J. Johnson, 1779.

Gibbon, Edward. *The History of the Decline and Fall of the Roman Empire.* Vols. 1 and 6. London: W. Strahan and T. Cadell, 1776 and 1788.

Godwin, William. *An Enquiry Concerning Political Justice, and its Influence on General Virtue and Happiness*. 2 vols. London: G. G. J. and J. Robinson, 1793.

———. *The Letters of William Godwin*. Edited by Pamela Clemit. 2 vols. to date. Oxford: Oxford University Press, 2011.

———. *Of Population: An Enquiry Concerning the Power of Increase in the Numbers of Mankind. Being an Answer to Mr. Malthus's Essay on That Subject*. London: Longman, Hurst, Rees, Orme and Brown, 1820.

Gouger, Robert, ed. *A Letter from Sydney, the Principal Town of Australasia, together with the Outline of a System of Colonization*. London: J. Cross, 1829.

Gourlay, Robert. *General Introduction to Statistical Account of Upper Canada, Compiled with a View to a Grand System of Emigration, in Connexion with a Reform of the Poor Laws*. London: Simpkin and Marshall, 1822.

[Graves, Richard]. "A domestic scene in rural life." In *Euphrosyne, or Amusements on the Road of Life*, 38–40. London: Dodsley, 1776.

Guthrie, William. *A New Geographical, Commercial, and Historical Grammar, and Present State of the Several Empires and Kingdoms of the World*. 2 vols. London: Charles Dillym and G.G.J. and J. Robinson, 1790.

Hansard, Parliamentary Debates of the United Kingdom. House of Lords: http://hansard.millbanksystems.com/lords; House of Commons: http://hansard.millbanksystems.com/commons.

[Hawkesworth, John]. *An Account of the Voyages Undertaken by the Order of His Present Majesty for Making Discoveries in the Southern Hemisphere*. 3 vols. London: W. Strahan and T. Cadell, 1773.

Heads of the Speeches delivered on 18th and 19th April, 1791. Liverpool, 1791.

Hibbert, George. *The Substance of Three Speeches in Parliament on the Bill for the Abolition of the Slave Trade*. London: Lane, Darling, 1807.

Home, Henry, Lord Kames. *Sketches of the History of Man*. 2 vols. London: W. Strahan and T. Cadell, 1774.

———. *Sketches of the History of Man*, 2nd ed. 4 vols. Edinburgh: W. Creech, 1778.

Humboldt, Alexander von. *Political Essay on the Kingdom of New Spain*. Translated by John Black. 4 vols. London: Longman, Hurst, Rees, Orme, and Brown, 1811.

Hume, David. *Essays, Moral, Political, and Literary*. Edited by Eugene F. Miller. Indianapolis: Liberty Fund, 1987.

———. *The Letters of David Hume*. Edited by J. Y. T. Greig. 2 vols. Oxford: Clarendon Press, 1932.

Jackson, Donald, ed. *Letters of the Lewis and Clark Expedition, with Related Documents, 1783–1854*. Urbana: University of Illinois Press, 1962.

James, Patricia, ed. *The Travel Diaries of Thomas Robert Malthus*. Cambridge: Cambridge University Press, 1966.

[Jay, John]. *A Circular Letter from the Congress of the United States of America to Their Constituents*. Philadelphia: David C. Claypoole, [1779?].

Jefferson, Thomas. *The Papers of Thomas Jefferson*. Edited by Julian P. Boyd, et al. 41 vols. to date. Princeton, NJ: Princeton University Press, 1950–.

———. The Papers of Thomas Jefferson: Retirement Series. Edited by J. Jefferson Looney, et al., 10 vols. to date. Princeton, NJ: Princeton University Press, 2004–.

———. *The Works of Thomas Jefferson*. Edited by J. Jefferson Looney, et al. 10 vols. to date. Princeton: Princeton University Press, 2004–.

————. *The Writings of Thomas Jefferson*. Edited by Albert Ellery Bergh. 20 vols. Washington, DC: Thomas Jefferson Memorial Assoc., 1907.

Jose, Nicholas, ed. *Macquarie PEN Anthology of Australian Literature*. Sydney: Allen and Unwin, 2009.

Journals of Congress: Containing Their Proceedings from January 1, 1779, to January 1, 1780. Philadelphia: Folwell's Press, 1800.

Lafitau, Joseph François. *Moeurs des sauvages ameriquains. . . .* 4 vols. Paris: Saugrain l'aîné, 1724.

Lansdowne, Marquis of, ed. *The Petty-Southwell Correspondence, 1676–1687*. New York: A. M. Kelley, 1967.

Lloyd, Charles. *Travels at Home, and Voyages by the Fire-side, for the Instruction and Entertainment of Young Persons*. 2 vols. Philadelphia: Edward Earle, T. and G. Palmer, 1816.

[Locke, John]. *Two Treatises of Government*. London, 1689.

Lowe, Joseph. *An Inquiry into the State of the British West Indies*. London: Baldwin, 1807.

Macaulay, Zachary. *East and West India Sugar; or, a Refutation of the Claims of the West India Colonists to a Protecting Duty on East India Sugar*. London: Lupton Relfe, 1823.

Machivaelli, Niccolò. *Machivel's Discourses upon the First Decade of T. Livius, Translated Out of the Italian; to Which is Added His Prince*. Translated by Edward Dacres. London: Thos. Dring, 1663.

Malthus, T. R. *A Letter to the Rt. Hon. Lord Grenville, Occasioned by Some Observations of His Lordship on the East India Company's Establishment for the Education of their Civil Servants*. London: J. Johnson, 1813.

————. *Essai sur le principe de population*. Translated by Pierre Prévost. Paris: J. J. Paschoud, 1809.

————. "An Essay on the Advantages of Colonies." In *T. R. Malthus: The Unpublished Papers in the Collection of Kanto Gakuen University*, edited by J. M. Pullen and Trevor Hughes Parry. Vol. 2, 275–77. Cambridge: Cambridge University Press, 2004.

————. *An Essay on the Principle of Population: Or, a View of its Past and Present Effects on Human Happiness: With an Inquiry into our Prospects Respecting the Future Removal or Mitigation of the Evils which it Occasions*. 2nd ed. London: J. Johnson, 1803.

————. *An Essay on the Principle of Population; or a View of its Past and Present Effects on Human Happiness; with an Inquiry into our Prospects Respecting the Future Removal or Mitigation of the Evils which it Occasions*. 3rd ed. 2 vols. London: J. Johnson, 1806.

————. *An Essay on the Principle of Population; or a View of its Past and Present Effects on Human Happiness; with an Inquiry into our Prospects Respecting the Future Removal or Mitigation of the Evils which it Occasions*. 4th ed. 2 vols. London: J. Johnson, 1807.

————. *An Essay on the Principle of Population: or a View of its Past and Present Effects on Human Happiness; with an Inquiry into our Prospects Respecting the Future Removal or Mitigation of the Evils which it Occasions*. 5th ed. 3 vols. London: J. Murray, 1817.

————. *An Essay on the Principle of Population; or a View of its Past and Present Effects on Human Happiness; with an Inquiry into our Prospects Respecting the Future Removal or Mitigation of the Evils which it Occasions*. 6th ed. 2 vols. London: J. Murray, 1826.

————. *An Essay on the Principle of Population; or a View of its Past and Present Effects on Human Happiness; with an Inquiry into our Prospects Respecting the Future Removal or Mitigation of the Evils which it Occasions*, edited by Patricia James. 2 vols. Cambridge: Cambridge University Press, 1989.

————. *An Essay on the Principle of Population; or a View of its Past and Present Effects on Human Happiness; with an Inquiry into our Prospects Respecting the Future Removal or Mitigation of the Evils which it Occasions*, edited by Donald Winch. Cambridge: Cambridge University Press, 1992.

————. *An Investigation of the Cause of the Present High Price of Provisions by the Author of the Essay on the Principle of Population*. London: J. Johnson, 1800.

————. *Principles of Political Economy, Considered with a View to Their Practical Application*. London: J. Murray, 1820.

————. *Principles of Political Economy, Considered with a View to Their Practical Application*. 2nd ed. London: W. Pickering, 1836.

————. *Reply to the Chief Objections Which Have Been Urged against the Essay on the Principle of Population*. Published in an Appendix to the Third Edition. London: J. Johnson, 1806.

————. *Statements Respecting the East-India College: With an Appeal to Facts, in Refutation of the Charges Lately Brought against it, in the Court of Proprietors*. London: J. Murray, 1817.

————. *A Summary View of the Principle of Population*. London: J. Murray, 1830.

————. *The Unpublished Papers in the Collection of Kanto Gakuen University*. 2 vols. Edited by J. M. Pullen and Trevor Hughes Parry. Cambridge: Cambridge University Press, 1997 and 2004.

[Malthus, T. R.]. *An Essay on the Principle of Population, as it Affects the Future Improvement of Society with Remarks on the Speculations of Mr. Godwin, M. Condorcet, and Other Writers*. London: J. Johnson, 1798.

————. "Newenham and others on the State of Ireland," *Edinburgh Review* 12 (July 1808): 336–55.

————— "Newenham on the State of Ireland," *Edinburgh Review* 14 (April 1809): 151–70

————— "Population," *Encyclopaedia Britannica*, supplement to the fourth edition 307–33. Edinburgh, 1824.

McDonnell, Alexander. *Considerations on Negro Slavery*. London: Longman, Hurst, Rees, Orme, Brown, and Green, 1824.

Melville, Lewis, ed. *The Life and Letters of William Cobbett in England and America*. 2 vols. London: John Lane, 1913.

Military Operations against the Aboriginal Inhabitants of Van Diemen's Land. London: House of Commons Papers, 1831.

Minutes of the Intended Arrangements between Earl Bathurst and the proposed Van Diemen's Land Company. London, 1825.

A Missionary Voyage to the Southern Pacific Ocean, Performed in the Years 1796, 1797, 1798 in the Ship Duff Commanded by Captain James Wilson. London: Chapman, 1799.

Montesquieu, Charles-Louis de Secondat, baron de La Brède et de. *The Persian Letters* (1721). In *The Complete Works of M. de Montesquieu*. Vol. 3, 191–. London: T. Evans and W. Davis, 1777.

————. *The Spirit of Laws* (1748). Edited by David Wallace Carrithers. Berkeley: University of California Press, 1977.

More, Hannah. *Slavery, A Poem*. London: T. Cadell, 1788.

More, Thomas. *Utopia*. London, 1516.

Muncaster, Baron (John Pennington). *Historical Sketches of the Slave Trade, and of its Effects in Africa: Addressed to the People of Great Britain*. London: Stockdale, 1792.

Nineteenth-Century U. S. Newspapers, Gale Digital Collections. http://gdc.gale.com/products/19th-century-u.s.-newspapers.

Oldmixon, John. *The British Empire in America*. 2 vols. London: John Nicholson, Benjamin Tooke, Richard Parker and Ralph Smith, 1708.

"On the State and Prospects of the Country" *Quarterly Review* 78 (1829): 475–521.

Ortiz, Tadeo. *México considerado como nacion independiente y libre: ó sean algunas indicaciones sobre los deberes mas esenciales de los Mexicanos*. Burdeos: C. L. Sobrino, 1832.

Overell, Richard, ed. *Early Book Purchases in the Melbourne Public Library: Redmond Barry's Instructions to the Agent-General, December 3rd, 1853*. Clayton, Victoria: Monash University Press, 1997.

Paine, Thomas. *Common Sense* (1776). Edited by Isaac Kramnick. London: Penguin, 1976.

Papakilo Database. Office of Hawaiian Affairs. http://papakilodatabase.com/pdnupepa/cgi-bin/pdnupepa?a=d&cl=CL2.

Park, Mungo. *Travels in the Interior Districts of Africa in the Years 1795, 1796 and 1797*. London: W. Bulmer, 1799.

Parnell, William. *An Inquiry into the Causes of Popular Discontents in Ireland by an Irish Country Gentleman*. London: Debrett, 1804.

Pemberton, Thomas. *An Historical Journal of the American War. Extracted from the Publications of the Massachusetts Historical Society*. Boston: Belknap and Pitt, 1795.

Petty, William. *Political Anatomy of Ireland*. London: D. Brown and W. Rogers, 1691.

———. *Political Arithmetick....* London: Robert Clavel and Hen. Mortlock, 1690.

Phillip, Arthur. *The Voyage of Governor Phillip to Botany Bay: With an Account of the Establishment of the Colonies of Port Jackson and Norfolk Islands*. London: J. Stockdale, 1789.

Political Economy Club, Minutes of Proceedings, Roll of Members, and Questions Discussed, with Documents Bearing on the History of the Club. London: Macmillan, 1921.

The Politician's Dictionary; or, a Summary of Political Knowledge. 2 vols. London: Geo. Allen, 1775.

Price, Richard. *Observations on Reversionary Payments*. London: T. Cadell, 1771.

Pullen, J. M., and Trevor Hughes Parry, eds. *T. R. Malthus: The Unpublished Papers in the Collection of Kanto Gakuen University*. 2 vols. Cambridge: Cambridge University Press, 1997 and 2004.

Ramsay, David. *The History of the Revolution of South-Carolina*. 2 vols. Trenton: Isaac Collins, [1785].

Ricardo, David. *Letters of David Ricardo to Thomas Robert Malthus*. Edited by James Bonar. London: Henry Frowde, 1887.

Robertson, William. *The History of America*. 3rd ed. 3 vols. London: W. Strahan and T. Cadell, 1780.

Rousseau, Jean-Jacques. *Correspondance complète de Jean Jacques Rousseau: édition critique*. Edited by R. A. Leigh. 51 vols. Geneva: Institut et Musée Voltaire, 1965–1995.

Sadler, Michael Thomas. *Ireland: Its Evils and their Remedies.* 2nd ed. 2 vols. London: John Murray, 1829.

Saint-Pierre, Bernardin de. *Paul and Mary, an Indian Story.* [Translated by Jane Dalton.] 2 vols. London: J. Dodsley, 1789.

Say, Jean-Baptiste. *Lettres à M. Malthus, sur différents sujets d'économie politique: notamment sur les causes de la stagnation générale du commerce.* Paris and London: Bossange, 1820.

Select Committee on Emigration from the United Kingdom, First Report (1826), Second Report (1827), Third Report (1827). London: House of Commons.

"Senex," "An Address." *Cobbett's Weekly Political Register* January 18, 1806, 65–79.

Shelley, Mary. *Frankenstein, or, The Modern Prometheus* (1818). Edited by Marilyn Butler. Oxford: Oxford University Press, 1993.

———. *The Last Man* (1826). Introduction by Brian Aldiss. London: Hogarth Press, 1985.

Smith, Adam. *An Inquiry into the Nature and Causes of the Wealth of Nations.* 2 vols. London: W. Strahan and T. Cadell, 1776.

———. *An Inquiry into the Nature and Causes of the Wealth of Nations.* 4th ed. 3 vols. London: W. Strahan and T. Cadell, 1786.

———. *Lectures on Jurisprudence* (1763), edited by Ronald L. Meek, David D. Raphael, and Peter G. Stein. Oxford: Clarendon Press, 1978.

———. *The Theory of Moral Sentiments.* Edited by D. D. Raphael and A. L. Macfie. Oxford: Clarendon Press, 1976.

Stephen, James. *The Slavery of the West India Colonies Delineated.* London: J. Butterworth and Son, 1823.

Stiles, Ezra. *A Discourse on the Christian Union.* Boston: Edes and Gill, [1761].

Swift, Jonathan. *A Modest Proposal for Preventing the Children of Poor People from Being a Burthen to Their Parents or Country, and for Making Them Beneficial to the Publick.* Dublin: S. Harding, 1729.

Symes, Michael. *An Account of an Embassy to the Kingdom of Ava in the Year 1795.* 2 vols. London: J. Debrett, 1800.

Tench, Watkin. *Complete Account of the Settlement at Port Jackson.* London: G. Nicol and J. Sewell, 1793.

Tocqueville, Alexis de. *Democracy in America.* Translated by Henry Reeve. 2 vols. London: Sanders and Otley, 1835.

Turner, Frederick Jackson. "The Significance of the Frontier in American History." *Annual Report of the American Historical Association* (1894): 197–227.

Vancouver, George. *A Voyage of Discovery to the North Pacific Ocean, and Round the World.* London: G. G. and J. Robinson and J. Edwards, 1798.

[Vincent, Philip]. *A True Relation of the Late Battell.* London: M[armaduke] P[arsons], 1637.

Volney, C.-F. *Les Ruines, ou méditation sur les révolutions des empires.* Paris, 1791.

———. *Voyage en Syrie et en Egypte, pendant les années 1783–1785.* 2nd ed., 2 vols. Paris, 1787.

[Wakefield, Edward Gibbon]. *England and America: A Comparison of the Social and Political State of Both Nations.* 2 vols. London: R. Bently, 1833.

———. *Sketch of a Proposal for Colonizing Australasia.* London: Dove, 1829.

Wakefield, Gilbert. *A Letter to William Wilberforce, Esq. on the Subject of His Late Publication.* London: A. Hamilton, 1797.

———. *Memoirs of the Life of Gilbert Wakefield, Written by Himself.* 2 vols. London: J. Johnson, 1804.

Wallace, Robert. *A Dissertation on the Numbers of Mankind, in Antient and Modern Times.* Edinburgh: G. Hamilton and J. Balfour, 1753.

Watson, Frederick, ed. *Historical Records of Australia.* Series 1, 26 vols. Sydney: Library Committee of the Commonwealth Parliament, 1914–1925.

Wilmot Horton, R[obert]. *Outline of a Plan of Emigration to Upper Canada.* London: F. Warr, 1822.

[Winslow, Edward]. *Mourt's Relation: A Journal of the Pilgrims at Plymouth.* Edited by Dwight B. Heath. Bedford, MA: Applewood Books, 1963.

Wrigley, E. A., and D. Souden, eds. *The Works of Thomas Robert Malthus.* 8 vols. London: Pickering and Chatto, 1986.

OTHER WORKS CITED (SECONDARY SOURCES)

Abbott, John Lawrence. *John Hawkesworth: Eighteenth-Century Man of Letters.* Madison: University of Wisconsin Press, 1982.

Adelman, Jeremy, and Stephen Aron. "From Borderlands to Borders: Empires, Nation-States, and the Peoples in between in North American History." *American Historical Review* 104 (1999): 814–41.

Albion, Robert Greenhalgh. *Forests and Sea Power: The Timber Problem of the Royal Navy, 1652–1862.* Cambridge, MA: Harvard University Press, 1926.

Aldridge, Alfred Owen. "Franklin as Demographer." *Journal of Economic History* 9 (1949): 25–44.

Almond, Philip C. *Adam and Eve in Seventeenth-Century Thought.* Cambridge: Cambridge University Press, 1999.

Altick, Richard D. *The Shows of London.* Cambridge, MA: Belknap Press, 1978.

Amory, Hugh, and David D. Hall, eds. *The Colonial Book in the Atlantic World.* Chapel Hill: University of North Carolina Press, 2007.

Anderson, Benedict. *Imagined Communities: Reflections on the Origin and Spread of Nationalism.* Rev. ed. London: Verso, 2006.

Appleby, Joyce. "Ideology and Theory: The Tension Between Political and Economic Liberalism in Seventeenth-Century England." *American Historical Review* 81 (1976): 499–515.

Appleman, Philip. "Introduction." In T. R. Malthus, *An Essay on the Principle of Population,* edited by Philip Appleman, xiii–xxxiii. New York: W. W. Norton, 2004.

Appuhn, Karl. *A Forest on the Sea: Environmental Expertise in Renaissance Venice.* Baltimore, MD: Johns Hopkins University Press, 2009.

Armitage, David. "The New World and British Historical Thought: From Richard Hakluyt to William Robertson." In Kupperman, *America in European Consciousness* (1995), 52–75.

Armstrong, Tim. "Slavery, Insurance, and Sacrifice in the Black Atlantic." In *Sea Changes: Historicizing the Ocean,* edited by Bernhard Klein and Gesa Mackenthun, 167–85. New York: Routledge, 2004.

Arnold, David. "Hunger in the Garden of Plenty: The Bengal Famine of 1770." In *Dreadful Visitations: Confronting Natural Catastrophe in the Age of Enlightenment*, edited by Alessa Johns, 81–112. New York: Routledge, 1999.

Atkinson, Alan. *The Europeans in Australia: A History.* 3 vols. Vol. 1: *The Beginning.* Oxford: Oxford University Press, 1997.

Attwood, Bain. *Possession: Batman's Treaty and the Matter of History.* Melbourne: Miegunyah Press, 2009.

———. "Returning to the Past: The South Australian Colonisation Commission, the Colonial Office and Aboriginal Title." *Journal of Legal History* 34 (2013): 50–82.

Ballantyne, Tony. "Remaking the Empire from Newgate: Wakefield's *A Letter from Sydney*." In *Ten Books that Shaped the British Empire*, edited by Antoinette Burton and Isabel Hofmeyr, 29–49. Durham, NC: Duke University Press, 2014.

Banner, Stuart. *Possessing the Pacific: Land, Settlers, and Indigenous People from Australia to Alaska.* Cambridge, MA: Harvard University Press, 2007.

Barker, Hannah. *Newspapers, Politics, and English Society, 1695–1855.* New York: Longman, 1999.

Barnes, Donald Grave. *A History of the English Corn Laws, from 1660–1846.* London: Routledge, 1930.

Barrell, John. *The Spirit of Despotism: Invasions of Privacy in the 1790s.* Oxford: Oxford University Press, 2006.

Bartlett, Robert. *The Making of Europe: Conquest, Colonization, and Cultural Change, 950–1350.* Princeton, NJ: Princeton University Press, 1993.

Bashford, Alison. "Malthus and Colonial History." *Journal of Australian Studies* 36 (2012): 99–110.

———. *Global Population: History, Geopolitics, and Life on Earth.* New York: Columbia University Press, 2014.

Bashford, Alison, and Stuart Macintyre, eds. *The Cambridge History of Australia,* 2 vols. Melbourne: Cambridge University Press, 2013.

Bateman, Fiona, and Lionel Pilkington, eds. *Studies in Settler Colonialism: Politics, Identity and Culture.* New York: Palgrave Macmillan, 2011.

Bayly, C. A. *Imperial Meridian: The British Empire and the World, 1780–1830.* London: Longman, 1989.

———. *The Birth of the Modern World, 1780–1914.* Oxford: Blackwell, 2004.

Beaglehole, J. C. *The Life of Captain James Cook.* Stanford, CA: Stanford University Press, 1974.

Belich, James. *Replenishing the Earth: The Settler Revolution and the Rise of the Anglo-World, 1783–1939.* Oxford: Oxford University Press, 2009.

Bell, David A. *The First Total War: Napoleon's Europe and the Birth of Warfare as We Know It.* Boston: Houghton Mifflin, 2007.

Bender, John, and David E. Wellerby. *Chronotypes: The Construction of Time.* Stanford, CA: Stanford University Press, 1991.

Bennett, Michael. "Smallpox and Cowpox under the Southern Cross: The Smallpox Epidemic of 1789 and the Advent of Vaccination in Colonial Australia." *Bulletin of the History of Medicine* 83 (2009): 37–62.

Blainey, Geoffrey. *Triumph of the Nomads: A History of Ancient Australia.* Melbourne: Macmillan, 1982.

Bolton, Herbert Eugene. *The Spanish Borderlands: A Chronicle of Old Florida and the Southwest.* New Haven, CT: Yale University Press, 1921.

Borgstrom, Georg. *The Hungry Planet: The Modern World at the Edge of Famine.* New York: Macmillan, 1965.

Brading, D. A. *The First America: The Spanish Monarchy, Creole Patriots, and the Liberal State, 1492–1867.* Cambridge: Cambridge University Press, 1991.

Braithwaite, Helen. *Romanticism, Publishing, and Dissent: Joseph Johnson and the Cause of Liberty.* New York: Palgrave Macmillan, 2003.

Brantlinger, Patrick. *Dark Vanishings: Discourse on the Extinction of Primitive Races, 1800–1930.* Ithaca, NY: Cornell University Press, 2003.

Braude, Benjamin. "The Sons of Noah and the Construction of Ethnic and Geographical Identities in the Medieval and Early Modern Periods." *William and Mary Quarterly,* 3rd ser., 54 (1997): 103–42.

Brewer, John. *The Sinews of Power: War, Money and the English State, 1688–1783.* New York: Knopf, 1989.

Briscoe, Gordon, and Len Smith. *Aboriginal Population Revisited.* Canberra: Aboriginal History Incorporated, 2002.

Brown, Christopher Leslie. *Moral Capital: Foundations of British Abolitionism.* Chapel Hill, NC: Omohundro Institute of Early American History and Culture, 2006.

Brown, Stewart, ed. *William Robertson and the Expansion of Empire.* New York: Cambridge University Press, 1997.

Brown, Vincent. *The Reaper's Garden: Death and Power in the World of Atlantic Slavery.* Cambridge, MA: Harvard University Press, 2008.

Browne, Janet. *Charles Darwin: Voyaging.* Princeton, NJ: Princeton University Press, 1995.

Buck, Peter. "People Who Counted: Political Arithmetic in the Eighteenth Century." *Isis* 73 (1982): 28–45.

Burke, Peter. "America and the Rewriting of World History." In Kupperman, *America in European Consciousness* (1995), 33–51.

Butlin, N. G. *Our Original Aggression: Aboriginal Populations of Southeastern Australia, 1788–1850.* Sydney: George Allen and Unwin, 1983.

Caldwell, John C. "Malthus and the Less Developed World: The Pivotal Role of India." *Population and Development Review* 24 (1998): 675–96.

———. "The Social Repercussions of Colonial Rule: Demographic Aspects." In *General History of Africa,* edited by Adu A. Boahen. 9 vols. Vol. 7: *Africa under Colonial Domination 1880–1935,* 458–86. Berkeley: University of California Press, 1985.

Cameron, Lauren. "Mary Shelley's Malthusian Objections in *The Last Man.*" *Nineteenth-Century Literature* 67 (2012): 177–203.

Campbell, Judy. *Invisible Invaders: Smallpox and Other Diseases in Aboriginal Australia, 1780–1880.* Melbourne: Melbourne University Press, 2002.

Cañizares-Esguerra, Jorge. *How to Write the History of the New World: Histories, Epistemologies, and Identities in the Eighteenth-Century Atlantic World.* Stanford: Stanford University Press, 2001.

Carpenter, Humphrey. *The Seven Lives of John Murray: The Story of a Publishing Dynasty, 1768–2002.* London: John Murray, 2008.

Carretta, Vincent. *Equiano, the African: Biography of a Self-Made Man.* Athens,: University of Georgia Press, 2005.

Cassedy, James H. *Demography in Early America: Beginnings of the Statistical Mind, 1600–1800.* Cambridge, MA: Harvard University Press, 1969.

Chapin, Helen Geracimos. *Guide to Newspapers of Hawai'i: 1834–2000.* Honolulu: Hawaiian Historical Society, 2000. http://www.hawaiianhistoricalsociety.org/ref/chapinpdfs.html

———. *Shaping History: The Role of Newspapers in Hawai'i.* Honolulu: University of Hawai'i Press, 1996.

Chaplin, Joyce E. *An Anxious Pursuit: Agricultural Innovation and Modernity in the Lower South, 1730–1815.* Chapel Hill, NC: Institute of Early American History and Culture, 1993.

———. *Benjamin Franklin's Political Arithmetic: A Materialist View of Humanity.* Washington, DC: Smithsonian Institution, 2008.

———. "Creoles in British America: From Denial to Acceptance." In *Creolization: History, Ethnography, Theory,* edited by Charles Stewart, 46–65. Walnut Creek, CA: Left Coast Press, 2007.

———. "Earthsickness: Circumnavigation and the Terrestrial Human Body, 1520–1800." *Bulletin of the History of Medicine* 86 (2012): 515–42.

———. *The First Scientific American: Benjamin Franklin and the Pursuit of Genius.* New York: Basic Books, 2006.

———. "Natural Philosophy and an Early Racial Idiom in North America: Comparing English and Indian Bodies." *William and Mary Quarterly,* 3rd ser., 54 (1997): 229–52.

———. "The Pacific before Empire." In *Pacific Histories: Oceans, Land, People,* edited by David Armitage and Alison Bashford, 53–74. New York: Palgrave Macmillan, 2013.

———. *Round about the Earth: Circumnavigation from Magellan to Orbit.* New York: Simon and Schuster, 2012.

———. *Subject Matter: Technology, the Body, and Science on the Anglo-American Frontier, 1500–1676.* Cambridge, MA: Harvard University Press, 2001.

Cheek, Pamela. *Sexual Antipodes: Enlightenment, Globalization, and the Placing of Sex.* Stanford, CA: Stanford University Press, 2003.

Christopher, Emma, and Hamish Maxwell-Stewart. "Convict Transportation in Global Context, c. 1700–88." In *The Cambridge History of Australia,* edited by Alison Bashford and Stuart Macintyre. 2 vols. Vol. 1: *Indigenous and Colonial Australia,* 68–90. Melbourne: Cambridge University Press, 2013.

Clendinnen, Inga. *Dancing with Strangers: Europeans and Australians at First Contact.* Melbourne: Cambridge University Press, 2005.

Cohen, I. Bernard. *Science and the Founding Fathers: Science in the Political Thought of Jefferson, Franklin, Adams, and Madison.* New York: W. W. Norton, 1995.

Cohen, Jeremy. *Be Fertile and Increase, Fill the Earth and Master It: The Ancient and Medieval Career of a Biblical Text.* Ithaca, NY: Cornell University Press, 1989.

Cohen, Michèle. "'Familiar Conversation': The Role of the 'Familiar Format' in Education in Eighteenth- and Nineteenth-Century England." In *Educating the Child in Enlightenment Britain: Beliefs, Cultures, Practices,* edited by Mary Hilton and Jill Shefrin, 99–116. Farnham, UK: Ashgate, 2009.

Cohen, Patricia Cline. *A Calculating People: The Spread of Numeracy in Early America.* Chicago: University of Chicago Press, 1982.

Coleman, Deirdre. *Romantic Colonization and British Anti-Slavery.* Cambridge: Cambridge University Press, 2005.

Colley, Linda. *Britons: Forging the Nation, 1707–1837.* New Haven, CT: Yale University Press, 1992.

Connell, K. H. "The Population of Ireland in the Eighteenth Century." *Economic History Review* 16 (1946): 111–24.

Connor, John. "British Warfare Logistics and the 'Black Line,' Van Diemen's Land (Tasmania), 1830." *War in History* 9 (2002): 43–158.

Cook, Alexander. "The Philosophy of Constantin Volney and its Roles in History: France and Britain 1788–1847." PhD diss. University of Cambridge, 2007.

Cook, Malcolm. "Bernardin de Saint-Pierre's English Correspondents during the French Revolution." In *British-French Exchanges in the Eighteenth Century*, edited by Kathleen Hardesty Doig and Dorothy Medlin, 18–21. Newcastle: Cambridge Scholars Publishing, 2007.

Cranston, Maurice. *The Solitary Self: Jean-Jacques Rousseau in Exile and Adversity.* Chicago: University of Chicago Press, 1997.

Cremaschi, Sergio. *Utilitarianism and Malthus's Virtue Ethics: Respectable, Virtuous and Happy.* London: Routledge, 2014.

Cullather, Nick. *The Hungry World: America's Cold War Battle against Poverty in Asia.* Cambridge, MA: Harvard University Press, 2010.

Daston, Lorraine. *Classical Probability in the Enlightenment.* Princeton, NJ: Princeton University Press, 1988.

Davis, David Brion. *The Problem of Slavery in the Age of Revolution, 1770–1823.* Ithaca, NY: Cornell University Press, 1975.

Dean, Mitchell. *The Constitution of Poverty: Toward a Genealogy of Liberal Governance.* New York: Routledge, 1991.

———. "The Malthus Effect: Population and the Liberal Government of Life." *Economy and Society* 44 (2015): 18–39.

Delumeau, Jean. *History of Paradise: The Garden of Eden in Myth and Tradition.* Translated by Matthew O'Connell. New York: Continuum, 1995.

Denevan, William M. "The Pristine Myth: The Landscape of the Americas in 1492." *Annals of the Association of American Geographers* 82 (1992): 369–85.

Dent, Joshua. "False Frontiers: Archaeology and the Myth of the Canadian Wilderness." *Totem: University of Western Ontario Journal of Anthropology* 21 (2013): 59–71.

Dent, N. J. H. *Rousseau: An Introduction to His Psychological, Social, and Political Theory.* Oxford: Basil Blackwell, 1988.

Dickinson, H. T. *British Radicalism and the French Revolution, 1789–1815.* New York: Basil Blackwell, 1985.

Dowd, Gregory E. *A Spirited Resistance: The North American Indian Struggle for Unity, 1745–1815.* Baltimore, MD: John Hopkins University Press, 1992.

Drayton, Richard. *Nature's Government: Science, Imperial Britain, and the "Improvement" of the World.* New Haven, CT: Yale University Press, 2000.

Drescher, Seymour. *Abolition: A History of Slavery and Antislavery.* Cambridge: Cambridge University Press, 2009.

———. *The Mighty Experiment: Free Labor versus Slavery in British Emancipation.* Oxford: Oxford University Press, 2002.

Drolet, Michael. "Democracy and Political Economy: Tocqueville's Thoughts on J.-B. Say and T. R. Malthus." *History of European Ideas* 29 (2003): 159–181.

Dubois, Laurent. *Avengers of the New World: The Story of the Haitian Revolution.* Cambridge, MA: Harvard University Press, 2004.

Dunn, Richard S. "Sugar Production and Slave Women in Jamaica." In *Cultivation and Culture: Labor and the Shaping of Slave Life in the Americas*, edited by Ira Berlin and Philip D. Morgan, 49–72. Charlottesville: University Press of Virginia, 1993.

Edmond, Rod, and Vanessa Smith, eds. *Islands in History and Representation.* London: Routledge, 2003.

Ekirch, A. Roger. *Bound for America: The Transportation of British Convicts to the Colonies, 1718–1775.* New York: Oxford University Press, 1987.

Embree, Ainslie Thomas. *Charles Grant and British Rule in India.* London: Allen and Unwin, 1962.

Emsley, Clive. "Repression, 'Terror' and the Rule of Law in England during the Decade of the French Revolution." *English Historical Review* 100 (1985): 801–25.

Everill, Bronwen. *Abolition and Empire in Sierra Leone and Liberia.* Basingstoke, UK: Palgrave Macmillan, 2013.

Fabian, Johannes. *Time and the Other: How Anthropology Makes its Objects.* New York: Columbia University Press, 1983.

Faragher, John Mack. *A Great and Noble Scheme: The Tragic Story of the Expulsion of the French Acadians from Their American Homeland.* New York: W. W. Norton, 2005.

Fenn, Elizabeth A. *Pox Americana: The Great Smallpox Epidemic of 1775–82.* New York: Hill and Wang, 2001.

Fergus, Claudius K. *Revolutionary Emancipation: Slavery and Abolitionism in the British West Indies.* Baton Rouge: Louisiana State University Press, 2013.

Festa, Lynn. *Sentimental Figures of Empire in Eighteenth-Century Britain and France.* Baltimore, MD: Johns Hopkins University Press, 2006.

Fichter, James R. *So Great a Proffit: How the East Indies Trade Transformed Anglo-American Capitalism.* Cambridge, MA: Harvard University Press, 2010.

Finkelman, Paul. *Slavery and the Founders: Race and Liberty in the Age of Jefferson.* Armonk, NY: M. E. Sharpe, 2001.

Finkelstein, David. "The Globalization of the Book, 1800–1970." In *A Companion to the History of the Book*, edited by Simon Eliot and Jonathan Rose, 329–40. Malden, MA: Blackwell, 2007.

Fitzmaurice, Andrew. *Sovereignty, Property, and Empire, 1500-2000.* Cambridge: Cambridge University Press, 2014.

Ford, Lisa. *Settler Sovereignty: Jurisdiction and Indigenous People in America and Australia, 1788–1836.* Cambridge, MA: Harvard University Press, 2010.

Franklin, Wayne. *James Fenimore Cooper: The Early Years.* New Haven, CT: Yale University Press, 2007.

Frost, Alan. "The Pacific Ocean: The Eighteenth Century's 'New World'." *Studies on Voltaire and the Eighteenth Century* 152 (1976): 779–822.

Fullagar, Kate. "Bennelong in Britain." *Aboriginal History* 33 (2009): 70–118.

———. *The Savage Visit: New World People and Popular Imperial Culture in Britain, 1710–1795.* Berkeley: University of California Press, 2012.

Furness, A. E. "George Hibbert and the Defence of Slavery in the West Indies." *Jamaican Historical Review* 5 (1965): 56–70.

Garrett, Aaron. "Anthropology: The 'Original' of Human Nature." In *The Cambridge Companion to the Scottish Enlightenment*, edited by Alexander Broadie, 79–83. Cambridge: Cambridge University Press, 2003.

Gascoigne, John. *Encountering the Pacific in the Age of Enlightenment.* Melbourne: Cambridge University Press, 2014.

———. *The Enlightenment and the Origins of European Australia.* Cambridge: Cambridge University Press, 2002.

———. *Science in the Service of Empire: Joseph Banks, the British State, and the Uses of Science in the Age of Revolution.* Cambridge: Cambridge University Press, 1998.

Ghosh, R. N. "The Colonization Controversy: R. J. Wilmot-Horton and the Classical Economists." *Economica* 31 (1964): 385–400.

———. "Malthus on Emigration and Colonization: Letters to Wilmot-Horton." *Economica* 30 (1963): 45–62.

Gibson, James Russell. *Americans versus Malthus: The Population Debate in the Early Republic, 1790–1840.* New York: Garland, 1989.

Gill, Natasha. *Educational Philosophy in the French Enlightenment: From Nature to Second Nature.* Farnham, UK: Ashgate, 2010.

Glacken, Clarence J. *Traces on the Rhodian Shore: Nature and Culture in Western Thought from Ancient Times to the End of the Eighteenth Century.* Berkeley: University of California Press, 1967.

Glasson, Travis. *Mastering Christianity: Missionary Anglicanism and Slavery in the Atlantic World.* New York: Oxford University Press, 2012.

Gliozzi, Giuliano. *Adam et le nouveau monde.* Lecques, France: Ed. Théétète, 2000.

Godelier, M. "Malthus and Ethnography." In *Malthus: Past and Present*, edited by J. Dupâquier, A. Fauve-Chamoux, and E. Grebenik. 125–50. London: Academic Press, 1980.

Grafton, Anthony. *The Footnote: A Curious History.* Cambridge, MA: Harvard University Press, 1997.

Grafton, Anthony, with April Shelford and Nancy Siraisi. *New Worlds, Ancient Texts: The Power of Tradition and the Shock of Discovery.* Cambridge, MA: Harvard University Press, 1995.

Graham, Kenneth W. *William Godwin Reviewed: A Reception History, 1783–1834.* New York: AMS Press, 2001.

Grove, Richard H. *Green Imperialism: Colonial Expansion, Tropical Island Edens, and the Origins of Environmentalism, 1600–1800.* Cambridge: Cambridge University Press, 1995.

Guest, Harriet. *Empire, Barbarism, and Civilisation: James Cook, William Hodges, and the Return to the Pacific.* Cambridge: Cambridge University Press, 2007.

———. "Ornament and Use: Mai and Cook in London." In *A New Imperial History: Culture, Identity and Modernity in Britain, 1660–1840*, edited by Kathleen Wilson, 317–44. Cambridge: Cambridge University Press, 2004.

Hackforth-Jones, Jocelyn, et al. *Between Worlds: Voyagers to Britain, 1700–1850*. London: National Portrait Gallery, 2007.

Hall, Catherine, et al., eds. *Legacies of British Slave-Ownership: Colonial Slavery and the Formation of Victorian Britain*. Cambridge: Cambridge University Press, 2014.

Hamilton, Annette. "Malthus, Yesterday and Today—and Tomorrow? A Brief Report." *Journal of Sociology* 17 (1981): 93–97.

Hargraves, Neil. "Beyond the Savage Character: Mexicans, Peruvians, and the 'Imperfectly Civilized' in William Robertson's History of America." In Wolff and Cipolloni, *Anthropology of the Enlightenment* (2007), 103–18.

Hartwell, R. M. "The Pastoral Ascendancy." In *Australia: A Social and Political History*, edited by Gordon Greenwood, 46–97. Sydney: Angus and Robertson, 1977.

Higman, B. W. *Slave Population and Economy in Jamaica, 1807–1834*. Cambridge: Cambridge University Press, 1976.

———. *Slave Populations of the British Caribbean, 1807–1834*. Baltimore, MD: Johns Hopkins University Press, 1984.

———. "Slavery and the Development of Demographic Theory in the Age of the Industrial Revolution." In James Walvin, ed., *Slavery and British Society, 1776–1846*, 164–94. Baton Rouge: University of Louisiana Press, 1982.

Hilton, Boyd. *The Age of Atonement: The Influence of Evangelicalism on Social and Economic Thought, 1785–1865*. Oxford: Clarendon, 1988.

Hinderaker, Eric. "The 'Four Indian Kings' and the Imaginative Construction of the First British Empire." *William and Mary Quarterly*, 3rd ser., 53 (1996): 487–526.

Hodgen, Margaret T. *Early Anthropology in the Sixteenth and Seventeenth Centuries*. Philadelphia: University of Pennsylvania Press, 1964.

Hodgson, Dennis. "Benjamin Franklin on Population: From Policy to Theory." *Population and Development Review* 17 (1991): 639–61.

———. "Malthus' *Essay on Population* and the American Debate over Slavery." *Comparative Studies in Society and History* 51 (2009): 742–70.

Hogg, Robert. *Men and Manliness on the Frontier: Queensland and British Columbia in the Mid-Nineteenth Century*. Basingstoke, UK: Palgrave Macmillan, 2012.

Hollander, Samuel. *The Economics of Thomas Robert Malthus*. Toronto: University of Toronto Press, 1997.

Hont, Istvan, and Michael Ignatieff, eds. *Wealth and Virtue: The Shaping of Political Economy in the Scottish Enlightenment*. Cambridge: Cambridge University Press, 1983.

Householder, Michael. "Eden's Translations: Women and Temptation in Early America." *Huntington Library Quarterly* 70 (2007): 11–36.

Howsam, Leslie, and James Raven, eds. *Books between Europe and the Americas: Connections and Communities, 1620–1860*. New York: Palgrave Macmillan, 2011.

Howsam, Leslie, and James Raven. "Introduction." In Howsam and Raven, *Books between Europe and the Americas* (2011), 1–22.

Hunter, Brooke. "Wheat, War, and the American Economy during the Age of Revolution." *William and Mary Quarterly*, 3rd ser., 62 (2005): 505–526.

Huzel, James P. "Malthus, the Poor Law, and Population in Early Nineteenth-Century England." *Economic History Review* 22 (1969): 430–52.

———. *The Popularization of Malthus in Early Nineteenth-Century England: Martineau, Cobbett and the Pauper Press.* Aldershot, UK: Ashgate, 2006.

Innis, Harold Adams. *The Fur Trade in Canada: An Introduction to Canadian Economic History.* Toronto: University of Toronto Press, 1956.

James, Patricia. *Population Malthus: His Life and Times.* London and Boston: Routledge and Kegan Paul, 1979.

Jasanoff, Maya. *Liberty's Exiles: American Loyalists in the Revolutionary World.* New York: Knopf, 2011.

Johnson, Sherry. "El Niño, Environmental Crisis, and the Emergence of Alternative Markets in the Hispanic Caribbean, 1760s–70s." *William and Mary Quarterly,* 3rd ser., 62 (2005): 365–410.

Johnston, Anna, and Mitchell Rolls, eds. *Reading Robinson: Companion Essays to Friendly Mission.* Hobart, Australia: Quintus, 2008.

Jones, David Shumway. *Rationalizing Epidemics: Meanings and Uses of American Indian Mortality since 1600.* Cambridge, MA: Harvard University Press, 2004.

Jones, Gareth Stedman. *An End to Poverty? A Historical Debate.* New York: Columbia University Press, 2004.

Jones, Peter, ed. *The "Science of Man" in the Scottish Enlightenment: Hume, Reid, and Their Contemporaries.* Edinburgh: University of Edinburgh Press, 1989.

Jonsson, Fredrik Albritton. *Enlightenment's Frontier: The Scottish Highlands and the Origins of Environmentalism.* New Haven, CT: Yale University Press, 2013.

Jordan, William C. *The Great Famine: Northern Europe in the Early Fourteenth Century.* Princeton: Princeton University Press, 1996.

Kipp, Julie. "Naturally Bad or Dangerously Good: Romantic-Era Narratives of Murderous Motherhood." In *Writing British Infanticide: Child-murder, Gender, and Print, 1722–1859,* edited by Jennifer Thorn, 236–64. Cranbury: Rosemont, 2003.

Konishi, Shino. *The Aboriginal Male in the Enlightenment World.* London: Pickering and Chatto, 2012.

———. "The Tantalising Cannibal: Rationalising Anthropophagy in the Long Eighteenth Century." *Signatures* 5 (2002): 60–84.

———. "'Wanton with Plenty': Questioning Ethno-historical Constructions of Sexual Savagery in Aboriginal Societies." *Australian Historical Studies* 39 (2008): 356–72.

Kupperman, Karen Ordahl, ed. *America in European Consciousness, 1493–1750.* Chapel Hill: Institute of Early American History and Culture, 1995.

———. "The Changing Definition of America." In Kupperman, *America in European Consciousness* (1995), 1–29.

Laidlaw, Zoe. "'Justice to India—Prosperity to England—Freedom to the Slave!' Humanitarian and Moral Reform Campaigns on India, Aborigines and American Slavery." *Journal of the Royal Asiatic Society* 22 (2012): 299–324.

Laiou, Angeliki E. "Economic Thought and Ideology." In *The Economic History of Byzantium: From the Seventh through the Fifteenth Century,* edited by Angeliki E. Laiou. 3 vols. Vol. 3, 1123–1144. Washington, DC: Dumbarton Oaks, 2002.

Lamb, Jonathan. *Preserving the Self in the South Seas, 1680–1840.* Chicago: University of Chicago Press, 2001.

Lambert, David. *Mastering the Niger: James MacQueen's African Geography and the Struggle over Atlantic Slavery.* Chicago: University of Chicago Press, 2013.

———. *White Creole Culture: Politics and Identity during the Age of Abolition.* Cambridge: Cambridge University Press, 2005.

Lawson, Tom. *The Last Man: A British Genocide in Tasmania.* London: I. B. Tauris, 2014.

Legacies of British Slave-ownership. https://www.ucl.ac.uk/lbs/claim/view/18607.

LeMahieu, D. L. "Malthus and the Theology of Scarcity." *Journal of the History of Ideas* 40 (1979): 467–74.

Lennox, Geoff. "The Van Diemen's Land Company." In *The Companion to Tasmanian History*, edited by Alison Alexander. Hobart, Australia: Centre for Tasmanian Historical Studies, 2005. http://www.utas.edu.au/library/companion_to_tasmanian_history/V/VDL%20Co.htm.

Lepore, Jill. *The Name of War: King Philip's War and the Origins of American Identity.* New York: Knopf, 1998.

Lourandos, Harry. *Continent of Hunter-Gatherers: New Perspectives on Australian Prehistory.* Melbourne: Cambridge University Press, 1997.

Lowes, John Livingston. *The Road to Xanadu: A Study in the Ways of the Imagination.* Boston: Houghton Mifflin, 1986.

Luster, Robert E. *The Amelioration of the Slaves in the British Empire, 1790–1833.* New York: Peter Lang, 1995.

MacCormack, Sabine. "Limits of Understanding: Perceptions of Greco-Roman and Amerindian Paganism in Early Modern Europe." In Kupperman, *America in European Consciousness* (1995), 79–129.

Madley, Benjamin. "Reexamining the American Genocide Debate: Meaning, Historiography, and New Methods." *American Historical Review* 120 (2015): 98–139.

Major, Andrea. "'The Slavery of East and West': Abolitionists and 'Unfree' Labour in India, 1820–1833." *Slavery & Abolition* 31 (2010): 501–25.

"Malthus and his Legacy: The Population Debate after 200 Years." Australian Academies Forum, Canberra, 1998. http://www.naf.org.au/papers.htm.

The Malthus Library Catalogue: The Personal Collection of Thomas Robert Malthus at Jesus College, Cambridge. New York: Pergamon Press, 1983.

Mancall, Peter C. *Deadly Medicine: Indians and Alcohol in Early America.* Ithaca, NY: Cornell University Press, 1995.

Manning, Patrick, and William S. Griffiths. "Divining the Unprovable: Simulating the Demography of African Slavery." *Journal of Interdisciplinary History* 19 (1988): 177–201.

Marchi, N. B. de, and R. P. Sturges. "Malthus and Ricardo's Inductivist Critics: Four Letters to William Whewell." *Economica* 40 (1973): 379–93.

Marouby, Christian. "Adam Smith and the Anthropology of the Enlightenment: The 'Ethnographic' Sources of Economic Progress." In Wolff and Cipolloni, *The Anthropology of the Enlightenment* (2007), 85–102.

Marshall, P. J. *Bengal: The British Bridgehead.* Cambridge: Cambridge University Press, 1998.

Marshall, P. J., and Glyndwr Williams. *The Great Map of Mankind: Perceptions of New Worlds in the Age of Enlightenment.* Cambridge, MA: Harvard University Press, 1982.

Martin, Andrew. "Surfing the Revolution: The Fatal Impact of the Pacific on Europe." Special issue, *Eighteenth-Century Studies* 41 (2008): 141–47.

Mayhew, Robert J. *Malthus: The Life and Legacies of an Untimely Prophet.* Cambridge, MA: Harvard University Press, 2014.

McCalla, Douglas. *Planting the Province: The Economic History of Upper Canada, 1784–1870.* Toronto: University of Toronto Press, 1993.

McCallum, John. *Unequal Beginnings: Agricultural and Economic Development in Quebec and Ontario until 1870.* Toronto: University of Toronto Press, 1980.

McCalman, Iain. *Darwin's Armada: How Four Voyagers to Australasia Won the Battle for Evolution and Changed the World.* Melbourne: Viking, 2009.

McCalman, Janet, and Rebecca Kippen. "Population and Health." In *The Cambridge History of Australia*, edited by Alison Bashford and Stuart Macintyre. 2 vols. Vol. 1, *Indigenous and Colonial Australia*, 294–314. Melbourne: Cambridge University Press, 2013.

McCormick, Ted. *William Petty and the Ambitions of Political Arithmetic.* New York: Oxford University Press, 2009.

McCoy, Drew R. *The Elusive Republic: Political Economy in Jeffersonian America.* Chapel Hill, NC: Institute of Early American History and Culture, 1980.

McLachlan, H. *Warrington Academy: Its History and Influence.* [Manchester]: Chetham Society, 1943.

McLane, Maureen N. *Romanticism and the Human Sciences: Poetry, Population, and the Discourse of the Species.* Cambridge: Cambridge University Press, 2000.

Meek, Ronald L. *Social Science and the Ignoble Savage.* Cambridge: Cambridge University Press, 1976.

Miller, J. R. "Petitioning the Great White Mother: First Nations' Organizations and Lobbying in London." In *Canada and the End of Empire*, edited by Philip Buckner, 299–318. Vancouver: University of British Columbia Press, 2005.

Miller, Perry. *Errand into the Wilderness.* Cambridge, MA: Harvard University Press, 1956.

Mills, R. C. *The Colonization of Australia, 1829–42: The Wakefield Experiment in Empire Building.* London: Sidgwick and Jackson, 1915.

Minchinton, W. E. "Agricultural Returns and the Government during the Napoleonic Wars." *Agricultural History Review* 1 (1953): 29–43.

Mintz, Sidney. *Sweetness and Power: The Place of Sugar in Modern History.* New York: Viking, 1985.

Mokyr, Joel. "Malthusian Models and Irish History." *Journal of Economic History* 40 (1980): 159–66.

Montes, Leonidas. *Adam Smith in Context: A Critical Reassessment of Some Central Components of His Thought.* Baskingstoke, UK: Palgrave Macmillan, 2004.

Mookini, Esther K. *The Hawaiian Newspapers.* Honolulu: Topgallant Publishing, 1974.

Moorehead, Alan. *The Fatal Impact: The Invasion of the South Pacific, 1767–1840.* New York: Harper and Row, [1966] 1987.

Morgan, Jennifer L. "'Some Could Suckle over Their Shoulder': Male Travelers, Female Bodies, and the Gendering of Racial Ideology, 1500–1770." *William and Mary Quarterly*, 3rd ser., 54 (1997): 167–92.

Mulvaney, D. J. "The Australian Aborigines, 1606–1929: Opinions and Fieldwork, Part One." *Historical Studies* 8 (1958): 131–51.

Naidis, Mark. "The Abolitionists and Indian Slavery." *Journal of Asian History* 15 (1981): 146–58.

Nally, David P. *Human Encumbrances: Political Violence and the Great Irish Famine.* Notre Dame, IN: University of Notre Dame Press, 2011.

Nash, Roderick. *Wilderness and the American Mind.* New Haven, CT: Yale University Press, 1967.

Ó Gráda, Cormac. *Ireland before and after the Famine: Explorations in Economic History, 1800–1925.* Manchester: Manchester University Press, 1988.

O'Brien, Karen. "Between Enlightenment and Stadial History: William Robertson on the History of Europe." *Journal for Eighteenth-Century Studies* 16 (1993): 53–64.

Oliphant, J. "The Cherokee Embassy to London, 1762." *Journal of Imperial and Commonwealth History* 27 (1999): 1–26.

Oliver, Douglas L. *Ancient Tahitian Society.* Honolulu: University of Hawai'i Press, 1974.

Pagden, Anthony. *The Fall of Natural Man: The American Indian and the Origins of Comparative Ethnology.* Cambridge: Cambridge University Press, 1986.

———. *Lords of All the World: Ideologies of Empire in Spain, Britain, and France, c.1500–c.1800.* New Haven, CT: Yale University Press, 1995.

Palmeri, Frank. "Conjectural History and Satire: Narrative as Historical Argument from Mandeville to Malthus (and Foucault)." *Narrative* 14 (2006): 64–84.

Paquette, Gabriel B. *Enlightenment, Governance, and Reform in Spain and Its Empire, 1759–1808.* Basingstoke, UK: Palgrave Macmillan, 2008.

———. "The Image of Imperial Spain in British Political Thought, 1750–1800." *Bulletin of Spanish Studies* 81 (2004): 187–214.

———. "José da Silva Lisboa and the Vicissitudes of Enlightened Reform in Brazil, 1798–1824." In *Enlightened Reform in Southern Europe and Its Atlantic Colonies, c. 1770–1850*, edited by Gabriel Paquette, 361–88. Farnham, UK: Ashgate, 2009.

Paugh, Katherine. "The Politics of Childbearing in the British Caribbean and the Atlantic World during the Age of Abolition, 1776–1838." *Past & Present* 221 (2013): 119–60.

———. "Rationalizing Reproduction: Race, Disease, and Fertility in the British Caribbean and the Atlantic World during the Age of Abolition, 1763–1833." PhD diss. University of Pennsylvania, 2008.

Perdue, Theda, and Michael D. Green. *The Cherokee Nation and the Trail of Tears.* New York: Viking, 2007.

Petersen, William. *Malthus.* London: Heinemann, 1979.

Petley, Christer. *Slaveholders in Jamaica: Colonial Society and Culture during the Era of Abolition.* London: Pickering and Chatto, 2009.

Pettigrew, William A. *Freedom's Debt: The Royal African Company and the Politics of the Atlantic Slave Trade, 1672–1752.* Chapel Hill: University of North Carolina Press, 2013.

Pitts, Jennifer. *A Turn to Empire: The Rise of Imperial Liberalism in Britain and France.* Princeton, NJ: Princeton University Press, 2005.

Plomley, N. J. B. *The Aboriginal-Settler Clash in Van Diemen's Land.* Launceston, Australia: Queen Victoria Museum, 1992.

Pocock. J. G. A. *Barbarians, Savages and Empires.* Vol. 4 of *Barbarism and Religion.* Cambridge: Cambridge University Press, 2005.

———. "Cambridge Paradigms and Scotch Philosophers: A Study of the Relations between the Civic Humanist and the Civil Jurisprudential Interpretations of Eighteenth-Century Social Thought." In *Wealth and Virtue: The Shaping of Political Economy in the Scottish Enlightenment,* edited by Istvan Hont and Michael Ignatieff, 235–52. Cambridge: Cambridge University Press, 1983.

———. "Gibbon and the Shepherds: The Stages of Society in the *Decline and Fall.*" *History of European Ideas* 2 (1981): 193–202.

Pomeranz, Kenneth. *The Great Divergence: China, Europe, and the Making of the Modern World Economy.* Princeton: Princeton University Press, 2000.

Pratt, Stephanie. *American Indians in British Art, 1700–1840.* Norman: University of Oklahoma Press, 2005.

Pullen, J. M. "Correspondence between Malthus and his Parents." *History of Political Economy* 18 (1986): 133–54.

———. "Introduction." In T. R. Malthus, *Principles of Political Economy,* edited by J. M. Pullen. Vol. 1, 11–69. Cambridge: Cambridge University Press, 1989.

———. "The Last Sixty-five Years of Malthus Scholarship." *History of Political Economy* 30 (1998): 343–52.

———. "Lord Grenville's Manuscript Notes on Malthus." *History of Political Economy* 19 (1987): 217–237.

———. "Malthus' Theological Ideas and Their Influence on His Principle of Population." *History of Political Economy* 13 (1981): 39–54.

Rao, Mohan. *From Population Control to Reproductive Health: Malthusian Arithmetic.* New Delhi: Sage, 2004.

Rao, Mohan, and Sarah Sexton, eds. *Markets and Malthus: Population, Gender and Health in Neo-Liberal Times.* New Delhi: Sage, 2010.

Raven, James. *London Booksellers and American Customers: Transatlantic Literary Community and the Charleston Library Society, 1748–1811.* Columbia: University of South Carolina Press, 2002.

Rawley, James A., with Stephen D. Behrendt. *The Transatlantic Slave Trade: A History.* Lincoln: University of Nebraska Press, 2005.

Rea, Robert Right. *The English Press in Politics, 1760–1774.* Lincoln: University of Nebraska Press, 1963.

Readman, Paul, Cynthia Radding, and Chad Bryant, eds. *Borderlands in World History, 1700–1914.* Basingstoke, UK: Palgrave Macmillan, 2014.

Reynolds, Henry. *A History of Tasmania.* Melbourne: Cambridge University Press, 2012.

Rich, E. E. *Hudson's Bay Company, 1670–1870.* 3 vols. New York: Macmillan, 1960.

Richards, Eric. *The Highland Clearances.* Edinburgh: Birlinn, 2008.

———. "Malthus and the Uses of British Emigration." In *Empire, Migration and Identity in the British World,* edited by Kent Fedorowich and Andrew S. Thompson, 1–47. Manchester: Manchester University Press, 2013.

Richards, John F. *The Unending Frontier: An Environmental History of the Early Modern World.* Berkeley: University of California Press, 2003.

Richter, Daniel K. "'Believing That Many of the Red People Suffer Much for the Want of Food': Hunting, Agriculture, and a Quaker Construction of Indianness in the Early Republic." *Journal of the Early Republic* 19 (1999): 601–28.

Riley, James C. *Population Thought in the Age of the Demographic Revolution.* Durham, NC: Carolina Academic Press, 1985.

Roach, Joseph. *Cities of the Dead: Circum-Atlantic Performance.* New York: Columbia University Press, 1996.

Robson, L. L. *A History of Tasmania: Van Diemen's Land from the Earliest Times to 1855.* Melbourne: Oxford University Press, 1983.

Ross, Ian Simpson. *Lord Kames and the Scotland of his Day.* Oxford: Clarendon Press, 1972.

Rothschild, Emma. *Economic Sentiments: Adam Smith, Condorcet, and the Enlightenment.* Cambridge, MA: Harvard University Press, 2001.

Rountree, Helen C. *Pocahontas, Powhatan, Opechancanough: Three Indians Lives Changed by Jamestown.* Charlottesville: University of Virginia Press, 2005.

Rusnock, Andrea A. "Biopolitics: Political Arithmetic in the Enlightenment." In *The Sciences in Enlightened Europe*, edited by William Clark, Jan Golinksi and Simon Schaffer, 49–68. Chicago: University of Chicago Press, 1999.

Russell, Gillian. "An 'Entertainment of Oddities': Fashionable Sociability and the Pacific in the 1770s." In *A New Imperial History: Culture, Identity and Modernity in Britain and the Empire, 1660–1840*, edited by Kathleen Wilson, 48–70. Cambridge: Cambridge University Press, 2004.

Ryan, Lyndall. *The Aboriginal Tasmanians.* 2nd ed. Sydney: Allen and Unwin, 1996.

———. "The Black Line in Tasmania: An Expensive Mistake or a Strategic Success." Paper delivered to the Australian Historical Association, Launceston, July 2011.

Sachs, Jeffrey D. "Are Malthus's Predicted 1789 Food Shortages Coming True?" *Scientific American*, August 2008.

Safford, Philip L., and Elizabeth J. Safford. *A History of Childhood and Disability.* New York: Teachers College Press, 1996.

Said, Edward. *Culture and Imperialism.* New York: Knopf, 1993.

Santurri, Edmund N. "Theodicy and Social Policy in Malthus' Thought." *Journal of the History of Ideas* 43 (1982): 315–30.

Schiebinger, Londa. *Nature's Body: Gender in the Making of Modern Science.* Camden, NJ: Rutgers University Press, 2004.

Schofield, Philip. *Utility and Democracy: The Political Thought of Jeremy Bentham.* Oxford: Oxford University Press, 2006.

Schofield, Robert E. *The Enlightened Joseph Priestley: A Study of His Life and Work from 1773 to 1804.* University Park: Pennsylvania State University Press, 2004.

Sebastiani, Silvia. *The Scottish Enlightenment: Race, Gender, and the Limits of Progress.* Basingstoke, UK: Palgrave Macmillan, 2013.

Sheridan, Richard B. "The Crisis of Slave Subsistence in the British West Indies during and after the American Revolution." *William and Mary Quarterly*, 3rd ser., 33 (1976): 615–641.

Simpson, A. W. Brian. *Cannibalism and the Common Law: The Story of the Tragic Last Voyage of the Mignonette and the Strange Legal Proceedings to Which It Gave Rise.* Chicago: University of Chicago Press, 1984.

Sivasundaram, Sujit. *Nature and the Godly Empire: Science and Evangelical Mission in the Pacific, 1795–1850.* Cambridge: Cambridge University Press, 2005.

Slotkin, Richard. *Regeneration through Violence: The Mythology of the American Frontier, 1600–1860.* Middletown, CT: Wesleyan University Press, 1973.

Smith, Bernard. *European Vision and the South Pacific.* Oxford: Oxford University Press, [1960] 1989.

———. *Imagining the Pacific: In the Wake of Cook's Voyages.* New Haven, CT: Yale University Press, 1992.

Smith, Keith Vincent. "Bennelong among his People." *Aboriginal History* 33 (2009): 17–69.

———. *Bennelong: The Coming in of the Eora, Sydney Cove 1788–1792.* East Roseville, Australia: Kangaroo Press, 2001.

Smith, Robert R. "The Reception of Malthus' Essay on Population in Spain." *Rivista Internazionale di Scienze Economiche e Commerciali* 16, no. 6 (1969): 550–62.

Smith, Simon D. *Slavery, Family, and Gentry Capitalism in the British Atlantic: The World of the Lascelles, 1648–1834.* New York: Cambridge University Press, 2006.

Smith, Vanessa. "Banks, Tupaia, and Mai: Cross-cultural Exchanges and Friendship in the Pacific." *Parergon* 26 (2009): 139–60.

———. "Crowd Scenes: Pacific Collectivity and European Encounter." *Pacific Studies* 27 (2004): 1–21.

Sokol, B. J. "Thomas Harriot—Sir Walter Raleigh's Tutor—on Population." *Annals of Science* 31 (1974): 205–12.

Solow, Barbara L., and Stanley L. Engerman, eds. *British Capitalism and Caribbean Slavery: The Legacy of Eric Williams.* Cambridge: Cambridge University Press, 1987.

Sonenscher, Michael. "Review Article—Physiocracy as a Theodicy." *History of Political Thought* 23 (2002): 326–39.

Spengler, Joseph J. "Alexander Hill Everett, Early American Opponent of Malthus." *New England Quarterly* 9 (1936): 97–118.

Stafford, Fiona J. *The Last of the Race: The Growth of a Myth from Milton to Darwin.* Oxford: Clarendon Press, 1994.

Stannard, David E. *American Holocaust: Columbus, Christianity, and the Conquest of the New World.* New York: Oxford University Press, 1992.

Stern, Fritz, ed. *The Varieties of History: From Voltaire to the Present.* New York: Meriden Press, 1973.

Strong, Pauline Turner. "Fathoming the Primitive: Australian Aborigines in Four Explorers' Journals, 1697–1845." *Ethnohistory* 33 (1986): 175–96.

Tachihata, Chieko. "The History and Development of Hawaii Public Libraries: The Library of Hawaii and Hawaii State Library, 1913–1971." PhD diss. University of Southern California, 1981.

Taylor, Alan. "'The Hungry Year': 1789 on the Northern Border of Revolutionary America." In *Dreadful Visitations: Confronting Natural Catastrophe in the Age of Enlightenment,* edited by Alessa Johns, 145–82. New York: Routledge, 1999.

Thomas, Nicholas. *Islanders: The Pacific in the Age of Empire.* New Haven, CT: Yale University Press, 2010.

Thompson Kelsay, Isabel. *Joseph Brant, 1743–1807, Man of Two Worlds.* Syracuse, NY: Syracuse University Press, 1984.

Toye, John. "Keynes on Population and Economic Growth." *Cambridge Journal of Economics* 21 (1997): 1–26.

Treasure, G. R. R. *The Huguenots.* New Haven, CT: Yale University Press, 2013.

Tyson, Gerald P. "Joseph Johnson, an Eighteenth-Century Bookseller." *Studies in Bibliography* 28 (1975): 1–16.

Vaidik, Aparna. "The Wild Andamans: Island Imageries and Colonial Encounter." In *The British Empire and the Natural World: Environmental Encounters in South Asia*, edited by Deepak Kumar, Vanita Damodaran, and Rohan D'Souza, 19–42. New Delhi: Oxford University Press, 2011.

Vanaclocha, Francisco J. "La recepción de Malthus en la España de 1834: Un ejemplo temprano de burócratas sensibles ante las amenazas del entorno." In *Historia y filosofía política, jurídica y social. Estudios de homenaje al profesor Gregorio Peces-Barba*, 1067–94. Madrid: Dykinson, 2008.

Vasconcelos, Sandra Guardini T. "From the French or Not: Transatlantic Contributions to the Making of the Brazilian Novel." In Howsam and Raven, *Books between Europe and the Americas* (2011), 212–32.

Vera, Eugenia Roldán. "'Learning from Abroad?': Communities of Knowledge and the Monitorial System in Independent Spanish America." In Howsam and Raven, *Books between Europe and the Americas* (2011), 233–56.

Walvin, James. The *Zong: A Massacre, the Law, and the End of Slavery*. New Haven, CT: Yale University Press, 2011.

Warde, Paul. "The Invention of Sustainability." *Modern Intellectual History* 8 (2011): 153–70.

Waterman, A. M. C. *Political Economy and Christian Theology since the Enlightenment: Essays in Intellectual History*. New York: Palgrave Macmillan, 2004.

Watson, Thomas D. "Continuity in Commerce: Development of the Panton, Leslie and Company Trade Monopoly in West Florida." *Florida Historical Quarterly* 54 (1976): 548–64.

Webb, Stephen Saunders. *The Governors-General: The English Army and the Definition of the Empire, 1569–1681*. Chapel Hill, NC: Institute of Early American History and Culture, 1979.

Wells, Robert V. *The Population of the British Colonies in America before 1776: A Survey of Census Data*. Princeton, NJ: Princeton University Press, 1975.

Whatmore, Richard. "Democrats and Republicans in Restoration France." *European Journal of Political Theory* 3 (2004): 37–51.

White, Peter. "Revisiting the 'Neolithic Problem' in Australia." *Records of the Western Australian Museum: Supplement*, 2011: 86–92.

White, Richard. *The Middle Ground: Indians, Empires, and Republics in the Great Lakes Region, 1650–1815*. Cambridge: Cambridge University Press, 1991.

White, Richard, and Patricia Nelson Limerick. *The Frontier in American Culture*, edited by James R. Grossman. Berkeley: University of California Press, 1994.

Williams, Glyndwr. "Seamen and Philosophers in the South Seas in the Age of Captain Cook." *Mariner's Mirror* 65 (1979): 3–22.

Williams, Michael. *Deforesting the Earth: From Prehistory to Global Crisis*. Chicago: University of Chicago Press, 2003.

Wilson, Kathleen. *The Island Race: Englishness, Empire and Gender in the Eighteenth Century*. London: Routledge, 2003.

———. "Thinking Back: Gender Misrecognition and Polynesian Subversion Aboard the Cook Voyages." In *A New Imperial History: Culture, Identity and Modernity in*

Britain and the Empire 1660–1840, edited by Kathleen Wilson, 345–62. Cambridge: Cambridge University Press, 2004.

Winch, Donald. *Classical Political Economy and Colonies*. Cambridge, MA: Harvard University Press, 1965.

———. *Riches and Poverty: An Intellectual History of Political Economy in Britain, 1750–1834*. Cambridge: Cambridge University Press, 1996.

Wing, John T. "Keeping Spain Afloat: State Forestry and Imperial Defense in the Sixteenth Century." Environmental History 17 (2012): 116–45.

Wokler, Robert. *Rousseau, the Age of Enlightenment, and Their Legacies*. Edited by Bryan Garsten. Princeton, NJ: Princeton University Press, 2012.

Wolfe, Patrick. "Land, Labor, and Difference: Elementary Structures of Race." *American Historical Review* 106 (2001): 866–905.

Wolff, Larry, and Marco Cipolloni, eds. *The Anthropology of the Enlightenment*. Stanford, CA: Stanford University Press, 2007.

Wolloch, Nathaniel. "The Civilizing Process, Nature, and Stadial Theory." *Eighteenth-Century Studies* 44 (2011): 245–59.

Woodley, Sophia. "'Oh Miserable and Most Ruinous Measure': The Debate between Private and Public Education in Britain, 1760–1800." In *Educating the Child in Enlightenment Britain: Beliefs, Cultures, Practices*, edited by Mary Hilton and Jill Shefrin, 21–40. Aldershot, UK: Ashgate, 2009.

Wrigley, E. A. *Energy and the English Industrial Revolution*. Cambridge: Cambridge University Press, 2010.

———. *Poverty, Progress, and Population*. Cambridge: Cambridge University Press, 2004.

———. "Standing Between Two Worlds." Paper presented at "Malthus and his Legacy: The Population Debate after 200 Years." Australian Academies Forum, Canberra, 1998. http://www.naf.org.au/papers.htm.

Wu, Duncan. *Wordsworth's Reading, 1770–1799*. Cambridge: Cambridge University Press, 1993.

———. *Wordsworth's Reading, 1800–1815*. Cambridge: Cambridge University Press, 1995.

Wykes, David L. "The Contribution of the Dissenting Academy to the Emergence of Rational Dissent." In *Enlightenment and Religion: Rational Dissent in Eighteenth-Century Britain*, edited by Knud Haakonssen, 99–139. New York: Cambridge University Press, 1996.

Wylie, Alison. "Invented Lands/Discovered Pasts: The Westward Expansion of Myth and History." *Historical Archaeology* 27 (1993): 1–19.

Wyman, Walker Demarquis. *The Frontier in Perspective*. Madison: University of Wisconsin Press, 1957.

Zall, Paul M. "The Cool World of Samuel Taylor Coleridge: Joseph Johnson, or the Perils of Publishing." *The Wordsworth Circle* 3 (1972): 25–30.

Zirkle, Conway. "Benjamin Franklin, Thomas Malthus and the United States Census." *Isis* 48 (1957): 58–62.

INDEX